CHRISTIANITY, DEMOCRACY, AND THE RADICAL ORDINARY

THEOPOLITICAL VISIONS

SERIES EDITORS:

Thomas Heilke
D. Stephen Long
and C. C. Pecknold

Theopolitical Visions seeks to open up new vistas on public life, hosting fresh conversations between theology and political theory. This series assembles writers who wish to revive theopolitical imagination for the sake of our common good.

Theopolitical Visions hopes to re-source modern imaginations with those ancient traditions in which political theorists were often also theologians. Whether it was Jeremiah's prophetic vision of exiles "seeking the peace of the city," Plato's illuminations on piety and the civic virtues in the Republic, St. Paul's call to "a common life worthy of the Gospel," St. Augustine's beatific vision of the City of God, or the gothic heights of medieval political theology, much of Western thought has found it necessary to think theologically about politics, and to think politically about theology. This series is founded in the hope that the renewal of such mutual illumination might make a genuine contribution to the peace of our cities.

FORTHCOMING VOLUMES:

Gabriel A. Santos
Redeeming the Broken Body: Church and State after Disasters

Christianity, Democracy, and the
RADICAL ORDINARY

Conversations

Between

a Radical Democrat

and a Christian

STANLEY HAUERWAS *&* ROMAND COLES

 CASCADE *Books* • Eugene, Oregon

CHRISTIANITY, DEMOCRACY, AND THE RADICAL ORDINARY
Conversations Between a Radical Democrat and a Christian

Theopolitical Visions 1

Cascade Books
A Division of Wipf and Stock Publishers
199 W. 8th Ave., Suite 3
Eugene, OR 97401

ISBN 13: 978-1-55635-297-3

Cataloging-in-Publication data:

Hauerwas, Stanley, 1940–.
   Christianity, democracy, and the radical ordinary : conversations between a radical democrat and a Christian / by Stanley Hauerwas and Romand Coles.

   xii + 366 p.; 23 cm. — Theopolitical Visions 1
   Includes bibliographical references and index (alk. paper)

   ISBN 13: 978-1-55635-297-3

   1. Religion and politics—United States. 2. Democracy—Religious aspects. 3. Wolin, Sheldon S. 4. Vanier, Jean, 1928–. 5. West, Cornell—Political and social views. 6. Baker, Ella, 1903–1986. 7. Campbell, Will D. 8. Gregory, of Nazianzus, Saint. I. Coles, Romand. II. Title.

BL2525 .H38 2008

Manufactured in the U.S.A.

We dedicate this book to

Ella Baker, Jean Vanier, and Sheldon S. Wolin

Contents

Preface

This is a *preface*, which means—following the Latin *praefatio*—that it is a "saying beforehand," or a "before speaking." And this raises questions: Before *what*? And how is this *before*, which as we all know is almost always written after what it precedes in a text, somehow to gesture toward something that really came before what the preface must be consigned to follow? In ecclesiastical contexts, a preface is a prayer of thanksgiving. Of what and to whom would we give thanks? We, who are each profoundly grateful yet frequently give thanks in such different ways?

Our book of essays that follows is an afterword. This preface speaks of that which came before. It gives thanks to events that came before this book yet find themselves inscribed here merely as traces of a much greater and more mysterious profundity whose name is friendship.

Toward the end of our work on this book we recorded some of our dialogues. With a sharp ear and great discerning patience, Carole Baker (research associate for Hauerwas) carefully transcribed one of these into written words, which we then revised into the form you will find at the end of our text. When Rom first *read* the unrevised transcription he was appalled! While he found that Stanley generally spoke in coherent sentences, Rom's voice tended frequently toward sentence-less deformations that contained ceaseless qualifications of qualifications, introjections, and strange twists. Rom somehow knew some of what he must have meant (and Stanley must have as well because he responded with precision) and revised his "speaking in tongues" into sentences he thought he would be less embarrassed to see in print. Yet before doing so he apologized repeatedly to Stanley, to Carole, and to others whom he imagined might one day come upon this transcription of his monstrous "thinking out loud."

A bit later however, he had the opportunity to *listen* to the actual recording of the conversations, at which point his reaction changed entirely. For what he heard, much to his astonishment, were the untranscribable sounds of friendship—sounds that could never find their way onto the following pages. Interweaving each other's words were "hmmms," "huhs," "whews," "yeses," "I sees," "waits!," "buts," collective pauses, collective hastiness, copious hilarity, shared sighs of mourning, almost inaudible invitations, questions, challenges, extensions, and incitements to the birth of each other's thoughts. To the extent that each of us finds ourselves saying new things in what follows, these new things are in an important sense an afterward to the friendship by which they have been born and carried along. The friendship is the thing, and we suspect that whatever is good in what follows is an afterward to the friendships that forged unexpected possibilities—friendships reaching across great strange differences and still underway. So in this "before saying" we wish to give a prayer of thanks to the spirit of a friendship that embodies an important kind of relationship to which radical ecclesia and radical democracy call us. We hope many traces have somehow survived our revisions.While every friendship is singular, we are of the mind that each one is entwined in a web of other friendships that have solicited, informed, supported, and in various ways challenged it.

We gratefully acknowledge that our friendship developed for a long period rather indirectly through friendships and dialogues with students (some shared and some not) who nurtured ventures of sensibility, thinking, questioning, and exploring that increasingly brought us into proximate orbits that called our friendship into being and on its way. For each of these friendships—that have often spiraled into many others—we can find no more profound words of gratitude than some of their names: Dan Bell, Winter Brown, Natalie Carnes, Bill Cavanaugh, Charlie Collier, Troy Dostert, Peter Dula, Brian Goldstone, Laura Grattan, Leah Hunt-Hendrix, Chris Huebner, Jeff McCurry, David Rice, Joel Shuman, Alex Sider, David Toole, Jonathan Tran, Joe Winters, David Clotier, Rosalee Ewell, Alex Hawkins.

We also need to thank Jeff Stout and Peter Euben not only for their friendship but for never letting us rest easy. Each has a capacity for asking hard questions for which we have no answer. But it must surely be the case that if there is a deep connection between Christianity and radical democracy it is that each requires us to live without answers. By so living hopefully we learn not only to need and trust one another, but even to be capable of love. This means we hope our book will find readers who will want to claim us as friends by doing better what we have tried to do. God knows we need all the help we can get.

Stanley Hauerwas
& Romand Coles
June 2007

Introduction

> What I have learned as a farmer I have learned also as a writer
> and vice versa. I have farmed as a writer and written as a farmer.
> This is an experience resistant to any kind of simplification. I will
> go ahead and call it complexification. When I am called, as to
> my astonishment I sometimes am, a devotee of "simplicity" . . . I
> am obliged to reply that I gave up the simple life when I left New
> York City in 1964 and came here. In New York, I lived as a passive
> consumer . . . whereas here I supply many of my needs from this
> place by my work (and pleasure) and am responsible besides for
> the care of the place. My point is that when one passes from any
> abstract order . . . to the daily life and work of one's own farm, one
> passes from a relative simplicity into a complexity that is irreduc-
> ible except by disaster and ultimately is incomprehensible. It is the
> complexity of the life of a place uncompromisingly itself, which is
> at the same time the life of the world, of all Creation. One meets
> not only . . . the wildness of the world, but also the limitations of
> one's knowledge, intelligence, character, and bodily strength. To
> do this, of course, is to accept the place as an influence . . . as a part
> of the informing ambience of one's mind and imagination.

—Wendell Berry[1]

This is a book about death—and life. Perhaps better put, this is a book
about the politics of death and life.[2] We hope that the politics exhibited

---

1. Berry, *Way of Ignorance*, 47–48.

2. In *After Christendom?* I (Hauerwas) wrote, "Genuine politics is about the art of
dying. That places the church at cross purposes with the politics of liberalism, built as it
is on the denial of death and sacrifice" (43). I am not sure I knew what I was talking about

in this book—a politics we try to enact with the joint authorship—is one that refuses to let death dominate our living. We believe that the people at the center of the book—Ella Baker, Bob Moses, Will Campbell, Jean Vanier, Ernesto Cortes; as well as the movements, organizing efforts, and communities such as SNCC (in its early days), the IAF, and L'Arche—represent a politics of life. They do so because they refuse the seduction of a politics that attempts to defeat death by promising "results." Even as the more frequently recognized ends for which they struggle (e.g., education, wages, jobs, health care, infrastructure) are of great importance, we find these people most exemplary for how, with patient intensity, they cultivate modes of attention and political engagement that perform a redemption that is otherwise than immortality.

We also believe that politics is slow and frustrating work. It is so because it is not finally about results (though good results, too, are difficult to come by in a world of subjugative powers). Politics is about relationships between people dead and alive, relationships that are as painful as they are unavoidable. Yet much of recent political theory, including accounts and justifications of democracy, has tried to avoid the subject of death and by so doing has put forward accounts of politics that are, ironically, insufficiently political. We are therefore very sympathetic with critiques of liberal political theory (such as Sheldon Wolin's and William Connolly's) that take liberalism to task for being insufficiently "political."[3] We think the liberal avoidance of the kind of politics we advocate

---

when I wrote those sentences, but I was under the influence of Augustine. I suspect I was continuing to reflect on the argument I had begun in *Naming the Silences: God, Medicine, and the Problem of Suffering*, where I tried to understand why the suffering and death of children seems to render our world unintelligible. Drawing on Alfred Killilea's *Politics of Being Mortal*, I argued that there was a relation between our use of medicine to try to get ourselves out of life alive, and liberal political theory and practice. I suggested that the fear of death is at the heart of the liberal democratic project just to the extent the liberal project tries to secure cooperation between individuals who have nothing in common other than their fear of death (123). As a result, one of the legitimating characteristics of liberal regimes is to provide "the best medical care available" to ensure that we will not have to die early. I wrote *Naming the Silences* before I had read Foucault, but I suspect his influence was in the air. In an odd way I regard *Naming the Silences* (renamed by the publisher using only the subtitle) as my most extended discussion of political theory. I should also point out that *After Christendom?*, which was given the subtitle, by the publisher, of *How the Church Is to Behave If Freedom, Justice, and a Christian Nation Are Bad Ideas*, was written in 1991. The 1999 edition has a new "preface" I wish some might read before they take too seriously the subtitle.

3. In *Beyond Gated Politics: Reflections for the Possibility of Democracy*, Coles offers a

has everything to do with the general tendency of much contemporary political theory and practice to avoid (if not to deny) the reality of death. Empire, global capitalism, the megastate, and even many forms of cosmopolitanism name systems of power that frequently proliferate death in the name of a life that would be free of it. No less pertinent are the quotidian practices of corruption and oblivion that are conditions of these systems' possibility and integral to (but not exhaustive of) the soulcraft through which we are all brought into being. The deaths we organize our lives to resist and escape, then, are not only the big ones that await each of us at the end, but are also (and relatedly) those that occur in the passing away of boundaries and identities in our vulnerable, lived encounters with the world of others and things.

That our subject is life and death should make less odd that this is a book written by a Christian (Hauerwas) and a sympathetic but non-Christian radical democrat (Coles).[4] Christianity, at least Christianity not determined by Constantinian or capitalist desires, is training for a dying that is good. Such good dying is named in the gospel as trial, cross, and resurrection. Radical democracy names the intermittent and dispersed traditions of witnessing, resisting, and seeking alternatives to the politics of death wrought by those bent on myriad forms of immortality-as-conquest. When it has managed to keep a critical reflection upon itself, radical democracy can be seen to be (in the words of Ani DiFranco) "working for the better good (which is good, at its best)."[5] Both radical democracy and Christianity are lived pedagogies of hope inspirited and envisioned through memories of the "good, at its best." Such training is

---

critique of political liberalism that focuses on the way liberalism seeks to secure a politics built on the denial of its own tragic finitude. In the Rawlsian account, this denial is paradoxically constructed by forcing all political phenomena through the transformative eye of a needle hollowed out by the frequent repetition of a particular account of ubiquitous death wrought by the wars of religion and of how we can avoid their return.

4. "Radical democrat" is a term that we try to display in our discussions of SNCC and IAF. It receives extensive theoretical treatment in the chapter on Sheldon Wolin. In brief, radical democracy refers to political acts of tending to common goods and differences. Such acts are dynamically responsive to a world that always exceeds our terms and settled institutional forms. They always exceed state formations that claim to be the exemplary shape of democracy. If "democracy" were not so persistently deployed as a rhetorical weapon to advance so many anti-democratic institutions and practices, we could simply say "democrat." "Radical democrat" is a rhetorical effort to distance ourselves from the erosion of the term "democrat" that results from this deployment.

5. DiFranco, "Grand Canyon."

a resource for sustaining the politics of the everyday, that is, the politics of small achievements. If Coles is right, radical democracy is the politics of small achievements. Such a politics takes time, which suggests that there may be some deep connections between Christianity and radical democracy. This is surely the case given the death-determined politics of our time, the politics of compulsory speed, which assumes that we do not have the time to take the time to listen to one another or to remember the dead.

Make no mistake: Christianity and radical democracy are revolutionary. Yet we are convinced that there are no revolutions (only histrionic returns of the same or the worst) that would be above and beyond—rather than through—the fine grains of the politics of micro-relationships and small achievements. We yearn for radical changes to systems that are destroying the world. We lend our bodies and minds to a number of efforts that seek such changes. Yet we believe that the locus of energies and intelligent visions for such projects are nourished in the textures of relational care for the radical ordinary. By radical ordinary we gesture to the ways in which the inexhaustible complexities of everyday life forever call forth new efforts of attention, nurture, and struggle that exceed the elements of blindness that accompany even our best words and deeds. And we think that nourishing these textures of relational care ought to be a chief aspiration of genuinely revolutionary (which is to say, "resurrectionary") politics. We think so, not just because these textures are sources for systemic change, but also because we take the devitalization of practices of relational care to be our deepest poverty. Yes, we are impatient for change. Yet we work to fashion this impatience into what Adrienne Rich calls a "wild patience,"[6] which we learn from Jean Vanier, Dorothy Day, Ella Baker, Myles Horton, and Michel Foucault, the last of which enjoined a "patient labor giving form to our impatience for liberty."[7] For we are convinced that the change we can call good—and paradoxically the quickest good change possible—will come largely from those who have time to take time to listen to one another and to remember the dead. And we believe that good changes will be those that nourish the futures of peoples who can give time, because they have time to take time.

6. See Rich's book, *A Wild Patience Has Taken Me This Far*.

7. Foucault, "What Is Enlightenment?," 319.

This book is about listening. We have had to learn to listen to one another. We have also tried to listen to voices that may seem speechless, believing that they have something crucial to say to us if we are to escape the politics of speed. Listening not only takes time, but it also requires a trained vulnerability that does not come easily. Vulnerability means that our life is not under our control, which means we must learn to trust others if we are not only to survive but flourish.

Such a politics is in sharp contrast to the politics of fear that characterizes current American life.[8] That such a culture of fear possesses Americans is, according to Talal Asad, not accidental. Drawing on the

8. For an astute analysis of the fear-driven character of American life after September 11, 2001, see Scott Bader-Saye's, *Following Jesus in a Culture of Fear*. Particularly important is Bader-Saye's "Appendix: The Deep Roots of Fear," in which he locates the current culture of fear after September 11, 2001, by way of Hobbes and Judith Shklar's work. Also worth reading is Geiko Müller-Fahrenholz's *America's Battle for God: A European Christian Looks at Civil Religion*. Particularly impressive is Müller-Faherholz's draft of a speech he wishes President Bush might have given in response to September 11, 2001. For example, he suggests what President Bush might have said:

> The assaults have shown us something we needed to know: we are vulnerable. . . . The experience of this immense cruelty is, at the moment of such great suffering, also our moment of truth about the vulnerability we share with others. For now we can empathize with other people who live through civil wars for years and even decades. . . . What follows from this kind of knowledge that we have brought so much grief? Should we try to close this window of vulnerability? To do that would turn our country into a prison. . . . So we should say to the world: We will try to learn from this bitter lesson. There is no special status for the United States. We are, together with all peoples, guests on this planet, finite and mortal beings who are connected to each other, dependent on one another. . . . This implies the acknowledgment—and this may be the hardest task I ask of you today—that our vulnerability is also an expression of our failure to meet peoples in other parts of the world as the honest brokers for their needs. We need to accept our share in the injustices that are causing so much suffering. The evil is not simply out there; it is also with us and within us. For a long time we have held onto our sense of national innocence. But it now lies buried under the rubble of the Twin Towers in New York. (95–96)

Müller-Faherholz then observes that "people who want to be invulnerable must make themselves impenetrable. Their search for invincibility must be paid for with the lifeless shield of numbed emotions and intellectual inertia. While suppressing their own insecurities and needs, they are forced to concentrate all their powers on fending off real and imagined enemies. This leads to false conceptions of the stranger, the other, and to a distorted sense of one's own identity" (99). For what might be considered an extended commentary on such impenetrability and, in particular, on how we fear the stranger because we are strangers to ourselves, see Eric Santer's *On the Psychotheology of Everyday Life: Reflections on Freud and Rosenzweig*.

work of Roxanne Euben, Asad suggests that the jihadis—that is, those who carry out suicide bombings—reenact something paradoxically analogous to Hannah Arendt's understanding of the profoundly this-worldly politics exemplified by the Greeks, in which men entered the public realm seeking something that they might have in common with others, in the hope of finding some permanence in life beyond their deaths. Arendt argued that this understanding of the world ended with the rise of Christianity and the fall of Rome, and that it cannot be resurrected. But according to Asad, Arendt rightly called our attention to the Greek understanding of political action that links human finitude, violent death, and political community, exactly because such linkages are so seldom acknowledged in liberal theory.[9]

According to Asad, the attempt to occlude the originating violence, an attempt that is at the heart of the founding of liberal states, hides from liberals the violence that founds the law. Even if liberals recognize the original violence that establishes the state, they assume such violence can be "redeemed by the progressive elimination of political exclusions." But they fail to acknowledge that

> violence is embedded in the very concept of liberty that lies at the heart of liberal doctrine. That concept presupposes that the morally independent individual's natural right to violent self-defense is yielded to the state, and the state becomes the sole protector of individual liberties: abstracting the right to kill from domestic politics, denying to any agents other than states the right to kill at home and abroad. The right to kill is the right to behave in violent ways toward other people—especially toward citizens of foreign states at war, and toward the uncivilized, whose very existence is a threat to civilized order. In certain circumstances, killing others is necessary, so it seems, for the security it provides.[10]

Suicide bombers, terrorists, become therefore crucial descriptions to legitimate the regimes of death characteristic of the "civilized" cultures that we know as liberal democracies. Such regimes take as a given that the distinction between terrorism and war is obvious, thereby legitimating the defense of civilizations that "value life" against barbarians who do not "value life."[11] Barbarians who do not value life are clearly "uncivilized,"

9. Asad, *On Suicide Bombing*, 57–58.

10. Ibid., 59–60.

11. Asad provides a devastating critique of Walzer's attempt to distinguish terror-

which means they must be defeated by those states that embody the advances in human subjectivity that stand against the darkness of death. Such a stance, according to Asad, means that the violence at the heart of liberal political doctrine (namely, the right to self-defense) cannot help but identify the liberal project as one committed to universal redemption. That is to say, "some humans have to be treated violently in order that humanity can be redeemed."[12]

Calling attention to Asad's understanding of the role suicide bombers play in the legitimating discourses of nationalistic fervor may seem "off subject" in a book committed to redirecting our attention to "small politics." We hope, however, that readers will find our attempt to reclaim the significance of the radical ordinary to be directly relevant if we are to find a way to challenge the politics of death shaping the American fear of the unknown. We are without hope if there are no examples of an alternative politics to the politics of death. This book is an attempt to hold up the kind of examples we think we so desperately need if we are to escape death-driven political necessities.

We are impressed with the speech Müller-Faherholz (in footnote 6 above) conjures for an imaginary leader far wiser than most of those currently in power. And we think that in important ways, such leaders would be less likely to perpetuate the worst violence of U.S. imperialism. Moreover, we have lent, and likely will again lend, our support to elect such statespersons to office. Yet for several reasons we do not find—nor do we place—our primary hopes in such efforts, leaders, and locations of state power. First, even if leaders such as those Müller-Faherholz imagines ushered forth with such speeches, we wonder: Would there be many people who could really hear them? Indeed, there have been voices saying similar things, and they have been most often too little and too poorly heard. Second, we think that holding positions of great power in the economic polity is a lot like wearing Tolkien's ring. The systemic forces of corruption dig deep into the soul and are enough to overwhelm most who—with good intentions—assume positions within the systems of power. This is not to deny that some good people are called to place their efforts there and should perhaps respond to such calls. Nor is it to deny

---

ism and war. See Asad, *On Suicide Bombing*, 31–32. I argued a case similar to Asad's in a chapter entitled "The Non-Violent Terrorist: In Defense of Christian Fanaticism," in *Sanctify Them in the Truth: Holiness Exemplified*, 177–90.

12. Asad, *On Suicide Bombing*, 62–63.

that important policy shifts for the better can be generated by people in such positions. Yet we think hope (even in terms of narrower instrumental goals, let alone in terms of deeper relational transformation) lies in the emergence of a multitude of peoples enacting myriad forms of the politics of the radical ordinary in ways that, first, displace and relocate our human efforts to tend to each other in our commonalities and differences away from the megastate and corporate power; and, second, struggle (with intransigent suspicion) to radically transform these powers—where we cannot entirely displace them—so as to make them increasingly responsive to the pressures of people cultivating knowledge, power, and hope through relationships of everyday attentive reciprocity. We think that it is most vitally in and through concrete practices of tending to one another that people find the sources of renewal and sustenance for a life-affirming politics—one that provides the most hopeful wellspring for defeating the politics of death. The politics of death is a dense, dynamic, and finely woven mesh of destruction and fear. An alternative politics that cares for the commonalities, differences, and emergent irregularities of life must also be dense, molecular, supple, mobile, and trickster-like in its modes. It must maintain its "heavy foot" in the complexities of the radical ordinary—in the memories and specificities of what is found there—if it is to avoid the fantasies of "seeing like a state" and of "being like a Wal-Mart," fantasies that not only threaten us but that are already plunging us into the new dark ages.

Memories. It is by collecting and retelling stories of radical ordinary political initiatives that have "done a new thing" and have resisted the politics of death that we inspire, nourish, and inform a dense and wild imagination, and an intransigent hope. Peacemaking, light-bringing, and joy are always already springing forth everywhere—in spite of the disasters. We must retrain ourselves to witness and give ourselves to these more hopeful modes of coexistence to which we are indebted beyond our wildest imaginations.

Accordingly, we trust that this is an imaginative and hopeful book. There is as strong a relation, we believe, between hope and imagination, as there is between imagination and the encounter with and memory of those who have lived with receptive generosity toward the radical ordinary. We could not imagine—*ex nihilo*—a Jean Vanier, an Ella Baker, or the IAF. Yet they exist, making possible a reality otherwise unimaginable. That they exist, moreover, means that we can be people of hope in a world too often devoid of it. Such hope is the resource necessary to help us see what otherwise might go unnoticed—that other worlds are indeed possible. Just as each of these exemplars has lived imaginatively and hopefully into the future, borne by their memories of past efforts and their mindfulness of "evidence of things not said" in the present, so might we. When resources like Vanier, Baker, and the IAF go unnoticed, we are condemned to cynicism and despair.

That this is a book about life and death we hope will counter the reaction some readers might have: that is, to think that because the book deals with small politics, it is not about the politics that really matters. The politics that really matters is typically assumed to be state politics associated with Washington DC. Again, we confess that the politics associated with Washington DC is not a prominent character in this book, but we certainly have no intention to ignore that politics. We have wearied, however, of what seems to be the endless attempts to provide ever-new accounts of "democracy" in order to ensure us that state politics remains or does not remain democratic.[13] Such projects now seem exhausted. Thus rather than offer another theory of the state, we attempt in this book to provide examples, drawn from actual democratic practices, that might enkindle imaginations dulled by the attractions of the state.

Kristen Deede Johnson quite rightly suggests that

> political theory is nothing if not an exercise of imagination, offering new or different pictures of collective life in the hopes of remolding, refashioning, or altogether altering contemporary arrangements. Indeed, the success or popularity of a political theory could be said to depend upon the extent to which it offers a picture of political society and life that is more attractive and persuasive than that of the status quo.[14]

13. In *Democracy: A History*, John Dunn puts the matter starkly: "When any modern state claims to be a democracy, it necessarily misdescribes itself" (18). He observes that what we should mean by democracy is not that we govern ourselves, but rather that "our own state, and the government that does so much to organize our lives, draws its legitimacy from us, and that we have a reasonable chance of being able to compel each of them to continue to do so" (19). We still consider C. B. Macpherson's work to be one of the best analyses of these matters. If Macpherson is right, it is not that democratic theory is exhausted, but that the attempt to subvert democratic practice by liberal theory is coming to an end. For a concise account of Macpherson's position see Macpherson, *Real World of Democracy*.

14. Johnson, *Theology, Political Theory, and Pluralism*, 22.

This is certainly not a book without theory. Indeed, in many ways the book turns on Coles's account of Wolin in "Democracy and the Radical Ordinary." The stories we tell of Will Campbell, Ella Baker, Jean Vanier, SNCC, and the IAF are shaped by what we have learned from Wolin. So we do not pretend that "theory" has not determined the shape of this book. However, as Coles, makes clear, without Ella Baker and SNCC, Wolin would not have been able to develop the theory we think so important for what this book is about.

What is the shape of this book? It is first and foremost a conversation originally initiated by students. Hauerwas's graduate students took Coles's courses in political theory and then tried to educate Hauerwas by teaching him what they had learned from Coles. Just as important as the content they learned from Coles was what they learned from him about reading texts. They learned to imitate Coles's reading, which, Hauerwas's students argued, was an exemplification of the politics they were also learning from Coles. Coles's reading of Rowan Williams in this book wonderfully exemplifies what Hauerwas's students meant.

From the other side, paradoxically, Coles found that year after year a couple of the most interesting students in his seminars on democratic theory, continental philosophy, critical theory, genealogy, phenomenology, hermeneutics, and deconstruction were deeply and tenaciously Christian PhD students from the department of religion, who had been sent his way by a "fideistic, sectarian tribalist" also known as Hauerwas.[15] These students were at once sympathetically swept up in many of the themes of the courses, yet also persistently raised difficult questions of practice, liturgy, church, tradition, and Christ in ways that simultaneously put pressure on these themes and increasingly pulled Coles into dialogue with the likes of John Howard Yoder, Alasdair MacIntyre, Hauerwas, and (more recently) Rowan Williams and Jean Vanier. Yet, interesting as these substantive themes and questions were, the dialogical performance of many of Hauerwas's students provided a very powerful exemplification of the vulnerable receptivity they saw in Jesus—and it was witnessing this, first and foremost, that drew Coles into a deepening engagement with them. And this engagement complicated Coles's thinking about the

15. Hauerwas was described as a "fideistic, sectarian tribalist" by one of his Yale teachers, James Gustafson. See Gustafson, "Sectarian Temptation."

possible relationships between radical allegiance and radical receptivity to differences.

Coles and Hauerwas therefore got to know one another through students. It is now the case, moreover, that many students doing graduate work in political theory also do work in theology. Instruction from all of these students finally led us to teach a course together on Christianity and radical democracy. This book is the result of that course, and we hope it maintains the dialogical character of our interactions made possible by students.

It needs to be said, however (or at least Hauerwas thinks it needs to be said), that this book is clearly more Coles than Hauerwas. This is not only the case in terms of material; just as important is the agenda Coles developed that has shaped what we have tried to do. Coles imagined "radical democracy." Moreover, Coles thinks that Christianity might matter for how radical democracy is understood and, more importantly, practiced. Hauerwas is less clear that he has a stake in "radical democracy," but given Coles's reading of Christian theologians, Hauerwas cannot and does not want to avoid being drawn into the lives of radical democrats.

"Coles imagined 'radical democracy,'" is a line written by Hauerwas, and it makes Coles squirm—not simply because it would be far better to say that Coles inherited streams of imagining radical democracy (as Hauerwas knows, for he too inherited these streams[16]). More importantly, Coles's imagination of radical democracy has been profoundly inspirited by the last two decades he has spent in Durham, North Carolina, for which even the novels of Flannery O'Connor could not prepare him. During most of this time, Coles has been engaged in a variety of radical democratic movements, organizing initiatives, and community-building efforts. And so he has found himself working beside prophetic people who understand their efforts as bringing the good news of the gospel to our city. He has found himself working within churches and listening to pastors and lay people proclaiming the glory of a God that Nietzsche had proclaimed was dead. Many of the most profound efforts to speak to questions of race in Durham have come from the mouths of black (and white) pastors channeling Christ and Moses, as have many of the most profound conjurings of Dionysian beloved community. Coles has

---

16. For some of Hauerwas's debts here, see his engagements with Wolin, Connolly, and others in *Vision and Virtue*.

written in passing elsewhere about the centrality of these experiences in the ongoing formation of his life and imagination, and he has no desire to construct a more systematic account here.[17] Yet it is important to note that more than anything else, in Coles's view, it has been the experience of working side by side with Christians in Durham that has nurtured this conversation with Hauerwas, nurtured Coles's capacity and interest in listening, and given it much of the depth it has. He repeatedly encounters difficulties translating what he has found here to those more comfortably lodged within the literal and discursive walls of secular university life. Translation is a slow, difficult, and uncertain process. Finally, if some of Coles's readings of, say, Yoder, Vanier, and Williams push on elements in Hauerwas, Coles suspects that he learned such things in no small part from engagements with Christians at work in Durham.

Yet along with our overlapping interests, questions, passions, and concerns, readers will discover that we make no attempt to conceal the tensions and conflicts that must be present if we are to be honest with one another. Hauerwas worries that Coles's generous willingness to take Christianity seriously could tempt Christians to ignore his unbelief.[18] Coles worries, moreover, as his letters make clear, that Hauerwas is never quite willing to expose his account of the church to the vulnerabilities that Coles thinks are the heart of radical democracy. Coles wants Hauerwas to live more on the edge, whereas Hauerwas is not even sure, given the character of the contemporary church, where the edge is. Yet Hauerwas believes that the center of the church's life requires that it live on the edge.

We do think there is a rationale to the way we have ordered the chapters. The book begins with an essay by Hauerwas that tries to establish the possibility of, as well as the problems involved in, trying to think through the relation of Christianity and radical democracy. Coles

17. See, for example, the introduction and chapter 7 in *Beyond Gated Politics*.

18. In *The New Measures: A Theological History of Democratic Practice*, Ted Smith provides an account of how Christian practices can migrate in the service of democratic forms that might still Hauerwas's worries. Smith observes, "If practices retain intentions, roles, rules, moods, and motives as they migrate across spheres, even when the conscious intentions of the users change, then reforms in one sphere can migrate to others. A Christian cultural critic might therefore treat the migration of practices between churches and other social spheres not as a rash of impurities that must be washed or wished away, but as a series of opportunities for critical engagement that do not require a church to abandon its first explicitly theological language" (30). Maybe, says Hauerwas.

responds with a letter in which the very notion of "haunting" is enriched by his directing attention to the remembrance of the dead. Particularly in this letter, as well as in the chapter that follows on West and Baker, Coles asks unavoidable questions about the way one views a past that was so wrong that nothing can be done to make it right. Race is, for us (and, we believe, for America), the fundamental challenge. Coles's appreciative critique of Cornel West through comparing West with Ella Baker sets the challenge before us. Hauerwas's celebration of Will Campbell at least raises the issue for Coles of whether he can have Baker without the theological language that makes Campbell's account of racism so compelling: racism is sin.

Many of these essays, both Hauerwas's and Coles's, were written for other occasions but with this book in mind. For example, the chapter on Campbell was written to inaugurate the Will D. Campbell Lecture at the University of Mississippi. The chapter on West and Baker was written in the context of a panel at the American Academy of Religion on Cornel West's *Democracy Matters: Winning the Fight against Imperialism*. We think it useful to keep the forms of the lecture and panel presentation for no other reason—in a book about the importance of locality—than that these forms do not try to hide from where they came. Moreover, that many of the chapters are followed by letters we hope helps to make the dialogical character of our work unavoidable.

The last part of the book is dominated by the work of Jean Vanier and the L'Arche movement. Some may well wonder what L'Arche has to do with politics. We hope the essays on Vanier and L'Arche will silence that wonder, as we explore the liturgical character of timeful friendship, peacemaking, and corporeal practices of receptivity. There is, however, a more pressing question raised by our calling attention to the significance of Vanier's work. It can be asked how a movement like the IAF or SNCC can be compatible with the work of L'Arche. Where the IAF and the SNCC were and are concerned with "results," even as they take the cultivation of relationships to be their primary work, nothing happens at L'Arche homes. Yet we believe this difference is exaggerated if politics is not about "doing something" for the poor and the marginalized, but about learning to be with the poor and marginalized. Central to our understanding of both efforts is learning to understand and live our situation—by which we mean our own poverty and richer political possibilities—in and through such relationships.

We think, moreover, that these issues are vital for thinking through the work that the university ought to be about. Universities are elite institutions that serve the relatively well off. If the work of radical democrats is to be sustained, the character of universities will need to take note. We do not pretend that we have any grand schemes for the transformation of the university, but we at least try to develop a few hints about where we might begin.[19]

The book ends with a dialogue that we hope makes evident the exchange that the chapters of the book have exemplified. And this returns us to questions of the edge between us, the topography of this encounter, and possibly the topography of the different modes that both inform and might be informed by it. Coles began an earlier book with the notion of "ecotone":"special meeting grounds" between two different ecological communities (for example, a forest and a meadow) that ecologists tell us are characterized by a particularly fertile "edge effect." Ecotone stems from the Greek *oikos* or "habitation," and *tonos* or "tension." "'Ecotone' and 'edge effect' call our attention to the life-engendering character of the ambiguous tension-laden dwelling . . . the pregnancy of edges."[20] The work of Rowan Williams allows us to deepen this metaphor significantly, such that it might evoke not simply an edge between different ecological or social communities or topographies, but the very transformation of our understanding of topography as such. Williams (as Coles discusses at greater length below) makes much of the idea that Jesus did not come here to be "a competitor for space in this world."[21] He does seek a kingdom, but not one that would be recognizable in terms of human territoriality, or even human territory. Rather, in his life "the human map is being redrawn, the world turned upside down" (52). Jesus' good news is that he "interrupts and reorganizes the landscape in ways that are not predictable" (40). He does so not as a simple reversal, but rather he "threatens because he does not compete . . . and because it is that whole world of rivalry and defense which is in question" (69). In this sense, the "unworldliness" of Christ's kingdom is "a way of saying 'yes' to the world by refusing the world's own skewed and destructive account of itself" (88).

19. For Hauerwas's extended reflections on the university, see *State of the University*.
20. Coles, *Self/Power/Other*, 1.
21. Williams, *Christ on Trial*, 6. Hereafter cited parenthetically.

In other words, we might say that Jesus lets the world truly be the world by refiguring our very sense of topography, such that the edge-effect, or ecotone, becomes the metaphor not just for the possible meeting ground between different communities, but, more importantly, for the character of generative life-giving places and modes of dwelling as such. In this sense, vulnerable edges are seen to run throughout different communities and landscapes in ways that—insofar as we live them vulnerably, which is at once our only possibility for living well and often a genuine danger—"are not predictable." It is the vulnerably undulating unpredictable landscape that is a constitutive dimension of the world into which Jesus (and radical democracy) would call us to recognize and work. This is to say, Hauerwas's not knowing "where the edge is" is something Coles (with Hauerwas) thinks is constitutive of generative places and modes of becoming in time—and therefore not a lack. We cannot know precisely where the edges are, because they are part of what and how we are called into being, and they run throughout our lives and works in ways that precede us and are multidimensional. We hope that this book might, at its best, offer encounters that are on their way toward exemplifying modes of being that are at once distinct and yet "not competitors for space in this world." Or distinct, precisely insofar as they are not competitors for space in this world—or, again, distinct insofar as we seek, through these engagements of our differences, to understand what it might mean to become noncompetitors for the world's space.

"Not competitors for space in this world" is a difficult aspiration for human beings, not simply because we are fallible or fallen but also because an ineliminable aspect of what we think it means to live well in this world is to have enemies, to name and struggle against the bad and sometimes the evil. This does not mean "demonizing," nor should "enemy" be ascribed as an immutable label. Nevertheless, insofar as a person or group struggles against particular practices or persons, there is a profound sense in which we are always competitors against particular patterns of territoriality. Yet does it follow from this that competitors against must be competitors for new modes of dominating space in this world? With Williams we would aspire toward new modes of becoming communities that at once oppose territoriality and aim toward more receptive and generous practices of coexistence. This is a never-perfectly-achieved and thus never-ending task, which will frequently err and will always be in need of rethinking, of reorganizing, and of new beginnings informed by histories of such efforts in the past.

It is a fine line—a fine edge—this distinction between competing against and struggling for something that is beyond the logic of competition. We frequently (and, to some extent, likely always) confuse one side of the line with the other, and often we even become invested in and systematize such confusions to the benefit of new conquests. The only possible remedy is "to turn the world upside down" and make ourselves unpredictable by deepening the strange and vulnerable dialogues that would confuse the confusions that keep us fixed within what Foucault called the blackmail of either "yes" or "no." Our dialogues are nourished by stories of, and shared visceral connections with, those who have devoted their lives to such efforts, including people such as Jean Vanier, from whom we paradoxically learn most about dialogue through the exemplary manner in which he explores wordless relationships. This is perhaps the deepest point of alliance between the radical-democratic trickster and the fool for Christ who converse in this book. We hope it inspires others toward hopeful folly. "Do not deceive yourselves. If you think that you are wise in this age, you should become fools so that you may become wise. For the wisdom of this world is foolishness with God. For it is written, 'He catches the wise in their craftiness'" (1 Cor 3:18–19 NRSV). Even the "unbeliever" among us hopes to become ever-more foolish in response to echoes of this call, and there is joy as well as haunting difficulty in responding to alien echoes.

We have enjoyed working on this book, and we hope readers will find enjoyment in reading it. We need all the help we can get, and we know that, without joy, such help will not be forthcoming.

CHAPTER 1

A Haunting Possibility:
Christianity and Radical Democracy

Stanley Hauerwas

WHY JOHN HOWARD YODER HAUNTS ROMAND COLES

Near the end of a chapter titled "The Wild Patience of John Howard Yoder," in his book *Beyond Gated Politics: Reflections for the Possibility of Democracy*, Romand Coles confesses:

> If I see Yoder's Jesus as a great story, it is not simply because it resonates so much with themes of dialogue and receptivity that I embraced long before my encounter with his writing. More importantly, it is great the way the sublime that is unconquered by sovereign subjectivity is great: It mightily calls into question my perception, sense-making, reach, direction, ethical and political faiths. Yoder haunts me. He is not an easy ghost, but I want to want him with me. I want him opening new doors and windows in my cave, offering new light and air, and occasionally rattling my walls until I feel in my bones "there's no place like home" and find myself engaged in a new thing.[1]

By exploring why Coles is "haunted" by John Howard Yoder, I want to open an investigation into the relation between the church and radical democracy. I want to want to do so, because I am haunted by Romand Coles. He is my colleague and friend. We have even co-taught a course on "Christianity and Radical Democracy." I admire Coles's willingness and

---

1. Coles, *Beyond Gated Politics*, 137–38. Coles also speaks of Yoder's work as a "haunting possibility" in the preface to *Beyond Gated Politics*, xxiv. References to *Beyond Gated Politics* will now appear in parentheses in the text.

courage to read theologians like Yoder and Rowan Williams and the challenge they present for how he thinks about politics and political theory. To witness Coles reading is a lesson in the generosity he argues is at the heart of the practice of radical democracy. I cannot pretend to possess the same reading habits, but I at least want to use this opportunity to engage Coles's worries concerning why and how Christian jealousy about Jesus might make Christians distrustful allies in the struggle for radical democracy. I hope I will be able to convince Coles (and myself) that Christians are able to make a constructive contribution to the development of radical-democratic alternatives.

Coles's worries concerning Yoder's "jealousy" about Jesus must be understood against the background of his account of radical democracy. According to Coles, the future of democracy depends on finding alternatives to the dominant forms of "disengaged liberal democracy" currently identified with the nations of the West (x). Coles argues that the very clarity characteristic of theorists such as John Rawls conceals liberalism's fear of our tragic finitude (26). Rawls's inability to acknowledge "tragedy's tragedy"—that is, the inescapable reality of the limits of our political vision—is exemplified by Rawls's setting aside as "extensions" questions of the identity and ethical substance of "a society" in the name of imposing a public reason we allegedly have in common (5). As a result, power is concealed by a flattened political process designed to disqualify in principle advocates of comprehensive doctrines that refuse to be domesticated or marginalized in the name of "peace."

By contrast Coles argues that democracy cannot be a "possession" but rather is a practice

> in search of itself, struggling beyond pasts and presents in which it was unrealized (both for many people and across many domains of life) and in the face of futures threatening to retrench its achievements and aspirations. Democracy happens primarily as a generative activity in which people seek to reinvent it in challenges and contestations concerning the questions of what it might become. Democracy is *democratization*. And when it has been brought to life historically (by abolitionists, feminists, antiwar activists, populists in the nineteenth century, the civil rights movement, Native American rights activists, grassroots community activists, and so on), it has always hinged upon those who sensed, in their myriad insurgent, inventive, and receptive ca-

pacities, that democracy was, is, and will be significantly beyond democracy as "we" know it in its dominant forms: beyond the arbitrary exclusions, subjugations, and dangers that accompany every democratic "we" and their "knowing" and disclose complacency toward present practices as a sham. Democratization has always depended upon those who embark beyond democracy's dominant forms to invent greater equality, freedom, and receptive generosity toward others. (xi)

"Tension-dwelling," therefore, becomes one of the essential characteristics of radical democracy, which leads Coles to quite a sympathetic reading of Alasdair MacIntyre. From Coles's perspective, MacIntyre's understanding of the conflict between traditions is a constructive alternative to capitalist cosmopolitanism. Yet he fears that MacIntyre's understanding of the "conflict of the faculties" lacks the basis for a generosity towards others that comes from "a sense of finitude wrought by vulnerable engagements with others whose differences bring it vividly into the foreground" (99). In contrast, Derrida—who at times evokes the radical responsibility for hospitality to the "new born child,"—begins to gesture toward the kind of dissymmetry necessary for democratic engagement.

Coles recognizes that some will find his account of radical democracy far too vague, but to counter such criticism he provides accounts of the concrete political work done by feminists of color as well as by the Industrial Areas Foundation (IAF). The IAF is particularly important for his case because, from Coles's perspective, the IAF's practice of the complex art of listening is constitutive of a politics that depends on organizing through the establishment of relationships.[2] Through such listening, what is radical about radical democracy becomes apparent: democracy has no stable "table" around which differences can be gathered. Rather the democratic table must move and be transformed in such a way that "the space and lines of separation and relation undergo repeated and unwonted change" (231).

2. It should be noted that Coles has been deeply involved in the IAF in Durham, North Carolina. In the "Acknowledgements" for *Beyond Gated Politics*, he notes that "during the past seven years I've been active with many scores of people in a grassroots democracy organizing project in Durham called Durham CAN. The myriad dialogues, struggles, and actions we perform together feed my imagination, thought, and judgment day in and day out. Thinking for me is impossible without hope. Without those who are daily bringing democracy to life in this small southern city I would muster little of either" (viii).

Radical democracy is, therefore, most determinatively exemplified by urban organizing practices that engage a wide spectrum of people by bridging political divisions. Coles does not assume that all forms of radical democracy will be local, but rather that local politics "provides a crucial learning ground for political work on many other scales, and, moreover, that analogous modes of receptivity will have to be invented at these larger scales if democratic efforts are better able to avoid problems of political disengagement, bureaucratic professionalism, and so on" (xxviii).

This finally brings us to why Yoder, whom Coles treats between his chapters on MacIntyre and Derrida, is so important for Coles's account of radical democracy. Coles, a member of no church, finds in Yoder "a vision of dialogical communities that brings forth very particular and powerful practices of generous solidarity precisely *through* creative uses of conflict and a vulnerable receptivity to the 'least of these' within the church and to those outside it" (110, emphasis in original). Coles notes that what particularly attracts him to Yoder, given the argument of *Beyond Gated Politics*, is the way Yoder combines bearing witness to his confessedly provincial tradition and remaining vulnerable and receptive to others who do not share his tradition (111).[3]

Coles acknowledges that he cannot avoid translating and developing Yoder's vocabulary (and Coles quite rightly knows that vocabulary is everything) into his own idiom. But Coles also refuses to try to "get around" Yoder's Christocentrism. For Coles recognizes that the characteristics he finds so admirable in Yoder's account of patience and vulnerability are inseparable from Yoder's understanding of what is entailed by being a disciple of Jesus. Yoder's commitment to nonviolence, and the

---

3. In *Seeing Like a State: How Certain Schemes to Improve the Human Condition Have Failed*, James C. Scott responds, in a manner similar to Coles, to the charge that his account of practical reason uncritically admires "the local, the traditional, and the customary." Scott argues that his point is not that practical knowledge is the product of some mythical and egalitarian state of nature, but that the kind of practical knowledge he describes is "inseparable from the practices of dominion, monopoly, and exclusion that offend the modern liberal sensibility" (7). The implications of the recovery of practical reason for political theory, particularly the implications of the recovery of Aristotle's understanding of practical reason through Wittgenstein, have not been adequately explored. Mouffe's attempt in *Democratic Paradox* to show that Wittgenstein underwrites a more "pluralistic" and conflictual politics is simply not very interesting. Using G. E. M. Anscombe's *Intention*, Mark Ryan begins the kind of analysis we need in his *Agency and Practical Reason: The Critique of Modern Moral Theory from Anscombe to Hauerwas*.

patience required to be nonviolent, are unintelligible if the practice of nonviolence as well as the corresponding virtue of patience are divorced from Yoder's understanding of the community gathered in the name of Jesus. The name for Yoder's politics is "church."

Coles is particularly impressed by Yoder's account of the necessity of the church's unending task of "reaching back" to Scripture to test again and again whether it is being faithful to Jesus. To "reach back" is not just another form of proceduralism but rather an expression of confidence that through the dialogical process of confrontation and reconciliation, the church will discern how it may have confused the gospel with worldly pretension. Yoder's name for the attempt to make the church safe by joining its destiny to worldly powers is "Constantinianism," which, drawing on his Anabaptist heritage, Yoder argues the church must disavow. That disavowal not only requires the church to give up claims of political, legal, and social establishment, but also, and more importantly, requires the church to abandon all attempts to secure the gospel through foundational epistemological strategies.[4]

Yoder argues that the church precedes the world epistemologically, but Coles rightly argues that does not mean that Yoder thinks the church has nothing to learn from the world. Rather it means that there can be no "politics of Jesus" that could be coercive, selfish, nondialogical, or invulnerable (121). Therefore, Christians, from Yoder's perspective, should welcome the diversity of peoples that Babel represents because only by engagements with different communities does the church learn what it means to be a community of truth and love.

Coles therefore admirably presents Yoder's understanding of the "politics of Jesus" as a refusal to confine the church to a private sphere. "Jesus is Lord" does not have the grammar of a private speech act. Nonetheless Coles worries that the confession "Jesus is Lord" might "constitute a radical deafness to nonbelieves and a confinement of prophesy to those within the church, so that the dialogic conditions of *agape* within give way to monological practices toward others outside in a manner likely to proliferate blindness and violence" (119). Coles therefore raises

---

4. This was the central argument of Chris Huebner in his dissertation written at Duke, titled *Unhandling History: Anti-Theory, Ethics, and the Practice of Witness*. Coles was one of the readers of this dissertation. Huebner's book, *A Precarious Peace: Yoderian Explorations on Theology, Knowledge, and Identity* develops this crucial point by unsettling the presumption that "Mennonite" is a given identity.

the question of whether there might not be an element of complicity between pre-Constantinian proclamations of "fidelity to the jealously of Christ as Lord" and the rise of Constantinianism (133, 135).[5]

Coles observes that even if these questions point to a problem, they are not, nor are they meant to be, devastating challenges to Yoder's position. Rather Coles's commitment to radical democracy makes him think it important to ask if Yoder's way of affirming Jesus as Lord might weaken his ability to engage in receptive engagements with "some forms of polytheism, atheism, and postsecular modes of enchantment, as well as with a lot of critical work being done by liberation theologians, critical race theorists, feminists, students of postcoloniality, and ecologists" (136). Noting that he has absolutely no authority to urge Mennonite Christians how to think about these matters, Coles nonetheless thinks Yoder would have benefited by engaging these other voices.

Coles ends his chapter on Yoder by articulating some of the challenges Yoder presents to radical democrats. He asks, for example, how radical democrats might develop, as Yoder has, enduring practices of resistance; Coles also asks if radical democrats can show how a certain jealousy might be unavoidable, necessary, and helpful in resisting odious forms of power. Might it even be the case that some account of jealousy infuses and enables every generosity? (138). In short, Coles turns to the critical tools developed through his close attention to Yoder in order to raise questions for radical democrats like himself. That he does so makes his challenge to Yoder, and to those like me who have been influenced by Yoder, all the more important. That challenge is, quite simply, whether we have something to learn from radical-democratic practice for the way we should understand the practice we call church.

YODER'S AUGUSTINIAN RESPONSE

Coles's account of Yoder is so sympathetic that he in effect answers his own challenge to Yoder in his exposition of Yoder's position. For example, Coles notes that in spite of Yoder's critique of Augustine's understanding of the invisible church, Yoder does not reify the visible body in a manner that identifies the church only with believers. Indeed, for Yoder, the

---

5. Coles is, I think, quite right to have this worry, but I think it should not be a worry. I have long argued that neither Yoder nor I are "sectarians." We are rather theocrats. It is just very hard to rule when you are committed to nonviolence. But we are willing to try. "Try," however, means that politics is always a matter of persuasion.

boundaries that constitute the church are permeable. Therefore, Yoder, as Coles observes, has no difficulty learning from Gandhi, Marx, or modern pluralism (128). Yoder's non-Constantianism means that he never assumes he can control who will want to be his conversation partners. The question is not whether Yoder would be ready to engage polytheists and atheists, but rather why they would want to talk with Christians, and what the conversation would be about.

In an essay titled "The Disavowal of Constantine: An Alternative Perspective on Interfaith Dialogue," Yoder observes that the attempt to develop a general theory or strategy for Christian engagement with other faiths or traditions can only reproduce Constantinian habits: "By the nature of the case," Yoder says, "it is not possible to establish, either speculatively or from historical samples, a consistent anti-Constantinian model. The prophetic denunciation of paganization must always be missionary and ad hoc; it will be in language as local and as timely as the abuses it critiques."[6] The way forward for Yoder is therefore always fragmentary and occasional. For the "affirmative alternative underlying the critique of paganization is the concreteness of the visible community created by the renewed message. The alternative to hierarchical definition is local definition."[7]

Yoder's appeal to the "local" as an alternative to Constantinianism is not unlike Coles's understanding of the work of radical democracy. Interestingly enough, I think Yoder's and Coles's attempts to recover the politics of locality depend on insights stemming from what each might consider the most unlikely of sources, namely, Augustine.[8] For I want to

6. Yoder, "Disavowal of Constantine," 250.

7. Ibid., 253.

8. Coles has written appreciatively of Augustine, though his worries about Augustine are similar to his worries about Yoder. He notes that Augustine argues that the Christian community is to embrace the uniqueness of each of its members, yet "*these forms* of Christian receiving, giving, and proliferation are based on an imagination profoundly blind to the possible being and value of radical alterity in people who live resolutely outside the Christian story" (see Coles, *Rethinking Generosity*, 2–3; emphasis in original). He also worries that Augustine's God is also a jealous God, leading to some of the same problems as Yoder's jealously for Jesus.

Yoder rarely had anything positive to say about Augustine, but Charlie Collier will soon have a dissertation finished in which he argues that there are some deep similarities between Yoder and Augustine. In his most recent book, *Christianity and the Secular*, R. A. Marcus provides a very sympathetic account of Yoder by suggesting that Augustine would have been profoundly sympathetic with many of Yoder's worries about Constantinianism.

suggest that the ability to sustain a local politics, whether it be Christian or radically democratic, requires an orientation toward death that grounds humility—the humility necessary to engage in the slow and painful work of sustaining a community capable of resisting the allure of significance that is the breeding ground of violence.

Robert Dodaro, in his extraordinary essay, "Eloquent Lies, Just Wars and the Politics of Persuasion: Reading Augustine's *City of God* in a 'Postmodern' World," argues that Augustine's critique of the deceptive language that the Romans used in order to claim political legitimacy was based on the core insight that the personal glory that motivates the behavior of all politicians

> is rooted in deception and is itself motivated by the need to cover up the fear of death. For the Augustine of the *City of God*, empire maintenance, with the attendant subjection of peoples and the religious, intellectual, and cultural props which legitimate it is the most grotesque social manifestation of this fear of death. However, just as the objective evil which empires sustain has to be veiled from the view of its practitioners, so too must the fear of death which motivates empire maintenance be veiled from view of all concerned. Hence, every act of political deception occurs on two levels: there is the lie or distortion itself which political authorities and their rhetors create and pass on to the public, and there is the self-deception which veils the lie from the officials who tell it.[9]

From Augustine's perspective, Satan was the first great politician, because Satan used eloquent and deceptive rhetoric to assure Eve that if she ate the forbidden fruit, she "would be like God" (Gen 3:5). For Augustine, the clue to the false security at the base of all political deception is the denial of death implicit in the rhetoric of glory. In *The City of God*, Augustine observes:

> Roman heroes belonged to an earthly city, and the aim set before them, in all their acts of duty for her was the safety of their country, and a kingdom not in heaven, but on earth; not in life eternal, but in the process where the dying pass away and are succeeded by those who will die in their turn. What else was there for them

---

9. Dodaro, "Eloquent Lies," 88–90.

to love save glory? For, through glory, they desired to have a kind
of life after death on the lips of those who praised them.[10]

In contrast to the Roman desire for political glory as the only way
to defeat death, Dodaro calls attention to Augustine's understanding
of martyrdom. For the martyr, fear of death was overcome by faith in
a reality that, from the Roman perspective, could not help but appear
"invisible." Yet the martyr's victory challenges the Roman understanding
of "politics," because the martyr does not depend on memory secured by
military or political glory. The martyr's memory is secured, rather, in the
communion of saints who died victorious because they broke forever the
fatal victim/victimizer logic.[11] The martyr cannot be a hero—whose glory
is his own—because the glory of the martyr is a reflected glory—a reflection of the glory of Christ—signaling an alternative political ethic.

Augustine contrasts the inability of Roman statesmen to confess
wrongdoing and seek repentance with the conscience made possible by
Christians' willingness to embrace death. Roman heroes cannot possess
the moral self-knowledge that comes from a right relationship with God.
They therefore fail to achieve "any progress toward a concomitant self-
forgetfulness, processes [i.e., love of God and contempt of self] which
Augustine believes are never absent from true virtue. Christians ought,

10. Augustine *City of God* 5.14 (Bettenson, 204). Hannah Arendt, of course, argued
that because Christians, and in particular Augustine, refused such glory, they were
determinatively nonpolitical. For Arendt, there can be no politics that does not try to
"transcend the life-span of mortal men." See Arendt, *Human Condition*, 55.

11. I wish Jeffrey Stout might have thought to include me in his commendation of
Augustinians in *Democracy and Tradition*, 39–41. In *After Christendom?* the book Stout
so deeply dislikes, I called attention to Augustine's understanding of martyrdom as the
basis for sustaining a politics of modesty. For example, I observed that "it was through
martyrdom that the church triumphed over Rome. Rome could kill Christians but they
could not victimize them. The martyrs could go to their death confident that the story to
which their killers were trying to subject them—that is the story of victimization—was
not the true story of their death. To Rome Christians dying for their faith, for their refusal to obey Caesar, was an irrational act. for the martyrs their dying was part of a story
that Rome could not acknowledge and remain in power as Rome" (38). Chris Huebner
rightly argues that martyrdom is an eschatological act through which the world as we
know it is stripped of its apparent givenness, and strange new possibilities emerge. In
other words, martyrs do not have a "solid identity" but rather call into question all our
assumptions that we can secure our identity through our actions. After all, the martyr
cannot know she is a martyr until God identifies her as such. In postmodern terms, the
martyr is the most determinative exemplification of the de-centered self. See Huebner,
Precarious Peace, chapters 8 and 12.

therefore, to read accounts of Roman heroism only as counter-examples, as signs pointing to the morally disastrous motivations which subvert good deeds as a matter of course."[12]

Accordingly, Augustine asks, "is it reasonable, is it sensible, to boast of the extent and grandeur of empire, when you cannot show that men lived in happiness, as they passed their lives amid the horrors of war, amid the shedding of men's blood—whether the blood of enemies or fellow citizens—under the shadow of fear and amid the terror of ruthless ambition?"[13] The only joy such people achieve has the "fragile brilliance of glass" and is outweighed by the fear of loss.[14] So the rich and the powerful are "tortured by fears, worn out with sadness, burnt up with ambition, never knowing the serenity of repose."[15] In contrast, the person of limited resources is loved by family and friends, enjoys the blessing of peace with his relations and friends; "he is loyal, compassionate, and kind, healthy in body, temperate in habits, of unblemished character, and enjoys the serenity of a good conscience."[16]

In short, a community shaped by the memory of the martyrs makes possible a patient people capable of the slow, hard work of a politics of place, because they are not driven by the politics of fear. Yoder's "wild patience" assumes that such a people must exist if the work of nonviolence is to be a radical challenge to the way the world is. What the church contributes to radical democracy is therefore a people who seek not glory but justice. Such a people have been made possible because they have been formed through liturgical action to be for the world what the world can become. Therefore, no bridge is needed between "church" and "politics":

> the will of God for human socialness as a whole is prefigured by the shape to which the Body of Christ is called. Church and world are not two compartments under separate legislation or two institutions with contradictory assignments, but two levels of the pertinency of the same Lordship. The people of God is called to be today what the world is called to be ultimately.[17]

12. Dodaro, "Eloquent Lies," 92.

13. Augustine *City of God* 4.3 (Bettenson, 138).

14. Ibid.

15. Ibid.

16. Ibid.

17. Yoder, *Body Politics*, ix. That *Body Politics* was originally published by Discipleship Resources is a telling indication of Yoder's politics—he wanted to write for

A people who seek justice rather than glory, a justice that is not driven by the fear of death, are not restricted to the church. The story Charles Payne tells in his *I've Got the Light of Freedom: The Organizing Tradition and the Mississippi Freedom Struggle* is the story of such a people.[18] Ella Baker, Miles Horton, and Robert Moses were and are such people.[19] They made possible the organizing that Payne shows was perhaps the greatest contribution of the Student Nonviolent Coordinating Committee (SNCC): they created a cadre of indigenous activists capable of recognizing existing leaders in the communities SNCC came to organize—leaders more than capable of assuming authority.[20] Yet as Payne makes clear, organizing is slow, and the injustices they sought to redress begged for quick resolution. It is therefore not surprising that SNCC was beset by internal strife, caused at least in part by an increasing need to take a more activist and black nationalist stance.[21]

Payne shows that many factors contributed to SNCC's inability to sustain the work of organizing. No doubt SNCC was victimized by its success, but Payne also points out that to explain what happened to SNCC in terms of victimization puts far too much emphasis on legal change, and not enough on local peoples' conception of freedom for education, jobs, and housing.[22] The more likely reason SNCC lost its way, according to Payne, is that once the work of SNCC was discovered by the national media, the stories necessary to sustain the everyday were lost, even among those doing the work of the everyday. But perhaps most disastrously, the work of organization was lost because, as Payne puts

---

nonacademics.

18. Payne, *I've Got the Light of Freedom*. Rom Coles told me to read Payne's extraordinary book. I was gratified that Payne holds in such high regard, as do I, Richard Kluger's *Simple Justice: The History of Brown vs. Board of Education and Black America's Struggle for Equality*.

19. In 1960 Ella Baker sent Robert Moses to Amzie Moore, who was vice president of the state conference of the NAACP, in order that Moses might learn what it meant to work in Mississippi. Payne reports that while "Moore was schooling Moses, he was doing a reading on him. In order to survive Mississippi, Moses feels, people like More had to become astute judges of character. As he initiated Moses into the Mississippi realities, Moore was also assessing Moses' character. Was this someone who could be relied upon? Someone who could stick it out?" (Payne, *I've Got the Light of Freedom*, 106). It must surely be the case that without people of character, radical democracy is not possible.

20. Payne, *I've Got the Light of Freedom*, 237.

21. Ibid., 365.

22. Ibid., 361.

it, "the undervaluation of the leadership role played by ordinary people corresponded to an overconcentration on the role of national leaders, Dr. King in particular."[23] In short, SNCC and the civil rights movement proved not to be immune from the pathologies that Augustine thought the Romans exhibited.[24]

I certainly would not suggest that if those engaged in SNCC's organizing efforts in Mississippi had read more Augustine and Yoder, they would have been more able to sustain their work over time. It is interesting, however, that in 1981 at Gammon Theological Seminary, Yoder gave a lecture titled "The Power Equation, the Place of Jesus, and the Politics of King," in which he worried that King's identification of the American dream with Christian hope might have negative results when success was not assured.[25] The problem, of course, was not how King understood the relation of the American dream with the Christian hope, but rather that those two quite different realities had been long been assumed by most Christians in America to be one and the same thing. This assumption (that is, that American democracy has a special place in God's providential care of creation) Yoder spent a lifetime trying to counter by helping Christians rediscover the hard, slow work of politics—the kind of politics on display in Payne's account of freedom summer in Mississippi.

CAN THE CHURCH BE RADICALLY DEMOCRATIC?

Some will find my use of Augustine to suggest how Yoder might respond to Coles to be an attempt to change the subject. I have no reason to deny this charge, but I hope by changing the subject I have at least suggested a way that Christians might contribute to the work of radical democracy. For I assume that such work requires the facing down of death, making

23. Ibid., 400; see also ibid., 93, where Payne quotes Ella Baker's wonderful observation: "Strong people don't need strong leaders."

24. There is no doubt something to Charles Marsh's argument (i.e., that the collapse of SNCC was due to a "retreat" from their original theological commitments), but this is probably to put the matter in too intellectualistic a manner. Payne sees, rightly I think, that the failure to sustain SNCC had multiple causes. That said, I think Charles Marsh's *The Beloved Community* exemplifies what a theological narrative should look like.

25. Yoder, "Power Equation," 125–47. Though noting that King's combination of Gandhi and Jesus is not wrong, Yoder thinks the risk in such an association is that the meaning of the cross cannot be adequately stated in Gandhian terms. Yet Yoder observes that King bore the cross through his "conscious choice of a path of vulnerable faithfulness, despite the knowledge that it will be costly" (147).

possible a politics alternative to the politics of glory. But the question remains whether the church itself can be understood to be radically democratic. For example, Peter Dula and Alex Sider have suggested that, in spite of the deep influence Yoder has had on my work, I (unlike Yoder) have expunged conflict internal to the Christian community by privileging an authoritative ministry and orthodoxy. Accordingly, Dula and Sider ask, "Is a radical democracy really compatible with an orthodox theology? If so, how?"[26]

In contrast to the protective habits characteristic of my account of the church, Dula and Sider contend that Yoder never assumed that the most fundamental conflicts for any existing church would be with the "outside." Rather, Yoder assumed that conflict would arise in the church as part of its being in time—thus the continuing debates surrounding the practice and status of the Eucharist.[27] Dula and Sider suggest that I fail to develop an account of the conflict necessary for the life of the church because of my animus against liberalism. Therefore, I at once identify with John Paul II and John Howard Yoder, because they each (to be sure, in quite different ways) provide modes of resistance to liberalism. In short, I have let the enemy overdetermine my understanding of church.

As a result, Dula and Sider, who are sympathetic with my criticism of liberal democracy, think I rarely take "the opportunity to give an alternative account of democracy," particularly as it might have implications for how the church itself is ordered.[28] In contrast, they suggest that Yoder's renunciation of violence, which is too often reduced to Yoder's resistance to war, as requiring the kind of receptive generosity necessary to radical democracy: "This is what it means to say that Yoder's refusal of war is inextricably tied to his refusal of anti-democratic mechanisms to guarantee the survival of the church"—a refusal that I have not made, according to Dula and Sider, because of my concern to sustain "orthodoxy."

So much depends on where you begin. Unlike Yoder, I did not begin from the margins. At least I did not begin ecclesially from the margins. I began as an outsider in mainstream Protestantism. But even as an "outsider," I am a mainstream Protestant. This "church" (that is, the mainstream Protestant church) has long been understood and justified

26. Dula and Sider, "Radical Democracy, Radical Ecclesiology," 495.

27. Ibid., 496.

28. Ibid., 494.

primarily by the contribution it will make to America. Accordingly, the fundamental practices and convictions that might sustain the church as a politics sufficient to challenge the violence of the world have been absent, or relegated to "religion." If, as Dula and Sider suggest, I have failed to emphasize the kind of conflict internal to the church—conflict that might be understood to be democratic—I have done so because of the "debilitating acculturation" of the church—an acculturation that has made it impossible for the church to challenge the politics of fear.

Dula and Sider suggest that "a dialogue is democratic when the terms of the conversation are not settled in advance by a framework given prior to the dialogue. . . . Democracy sheds all guarantees and takes the risk of keeping nothing safe."[29] Yet they observe that Yoder's account of the vulnerability of the church is based, as Coles sees clearly, on the nonnegotiable lordship of Christ. I have assumed that "orthodoxy" but names the developments across time that the church has found necessary for keeping the story of Jesus straight. Therefore, rather than being the denial of radical democracy, orthodoxy is the exemplification of the training necessary for the formation of a people who are not only capable of working for justice, but who are themselves just.

I hope therefore that it might be possible to tell the story of the church across time and space as the story of conflict that makes possible a political alternative otherwise not available. No doubt the church has often betrayed this "politics" by imitating the diverse forms that the politics of fear can take. Yet Christians rightly believe that God has never left the church without faithful witnesses capable of identifying and challenging our accommodation to the powers. If it is useful to call this process "radical democracy," I certainly have no objection.

But just as important as the question of whether the conflict across time (called "orthodoxy") exemplifies "radical democracy," is the question of whether Christians will continue to be involved in the kind of work exemplified by SNCC and the IAF. These are the stories we desperately need if our political imagination is to be shaped by the gospel. I take it that Rom Coles understands his task to be nothing less than not letting us forget such stories. That is why Rom Coles haunts me. That is why I want him with me.

29. Ibid., 496.

CHAPTER 2

Letter of July 17, 2006

Romand Coles

July 17, 2006

Dear Stanley,

I'm sitting on an isolated north-facing deck of my mother-in-law's house, right in front of the moss- and lichen-covered trunk of an oak tree that grows through a hole in the deck, overlooking miles and miles of northern California ridges shrouded in oak, fir, and redwood, a lake in the valley below, the smell of baking golden-brown grasses, buzzards soaring lazily, osprey occasionally sounding in the distance—a slight breeze. I'm more aware of time happening in a very different way out here. So, when the rats gnawed the phone lines so that now you can only occasionally "sort of" hear voices on the other end through the static—but not get a smooth enough connection to sustain internet/e-mail access—I have not bugged my mother-in-law to fix it. I've relished the distance. Supposedly, someone is coming later today to run some new lines, and I may be able to send you this letter. I miss our conversations.

Have you ever read Annie Dillard's *For the Time Being*? She writes there in a way that repeatedly evokes the unfathomable numbers of dead humans and nonhumans in the earth underneath our feet.[1] As I sit here— looking, smelling, listening, and tapping on this laptop—I'm frequently overtaken by this sensibility. By a sense of the dead everywhere around me (beginning most closely with Kim's dad); by a sense that responsibility travels backwards, first toward the dead—their works, their unfulfilled

1. Dillard, *For the Time Being*.

dreams, their memories. Walter Benjamin has that very poignant passage about how even the dead are not safe from the "victors" who are continually rewriting history-as-conquest.[2] For the dead are again and again redying death at their hands. He also writes indebted to the Jewish proscription against interpreting responsibility as first and foremost futural. It is, rather, not our grandchildren but our dead ancestors who should be the focus of our responsibility. It is not that he has any disregard for the future, of course, just that the future can only be cared for obliquely, looping through the "weak messianic" shards of the past.[3] Get wrapped up in the present-tending-toward-the-future, I think he means, and you both vitiate the energies and insights from which ethical responsibility might be rendered less unintelligent, and you go mad trying to control "progress." The madness and murderous touch of being or trying to be "the victor." Of course, Benjamin didn't always stay with this thought, for example, when he wrote of the possibility of "divine violence,"[4] but he put it on the table for others to work to free from the magnetic field that sometimes stole his sense of direction in spite of all the brilliant work he did to help (re)claim another compass that discloses other possibilities. In more vernacular terms, you could say all this by saying, "Keep an eye on Ella Baker, who was keeping an eye on her parents and grandparents."

As I see it, this thought that we care for the world as we care for the dead is at the heart of what we might call a radical-democratic relation to time that begins to respond to the crucial question you raise (with Augustine—in a way very proximate to some of the themes in Williams's essay on Augustine and Arendt[5]) about the death/glory matrix that so (most) often captures politics and bends it toward violence.

What does it mean to be responsible to the murdered (or, less dramatically, to the otherwise dead) so that they might not be killed yet again—or for the first time murdered? It cannot mean to protect them from physical violence—because they've already gotten the maximal dose possible, or, if they managed to avoid physical violence in their deaths, they are now and forever free from it. No, responsibility to ancestors must mean something else.

---

2. Benjamin, "Theses on the Philosophy of History," 255.

3. Ibid., 254.

4. See Benjamin, "Critique of Violence."

5. See Williams, "Politics of the Soul."

The first thing it means, backing up a bit, is that the focus of responsibility shifts from an exclusive—or perhaps even primary—emphasis on trying to save a present-to-future moment from disaster. *The disaster has already occurred.* Benjamin is clear about that, as is the angel he writes about, looking back toward paradise, wings spread, trying to return, but blown backward by the winds of history piling up disaster.[6] (SNCC imploded, Medgar Evers was gunned down, Martin Luther King Jr. was assassinated, the civil rights movement became "Martin Luther King Day," for which Bush performs the oratory of annual reassassination, etc.) The question, then, is how do we live haunted by the disasters that have already occurred to those who were more hopeful than what befell them? And how do we live haunted by the dreams that are never killed if we remember them in the way we attempt to live? Evers is already dead. So are most of the Pomo Native Americans who once filled this valley. No sword can save them from their past deaths and potentially present remurders. So what does it mean to live responsibly in a such a tradition of murder-struck hoping? I think it means something like this: If the locus of responsibility—even responsibility to the future—lies in facing violence that has *already* happened, much of which, on top of everything, we find ourselves implicated in, the question concerns a certain reclamation and rehabilitation of something that exceeds this violence. Benjamin speaks of "hope," "redemption," and "weak messianic power."[7] With these words I want to say that whatever "lives on," or exceeds murder and even death as such, is the hopeful working of peacemaking by selves and (what I think of as) radical-democratic communities of various kinds. To be responsible for preventing re-murder is to be responsible to the memory of this hope, and one cannot do so with violence. How one *can* do so is the most challenging question we face, but maybe it is the only question that matters at the end of our days. What merits living on in and beyond us is our capacity to participate in bringing forth a future through such caring for the past-fallen. This is some of what a tradition of radical democracy calls from us. Not glory—at least not the kind about which Augustine rightly worried.

In January 2004 I gave a talk to a CAN-delegates assembly of a few hundred folks gathered in Mt. Zion on the way-east side of Durham. This

---

6. Benjamin, "Theses on the Philosophy of History," 257–58.
7. See Benjamin, "Theses on the Philosophy of History."

was Rev. Michael Walrond's church (who has since gone to Harlem to re-gather the nearly empty but largest church there), and he is one of the best speakers I've ever heard, so lifting a word in that room felt profoundly foolish to begin with, but after that beginning I was free to say whatever I could muster. So I said this, at the end of what surely must have been a "white boys can't jump" kind of speech (though a number of black pastors came up to me afterward with a twinkle in their eyes and said that was more of a sermon than they'd ever heard from a white Duke professor—so all must not have been lost):

> *Democracy is a struggle across centuries.* It's reverberating and brewing within the walls of rooms like this one. And I think, that if we really *listen*, if we *really* listen, up in the corners of this room, we can *hear the echoes of cries and dreams* of those who gather here, and all over Durham—even echoes of those who are no longer with us, those not yet born. I say to you: *we are here to create a power that will hear and respond to these voices.*[8]

I take it that this is the sort of thing that inspired Ella Baker and Bob Moses and Amzie Moore and Septima Clarke. Medger Evers. I take it that if there is radical-democratic "glory," it comes through our picking up the trail they were on. We must become trackers of nearly vanished footprints across the Mississippi delta—the sands of South Carolina's outer banks. Just like they were trackers of re-memories of radical-democratic reconstruction communities. Just like Howard Fast and Toni Morrison. You can't do this with a sword. It remains to be seen how or to what extent it is possible to win such a struggle—or what winning means, exactly, in such a struggle, especially if you don't have the slightest faith in a victorious ending. Especially if a big part of what you mean by victory is "going under," in Nietzsche's terms—not being a "victor."[9] What would it mean to devote one's life thus, on this thin surface of biosphere that may become cinder much sooner than we can imagine? I suspect I will die without an answer. Nevertheless, at some point one gets swept up in a tradition of radical-democratic struggle such that living toward these unanswered questions matters more than the other struggles, victories, ways of winning. It can be exuberant sometimes, and sometimes it can be

---

8. Coles, "Talk to Durham Can Assembly," January, 2004, in author's possession.

9. See Nietzsche, *Thus Spoke Zarathustra*. See my discussion of this Nietzsche on receptive generosity in *Rethinking Generosity*, 15–23.

like an attunement to the "lonely center of the spinning earth," as Marsh quotes Jane Stembridge.[10]

Ella Baker and Bob Moses and Amzie Moore and Septima Clarke. Medger Evers. You're exactly right: I think that among the deepest things you and I share is a passion not to let us forget such stories. I have always taken a great pleasure in you as a storyteller, and especially perhaps in relation to the stories I wouldn't have guessed I'd like all that much until I heard you tell them. So a question arises: Just what kind of stories are these? Are they ultimately stories of Christian characters who, because they were Christian, provided the patience without which practices I call radical-democratic could not have transpired? This is a possibility from which I should remind myself not to hide. And I see the centrality of Christian characters all over these stories. Nevertheless, I think you too would do well to dwell patiently with some other possibilities than the ones that are more comforting to you.

In your essay, which is quite wonderful and has sparked a lot of thinking out here in response, you ask early on what Christians might learn from radical-democratic practice. I see you suggesting in this essay how Christians via Yoder and Augustine are what you do not object to calling "radical democrats," if it is useful to do so (paraphrasing you). I also see you saying at the end of the essay, "I take it that Rom Coles understands his task to be nothing less than not letting us forget such stories. That is why Rom Coles haunts me." But it remains unclear to me what you mean by "haunts" here. And it remains unclear what you might be saying you have to learn from radical-democratic practice. These are not mainly rhetorical questions, but rather real ones. Perhaps you could say more to clarify? With an edge, one could wonder, what and how does Hauerwas learn from radical democrats if what he learns is that Christians have always been, insofar as they were Christians, what could be called radical democrats, if that is useful? One could wonder this precise question without any edge, too. I'm curious what you mean to say here.

Similarly, by "haunting," I mean—as I think the word means—something profoundly discomforting, even if one can certainly want a ghost's presence, as one might wish, for a time, for the ghost of a passed friend or relative. Yoder is profoundly discomforting to me, because he raises a number of challenges to which radical democrats of several non-Christian

10. Quoted in Marsh, *Beloved Community*, 93.

varieties have not yet sufficiently responded, and there are no certainties that we can, even if I have more than a little faith we *might*. Is there any analogous type of haunting in your relation to radical democrats? Maybe not? Cultivating a capacity to be haunted, or rather a capacity not to deny being haunted, is integral to what I think of as tension-dwelling. Perhaps Christians simply have other means that they find to be sufficient, for seeking goods that they take to have some analogy with some of the goods radical democrats discuss? But could those swept up in a tradition of the Holy Ghost claim to be beyond the need of a haunt? So, what do you mean by haunting? What role might it play generally in Christian communities? What might be some of its very specific manifestations in relation to radical democrats?

Beyond the "Christian characters enabling the patience requisite to radical-democratic practices" narrative that you suggest (and I like, but perhaps find it to be insufficient; and maybe I like it more than I think you should like it—or at any rate settle into it—*in this specific context . . .*), two other narratives immediately suggest themselves. Each would be more haunting for you, I would guess. The first is that what we see in a number of insurgent struggles is a radical-democratic tradition that is (becoming) distinct from Christian tradition and yet cultivating many proximate virtues and communities of character. Perhaps Bob Moses suggests this more haunting possibility, as may Myles Horton, Howard Zinn, Audrey Lorde, Judith Butler, Larry Goodwyn, Adrienne Rich, Tom Hayden, Saul Alinsky (somewhat), Charles Payne, and a plethora of emergent radical-democratic communities reverberating across time. The haunting possibility is that there are traditions of radical-democratic practice that are arising, which, though indebted to several theological practices and visions, are developing admirable and possibly enduring capacities for seeing and moving through the world. I love the term you use, "distrustful ally," and I would—or should—want not to want more than this. And yet perhaps part of what sustains some distrustful alliances is a sense that those one distrusts in some ways may have even more going for them than "we" would like to acknowledge. That, at least, is my sense in relation to Yoder, Williams, and you.

There is a second possibility that might be more haunting than the main narrative you provide. This possibility seems more likely to me— that is, it seems more likely that this ghost may be recognized by you (and Christians similar to you), such that haunting takes on a specific density for you in relation to radical democrats. In fact, this second possibility is probably mainly a subtler and sharper articulation of the first possibility, which doesn't quite state the case properly. It is more haunting to me, perhaps, from the other side of a syncretism. (And what, at this point, I ask myself, am I doing, sitting here writing in what is now 104-degree shade? Am I begging to be someone's ghost . . . ? What kind of friendship—haunted? And why do I not seek the other side of the window to my back, where it is about 30 degrees cooler?) The second possibility is that what Baker and Moses and Moore and Clarke embody is a form of syncretic radical-democratic community that significantly exceeds what either Christianity or non-Christian modes of democracy embodied before them. Or, at any rate, they embody something that exceeds that which they brought from each of these traditions by combining them in ways more admirable than much of what they inherited from each on more separate lines. What if you're right, from the Black Church they inherited modes of patience, time dwelling, virtues and a vision of beloved community, and so forth, that greatly enabled a struggle of nonviolent vulnerability and enemy love that is very difficult to imagine having been born in absence of this tradition? *AND*, what if the distinctive "experimentalism," "openness to experience," "a profoundly antihierarchical ethos," "generous (as opposed to flattened stingy) pluralism" in relation to atheists, Jews, mystics, and others who were profoundly invested in the struggle, and so forth, were engendered very significantly by streams of radical-democratic tradition that were irreducible to Christian debts and nevertheless crucial to much of what is admirable in early SNCC and current IAF practices? It is hard to even say it this way. Maybe it would be better to say that each side of this development (labeled Christian or democratic) was enabled by a syncretic relationship with the other—a generative fusion that harbored many questions, tensions (a work in progress?)—a haunted work, no less beautiful for so being? The point here wouldn't be that Christianity *couldn't* be "by itself" the characteristics I place more on the radical-democratic side. It is just that in *this* particular emergent undercurrent of democracy in America, radical democracy is developing intensities, practices, vision, and ethos that are irreducible to its Christian inheritance.

You may *not* be haunted by this? Are you? *I am*. I am haunted by the possibility of being profoundly committed to a historical development, a strand—and a strand only—which I carry forth [in such a way] that does not exhaust the whole growing fabric of this emergent tradition. I am haunted that many of the goods I admire and seek to nurture might require strands that I cannot claim to endorse entirely but nevertheless rely upon and even love-at-a-distance. I am haunted that aspects of radical democracy to which I am closer (which I find less often or less intense in many forms of Christianity that I see) may, oddly enough, be indebted to this very Christianity—which at the same time I see doing miracles I can barely fathom. What a strange thing. And how wondrous its appearance in Baker, Moses, Moore, Horton, Clarke, and so many others. To endorse this strange and beautiful thing while recognizing that the strands one finds oneself most claimed by seem to be indebted to others that one is less enamored of, or enamored as much by but at a distance to, or somewhat distrustful of—all this!—*this mode of engaging a historical struggle is what I take to be a part of a radical-democratic "unhandling of history."* I do not know if it is too much, or too little. Is it a new mode of hopefulness? Or hopelessness unaware of itself—in its latest disguise? I have no definitive answers, but it seems like the best, or at least most honest, mode from where I am working—with others who are like and unlike me toward these strange relationships sometimes called "radical democracy" and "receptive generosity." Sometimes "beloved community."

Now let me express some worries: You write, "No doubt the church has often betrayed that 'politics' by imitating the diverse forms the politics of fear can take." What work does the word "imitate" do here? Does it put "the original"—or the generative element—of the politics of fear definitively somewhere else, somewhere outside of Christianity? Might not doing this risk preventing or discouraging certain critical reflections on possible sources of such fear that reside "inside" the Christian story/body/practices? Sources that might lie in *potentia* in the heart of some of its highest aspirations, needing to be kept at bay repeatedly? To be sure, I think Connolly offers a sometimes reductive reading of Augustine on this point.[11] But it is also and at the same time an illuminating reading of Augustine. I would think Christians would want to keep some such reflections alive as conditions of their own flourishing? To say that there are sources of a politics of fear within Christianity is not to damn Christianity, but rather potentially to call for it to recognize and work to

---

11. See Connolly, "A Letter to Augustine."

resist dangers that can be spawned by it. (Radical democracy has many of those dangers too. This isn't a move to "gain an upper hand.")

On King, Christianity, and the American Dream: which American Dream? I don't think Martin Luther King Jr. is talking about the dominant dream, even as he quotes the founders. I think he's clearly got his heavy foot in the Baker-Horton dream (as I'm sure you know, with Parks, Martin Luther King Jr. visited Highlander on a number of occasions prior to Montgomery). I also don't think he's writing about progress on an American–nation-state, temporal scale. People often hear only the last four words of King's phrase, "*the arc of the universe is long* but it bends toward justice."[12] I think he's much closer to Yoder here. But these are maybe not ultimately very important questions in the context of this essay. . . .

Back to worries. You write:

> Coles is, I think, quite right to have this worry, but I think it should not be a worry. I have long argued that neither Yoder nor I are "sectarians." We are rather theocrats. It is just very hard to rule when you are committed to nonviolence. But we are willing to try. "Try," however, means that politics is always a matter of persuasion.[13]

Now, as you might suspect, "theocrat" and "willing" to "try" to "rule" continue to make me very worried. Nonviolence doesn't dispel the worries. Lots of what I fear most in the "-ocracies" of our day is "nonviolent." Shopping malls (if you exclude the sweatshops . . . which you of course can't) are nonviolent, I suppose, but hell-bent on absorbing every corpuscle of flesh-desire that enters them, to largely—though not simply—odious ends. They seek total rule. Exclude the violence of sweatshop regimes and they'd still be odious. My work in relation to Yoder, and my questions about haunting, above, are less singularly about violence (though, too, they are very much about *that*) than they are about the "willing to try to rule" frame. I'd even say that the hope of a better "haunted community" is an effort to explore an alternative to "willing to try to rule." Read it in this context. Or at least the close proximity of "will" and "rule" makes me very nervous about likely incapacities of receptivity that will be engendered in

12. This is a phrase Martin Luther King Jr. used repeatedly in speeches over many years.

13. See page 22 above, note 5.

such "willing"—and about the undesirability of relationships constituted along those lines. Do you still seek handles on history? Just nonviolent handles? Maybe learning to live well requires a more radical unhandling? Do you think Ella Baker was a theocrat who willed to rule nonviolently? Should she have been more so? How so and how not so? Maybe some dose of haunting that somewhat unhandles even nonviolent unhandling would be preferable to the stance you suggest in this footnote I quote above? Perhaps this might support cultures that help us become less dishonest? Of course, in relation to what and to whom? And that raises all those questions about jealousy—the ones I put to you, and the ones you put to me. Perhaps all I could ask of you here is for more discomfort about even nonviolent theocracy? A discomfort in which you pause and linger more with these questions. And what does it mean to request such discomfort from another—from you?

Let me flesh out these worries a bit in relation to a book I recently read that is profoundly indebted to you and to the body of literature hugely indebted to you (including Cavanaugh, Shuman, Toole, and others, in each of whose dissertations/first books I am significantly implicated . . . strangely enough . . .): Sam Wells's *Improvisation: The Drama of Christian Ethics*. This is a book I really enjoyed reading, and I learned a lot from it. (Interestingly, among its rich and lasting echoes in my life is its contribution to my thinking about certain blocking habits in my daughter, and certain blocking habits I have in relation to her blocking habits, and how I might think about modes of overaccepting that nudge her toward overaccepting and other varieties of improvising with others . . .) Much of his discussion of improvisation, imagination, *la disponibilité*, questioning givens, ethics as done by people on the *receiving* end, etc., is really illuminating—and I like much of what he does with the idea that "blocking assumes that heaven has walls" (108).[14] But I think, finally, I have a number of worries about several of its central arguments, including the central place of "overaccepting" itself in his project. If I were address-

14. But there is at the same time a lot that I want to block. Or to "block in part," at the same time that I do other things in relation to them. Blocking is not taboo to me. It is, in fact, a crucial virtue, but one that should be used sparingly. Still, a virtue. There is much that calls to be blocked; the question is how to do so without closing down relationships. Blocking does not have to be violent, or "simply blocking" as Sam sometimes caricatures it. Blocking can be integral to opening, I think. Excommunication in Chile is certainly a form of blocking—among other things—and I don't think Sam comes clean in his discussion at this point in the book. But these are thoughts to discuss elsewhere. . . .

ing this book publicly, I'd probably do so in the form of "overaccepting overaccepting"—and that is in fact the spirit of the remarks that follow, but the modality is briefer and maybe more edgy in this communication between the two of us.

So: in the midst of so much with which I'm sympathetic, let me play you some samples and discuss:

> Overaccepting is accepting in light of a larger story. Overaccepting is an active way of receiving that enables one to retain both iden-tity and relevance. It is a way of accepting without losing the ini-tiative. This often involves a change of status. (131)

> When the Christian community is faced by offers coming to it from the society in which it lives, it overaccepts in the perspective of a story that stretches from creation to eschaton—a far larger story. The method has much in common with what Milbank de-scribes as Christianity's ability to "outnarrate" all secular narra-tives. . . . Overaccepting fits the remarks of the previous actor in to a context enormously larger than his or her counterpart could have supposed. This is exactly what the Christian community does with offers that come to it from wider society. It overaccepts in light of the church's tradition and story seen in eschatological perspective—a perspective much wider than urgent protagonists may have imagined. (133)

> The church has ample resources for every eventuality it faces and it finds those resources among the discarded elements of earlier parts of its story . . . , good examples. . . . Bad examples. (151)

Now, you know me well enough—and regrettably I am predictable enough—that you can probably imagine much of my response to this. In spite of the humble and receptive stance that Sam wonderfully strikes and performs at many points in the book, this metanarrative is troubling. And it is troubling to me, precisely because of what it shares with your footnote to which I took issue on "willing to try to rule." It is the posture of nonviolent rule (though evoking Milbank in this context seems deeply problematic—I've addressed that elsewhere and let it go here . . .).[15] Nonviolent rule as "retaining identity," not "losing the initiative," main-taining possession of the "far larger story," "outnarrating" the other sto-ries, fitting the other into one's own context that is far larger than the

15. See Coles, "Storied Others."

other could have supposed, maintaining a confidence that the church
has within its history ample resources for every eventuality it faces. If I
were to change directions very abruptly—so abruptly as to risk appearing
with the crudeness of "simply blocking"—I'd gather some of my earlier
reflections to wonder: *Might not ethical practice hinge very significantly
on slackening the will to "retain identity"?* I'd say Rowan Williams offers a
reading of the gospel in which this central motif in the "Milbank-Wells"
story (I use this hyphen to confine my critique to one, albeit very significant, part of Sam's text) is radically called into question—in which the
gospel is read to lean in a very different direction, toward a much greater
vulnerability of identity being *vital* to cross and resurrection. *Should one
seek always not to lose the initiative?* I doubt it. There are many ethical
relations where the most important effort we can make is to step away
from initiative, let others take it from us, let them radically call us into
question, let them call us to pause indefinitely. The SNCC story is full
of this central concern shared by believers of beloved community and
radical democracy. Initiative and ceding initiative ought to be entwined
in much more difficult and indeterminate manners than Wells's account
would have it, I think. *Should we—Christians, radical democrats—have
confidence that we have the "far larger story," that our task is to outnarrate
all the others?* Again, I'd draw on so many readings of Rowan Williams to
draw this into question, to suggest that ethics requires often enough, and
crucially, a very different yearning and practice. And the idea that there
are in a single tradition (if it reincorporates good and bad examples from
its past) sufficient resources to face every eventuality—this faith strikes
me as one that may well shut the door to other peoples' traditions and
stories, from which Yoder and Williams, for example, provide far more
resources and impetus for Christians to learn. *Don't we need to cultivate a
more radical notion of insufficiency here than does Wells?*

In all of this, there is in the theatrical/dramatic imperative to "keep
the story going" a certain insinuation of quite fast pacing—a hasty temporal aura like that of witty dramatic improvisation—that I also find highly
problematic as a central motif for ethical reflection/action. Not knowing
what to say and knowing one does not know—perhaps for a very long period of time—*and dramatizing* the fact that one is confronted with something for which one knows that one does not yet have the words: this is a
very important ethical capacity. (Socrates comes to mind here, of course.
But in different ways, Williams's account of Matthew's account of Jesus is

full of this.) Maybe it is among the most important. "Block v. overaccept," which governs so much of Sam's account, neglects a host of other crucial capacities and ethical strategies. All those themes in Marsh's discussion of SNCC—of radical patience, stillness, "acting out of the deepest silence," sitting around on front porches with no plan of action and resisting imperatives for quick improvisations—these are among the most important political motifs I know of. In those space-times we slacken the insistence to outnarrate, and perhaps for the first time assume an ethical stance toward others. We provoke and let be the initiative of others. Beyond accept/block/overaccept, we *ask the other(s) questions. We allow ourselves to be called into question in ways that perturb our energies and insistences to outnarrate and try to rule. We allow ourselves to sense that we don't know where this is going, that ethical action calls for uncertain discernment. We discover long pausing as frequently the most profound ethical art in difficult situations. We cultivate arts of pregnant waiting.*

Now it would be easy to overaccept Sam's book in a way that opens toward and pronounces these themes. Hence, the idea that we're in Act Four, that Act Five is not ours to write/perform—this would suggest that the trope of outnarrating is a simplifying strategy in relation to God's divine drama, and probably a violent one, even if it is a nonviolent violence. Similarly, when Wells writes of imagining what it means for Act Five to be made up of the discarded material from Act Four (e.g., 145), he might push beyond the standard "hungry, thirst, homeless, naked, sick, or prisoner" to consider the myriad Native American cultures-histories-stories (which Christians frequently helped destroy, for example) that might ultimately be reincorporated by God in ways that syncretically torque Christian narratives beyond present Christian imaginations such that "outnarrate" comes to seem barbaric. What if the development of the Christian story ends up being the development of one among other things—say, the Nez Perce/Lakota/Christian story—such that each of these narratives is profoundly *thrown out of joint,* out of narrative structure, even out of an improvisational narrative structure, and what develops comes to be seen as essentially unexpected newness born of an unexpected encounter? Newness beyond narrative, and "outnarrating." I'd say that if we're in Act Four—we ought to learn to expect that unexpectability and come to view the cultivation of Christian virtues as those that engender and protect that expectation. Might not Christian ethics that moved in this direction then come to view "outnarrating," and haste made normative, as idolatry?

Again, I am aware of so much more that is of great value in *Improvisation*—so much that moves in counter-directions. But like the call to discern possible dangers in Augustine—amidst the incredibly rich resources that you and others have identified—that might, if unrecognized and unresisted, inadvertently nurture the politics of fear he sought to move beyond, I want to flag some dangers that seem operative in the text—especially operative in ways that maybe suppress embracing other important ethical motifs and issues (for example, why no discussion of something analogous to the Nez Perce/Lakota/Christian relation in the last section of the book—given the weight of this historical problematic, and given its relevance to the question of living a story in a heterogeneous world?).

OK. I need to go try to find a line where I can send you this letter. The rats re-chewed through a line that had been "fixed," so we're again without electronic connection.

Let me know your thoughts on these scattered thoughts!

peace,

rom

CHAPTER 3

"To Make This Tradition Articulate": Practiced Receptivity Matters,
Or Heading West of West with Cornel West and Ella Baker[1]

Romand Coles

With West, West of West.

We must, Cornel West writes in *Democracy Matters,* "look unflinchingly
at the waning of democratic energies and practices in our present age of
the American empire."[2] And like a conjurer, West employs his remarkable
rhetorical arts, acute sensibility, infectious generosity, and manifold powers of critical cognition to enjoin us to "learn from the blues people how
to keep alive our democratic energies in dark times"—listen to those who
forged their sounds on "the night side of America" (*DM* 21–22).

In the halls that I frequent more often than those of the American
Academy of Religion, namely, those of various political science meetings,
Cornel West is greatly appreciated by radical democrats for the wisdom,
passion, and resonance of his engaged and engaging *voice.* And I too like
to hear West speak. Yet I relish it most when I hear him *listening,* which
he does across a vast range of expression. Hence some of my favorite texts
by West are those that record his *dialogues,* perhaps best exemplified by
his conversations with bell hooks, in *Breaking Bread.*[3]

---

1. Prepared for the American Academy of Religion Annual Meeting, Washington
DC, November 19, 2006. Revised, May 2007. The phrase "to make this tradition articulate" is from James Baldwin, "Many Thousands Gone," 73.

2. West, *Democracy Matters,* 2. Hereafter cited as *DM* in parentheses in text.

3. I think bell hooks makes an analogous point when she reflects that even more than
the substance of her public conversations with West, she values the performance of the
dialogues themselves: "I think the most powerful impact that we had . . . was not even

As the many blurbs on the dust jacket repeatedly tell us, *Democracy Matters* is a work of prophetic *voicing*. Yet I read it more as a work of prophetic listening, prophetic receptivity toward those who have already spoken—prophecy as generous receptivity. And is there any genuinely prophetic voice that was not this in the first instance? Were not Jeremiah and Jesus most profoundly astonishing listeners before they spoke their first unwonted and unwanted words?[4] Somewhere Walter Benjamin dreams of writing a book that would inscribe nothing but the art of illuminating juxtapositions—stringing together incisive quotations from others, one after another, cultivating perception and energy through uncanny resonances to which he, and we, might listen. No doubt *Democracy Matters* lays West's own words on the page, yet some of the sections I relish most are those where he powerfully juxtaposes passage after passage from the likes of Morrison, Melville, Emerson, Baldwin, and others, such that they ring newly, and perform what Toni Morrison calls an "*aural literature*"[5]: one demanding that *he* listen closely in order to inspire and inform the words he then weaves around them as expressive listening that enjoins *us* in turn to listen and awaken.[6]

---

so much the words we said but the manner in which we conducted ourselves—two individuals in solidarity . . . [not] talking at one another . . . but . . . really having a conversation" (hooks and West, *Breaking Bread*, 110 and 112). You can also listen to him listening to hooks when he writes, in *The Cornel West Reader*, introducing a re-release of his essay "The Dilemma of the Black Intellectual," that bell hook's "Black Women Intellectuals" "is a devastating critique of this piece. I recommend that people read them together" (302).

4. Reader: These two question marks were placed intentionally and with care. But the weight of each one is too great and pierces through any page. All we can do is return again and again to their trace and the tensions they mark, which return to haunt the ending of this chapter.

5. Davis, "Interview with Toni Morrison," 230.

6. My favorite essay by Cornel West is "Black Strivings in a Twilight Civilization" (though one has to read this essay not alone, finally, but as a point in a constellation of discordant essays that West has written, each of which is an invaluable supplement to the others—and I would recommend in this regard the chapter on Emerson in *American Evasion of Philosophy* for its discrepant themes). "Black Strivings" is performed as "aural literature," juxtaposing long paragraphs by others, to which he responds with insightful words of his own, which surround them like tear-soaked lace. This essay is originally from *Future of the Race*, by Henry Louis Gates Jr. and Cornel West. Interesting is that in his prefatory remarks to the essay reprinted in the *Cornel West Reader*, he writes, "If all of my writings but one had to disappear, this essay is the one piece I hope would survive" (87). I think this indicates West's own sense of the dialogical character of his very best work, as well as the ineliminable importance, vitality, and one should also say *truth*, of episodic *exaggeration* both tragic and utopic for democratizing intelligence and struggle.

Over the years I have found courage and animation, as well as insight, from West's words. Yet perhaps our deeper solidarity might be found less in the proximity of our *voices* and more in where and how and to whom we *listen:* With West, for example, I am brought to the deepest depths in Coltrane's *Alabama*—cross—and the highest heights in his *Love Supreme*—difficult resurrection. I suspect that ultimately whatever we seek to express, we hear there.

And thus, so closely drawn in listening, the question emerges: How might I fulfill the task set by the title of this panel and offer "critical reflections"?[7] And how to do so such that the *gravitas* of what we hear and what matters—radical democracy matters—might thwart the assimilation of a critical engagement to the endless professionalized academic games and pseudo-differentiations that West compellingly exposes as a nihilistic power sham?[8] Yet how to evade *this* trap without falling into an equally problematic trap of tensionless, lifeless, unedifying solidarity? In the face of these questions, I want to strive to be with West in the effort to work upon certain limits I find in his work. Thus my critical motif emerges

As Jeffrey Stout notes in *Democracy and Tradition* (57, 324), "Black Strivings" is the essay of West's from which Stout most departs, due to its "extreme highs and lows." Stout says he much prefers West and Roberto Mangabreira Unger's *The Future of American Progressivism*, a view from which I also must depart. Though at some points *The Future of American Progressivism* stands as an important corrective to certain dogmas prevalent on the left, I must confess that I worry about some of the central motifs of this book. The nutshell of my critique is sketched briefly in the "postscript" to this chapter. A conversation between West, Stout, and Coles is just beginning concerning the intertwining of exaggeration, temporality, and the possibilities for democracy. A couple first steps can be found in Coles, "Democracy, Theology, and the Question of Excess: A Review of Jeffrey Stout's *Democracy and Tradition*," 301–21; and Stout, "Spirit of Democracy and the Rhetoric of Excess," 9–21.

7. The AAR session at which this paper was presented was titled: "Critical Reflections on Cornel West's *Democracy Matters*".

8. Among West's essays exploring the problems of professionalized cooption and insurgent possibilities in contemporary intellectual production, I find "The New Cultural Politics of Difference" and "The Dilemma of the Black Intellectual," in *Keeping Faith: Philosophy and Race in America*, as well as "Decentering Europe" and "The Black Underclass and Black Philosophers" in *Prophetic Thought in Postmodern Times*, to be crucial starting points for reflection—among white people as well as black people. The need to cultivate connections with associations beyond the academy—as a condition of possibility for thinking—is a theme articulated in these works in ways that inspire some of my critical resistance to what I take to be shortcomings below. Or, one could say, I seek to radicalize further paths that West suggests but does not, to my mind, sufficiently articulate or perform.

precisely where I discern what is most exemplary in his critical performances: the thematic of listening. Generous receptivity as the most radical-democratic practice. In a sense, then, the work of critique here would be that of striving to go West of the West who frequently and much better than most—politically and theoretically—crosses divides with engaged receptivity. Perhaps what follows is less a "critique" of West and more like a jazz improvisation in which we're "trading eights."

In what I take to be the most compelling moments of *Democracy Matters*, West not only listens to others, but he explicitly calls us to listen and insists that doing so is central to the practice of radical democracy. Thus, in his chapter on engaging youth culture, he enjoins us that, "it is imperative that young people . . . see that the older generation in the academy cares about them, that we take them seriously, and that we want to hear what they have to say" (*DM* 199–200). Similarly, he lets ring Emerson's incisive words in "The American Scholar": "The literature of the poor, the feelings of the child, the philosophy of the street, the meaning of household life, are the topics of the time. . . . I embrace the common, I explore and sit at the feet of the familiar, the low" (*DM* 70–71).[9] Yet these moments are positioned within an overall emphasis on prophetic *voices or writings* that tend too little to the *lived and practiced receptivity* that is the greater part of the life and materiality of democratic relationship, struggle, and power. In West's texts there is too little strenuous attention to the specific textures of democratic struggles and organizing modes, to the movements in churches and community centers, to the movements in the streets, on front porches, at kitchen tables; the practice of saying carefully what is found there with, say, the subtlety that he musters in relation to Emerson, Morrison, or Baldwin. These practices of moving (on) the ground are very much the *matter* of democracy—the liturgies in which radical democracy discerns and manifests its living and dying. West's work (at its best) builds an expectation for more than it delivers in terms of learning from this liturgical element (practiced, performed, ritualistic—about which more below) and re-inflecting the theory and practice of prophetic scholarship by cultivating a greater attentive receptivity toward it. When West episodically calls us in these directions, he

9. Indeed, one could say that *one* of the most crucial currents of his work is best articulated when he writes, "the condition of truth is to allow the suffering to speak" ("Beyond Eurocentrism," 4). The ultimate source for this insight in West's thinking is, of course, Jesus.

does so in ways that are far *too general* (such as with vague calls for energetic participation) and in ways that sometimes elide crucial distinctions
and difficulties with which we must linger and from which we must learn
(such as the many times when very different political people, including
Martin Luther King Jr. and Ella Baker, are separated by only a conjunction
or a comma). By repeatedly foregrounding how "th[e] love of democracy
has been most powerfully expressed and pushed forward by our great
public intellectuals and artists" *(DM 15)*, West's textual practice perhaps
inadvertently risks shifting to the background the endlessly powerful and
informative expressions of lived artistry and philosophizing bodies in the
democratic practices that receive very little comparable engagement in
his work.[10] I think the emphases and accents are somewhat off in ways
that might be reworked to the benefit of radical democracy.

Perhaps this claim arouses suspicions concerning the tyranny of
small differences. I am aware that the task of heading critically West of
the West who does better than many scholars the very things I am criticizing him for not doing enough, may appear strange. Hence, to clarify
the political and theoretical stakes (a certain gestalt-shift of prophetic
democratic theory and practice), let me cut to the chase with a few strong
claims, then try to substantiate them, and finally take some steps in alternative directions.

1) West (like those blurbing the covers of his books) tends, more
   often than not, to misconstrue or misaccent the vocation of
   prophecy (and the prophetic dimension of public intellectuals as
   "insurgent" "critical organic catalysts") too much toward *voicing*.
   Though he very rightly seeks connection and roots in associations beyond the academy and thinks they are crucial as sources
   of courage and nourishment, he tends to frame these connections
   in ways that overemphasize the element of voice in comparison
   to those profound, entwined, and (in certain senses) primary
   modes of prophecy that are receptive. Public intellectuals are thus
   understood more often as speakers than as listeners to and with
   democratic publics. West tends to emphasize the vocal element in
   ways that significantly underplay its massive debts to (and consti-

---

10. Once, in *Democracy Matters,* "activists" join intellectuals and artists in a similar
sentence of praise (67).

tutive relationship with) radically receptive modes and textures of prophetic being.

2) On a related point, West often underplays the centrality of pains-taking receptive arts and relationship building in the liturgies and body practices of democratic life. Generally, he focuses on the (also crucial) ways in which democratic movements articulate voice and vision, or on the ways in which they take power from elites and hold them accountable. While drawing our attention to a vital aspect of radical-democratic practice, West underplays the receptive body practices that might make such voicing, vision, and power more possible and desirable.

3) Points 1 and 2 tend to coalesce in a self-perpetuating dynamic: Insofar as West and others accent the vocal dimension of prophetic public intellectuals, their predominant energetic investments will likely disproportionately occur in speaking to publics more than in painstaking receptive attention to what might be learned from them in order to critically engage and give expression to these things. Thus, we will be less likely to encounter surprising and in-teresting phenomena in our relationships with nonacademic pub-lics from which we might learn—which, in turn, tacitly reinforces the vocal accent we initially brought to the relationship. Caught in this circle, we will likely conceal the receptive body practices that are integral aspects of the best radical-democratic organizing. Thus we will remain oblivious to the primacy of learning from the moving ground—not only about democracy on the ground but about what it might take to reenergize and reinvent the meaning, possibility, and desirability of insurgent prophetic scholarship.

The issues go back to some of West's earliest writing. In his profound and illuminating effort to articulate and extend hope for African Americans and for broader humanity at the intersection of Christianity and Marxism in *Prophesy Deliverance!* he rightly describes the black church (especially in its Baptist and Methodist forms) as a locus of relatively antihierar-chical and loosely bounded organization,[11] as well as a chief association engendering "organic intellectuals," in the Gramscian sense (*PD* 121). Yet

11. *Prophesy Deliverance!: An Afro-American Revolutionary Christianity*, 36. From here on, cited as *PD* in the text.

he gives flesh to these points in ways that focus almost exclusively on the theoretical/practical *voicing* potentials of male "Black religious leadership": "Black preachers and pastors are in charge of the most numerous and continuous gatherings of black people. . . . [Their] freedom . . . is immense. . . . The contributions of black religious leaders can be prodigious, as exemplified by the great luminaries of the past" (*PD* 121). The beacons of hope at the end of the book are all male, and West's focus is upon voices. With this emphasis, he sets a course of overaccenting voice and underaccenting relational-receptive body practices in the work of both prophetic public intellectuals and democratic organizing; though West sometimes peers around and gestures beyond these limits, his emphasis on voicing at the expense of relational-receptive body practices continues to infect his work to this day. For this reason, I believe, he claims that Martin Luther King Jr. was "the most effective black prophetic Christian leader"(*PD* 103) and makes no mention of Ella Baker and the early SNCC—who practiced a very different (yet an at least as effective) kind of prophetic leadership and organic intellectuality profoundly rooted in receptive relational practices that Martin Luther King Jr. barely grasped.[12] Similarly, in "The Dilemma of the Black Intellectual," when West refers to "two *organic* intellectual traditions in African American life" (i.e., Christian preaching and musical performance), what goes unspoken is the wildly generative practices of knowledge production among black women who were not preachers in the church, and who cultivated intense receptive arts of radical-democratic organizing, even though many were also great speakers.[13]

In later works, as West increasingly listens to and begins to be reworked by (especially black) feminist theory, engagements, and sensibilities, Ella Baker's name occurs more frequently in the mix, but she never receives serious discussion. Indeed, he tends to evoke her in the same breath as Martin Luther King Jr., in ways that eclipse the very different understandings of democratic practice, prophetic activity, and leadership she articulated—thereby concealing the need to focus very carefully on what we might learn from her distinctive example of lived philosophizing.[14]

12. Septima Clarke offered a critique of King and SCLC that is rooted in a tradition of black women and is similar to the one I discuss below.

13. West, "Dilemma," 72–73. Emphasis is West's.

14. She is mentioned twice in *Democracy Matters*: once as one from whom, along

This weakness tends to be associated with a diminished sense of the kinds of receptive organizing efforts that are—decades later—deeply indebted to the traditions that Baker received, deepened, and extended. I am sympathetic to West's affirmative gesture toward "the Industrial Areas Foundation efforts of BUILD in Baltimore" in his essay called "The Crisis of Black Leadership" in *Race Matters*. Yet all we learn there is that they are "engaged in protracted grass-roots organiz[ing] in principled coalitions that bring power and pressure to bear on specific issues" even as they embrace "critical dialogue and democratic accountability"(45).[15] Similarly, more often (and before most men have), West gestures toward the importance of engaging the organizing work of Black women—as a most vital source of hope.[16] Yet one is left hungering, in the discrepancy,

---

with Martin Luther King Jr. and others, we might learn to "remain open to solidarity with people who hate you" (an absolutely vital point, though it leaves me yearning for theoretical development that is not provided) (217); and once (again with Martin Luther King Jr.) as one who (in contrast to "blues and jazz" that "recast[s] the contours of democratic vision and re-creat[es] the contents of democratic modes of existence") was seemingly organizing to deepen democracy as "simply a matter of the expansion of rights and liberties. . . ."(92). This misses vital aspects of what Baker (or, for that matter, King) was really about, and since I know that West knows and pronounces this, I suspect all we have here is a matter of infelicitous phrasing in a context where West intends to praise the blues, not to offer a reductive reading of these social movements. But in a way I want to say that the possibility of this latter paragraph lies in a perception that really undertheorizes, underappreciates, and is insufficiently *swept up by* the traditions of Baker's difficult belonging and complex leadership. Otherwise, I suggest, it could not have been written. Some other places where West runs King and Baker problematically together in the same breath that conceals questions we will ask below include *Breaking Bread*, 43; *Race Matters*, 38; and "Cultural Politics of Difference," 27. (His discussion in "The Paradox of African-American Rebellion" in *Keeping Faith* is a bit more suggestive of questions that need to be asked, even as West does not sufficiently pursue them, as I discuss below).

15. The IAF's deep debts to Baker and to the early SNCC can be seen in, among other things, the fact that Charles Payne's magisterial *I've Got the Light of Freedom*, focusing on early SNCC organizing and on Baker's pivotal role in it, is required reading for organizers and grassroots leaders in the network.

16. E.g., in "Cultural Politics of Difference," 19, West alludes to how the "Black women's movement" breaks up homogeneous discourses on race, but we don't learn much about the arts of receptivity that were associated with this breakup, and then that radically reinflected radical democracy in light of these arts. In "Black Strivings," West writes that "a visionary (disproportionately woman-led) radical-democratic camp" is "maybe the last hope" (*Cornel West Reader*, 117)—and I think he is right but want to know more about the specific textures of this hope, how it lives and breathes in the suffocating atmosphere that West evokes so powerfully, in no small part in relation to Toni Morrison. In the same essay, West criticizes Dubois's "Talented Tenth" strategy by noting that, in fact,

between how frequently this gesture occurs and how comparatively thin the engagement remains to date.

If we were to move West of West—informed and emboldened by West's own occasional gestures toward receptive prophetic modes of public scholarship and radical-democratic practice—gestures that not only "tell unpleasant truths" and "bear prophetic witness" but also let themselves be "organized and mobilized by" the least of these;[17] gestures that cultivate roots in civil society in part so that "your insight can be informed by the very folk who you're talking to, because they have a wisdom to bring"[18]—how might we see and act differently? What difference might it make for radical democracy and radical ecclesia?

Ella Baker's New Light in the Tradition of Radical Democracy and Radical Ecclesia: "Now Who Are Your People?"

Ella Baker—first among equals because she had the deepest and longest history of cultivating empowering arts of democratic receptivity across a vast array of differences (along with Bob Moses, Amzie Moore, Fannie Lou Hammer, and countless others), took radical democracy "to another level" with SNCC in the early 1960s. Charles Payne, the early SNCC's most acute interpreter, insists that in conjunction with what is often read only as a political legacy, we must attend carefully to the "distinct philosophical heritage" in which SNCC creatively imagined, practiced, and conceptualized new and important modes of democratic relationship and collective leadership.[19] (I suggest that we should read Payne's historical work on SNCC as itself profound philosophy and democratic theory in narrative mode—as if history mattered.) Baker's biographer, Barbara Ransby, recognizes a similar intellectual legacy, in spite of the fact that Baker wrote little, when she writes: "Baker's theory of social change and political organizing was *inscribed in her practice*. Her ideas were written in her work: a coherent *body of lived text* spanning nearly sixty years."[20]

---

it was not the educated elite who were leading, but groups based in civil society like Ida B. Wells-Barnett's black women's club—but the conversation moves quickly, and we learn little about this, though we stand to learn much (ibid., 95).

17. West, "Black Strivings," 116.

18. West, *Prophetic Thought in Postmodern Times*, 100.

19. Payne, *I've Got the Light of Freedom*, 67.

20. Ransby, *Ella Baker*, 1. Emphasis mine. Cornel West is familiar with this book

Read in this way, perhaps Baker—with, say, Sheldon Wolin—is among the most important democratic theorists as well as activists in the latter half of twentieth-century America.[21] Both understood the intricate connection between radical democracy and memory.

And it is precisely the self-consciously historical and situated character of this "body of practices as lived text" that demands that our understanding of what is new and distinct with Baker—"natality," in Arendt's sense—must be situated in the broader histories and stories in which it is intelligible as a birth and response. Indeed, this historical sensibility and the questions that accompany it animated the pulse of Ella Baker's relationship to the world; and even after Alzheimer's had rendered her incapable of responding to it, she would repeatedly query: "Now who are your people?"[22] We owe her the question.

Those who have studied her agree that two situations contributed most in a constructive sense to Ella Baker's development: the network of turn-of-the-twentieth century strong black church women into which she was born, and her experience of the teeming heterogeneous practices of radical democracy that flourished in Harlem during the Depression. As each has everything to do with our interpretation of prophetic practices of radical ecclesia and radical democracy, I want to linger with them a bit. The doubled syncretic character of these sources may disturb both those secularists and those Christians who wish to claim for what is highest a tradition that is not haunted by irreducible heterogeneity and "others" who helped make it possible. If so, this is all the more reason to linger.[23]

---

that bears his acclaim on the front cover: "A magisterial rendering of one of the greatest radical Democrats in the twentieth century."

21. West concurs with this assessment of Wolin in his powerful tribute to Wolin, "Afterword." West's reflections on Wolin's emphasis on the importance of memory for the possibility of future waves of democratization is very much in the spirit of what I am arguing and trying to practice in the present essay.

22. See Ransby, *Ella Baker*, 13–14. This was Baker's response to Paula Giddings, who came to interview Baker for her book on black women's history and had to face the fact that all that was left was Baker's own deep historical sensibility and the curious love to ask this question.

23. See Chappell, *Stone of Hope*, for an insightful corrective to secular liberal readings of the civil rights movement. His book accents the centrality of the role of black (and, differently, white) prophetic Christianity in making possible and sustaining the civil rights struggles and victories of the 1950s and 1960s. Unfortunately, Chappell not only interprets the prophetic church in a manner that greatly underplays the practiced (disproportionately female) networks that were so integral to this prophetic tradition and

A great deal of fascinating work and debate has emerged in the past couple of decades on the networks, practices, and ethos of black Baptist women in the South, and as it is well beyond the limits of the current discussion to review these in detail, I will focus only on what I take to be most crucial for "making articulate" this tradition of practiced receptive generosity. It is well known that Baker and many other black women had a tension-filled relationship with the Southern Christian Leadership Conference (SCLC) over styles of prophetic leadership. The SCLC tended to focus organizational leadership in the circle around Martin Luther King Jr. and to understand church involvement in a way that accented pastoral leadership. Baker and those who eventually formed SNCC had a much more group-centered understanding of leadership, and understood church involvement much more in terms of grassroots networks within (and beyond) churches. These differences are importantly rooted in long traditions of gender-structured practices in black church life and society. Though West is aware of these differences and critical of the undemocratic elements of King's legacy,[24] I am suggesting that the lack of textured, strenuous engagement in his writing with the lived works of black women who were critical of the SCLC and integral to the formation of SNCC's alternative, may itself be partly due to the weakened yet still-significant legacy of these differences (and to related modes of inattentiveness) that continue to impede the reflective work through which each might learn from the other.

Baker's differences with King must be grasped in terms of their different understandings of church and community. King understood

---

its conditions of possibility, but he also frames the interpretive question as one between either liberalism or prophetic Christianity, almost entirely missing the vibrant traditions of radical democracy that were irreducible to either and equally important. His deafness in this regard finds painful expression when he writes lines such as, "Ella Baker, whose contributions were by all accounts organizational rather than philosophical or strategic" (67). Still, though significantly blind to prophetic practice and radical democracy, Chappell's book remains a major contribution.

24. In *Race Matters*, West briefly notes the "undemocratic nature of MLK Jr.'s organization" (46). In "The Paradox of African-American Rebellion," in *Keeping Faith*, he notes the rift between Martin Luther King Jr. and SNCC, and further argues that King's organization was nearly dead when King himself was murdered. Yet West never really takes up the textures of SNCC's challenge, or the alternative it presented (276–81)—which would be so crucial to advancing the aims of his essay. Relatedly, the many ways in which SNCC went beyond bourgeois liberalism—in terms of practice and economic policy exploration—remain unarticulated.

church very significantly from the vantage point of a male-pastor tradition that cultivated extraordinary rhetorical skills and accented top-
down leadership.[25] Yet the young Baker was led largely by the example of
a different type of voice and mode of leadership, namely, that of her very
active mother and the Littleton, North Carolina, community of "strong,
hard-working, deeply religious black people—most of them women . . .
who . . . pledged themselves to serve and uplift those less fortunate."[26]
The pledge was practiced, visceral, and highly organized into women's
auxiliary associations, as well as local and state chapters of the National
Woman's Convention, which played an assertive and largely autonomous
role within the black Baptist church. Baker's childhood recollections are
replete—like those of many black girls of her day—with memories of
tagging along at such meetings, and her stories also exemplify the daily
practiced-meaning of her mother's injunction at a statewide convention
to "stay on the job for Christ"[27]: Not only were women in her family and
community deeply involved in an association that "sponsored an orphan-
age, aided the sick and elderly, funded scholarships for black college students and provided aid to local, church-affiliated grammar schools,"[28] but
these women also sought to proliferate Christian community through
"home visits and reading groups called Bible bands, [as] they forged
personal, cross-class relationships with the poor and illiterate members of their communities." Beyond the edge of the church, they were
involved in a variety of secular causes: for women's suffrage and against
lynching, segregation, and drinking. They endorsed what might be con-

25. Of course, in the mid-1960s King moved more and more toward efforts at deep
democratic grassroots organizing. Perhaps the extent to which he too weakly grasped
the practices of church and community traditions, with which Baker was imbued and
from which he might have learned and employed a great deal, can be assessed in his
late book *Where Do We Go From Here: Chaos or Community?* When elaborating upon
the imperative that blacks "need to become intense political activists," King employs the
example of the tradition of Jewish social action in the United States. While he is right that
this is a rich tradition, and strategically correct to affirm the alliance with Jews by use
of their example here, it is striking that there is no mention of the practices of the black
church life, nor any of the black radical-democratic tradition in Harlem and elsewhere.
He would have had to tap deeper into these historical currents of wisdom, relationship,
and action to proceed down the paths he nevertheless so brilliantly evoked. See King,
Testament of Hope, 609–11.

26. Ransby, *Ella Baker*, 14.

27. Quoted in ibid.,16.

28. Ibid., 17.

ceived as a tacit feminist theology that held women to be "the key to social transformation."[29] For Baker, this included daily care and "intimate identification" with people in need in her community. As Ransby puts it, "they were not some reified and depraved 'other,' but rather an extension of self."[30] Or, as Baker puts it in more direct terms with Eucharistic resonance: "If you share your food with people, you share your lives with people."[31] The broader Littleton community practiced "mutual aid" in a wide range of activities, from land use to farm tools to collective practices of mothering.

All of this suggests a mode of Christian prophetic discipleship that was profoundly quotidian, engaged, bodily, specific, discerning, relational, and cultivated primarily by women. It developed according to reflective lived-logics of what Sheldon Wolin calls "tending":

> to apply oneself to looking after another. . . . active care to things close at hand, not mere solicitude. . . . tendance is tempered by the feeling of concern for objects whose nature requires that they be treated as historical biographical beings. . . . attentiveness to differences between beings within the same general class. . . . centers politics around practices . . . habits . . . beliefs. . . . the product of intimate political experience which Americans acquired in their everyday existence.[32]

In other words, the faith practices through which Baker came of age—the practices that significantly engendered who she became—were not abstract but experientially substantive, up-close; they hinged significantly on listening and responding to the expressions of need and yearning of those to whom her Christian vocation called her to tend. Hence one of her biographers writes that as a child, "Ella, as part of her weekend 'pleasures,' went to round up the rambunctious children of a neighboring widower to bathe them and retrieve their clothes for laundering. 'We'd chase them

29. Higginbotham, *Righteous Discontent*, 120–21.

30. Ransby, *Ella Baker*, 20.

31. Grant, *Ella Baker: Freedom Bound*, 12.

32. Wolin, *Presence of the Past*, 89—the "everyday" here is a reference to Tocqueville. If Wolin so eloquently theorizes such practices, it is in no small part due to the pivotal debts his own theorizing owes to SNCC and movements that spun off from SNCC—but that is a point I make in another essay. In "Ella Baker and the Origins of 'Participatory Democracy,'" Carol Mueller makes a related point concerning a genealogy of participatory democracy, though the specific connections between SNCC, spin-off movements, and related theoretical work need further development.

down, and bring them back, and put 'em in the tub, and wash 'em off, and change clothes, and carry the dirty ones home, and wash them. Those kinds of things were routine."[33] Discipleship as she learned and lived it occurred at the fructiferous intersection of a tradition of responding to the stories of the gospel *and* responding to the specific stories and lives of those to and with whom the gospel called her to tend. Again in Wolin's terms, the attention to differences, which is integral to the possibility of tending,

> signified exception, anomaly, local peculiarities, and a thousand other departures from the uniformity that a certain kind of power prefers. Difference rejects the notion of a single narrative history and a unifying single purpose. It favors a pluralistic conception of history, or histories rather than history. Difference is not about a unified collective self but about the biography of a place in which different beings are trying to live together.[34]

A discipleship of tending works at the intersection of the teleological and the ateleological[35]—between preconceptions and the stories of a tradition, on the one hand, and the surprising substantial textures of the world we encounter, on the other. The ateleological here can be glimpsed in patterns of quasi-socialist community and cooperative help, in democratizing struggles about race and gender, and in Baker's own emphasis on receptive practices. Part of the ateleological register involves a capacity to be interrupted. However much Baker's mother was a leader with a vision on numerous fronts, and however much she could be "sort of snobbish," she was simultaneously someone deeply swept up in patterns of spontaneous responsiveness: "If you follow Mama's pattern we'd all be home watching the sick and nobody would be ready to bury the dead because nobody had made any money to pay for the burial."[36]

It is clear that very early in her life, Ella Baker began to develop a critique of church understood as the giving and receiving of relatively abstract sermons—stories cut off from the living practices and struggles of a community striving toward mutual tending. As Joanne Grant puts

---

33. Grant, *Ella Baker: Freedom Bound*, 17.

34. Wolin, *Presence of the Past*, 93.

35. I address the tension between teleology and ateleology throughout *Beyond Gated Politics*.

36. Grant, *Ella Baker: Freedom Bound*, 17.

it, "she disdained the preacherly speech, which often lacked content but had cadences"[37]—resonating with Adorno's line that "to want substance in cognition is to want a utopia."[38] It is not that she was against rhetorical arts—her own skills in this regard were substantial—but that she was profoundly suspicious of concepts, narratives, and purveyors disconnected from the *practiced work* of the corporeal beloved community. Nor should her position be conceived as anti-intellectual, or mere unreflective service. Indeed, Baker's literary education was very strong from the beginning and continued through and beyond the 1930s as she devoured a vast range of progressive literature in Harlem. We would do much better to understand her work and call here in terms of another model of the insurgent public intellectual: one that was engaged in reflective intellectual production close to the ground, in the thickets of receptive relationships, and highly suspicious of those that were produced by (and claimed privilege and leadership in terms of) their distance from such daily liturgies. What could one offer in absence of these, she might ask?

Relatedly, the notion of leadership that infused (the best of) black women's "uplift" practices did not seek to accumulate power at the apex of a pyramid but rather to disperse it through a model of "education as empowerment"; bestowing authority on those who understood that the "purpose of leadership is to build more leadership."[39]

Of course, it is easy to romanticize the social world in which Baker came of age, but we should not. Aspects of class status were sometimes closely interwoven with displays of service to the poor, and many of the moralizing and policing dimensions in this missionary work appear to stretch well beyond the limits of relationships that might be called receptive.[40] Moreover, as bell hooks has argued, the "black woman as server"

---

37. Ibid., 19. It is important to note that her grandfather was a preacher and was similarly critical of histrionics without content. His profound influence upon Baker may have contributed to what I take to be a weakness she carried with her, as well as so many strengths: a revulsion to the more Dionysian aspects of black church life. Perhaps this revulsion inhibited her ability to appreciate aspects of Martin Luther King's vision and practice from which she might have learned?

38. Adorno, *Negative Dialectics*, 56.

39. Nikki Giovanni, quoted in Collins, *Black Feminist Thought*, 157.

40. See Higginbotham, *Righteous Discontent*; and Gaines, *Uplifting the Race*, for further discussion of these points, as well as Gilmore's discussion in *Gender and Jim Crow* for an accounting of the strategic ways in which black women deployed class symbols vis-à-vis whites, and simultaneously sought the uplifting of blacks in ways that exceeded

ethos has certainly operated in ways that can stifle female scholarly activity when it engenders charges of "selfishness" in the face of black women seeking the solitude that is *also* necessary for scholarly work.[41] Nevertheless, what Baker inherited from the textured practices of early-twentieth-century life in Littleton was to a great extent a practiced, relational, receptive understanding of the prophetic work of world transformation, leadership, and knowledge production—lessons in and spurs toward humility, patience, dialogue, and generosity.[42] It is not that these virtues and practices were somehow "pure," but rather that life in this tradition gave energetic expression to them in ways that made them prominent contenders in "mixed-bag" inheritance. Some of the weaknesses and potential undersides of this inheritance were eroded by the radical-democratic milieu that she entered in Harlem. Nevertheless, her life in Littleton seems to have engendered a hunger as well as dispositions and practices for the receptive encounters with the vast range of differences in Harlem that, in turn, pulled her toward further transfigurations.

Baker, in later years, looked back enthusiastically at Harlem in the 1930s as a "hotbed of radical thinking" and activity.[43] The rich tapestry of political philosophies, polemics, and dialogues was extraordinary: communist, socialist, liberal, various stripes of Christian, anarchist, black nationalist, pacifist, and many shades between. From the beginning, Baker read widely and engaged in discussion with folks from vastly different positions, many of whom would not talk to each other. *Bricoleur* is the term that comes to mind as Baker's thought and imagination traveled with open, eclectic, mobile subtlety in relation to differences of experience and political practice. Political debates were widespread—sponsored by libraries; emerging in dynamic soap-box, street-corner political oratory that came with Caribbean immigrants; emerging in speeches at rent strikes, picket lines, boycotts, marches; in churches, classrooms, union

the limits of class interest. It is virtually certain that both class and transclass solidarities and dynamics were significant historically, and it was likely that Baker's family, community, and church experiences leaned significantly toward the latter.

41. See hooks, "Black Women Intellectuals," 147–64.

42. In *Black Feminist Thought,* Patricia Hill Collins similarly summarizes a long tradition of black feminist practices and thinking (including the period under discussion) to identify "concrete experience," "narrative," "dialogue," and "care," as among the prominent modes of knowing and engaging others.

43. My account here is primarily indebted to Ransby's discussion in chapter 3 of *Ella Baker,* 64–104.

meeting halls, private homes; in a plethora of forums sponsored by the organizations such as the Workers Education Project and many others. Baker developed an insatiable hunger for engagement in the thick, manifold, and expressive public sphere, fired by a mixture of organized and studied hopes as well as by depression-era suffering. She is even said to have had a passion for "the fine art of strolling," in which she would initiate discussions (often political) by "accost[ing] people" passing by with her familiar, "Hello, brother, and where do you hail from?"[44] Baker's account of these years has many more political textures, colors, and sharp edges than the more familiar folkloric accounts of the Harlem Renaissance.

For every political conversation, there were a host of local practices experimenting in modes of radical democracy: trade-union struggles, church organizing, political mobilizing, a host of journals and pamphlets, active associations of tenants, antilynching campaigns, self-organized groups concerned with parenting, those pursuing education projects. In the same way that she was intellectually mobile, Baker was organizationally mobile and had highly significant involvements in several of the above. Yet Baker's most intensive investments during her decade in Harlem were in the Young Negro Cooperative League (YNCL), founded in the 1930s in order to address depression-period suffering and to educate people in practical as well as in theoretical ways about socialist alternatives (the cooperative movement aimed ultimately at producer co-ops as well as consumer co-ops). These cooperatives practiced participatory democracy, fostered leadership in youths, and emphasized inclusion and equality for women. For Baker and others involved, the co-ops were small-scale embodiments of the democracy and mutual aid that had a long tradition in many black communities; Baker and those with her hoped the co-ops would engender "the values of interdependency, group decision making, and the sharing of resources"—to be used for the common good. For Baker, as Ransby argues, "social change must transform the individuals involved, the values, priorities, and modes of personal interaction." The daily activity in and around co-ops functioned as a sort of *liturgy* (*laos* [Greek for "public" or "people"] and *ourgia* ["work"]): a regularized public practice in which the most crucial work done was the formation of a public in the sense of people capable of responding and tending to each other and the possibility of common goods: "changing

44. See Grant, *Ella Baker: Freedom Bound*, 27.

themselves, each other, and the world around them simultaneously."[45] It was during this time that Baker came to understand transformation in terms of the effort to proliferate dialogical practices and spaces in which more hopeful selves and communities might be engendered, supported, and sustained. This understanding of social change, elaborated during her years in Harlem, and her leadership in the YNCL were crucial to the vision of radical democracy she brought to SNCC over two decades later.[46]

In Harlem, then, Baker radicalized, diversified, and explored new forms for many of the dispositions, practices, and visions that she first acquired in Littleton, North Carolina. The practices of quotidian tending that she inherited became more explicitly and intensely egalitarian through her engagement with a variety of radical-democratic and socialist frameworks that moved critically beyond class power. Radical democracy became a central motif in her vision of the beloved community, and she came to understand the world-transformative work for which it called in terms of building alternative practices from the microlevel on up. This path required studied receptive patience—without which larger visions would be relentlessly undermined from within by new forms of odious power.

Baker continued to attend church, as well as to speak and sing at services during her Harlem years. Though her critique of the hierarchical leadership of male pastors intensified in the 1950s, her sense of the ethical and strategic vitality of much of the Christian tradition that she inherited as a black woman in the early part of the twentieth century remained strong (one could say that significant aspects of it deepened) and continued to be the most animating part of SNCC in its early years. Yet a more radical capaciousness came to infuse the sensibility that she and others brought to SNCC. SNCC organizers were nothing if not evangelical and missionary in their work. Yet they were so in a manner that focused less on an insistent necessity of expressions of Christian faith, and more on building practices of patient dialogical engagement in ways that *both* drew from and gave profound expression to this Christian tradition,

45. Ransby, *Ella Baker*, 90; see 75–91 more generally.

46. It is interesting to note that one reason the cooperatives may have eventually collapsed, according to Ransby, is that George Schuyler (a central person in the movement with whom Baker worked and from whom she learned significantly) was very antireligious and may have alienated a large portion of the black middle class.

and simultaneously made space for and learned from the Jews, Gandhi's teachings, atheists, and mystics who also played important roles.

There was a specific dynamic mixing of Christian and radical-democratic traditions (each already with a history of reciprocal influence yet irreducible to the other) that made possible one of the most creative, powerful, and hopeful moments in the history of each. To recall this is to cultivate a hospitality toward and nurturance of analogous collaborations in the present and future.

Baker played a pivotal role in the first gathering of people who would become SNCC organizers in 1960, following the initial wave of sit-ins. Yet her aim was to nurture the dialogical autonomy of the younger people such that they might resist being assimilated by the more established, conservative, and less-democratic civil rights groups, and thus embark on a more radically democratic path. One of her chief objectives was to participate in building an organization in which teachers would above all "teach their capacity to learn," and leaders would aim to engender more leaders. Hence, Baker sought to cultivate a profound "openness to experience" on the part of the organizers she helped teach: a strong sense that this was a chief quality that they themselves should seek to practice and engender in their efforts to organize radical-democratic communities of struggle.[47] First and foremost, to change the world meant developing a practiced culture of people with discerning eyes and ears for present-yet-subordinated possibilities—for hopeful latencies—in self, in others, and in the surrounding world, possibilities that might be explored and refigured toward the "beloved community." Baker enjoined organizers to learn to see and solicit latencies: to "be able to look at the sharecropper and see a potential teacher . . . a conservative lawyer and see a potential crusader for justice."[48] Yet to see, solicit, and nurture such latencies—and a sense of hopeful possibility *as such*—SNCC organizers had to strive to exemplify a mode of engagement that was receptive and vulnerable to the *manifest* as well as to the latent specificities of the others one faced, rather than to seek to bend the world to fit rigid ideological frames. As SNCC organizer Mary King puts it profoundly, years later, "We had a stern insistence that our conceptualization, our thinking, our framework, should grow from engagement with the people that we were working with rather than any

47. Payne, *I've Got the Light of Freedom*, 67 and 127.
48. Ibid., 89.

doctrine or any ready-made philosophy." This was not only the way that "substance might come to cognition" (echoing Adorno again, and thinking of the conditions of possibility for thinking, and most especially on the part of "public intellectuals" and radical-democratic leaders), but was also key to an individual and group *politics of exemplarity* aimed at soliciting and nurturing listening, voice, and radically receptive dialogical modes of leadership in each of those they engaged: "We thought of leadership as a matter of development, a process, a matter of becoming, and that our role was to help it emerge and flourish, [in everyone, 'even the least of these']."[49] In the first instance, then, SNCC's work required a pedagogy of striving for exemplification from both the individuals participating in SNCC and from the group as a whole. We should read Baker's efforts (and the efforts of many of her best colleagues) not only as receptive democratic practice but also as fundamental epistemological modes for generating knowledge about the world beyond the limits of white supremacy and hierarchy more generally: pivotal (but not the only) understandings for practicing public scholarship.

Thus, in the accounts of Baker's participation in the 1960 conference in which SNCC was officially formed, one finds a repeated motif about her "listening patiently," "asking questions," and "warning against dogmatism": "'Ask questions, Mary', she would say." People referred repeatedly to her "personal connection" and "care," and it is clear that she sought to teach as a solicitous exemplar of the radical-democratic ethos she preached.[50] As an SNCC member put it: "'She was the consummate teacher, never pounding us, "You must do this, you must do that," [but simply] by raising questions.' So what are we trying to accomplish? she would probe. Are we all in agreement? What do we really mean by that? These were her kinds of questions."[51] Observers of Bob Moses—a protégé of Baker, and himself revered by his cohort as an exemplar of receptive thinking and leadership—noted that he would "convince by his example,"

49. Mary King, reflecting on the occasion of SNCC's twenty-fifth anniversary, in Greenberg, *A Circle of Trust: Remembering SNCC*, 25.

50. Payne, *I've Got the Light of Freedom*, 97.

51. Ransby, *Ella Baker*, 328. See also Grant, *Ella Baker: Freedom Bound* for a discussion of Baker on the pedagogy of listening for the gift in everyone. Grant quotes SNCC organizer Charles McDew's remarkable comments on this point: "Somebody may have spoken for 8 hours, and 7 hours and 53 minutes was utter bullshit, but 7 minutes was good. She taught us to glean out the 7 minutes" (137).

and "led by seeming only to respond," asking questions at key moments and seeking to ensure that all were heard.[52] The SNCC Freedom Schools that opened in the summer of 1964 sought to cultivate such a pedagogy and engagement.

While Baker's own commitment to radical nonviolence is frequently said to be more tactical than philosophical, she nevertheless argued that for most in SNCC, nonviolence—beyond being a tactic—was understood as integral to engendering more receptive relations with and acknowledgment of others: early organizers, she said, "were so keen about the concept of nonviolence that they were trying to exercise a degree of consciousness and care about not being violent in their *judgment* of others."[53] While Baker (and many in SNCC) had doubts about telling local individuals and families not to shoot back in the face of vigilantes who stormed their homes with guns, ropes, and firebombs, nonviolence was not only an organizational position she affirmed but also a dense fabric of peacemaking practices in everyday life.[54] Nonviolence, in other words, was a set of microdispositions and micropractices lodged in relationships with others both within and beyond SNCC. Nonviolence is the myriad small ways of engaging people that stitch the fabric of what Howard Zinn, decades later, calls "connections [that] go on and on over the decades and over the generations . . . the importance of the little things we do that carry on the struggle," and that are also the wellsprings of relationships through which we might experience "that sense of coming alive in a movement."[55] It was everyday epistemology. Their commitment to nonviolence centered on upbuilding radical-democratic (and for many, Christian) liturgies: quotidian rituals engendering individual and collective cultivation of responsive democratic character, and an engaged sense of the sacred. Way beyond "an absence," early SNCC member Diane Nash thought of nonviolence in SNCC's work as an active process of "whole spectrum" peacemaking, which involved not only the "five steps" through which

52. Burner, *And Gently He Shall Lead Them*, 7.

53. Ibid., 373. My emphasis.

54. Baker rejected absolute nonviolence as a doctrine or way of life not only because she could not reject individual self-defense but also because she worried that "pacifism" often had an insufficiently robust vision of social transformation and of the enduring conflicts necessary for transformative work. Her well-known comments in which she puts pacifism at a distance ought to be read, I think, in this context. See, Ransby, *Ella Baker*, 193–94. She was clearly an ardent peacemaker in the senses that I am developing here.

55. See Zinn's chapter in Greenberg, *Circle of Trust*.

SNCC would lead communities (i.e., investigation, education, negotiation, demonstration, resistance)[56], but also a way of being together that fostered growth through patience and vulnerable collaboration. During the most exuberant period, Diane Nash recalls, "there was nothing we were afraid to discuss. We asked astounding questions of each other."[57]

Charles Payne suggests that practices of receptive engagement were not only key to organizers' abilities to teach others "their own capacity to learn," but were also the ongoing source from which organizers themselves relearned and intensified their own capacities to learn and to become a beloved community. It is worth quoting Payne at length on this point:

> We have to remember that they immersed themselves in their communities—Bob Moses liked to call them deep-sea divers—learning those communities from the inside and developing relationships in which people learned to care about one another as individuals in ways that cut through issues of ideology and social status, militating against the tribalism that worked so much evil in the later movement. We have to remember how much of themselves they invested in learning, slowly and painstakingly, how to help other people recognize and develop their own potentials. We have to remember their persistence and their willingness to do the spade work, the undramatic, actual work of organizing.[58]

Diving repeatedly into the depths of places and people engendered in organizers a resistance to their own tendencies to flatten and objectify the world into neat ideological boxes. This resistance was key to their capacity to *theorize*, to remain cognitively mobile, from the perceptual register on up. As Payne puts it, again echoing Moses, "So long as organizers were living in daily contact with local people, they were forced to confront the complexities and contradictions of flesh-and-blood people" in ways that resisted the development of tangents oblivious to the intricacies of the ordinary.[59] Baker sent Moses to long-time Mississippi organizer Amzie

56. Ibid., 21–22.

57. Ibid., 226.

58. Payne, *I've Got the Light of Freedom*, 404. See also Michael Thelwell's reflections on "the drudgery, the tedium of it. It wasn't always excitement, but there was a willingness to do the back-breaking, slow, unglamorous, serious work of working with and organizing people" (Greenberg, *Circle of Trust*, 202).

59. Payne, *I've Got the Light of Freedom*, 200.

Moore to learn these lessons himself. In Moses's reflections years later upon these experiences with Amzie, the receptive aspect of radical democracy is striking: "That was how I learned to organize. . . . I heard my way through the world. I listened to Amzie. I just listened and listened. I watched him, how he moved."[60]

It is important to emphasize the centrality of the bodily dimensions of the dialogical work that SNCC sought to do. Both letters and later reflections repeatedly emphasize—as do Moses' words on "hearing his way through the world" and "watching how Moore moved"—the ways in which SNCC's liturgies of radical democracy had everything to do with how they fashioned bodily modes of dwelling and moving in places, as well as distinctive temporal modes of being. When, early on, white organizer Jane Stembridge wrote that "it all boils down to human relationships . . . whether there shall be a we . . . It is a [*sic*] *I am going to sit beside you* . . . . Love alone is radical," she was speaking literally and corporeally.[61] "SNCC organizers shook hands with sharecroppers who had dirt under their fingernails and sat at the feet of workers with dust on their boots. They sat on the front porches of ramshackle tenant houses not only to teach but to learn." Barbara Jones says that Baker's example set "a tone that said, 'you've got your education, now sit and learn.'"[62] Another organizer, John Lewis, puts is thus: "We were meeting people on their terms, not ours. If they were out in the field picking cotton, we would go out in that field and pick cotton with them. . . . Before we ever got around to saying what we had to say, we listened."[63] Organizing in Greenwood, Mississippi, "with dogged perseverance," Sam Block, "walked the streets and met local people." He not only talked with them about SNCC's vision but also "listened to the locals talk about their fears, concerns, and aspi-

60. Ransby, *Ella Baker*, 302–3. Though Eric Burner in his wonderfully titled book, *And Gently He Shall Lead Them: Robert Parris Moses and Civil Rights in Mississippi*, generally overaccents an existential solitary interpretation of Moses, he sharply evokes some similar themes when he writes of the "slow, methodical, and often inconclusive [discussion]" that was "SNCC's distinctive modus operandi" (126), and when he notes that "Bob Moses and his staff spent most of their time listening to people; programs geared to those needs . . . were slowly developed—or discovered" (127). In a letter addressing growing tensions concerning students coming from the north, Moses wrote poignantly: "If we lose dialogue then we will be lost" (137).

61. Zinn, *SNCC: The New Abolitionists*, 7.

62. Ransby, *Ella Baker*, 305.

63. Ibid., 282.

rations. Eventually, he asked people to come together in small meetings at the Elks Hall, where at first all they did was sing freedom songs."[64] If adults were too scared to talk, you played basketball with their kids. In contrast to the "normal" geographical movement of bodies toward the centers of power, SNCC's work hinged on corporeal movement toward the "backwaters"—then, from backwater to backwater, striving by example to move bodies, imagination, and thought toward further backwaters searching for warmer currents of possibility struggling amidst the dominant subjugative currents there. Integral to their sense of social transformation was the task of soliciting and swerving flows of people off of the courses dictated by and reproductive of the dominant *habitus* of white supremacy in America—beginning with their own highly vulnerable bodies.

Intertwined with these new movements of bodies in space were distinctive modes of temporality. Charles Marsh—who as a Christian theologian and historian of "lived theology" is especially attentive to the liturgical aspect of SNCC community organizing—puts it like this:

> It is easy to forget that so much of a civil rights life involved sitting around freedom houses, community centers, and front porches with no immediate plan of action. The *discipline of waiting* required *uncommon patience* even as it sustained humility and perspective, resisting the cultural paradigm of efficiency. SNCC's genius was its ability to demonstrate . . . the strategies available to social progress within an unhurried and sometimes languorous emotional environment. As such, a condition for achieving beloved community was *a certain kind of stillness* in a nation of frenetic activity and noisy distractions, *learning to move at a different pace. . . .* an attempt *to live into a new and distinct kind of time. . . . waiting as a discipline.*[65]

Marsh views these practices and the dispositions they cultivated as "contemplative disciplines" akin to a "free-floating monastic community."[66] Many may find it tempting to push this mode of being into a box that is folkloric, or to think of it as nostalgic yearning for a localism that verges on (what later and very different SNCC organizers branded) parochial "local-people-itis," or to frame it as nostalgic "slow time" hope-

---

64. Payne, *I've Got the Light of Freedom*, 307.

65. Marsh, *Beloved Community*, 93. Emphasis mine.

66. Ibid.

lessly oblivious to the necessities and possibilities of postmodernity's hyperspeed, or to dismiss it with quips like, "nice ethics, but not politics." But these interpretative temptations really miss the nuanced radicality of SNCC's efforts. SNCC crafted these modes of engagement in the midst of what was effectively a war zone in which insurgent black people and sympathetic white people were being shot, bombed, lynched, clubbed, chained, beaten, bitten, burned, hosed, and jailed with great regularity. It was *here*, in the least folkloric situation imaginable, that SNCC manifested the unthinkable audacity to forge a radically democratic organization that dramatically began reworking relations of race, class, gender, and much more within their organization. Simultaneously, they forged a political movement that was one of the major forces to significantly transform not only the Jim-Crow South but also a variety of other oppressive modes of power, as aspects of their model, courage, and sense of possibility spread widely to other movements across the U.S. and beyond. At the very least, we ought to hesitate to confine this practiced vision to "slow-time," given that SNCC's "slow" paradoxically helped move U.S. history more quickly than it had moved on questions of race, gender, and class in centuries of nation-time, which was and is becoming increasingly frenetic, and thus stuck. Moreover, the early SNCC worked on a variety of practical temporal modes even as it maintained the center of its *paideia* in the liturgies discussed above. Thus, for example, it sought to use the court and aspects of the state to protect the spaces in which it could organize, as well as to press for quicker changes to the legal structure in which Jim Crow was lodged.[67] The SNCC's work urges us to rethink the complex and entwined temporalities of radical democracy in ways that far exceed the polemics that sometimes frame debates in political theory.

Similarly, though moving into and dwelling patiently and receptively in local communities was certainly a crucial aspect of SNCC's work, it was only one aspect of the way SNCC tried to rework the possibilities of bodily movement as a condition of radical-democratic transformation. Rather than interpreting SNCC's struggle as an overly "rooted" project of dwelling (even as such dwelling was itself a mode of moving, within communities), we would do better to locate the vitality of SNCC at the contrapuntal intersection between "roots" (dwelling or traveling locally)

---

67. Clayborne Carson's *In Struggle: SNCC and the Black Awakening of the 1960s* is very informative on these strategic and programmatic aspects of SNCC organizing.

and "routes" (traveling among different communities and across vaster terrain).[68]

For example, as we've seen, SNCC's work hinged on empowering flows—against the currents of power—of people with generally greater organizing experience, greater radical-democratic receptive learning, and greater capacities to teach such learning, into communities that were generally less developed. As SNCC did so, organizers sought to identify people with significant capacities, to cultivate these potentials, and to inspire people in turn to circulate further and analogously cultivate others within their communities. Simultaneously, however, as SNCC discerned people with significant leadership potential, they often sought to employ a very different form of traveling. In order to further provoke radical-democratic transfigurations of perception, consciousness, and organizing skills, SNCC would send them to visit other regions or gathering centers: "When such people were identified they were often sent to Septima Clark's citizenship training center in Dorchester, Georgia. The trip helped people develop a sense of the larger movement and of themselves as movement people."[69] According to Moses, practices of traveling and receiving travelers played an important role in broadening sensibilities, expanding a sense of empowerment, and cultivating a sense of the possibility of beloved community or of utopian possibility:

> It can't happen if the framework is narrow. You've got to be exposed to a lot. Part of what the Movement did is just expose people to a lot. Exposing people to all different kinds of people who were coming in and out of Mississippi . . . all people who are somehow part of this movement culture, sharing certain values, talking about certain things. . . . If all those activities are really trying to get across the same message which is that people have to take ownership over what they are doing, they have to commit themselves and there has to be this element of persistence and also an element of trying to figure out how to work with other people. If all this is happening everywhere then it gets to be more than just the sum of the parts.[70]

68. The following insights are partly informed by James Clifford's critical discussion of overly rooted anthropological paradigms, in *Routes: Travel and Translation in the Late Twentieth Century.*

69. Payne, *I've Got the Light of Freedom*, 249.

70. Ibid., 333.

Hence, the travel-induced accumulation of a sense of many small resonant efforts created a sense of possibility that was qualitatively different—and in important ways grander—than developments in any one place alone. At the same time, the encounter with *differences* to which travelers were exposed between places and persons also played an integral role. Highlander Folk School in Tennessee, as well as other meeting grounds, brought people together from vastly different backgrounds, places, and perspectives; and in excess of the radical-democratic ethos that Highlander explicitly sought to convey, these differences as such were enlivening aspects of the Highlander experience: "The advice the young people received from the older organizers was often divergent, even contradictory, but from Highlander's viewpoint that was not a problem. The intent was to expose the kids to as rich a body of concrete experience, to as wide a variety of perspectives as possible." This was an integral part of the preparation for learning to "listen to the people" in the communities to which they would once again travel.[71] The SNCC, in the early years, had a profoundly experimental approach, hence the knowledge gained from myriad local organizing efforts was pooled together into a comparative milieu through which a democratic ethos and set of strategies unfolded.

For several years, this ethos—could we call it an "ever-emergent cosmopolitanism," engendered at the dialogical intersection of myriad provincialisms?—managed not only to resist lifting itself hubristically above the provincial experiences from which it grew, but also to understand its significance in relation to how it enhanced movement-wide capacities to go receptively toward and sink deeper ("deep-sea diving") into the lives and places to and from which they traveled, learned, and organized. Whether we think of an ever-emergent cosmopolitanism that thrives only in a persistent refusal to claim a position of privilege, or whether we think of "localists" who refused to be "parochial,"[72] what SNCC suggests is that the condition and vitality of radical-democratic theory and practice lie in cultivating modes of bodily travel at the mobile intersection of routes and roots—routing and rooting. If we recall that *theoria* is the Greek root of both "theory" and "travel" (a root that expresses the tight, if unsettled and manifold, relationship that theory has had with travel since

71. Ibid., 144.
72. Payne's distinction; ibid., 101.

Herodotus[73]), SNCC might lead us to venture that a different body politics would be more a *condition* of radical-democratic public intellectual work rather than the *result* of scholarly voices and leadership, as many academics still somehow imagine. Or, better, partaking in the receptive liturgies and flows of alternative body politics would be an invaluable condition of scholarly voices and works that hold out much hope of making distinct, important, critical, and constructive contributions. Without such voices and visions, the chances for radical-democratic politics are, to be sure, greatly diminished. Of course, bell hooks is certainly correct to underscore the necessity of solitude and distance from such ethical and political work (especially in relation to those who have been historically denied these) as also a condition for the distinct type of work that scholarly reflection and production involves.[74] My point is not to recommend compulsory and relentless engagement as a cure for the compulsory and relentless lack of engagement that tends to undergird so much of the "motionless motion" (to borrow from Fanon) of "critical" theory in contemporary U.S. universities. My point is simply that the critical mind and imagination are profoundly historical, bodily, relational, and practiced. When thinking is radically disconnected from receptive involvement in these latter modes, it becomes increasingly empty *and* blind.

And impotent. My suspicion is that the mode(s) of power with which SNCC experimented in the early 1960s are a lot like the possibilities of solar energy—for the most part studiously ignored, largely untapped, yet absolutely crucial to our future flourishing. The SNCC's practices generated a great deal of power, largely insofar as they formed the magnetic infrastructure of one of the most intensive forms of coalition building in U.S. history. Baker's own relationships were an exemplary indication of this power: She had many political friendships and associations with people who were vastly different from one another and from herself, and she maintained many of these connections for decades. On top of the power in manifold bridging relationships and in practices of mobile and textured knowledge production, much of SNCC's power lay significantly in the ultimately disarming effects of not bearing arms, of not demonizing their enemies, of cultivating capacities to "remain open and ready for meaningful solidarity with the very people who hate you," as Cornel West

73. On this point see J. P. Euben, "Creatures of a Day," 28–56; Wolin, *Tocqueville*; and R. Euben, "Traveling Theorists and Translating Practices," 145–73.

74. hooks, "Black Women Intellectuals," 147–64.

puts it (*DM* 217). Historically, these qualities seem to have an attractive force that can erode subjugative power quite unexpectedly. We ought neighter romanticize this force, nor think that it makes our work easy. It does not; the abuse that those involved in SNCC often suffered amply indicates this. Yet even among many of those who would remain quite hostile, such nonviolent solidarity often has certain disarming effects that can be very significant, as David Chappell's work illustrates.[75] Even those many white church leaders in the South who would have been quite fine leaving Jim Crow in place for ages to come found vigorous opposition to civil rights difficult to muster. As Chappell emphasizes, this is partly because explicit and combative theological racism is not easy to square with the gospel. But this difficulty in mustering anti-civil rights opposition is equally due to the fact that early SNCC organizers were acting a lot like . . . Jesus. Those addicted to seeking other forms of power—be they defenders of Jim Crow or left-intellectuals dreaming of neo-neo-Constantinian modes of rule over others[76]—rarely recognize the powers of SNCC-like organizing. But it is there and discernable for those who will look.

Returning West of SNCC

Yet for all that early-SNCC people did, and for all the different theoretical work and political movements they spawned in the following decades, SNCC lost most of its soul and power quickly—certainly by 1965. The reasons for this loss appear to be manifold. There were very uneven and contradictory ethical and political commitments among the earliest SNCC organizers that remained unsettled and that were drawn into destructive conflicts in later years as new events created new challenges. The sheer stress of facing endless violence and threats year in and year out took a tremendous toll politically and personally on many of those involved. There was a huge influx of people who had little education in the traditions and practices that SNCC drew upon and extended. Many of these people were white, and great tensions arose as the naive paternalism of many whites intersected with centuries of suppressed anger among many blacks. Some key leaders began to lead the organization away from the types of work discussed above. As they did, ideologies that were

---

75. Chappell, *Stone of Hope*, especially chapter 6, 105–30.

76. For a gloss on modulations of Constantinianism, see Yoder, "Christ the Hope of the World."

more abstract and dogmatic increasingly came to the fore. With SNCC's growth, the challenges of scale also mounted. Key figures became media televisual pop stars, and this celebrity greatly distorted the relationships, dynamics, tempos, movements, and ways of dwelling within the organization. Televisual space-time was hard on SNCC. By the mid-1960s, a larger SNCC organization with more lucrative opportunities attracted new people with very different aims from those organizers who initiated SNCC, sometimes leading to corruption. Thus, SNCC faced myriad problems of such severe weight that it would have been yet another miracle if SNCC had survived with vitality much longer than it did.

But these factors are not the only ones that came to bear, and with this next point, I return to themes more obviously touching upon the questions I raised in the beginning of this engagement with West. The SNCC's strengths were born of traditions struggling mightily, as we have seen, with hierarchical, undemocratic modes of power. Some modes, like racism, were violent and oppressive; some, like the SCLC, were infinitely more benevolent and benign but were perceived as hugely problematic nevertheless. This straining generated both what was perhaps the grandest experiment in radical democracy in U.S. history and simultaneously deleterious expressions upon which insurgent intellectuals must critically reflect: for although it led to what might be thought of as an "over-suppression" of elements it was nevertheless right to resist in important respects because of their dominance and effects at the time. I have in mind two related things.[77]

77. Actually, there is a third (to which I return below). Baker's suspicion of histrionic but empty preaching was profoundly important, but her intense struggle against it seems to have greatly diminished her sense of the intercorporeal effects and possibilities that great speakers such as King can have in terms of generating hope, insight, solidarity, motivation, and action. I take this to be self-evident both in terms of many stories in books such as Marsh's *Beloved Community* and Chappell's *Stone of Hope,* and also in terms of some of my own experience in call-and-response–reveling IAF assemblies in Durham, North Carolina. For an account of the last, see Coles, "Wild Patience of Radical Democracy: Beyond Zizek's Lack." Baker is right that this power poses great threats to democratic organizing, but she is wrong to deny its power and elements of hopeful promise. Serious reflection needs to be given to the uses and abuses of great speakers, and to the tremendous possibilities and tensions involved between them and those organizing on the ground, so that we might better navigate what are inexorably difficult waters here. Critical scholars are situated to do important work here, but only if they are deeply attentive to the traditions of receptive relational prophetic practice that informed the likes of Baker and Septima Clarke and their suspicions of the Southern Christian Leadership Conference (SCLC). Otherwise we will enact precisely the voice-accented modes that

First, in its resistance to modes of "democratic," "left," and "Christian" practice that marched in overly rigid fashion to a future scripted far in advance of those who were to be recruited to it, SNCC tended to adopt a hyper–anti-ideological stance that was problematic because this stance tended to weaken efforts to explicate and elaborate the theological and philosophical sources from which SNCC's work drew its nourishment and direction. Taking this stance diminished SNCC's capacity to gain and sustain traction in the historical struggles. With insufficient voice and vision, SNCC weakened its capacity to resist these powers and to extend receptive democratic power. Eric Burner refers to Bob Moses as "a figure who spoke by silence."[78] I have already discussed some of what I see as the profound virtues of this mode. Yet its defect was that it left much too (or much too persistently[79]) inaudible the distinctive modes of ethical and political being that SNCC sought to cultivate. In a world of selves born and overwritten with a plethora of governing political discourses (and with accompanying dominant practices), one result of giving SNCC's practices too little expressive deliberation and development was that the practices were increasingly misunderstood and assimilated to more established modes of ruling. The force of this dominant history of discursive and practical power needed more resistance in the form of explicitly elaborated visions of alternative modes of being that more explicitly drew upon the traditions of living practices and struggle from which they grew (especially from radical-democratic and black church practices, understood in ways that accented relational, prophetic work done disproportionately by women). Such envisioning might have helped

---

preclude listening, modes that they criticize. So we will once again be oblivious to the powers of their practices, and therefore unable to make serious informed contributions, and unworthy of being seriously considered by those to whom we remain largely deaf and blind. This chapter can be seen in part as an effort to modulate the voices of prophetic organic intellectuals and great speakers by calling their ears to attend to the receptive "spade work" such that their voices might then henceforth ring with key elements of perspicuity they might otherwise lack. I discuss at greater length the entwinement of the "male" (call and response) and "female" (response and call) traditions of prophetic practice in "Awakening With King, or, Refusing Political Soporifics," delivered at a symposium at Grinnell College, September 25, 2007, celebrating the fortieth anniversary of King's talk at Grinell, "Remaining Awake Through a Great Revolution."

78. Burner, *And Gently He Shall Lead Them*, 7.

79. This word is key: silence is an integral *element* in SNCC's ethos and the arts of leadership. The question concerns how to modulate: how to entwine silence and voice in ways that enhance and deepen radical-democratic modes of being and insurgency.

to orient those involved in SNCC in ways that would have given them a greater sense of direction, endurance, and a history of textured practices across time with which to dialogue. Unfortunately, in the absence of these practices, it appears that many of those who continued to vaguely resist the assimilation of SNCC to ideologies of exclusion, force, and hierarchy were left without—or with too little—language. A radically democratic future then hinged and now hinges on emergent *discursive* practices: the dynamic and generative intertwining of language, body practices, and political and economic visions: each articulating in relation with the others. When practices and language do not develop together, each tends readily to wither. With too little language, the practices were deprived of a certain orientation and traction (let us distinguish between "traction" and "handles" in Yoder's sense of trying to take total control of history[80]). Surely when the rising nationalist elites in mid-1960's SNCC dogmatically dismissed as "floaters" the grassroots practitioners who resisted the group's will-to-power trends, the elites committed an awful distortion. Yet perhaps the charge was not without a moment of truth. The vital question remains: Are there paradoxical arts that might enhance our capacities to combine dialogical language, silence, body practices, and political and economic policies in a way that, in Derrida's words, seeks "to render [a place—to make a responsive *'place,'* instead of objectified *space* fit for rule], to render it habitable, but without killing the future in the name of old frontiers"?[81]

We need to move far beyond the conflict between dogmatists and floaters; but, truth be told, perhaps we have yet to travel very far at all on these more promising paths. The traditions of black church women engaging in more receptive prophetic modes, along with the heterogeneous practices of radical democracy in Harlem, continuing syncretically through SNCC organizing and beyond, offer us a great deal that could inform the efforts of public insurgent scholars who seriously seek to respond to these problems. And, in turn, organizing efforts on the ground could likely benefit from engaging the critical, reflective works that sustained scholarly attention to such questions would probably spawn. All of this is to suggest that SNCC's oversuppression of the tradition of vocal-articulate prophetic envisioning and *theorizing* needs to be rethought

80. See Yoder, *The Politics of Jesus*, especially chapter 12, "The War of the Lamb," 228–47.

81. Derrida, *Specters of Marx*, 169.

and revised. The work of prophetic organic scholarship as voicing has a vitally important role to play—both in diagnosing this problem in the first place and in taking up the task of explicating, naming, and emphatically envisioning pragmatic paths and utopian possibilities of beloved community.

This type of relationship, it seems to me, would be a vital condition for reviving receptive public scholarship and receptive radical democracy. It just might awaken us from the deep dogmatic slumbers that endlessly "new" forms of "critique" seem less and less capable of disturbing. So, I am saying: Those rooted in receptive liturgical work need to become more affirming of the work of vocal prophetic envisioning, and the latter mode needs to become more receptive and to cultivate its own voice in relation to everyday struggles—and in relation to the centrality of receptivity to these struggles. Receptive liturgical work and receptive prophetic work do not join in harmony, because each risks endangering the other in its efforts to nurture its own possibility. What we need is a more responsive relationship between prophetic scholars and receptive prophetic struggles: a relationship of endless tension that must repeatedly be reevaluated and rearticulated.

This also suggests another mode of thinking about leadership and authority—a mode of thinking that pertains to the second related problem I want briefly to discuss in relation to weaknesses of SNCC. In struggling so mightily against top-down modes of leadership, perhaps SNCC overstrained, and hence paid insufficient attention to explicitly formulating visions and practices of leadership that might enhance its capacities to bring a "new thing" to flourish and endure in the world. Decades after her involvement in SNCC, Diane Nash reflects that the dissipation of SNCC was not due primarily to the influx of many northerners so much as it was to the fact that "we did not devote enough time and energy into the education of the people coming in."[82] In another set of reflections, Tom Hayden notes "it is difficult to sustain a revolutionary commitment without roots for very long."[83] Perhaps what SNCC failed to cultivate sufficiently—given its fear of modes of leadership and authority in other organizations—were practices of pedagogy and training that might draw people into relation with historical narratives of those struggling roots:

82. Greenberg, *Circle of Trust*, 21.
83. Ibid., 32.

e.g., the arts and techniques of "sitting at the feet" of the least of these; instilling a sense that this has been a long struggle; offering textured historical sources for dramatic hope; and also cultivating a wizened sense that there will be painful setbacks, trials, dry periods, failures, and corruption—a sense that serious hopes for radical democracy and radical ecclesia must cultivate an expectation of these too lest we wither in the face of each new challenge.

Critical insurgent intellectuals could play a major role in offering reflections upon these issues and upon the inevitable tensions we will need to sustain in order to better negotiate them. But we will have little interesting to say unless we study with great care the promises, tensions, and pitfalls of people practicing grassroots democracy in myriad contexts of struggle. Why should any struggling people listen to what we might say unless we demonstrate in the most textured of ways that we are learning that the aim of leadership should be to create capacities of leadership among those who would be led? Why should any struggling people listen unless we demonstrate that the legitimacy of authority should be related to the extent to which it can disperse itself and empower the gifts of those who would be called to acknowledge it? To be learning these things is to be receptively engaging with struggles beyond the walls of the academy as well as within them. To learn these things is to become aware that they are a crucial condition of most valuable democratic scholarship. Engagement is surely not the only condition of scholarly reflection, and too much engagement can risk threatening reflection as well as enabling it. But lives devoid of such engagement and of proximity to those more ensconced in daily democratic organizing and struggle rarely nurture democratic theory.

To venture toward receptive engagement is, to be sure, to embark upon learning the most difficult, paradoxical, and elusive things about existence, philosophy, ethics, politics, and theology. Questions of being and time, spatiality and bodies, identity and difference, teleology and ateleology, the character of prophecy, Jesus and the Trinity—these need not be "dumbed down" as we sink our receptive hands into the soils of living struggle. We learn that *democracy matters*—not only as a condition of struggling for what may be highest, but also because receptive democratic engagement is the condition of democratic thinking as such.

Kierkegaard is famous for saying that a "thinker without a paradox is like a lover without feeling."[84] This remains true, in spite of legions of sterile academics chattering about paradox in modes that increasingly lack trembling substance, life, tension—and paradox. SNCC-like struggles offer us a mode of receptive engagement that is at once a condition for thinking, for democracy, and perhaps for aspects of a non-Constantinian politics of Jesus. And they are *paradoxically* so insofar as they also contain and confront conditions that can lead to thoughtlessness and to the death of much of what is most promising in them. To turn our inquiring energies to such things is to inhabit the *paradoxical character of the ordinary*, which is the *only* dislocated location in the midst of which paradox genuinely emerges and will not let us be.

Hence, entwined with this chapter's detouring through practices to which West sometimes gestures but insufficiently tends, is a returning to an affirmation of the importance of the initiative and insight of public prophetic vocal intellectuals whom West names so well. But only if we, in turn, receptively draw our eyes, our ears, and our touch to the textures of history and of living democratic initiative as the conditions of possibility for voices and times in and for which democracy matters.

INTERRUPTION

I am sitting quietly, on a day that follows a weekend in which Cornel West and I (along with Jeffrey Stout and Amina Waddud) engaged in public conversation and debate that included a greatly shortened presentation of this engagement with his work.[85] And our conversation—it reminds me, again, that one cannot discuss sufficiently well that to which one has insufficiently borne witness.

In a way that few others can, West's voice fills a room that can seat seven hundred people. It is like listening to a scholarly version of Coltrane (and his right hand moves, sometimes with frenetic grace, as if he were conducting an incredible improvisation, or being pulled by one that most cannot hear except through him). I am not speaking simply of incredible passion and charisma but also of a level improvisational insight, scholarly repertoire, power, and coherence that is profoundly humbling. Swept up

---

84. See Kierkegaard, *Philosophical Fragments*, 46.

85. We also engaged in nonpublic conversations, which significantly informed the character of this "interruption."

in this vortex of intensity, I am hurled back into footnote 77 above. I am wishing I had underlined it, put it in bold, in italics, in "caps," developed it in the body of the text. *This is a gift.*

Among the many things West said that continue to reverberate were his intense declarations that in his view, listening, voice, and body practices are not separate but deeply entwined—deeply entwined across time such that his performative mode *is* an incarnation of a long history of black expression and struggle in the midst of the centuries-long catastrophe that black people have endured. He suggested that a call to diminish black voice was difficult for him to hear because of the long history in which voice was frequently the only thing black people have had with which to resist annihilation: the power to cry out, to give voice in myriad media to the catastrophic suffering, so that it may not be the last word.

I am *stopped*, for a time, not only because of *what* West is saying but because he is *doing* the thing he is saying, and doing so in a way that brings into the room things that must be there: important things that no one else is bringing in the same way or with the same power. You can hear and feel the listening in his voicing. He is voicing and leading in ways that I would not want any "we" to be without. So I am stopped. The "repeated reevaluations and rearticulations" I emphasized toward the end of the previous section are beginning to rearticulate my bones.

I am stopped in a number of conflicted ways. And after a while, my response to him in the public conversation—and continuing now—becomes something like this. I would not want anything I have said or written to be read to imply that I seek to diminish voice, nor to eclipse the vital role such voices might play in leadership. In a sense I am saying precisely the opposite. I am asking about conditions of possibility for democratizing voice, about conditions of radical-democratic leadership. The questions I raise—that Ella Baker raised—concern modes of *informing* and *empowering* voices, modes of becoming more resonant bodies that, in turn, resound with the voices and intelligence of others in our own words and blues and exuberant jazzlike vision. The questions I raise concern who is "part of the band" to which one responds and with which one improvises, and Baker and I are suggesting that those engaged in everyday liturgies of receptive democratic insurgency are crucial; that the voices of tremendous soloists must develop a new sound that is more discerning and attentive toward such everyday liturgies. Informed and animated by them.

The broader issue is, what kind of democratic voicing (or, better, what kind of democratic resonance) are we performing and talking about when we gesture and work toward the beloved community? If one will linger for a moment with a metaphor informed by a life-long love of guitars, let me put it this way: Deepening democracy is in no small part about developing relationships that enable and are enabled by resonant bodies. Relational resonance. Yet most of us have become bodies that, like bad guitars, dampen and distort the sounds of even the brightest strings and melodies coming through our sound holes and along the surface of the instruments that we are. The sounds of others do not linger well within us but are absorbed into the deafening silence of egoistic pursuit. Nothing is more important to radical democracy today than cultivating relationships through which more and more people might become a "we" of more resonant bodies: picking up the tones, overtones, and undertones of others; listening and resonating so provocatively that new tones in others are reverberated into being; listening and resonating so profoundly that old tones in others, days and years and centuries gone by, still resound, perform, and ignite within us.

Cornel West is nothing if not such a resonant body, and nothing if not a weaver of relationships that nurture such resonance in others. And as I listened to his voice, and walked the streets of Washington DC with him—from dinner to lunch—I was struck by the multitude of people (of every color, but especially black people) politely interrupting him with praise, requests for autographs, the brief sharing of stories. One person even walked up and announced that he and others had recently started a "Cornel West Center for Leadership Development" (this person handed him an official card bearing this title), about which West had been unaware. In response to each of these interruptions, West responded graciously and receptively, with questions, praise, shared joy, and encouragement.

And so I am stopped—by a sense of how much the voice with which I have wrestled here still richly exceeds and differs from my experience and grasp. I could revise this essay to incorporate these new insights and sensibilities, but that would obscure the finitude of my voice in a way that would betray it. I still think that Cornel West has a great deal to learn from Ella Baker and from Bob Moses (whom West publicly and playfully mocked for his avoidance of TV cameras[86] even as he expressed

---

86. To which I later responded that the better part of an altered relationship between

great appreciation for Moses in private conversations later). I still think, in fact (perhaps "still" should be replaced by "more than ever"), that no small portion of *Democracy Matters* hinges on West and others like him receiving such lessons and repeatedly *returning* to that schoolhouse—to learn and to teach. [87] Yet I have deeper sense that the relationships that spur and develop in these returns will draw upon many sources, take many forms, and exceed any of our imaginations.

POSTSCRIPTUM

In a footnote above (6), I alluded to a certain dissatisfaction I have with Unger and West's *The Future of American Progressivism*, even as I am sympathetic to several themes that are central to it, such as radicalizing democracy, equality, experimentalism, the genius of ordinary people, and so forth. It is well beyond the scope of this chapter to get into a lengthy discussion of the details of the political and economic reforms that West and Unger propose in this book. And yet, if receptivity matters, how might it pertain to the most basic motifs of this text?

The *Future of American Progressivism* has a breathlessness to it that strikes me as more Unger than West—and many of the social-theory and policy motifs expressed are closely akin to those articulated in Unger's earlier and later works.[88] Social theory owes much to Unger's insightful critique of "necessity" and to his theorization of "plasticity." But my sense is that increasingly Unger comes to fetishize high-speed plasticity, almost as an end in itself. Frequently, too, this seems to be the case in the book that he and West coauthor. West and Unger situate their project in the stream of the American "religion of individual and collective possibility: the belief that Americans can make themselves and remake their society,

---

prophetic voices and prophetic receptivity could be summed up in the hope that Bob Moses receive infinitely better treatment than that.

87. And I confess that among the many things that I experienced in West's public response was a fear that Baker's criticism of a certain deafness (to Baker's concerns . . .) —a deafness that is frequently entwined with a certain brilliance of voice—was at times justified by West's performance.

88. See, for example, Unger, *False Necessity*, which is among the most powerful works of social theory in decades, and most recently, *What Should the Left Propose?* in which Unger develops many of the themes in *Future of American Progressivism* in a more differentiated global context.

that they can make everything new," echoing Tom Paine.[89] This religion of possibility takes its distinctively American twist through a particular articulation of being and time that frames the book itself: "In America, men and women have placed hope above memory."[90]

This is a weird and highly un- or, I would even say, anti-Westian way of putting it. It splits apart and prioritizes what West generally and more wisely intertwines in complex and mutually informing ways. Hence, in *Democracy Matters*, he suggests a more complicated and compelling temporality insofar as he loops back to ancient prophetic, Socratic, and blues traditions in order to help recover the past in a revivified present that might participate in opening the future as gift. The temporality of *Democracy Matters* is inexorably more like a *pulsing* than a *ceaseless flowing* (echoing Bloch's critique of Bergson, and the key motif of *The Principle of Hope*).[91] Radical-democratic time, on this reading, is endlessly errant: It falls again and again, gets blocked and blocks itself, and goes astray, even as it dreams and works toward the "not yet" of verbal democracy. To move toward the "forward dawning"[92] of democratic dreaming, then, is not to remain in compulsory fashion on the leading edge of time (as Benjamin showed us so poignantly) in an effort to bolster a "progressiveness" that is already in process. Progressive process is often (not always) a trap saying, "Another world is impossible"; "stay the course." Rather, more complicated strategies and temporalities are needed, likely entwining modes such as:

- looping back (e.g., Yoder)

- blasting open the "progress" of oppressive times with complex resonances across discrepant moments (e.g., Benjamin)

- developing *some* progressive tendencies (West)

- pausing in radically patient and indeterminate silence (famed Quaker meetings)

- cultivating traditional slow-time routines that appear to contain historical soils of flourishing (Wendell Berry)

89. Unger and West, *Future of American Progressivism*, 3.
90. Ibid., 70.
91. Bloch, *Principle of Hope*.
92. The phrase appears repeatedly in *Principle of Hope*.

- cultivating a memory of the political in order to engender future radical-democratic possibilities (Wolin)
- juxtaposing in tension critical, monumental, and traditional histories and temporal modalities (Nietzsche), and so on.

Complex "pluri-time" is time that solicits patient receptivity and new possibilities for political relationships and action.

Yet at the heart of Unger and West is a relentless compulsory progressiveness, an unquestioning allegiance to the cutting edge of the present leaning into the future (something Karl Polanyi brilliantly criticized).[93] Progressive ideals are to be figured and enshrined in terms of a temporality that becomes the inescapable home of democracy rather than the object of democratic dialogue, struggle, and irreducible heterogeneity. It is a market temporality that dreams of a world such that, in Marx and Engel's words, "all that is solid melts in the air": pure flow.[94] Unger and West dream of a world like "a thousand little Silicon Valleys, where a new logic of practical collaboration and restless experimentalism" reigns; where there is "a logic subordinating routine to innovation."[95] Of course, the problem, in their view, is that currently these practices are entwined with logics of exclusion and inequality. The solution they propose is to universalize these islands of the economic vanguard, remaking the world in its image so that all are included and the flows are released from their oligopolistic constrictions so that opportunity circulates in far more egalitarian fashion. We must overcome the gap between these "rearguard" and the "vanguard" modes of production in order to create an economic geography such that the entire present is breathlessly propelled into the future on its own cutting edge, as we "quicken the tempo of democracy"[96] and promote an "anti-conservative" education that "promotes the voice of the future," which is, it seems, none other than *pure futurity as such*: permanent innovation.[97]

93. See chapter 12 below for a more extended discussion of Polanyi's critique.
94. Marx and Engels, "Communist Manifesto," 476.
95. Unger and West, *Future of American Progressivism*, 38.
96. Ibid., 85.
97. Ibid., 70.

Whither receptivity? Is keeping a receptive memory of Jesus, Socrates, black-church traditions, SNCC, and Ella Baker conservative? Or radical? Or *both*? And if it is the last, are we not drawn into negotiating a very different temporal situation than the one proposed by Unger and West? Is lingering slowly on front porches and at the feet of sharecroppers "rearguard" temporality? Is ending a democratic meeting that surfaces intractable differences, opaque complexities, tradeoffs, and irreducibly particular attachments—is ending such a meeting with *indecision* a thing necessarily to be biased against in the name of "quickened tempo"? Is ending it several times this way necessarily bad? Should we orient all our institutional and soul-craft investments toward "thriving in the midst of change," or rather ought this not be an ongoing question instead of the supposition and ground of radical democracy? Perhaps we should cultivate selves that insist and struggle in order that many things *not* be subject to compulsory change: that we design economic practices that allow us to live in proximity to the same friends and strangers over a lifetime if we want; practices more likely to engender this want; practices that allow us to live in community for many decades so that we develop attachments, knowledges, connections, textured historical senses of place, political capacities, and so forth, that are so often important aspects of radical-democratic flourishing and possibility. Perhaps we should cultivate our days so that we have ample time to linger in manifold modes of tending that *require* ample time. Perhaps many different values and visions ought to be viewed in agonistic *tension* with a vision of restless innovation. Perhaps many are higher. Or perhaps we want some mix of these things alongside some of the features Unger and West suggest. Or, better, perhaps we want different mixes at different times and in different places: Mixes we adjust in light of specific problems and opportunities we are facing, in light of different goods for which we are striving, in light of different dangers we seek to avoid.

If receptivity matters, I suspect we will likely seek to foster vast regions for Tolkien's *Ents* (the very slow, treelike creatures in *The Lord of the Rings*), and for the *Ent* in each one of us. We will seek not an entire land of *Ents*, but vast regions and modes. As we have seen, receptivity is *both* slow and fast. Yet it cannot thrive in a world that takes the innovation Unger and West describe as an underlining motif for social transformation. Radical-democratic economics, politics, and education for engaging the complexity of the ordinary demand a much more subtle relation to the question of time, because every particle of complexity leans in different temporal directions—along paths of different teleologies—and moves at different paces and rhythms. Radical democracy is the ongoing negotiation of *manifold and often agonistic* temporalities. It is the questioning of time, and it requires time for this questioning. Strategies that seek to found radical democracy unquestioningly according to a single temporal motif will kill it—especially when the motif is entwined with so many tendencies that historically have had antidemocratic effects. Surely, there are issues that call for the restless innovation that West and Unger articulate: alternative energy, public transportation, water conservation, energy efficiency, and the like. But to acknowledge this is a far cry from adopting "the future of American progressivism."

Time is a complicated ever-changing pulse, not a flow. We should conceive of time and should seek to live it thus—not just now, in dark times, but in perpetuity. And precisely because we are, as West shows so profoundly, tragic beings ("crooked timber"), we endlessly and erroneously fetishize what we take to be vanguard—in our day, we even fetishize the vanguard as such as a fundamental temporal motif. Worshiping at the feet of vanguard temporality leads to the land of "no exit." It is the dominant form of contemporary Constantinianism (which, as Yoder shows us more deeply than West does in *Democracy Matters*, is fundamentally the effort to define, control, reduce, and thereby domesticate time). Rather than at the feet of vanguard temporality, we should conduct worship at the feet of the least, which is precisely *not* to say, "follow them blindly." And so, with a postscript I am calling "West back West from Unger and West." The shape of such a place I shall discuss more fully below in relation to the work of Sheldon Wolin, whom West names as one of his greatest teachers.

CHAPTER 4

Race: The "More" It Is About: Will D. Campbell Lecture
University of Mississippi, 2006

Stanley Hauerwas

"Time takes time—sometimes too long—but it is all we have."
　—Will Campbell[1]

HOW DID TWO MEN, ONE FROM MISSISSIPPI AND ONE FROM TEXAS, END UP ON THE SAME SIDE?

I am deeply honored to inaugurate the Will D. Campbell Lecture Series on Faith and Social Justice at the University of Mississippi. It is not clear, however, whether I should be honored to give this lecture. Campbell has quite rightly reminded us that honor is a virtue that is more stoic than Christian: one often used for manipulation and deception.[2] Nor is it clear whether anyone giving this lecture can honor Will Campbell and at the same time explore the relation between faith and social justice.[3] Anyone

---

1. Campbell, *Brother to a Dragonfly*, 151.

2. Campbell, *And Also With You*, xi. Campbell observes that honor is "nevertheless a virtue unto itself. After the battles were over, won or lost, when the Blue and the Grey lay together, when Gettysburg was again quiet for they had all gone away, honor, we have been taught, remained. Remained, though perhaps badly violated. Still and yet: honor." On the statue of the confederate soldier in the center of the University of North Carolina is written: "To the sons of the university who entered the War of 1861–65 in answer to the call of their country and whose lives taught the lesson of their greatest commander that duty is the sublimest word in the English language."

3. I also suspect that Campbell, the man who has always had an animus against insti-

who has read Will Campbell has learned that appeals to justice are often attempts to subvert our faith in Jesus by confusing Christianity with some variety of humanism.

For me, however, the invitation to give this lecture could not have come at a better time. This is so because, as I will explain, it provides me with the opportunity to blame Will Campbell for screwing up my life. In his book, *Will Campbell: Radical Prophet of the South*, Merrill Hawkins reports that after Campbell's speech in 1962 in Chicago at the National Conference on Religion and Race, Campbell had reached the point at which he was "consistently offending everyone."[4] He had done so because, in an effort to suggest that race might have something to do with sin, he left in the media version of his speech this sentence: "If I live to be as old as my father I expect to see whites marched into the gas chambers, the little children clutching their toys to their breasts in Auschwitz fashion, at the hands of a black Eichmann."[5]

Of course it is hard, he said ironically, to imagine that anyone might be offended by that sentence, but it turns out that it is still possible to offend people by insisting that Christian language might make a difference for how we understand the world.[6] For example, like Campbell, I

---

tutions, may worry that a lectureship in his name means he is becoming an institution. I do not think, however, that Campbell's anti-institutional stance denies the necessity of habits for sustaining the memories that enable our faithfulness to the gospel. Will Campbell will soon be dead, so we will need this lectureship not only to remember him, but also to remember everything he has taught us to remember.

4. Hawkins, *Will Campbell*, 46.

5. Ibid., 45. Never one to use a good sentence only once, Will used a version of that sentence in his *Race and the Renewal of the Church*, 6. What might be described as *the sentence* reads: "The Christian understanding of sin makes it highly probable that our generation will see white children marched into gas chambers by dark masters, clutching their little toys to their breasts in Auschwitz fashion." The sentence as it appears in *Race and the Renewal of the Church* is better written. I make this observation only because it should not be overlooked that Will Campbell is first and foremost a writer who pays close attention to his craft. He comes from Southern poor folk, but he has taught himself how to write. Of course being poor in the South is a great resource for learning how to write because of the expressive character of the language that constitutes your life. Stories are all you have, but the stories you have are irreplaceable.

6. Reflecting on the reality of Tchula, a town that had become 95 percent black, in his book *Providence*, Campbell observes that his prediction, "that Negroes, being fully human, would behave with comparable power as white power had behaved—had not come to be. If equally good, then equally evil, I had argued. It had not occurred here. Why not? I wondered" (108–9). His tentative answer is the power that comes from owing the land,

am accused by some of failing to adequately support calls for justice and democracy, and as a result some think I have not sufficiently dealt in my work with the continuing challenge of race. So by exploring and defending how and why Campbell has managed to offend some folks because of his theological commitments, I hope at the same time to show that his influence has put me in the same boat.

I went to Yale Divinity School in the same year, 1962, that Will's book *Race and the Renewal of the Church* came out. I suspect that I was led to read the book because Will came to the Divinity School that year to give a lecture. "Give a lecture," of course, is a misleading description. Rather, he sat on a table in the common room, surrounded by portraits of Yale Divinity School greats, and told stories. He was not wearing a coat or tie, and I am pretty sure that he was chewing tobacco, which he spit into an empty coke bottle. I do not remember much that he said, but I do remember thinking that this is my kind of guy; that is, someone who "did not harness well."[7]

The argument he made in *Race and the Renewal of the Church*—that is, that race is fundamentally a theological problem—left a decisive impression on me. For example, at the beginning of *Race and the Renewal of the Church* Campbell notes that his book has little to say about how the world might be reformed to be more free, just, or democratic. He doubts that such a project was ever the church's responsibility, but even if it were, such an opportunity has passed it by. Yet the church, in an effort to still show her relevance, imitates governmental authority by adopting a largely humanitarian approach: by advocating law and order, democracy, the rights of man, human dignity, constitutional process, and public schools. Campbell acknowledges that

> these things are good, but are they the most basic, most distinctive, concern of the church? In these pages, we will try to determine whether our concern is not something far more basic and more radical than anything the state has said. In the process we will attempt to establish that the church's failure in the racial crisis has been not functional but organic, not sociological, but theological. In effect, we have been asking the wrong questions. Instead of demanding, What can the Christian *do* to improve race

but I suspect this is but shorthand for the story he tells in *Providence*.

7. Campbell, *Providence*, 231. Campbell uses this wonderful phrase to describe Gene Cox, who in many ways is the hero of the story Will tells in *Providence*.

relations? we should be asking, What must the Christian *be*? As the body of Christ the church first of all must be the redeemed community. Then will it be empowered to redeem the world, and not before. The sin of the church is not that it has not reformed society, but that it has not realized self-renewal. Its sin is that it has not repented. Without repentance there cannot be renewal.[8]

I could have written those lines. In fact, I have spent a lifetime writing and rewriting those lines. I have done so, moreover, forgetting from whom I first learned them, namely, Will Campbell (and William Stringfellow). So it gives me great pleasure to acknowledge the debt I have long owed to Will Campbell. He not only taught me that race is first and foremost a theological problem, but also how addressing such a theological problem requires that we learn how to tell the stories that constitute our lives.[9] This means that I need to tell you some of the stories that have shaped my life in order to explain why Will Campbell's story, as well as the stories that he tells, have been so important for me. I have no way to know if those who invited me to give this lecture did so knowing that we are "biographically connected," but it may even be the case, as is often the case in Mississippi, that Campbell and I are "kin."

By "biographically connected" I do not mean that I have been fortunate to know Will other than through his writing. We did, if I remember rightly, have a brief meeting during one of Will's visits to Durham. Will, moreover, is from Mississippi, and I am from Texas. Those external to the South usually do not understand that Texas is not the South. I do not need to tell people from Mississippi that Southerners usually do not think fondly of Texas. For example, I love the conversation Will reports between Duncan Gray, the priest who is the hero of *And Also With You*, and General Walker, the retired general from Texas who had come to aid those protesting James Meredith's entrance to the University of Mississippi. Gray is pleading with the general to use his influence to stop

8. Campbell, *Race and the Renewal of the Church*, 3–4.

9. Campbell, like all great Southern storytellers, knows that one story is not one but many. *Brother to a Dragonfly* is the story of Joe, but it is also the story of the pathos of being poor and white in the South. Campbell knows well that one of the great tragedies of the South is the loss of voice for those who are poor and white. Crews, *Childhood*, is an attempt to give voice to those who seem robbed of any story about who they are apart from their not being black.

the riot, but instead Will reports that Walker turned on the priest and demanded,

> "Just who the hell are you anyway? And what are you doing here?"
>
> "My name is Duncan Gray. I am the rector of the local Episcopal Church," the priest replied. "This is my home and I am deeply hurt to see what is happening to the university and the state. I am here to do anything I can to stop the rioting and keep any more people from getting hurt or killed."
>
> The general became even more angry, moving toward Mr. Gray and exclaiming, "You're the kind of minister that makes me ashamed to be an Episcopalian!"
>
> Mr. Gray, realizing that he was on the verge of losing his temper, tried to remain calm, explaining that he was on home ground. "I have a proper concern and interest in keeping law and order. You, sir, are a Texan and have no business here. Your very presence here is making matters far worse. You should have stayed in Texas. We have enough problems of our own."[10]

I am, no doubt, more Texan than Southern, but like Will I also inherited the Christ-haunted genes of Mississippi. My mother, Joanna Gertrude Berry, was born and raised in the unforgiving, hardscrabble land surrounding Kosciusko. When she was ten, her mother died, and her father, a cotton-gin drunk and member of the Klan, married his cousin, resulting in my mother's and her sister, Wildean's, running off to be raised by their mother's brother, Uncle John Andrew and his wife, Ophelia. The

10. Campbell, *And Also With You*, 26. I love *And Also With You* and think that in many ways it is Campbell's best book. It may be that I like the book because in it we see how those of us with Anabaptist convictions are drawn to the liturgy of the *Book of Common Prayer*. Campbell was drawn to Gray because Gray was just a "good man." Late in the book, Will asks what the mark of a good man is. Scanning the *Book of Common Prayer*, he observes how often the words *joy* and *joyous* appear, and that those were the same words many used to describe Gray. Will observes, "A good man, I concluded, will be a man of unceasing joy. Joy in the biblical and *Prayer Book* understanding. Not joy as happy-go-lucky for he is capable of deep sadness. Over the years, through trials and tribulations, good times and bad, victories and defeats: joyous. Springing from assuredness that God has intervened in human history. Advent. Easter. Pentecost. Joy not dependent on highs and lows of feeling or changing conditions of affluence or misfortune. A person close to Gray had said, 'Duncan is what the Episcopal Church would be if everyone in it believed (lived by) the words they repeat every Sunday.' The radicalism of the liturgy had made an ordinary man good. Joyous. And a truly joyous person is never up to anything" (245).

names are enough to indicate that I have some sense of what it means to be from Mississippi.[11]

Like Will I learned from my mother, who taught me how to grow and peddle black-eyed peas and okra, and from my father, who taught me how to labor and lay brick, that life is just another name for hard work. Also like Will, I grew up in a segregated society, but segregation did not mean separation. I was a laborer. I was one of the few white men who labored, meaning that I was bonded with black men against a common enemy—bricklayers. Yet even after I learned to lay brick, I did not know enough to refrain from teaching a man I had labored with for years how to spread mud. I knew vaguely that black men were not allowed to learn to lay brick, but at the time it seemed more important to me to get the job finished. I suspect that is how segregation was undermined, that is, by those who were insufficiently schooled in how to maintain the rigid lines between the races.

Moreover, like Will, I was destined not to be able to escape God. Having married late, my parents had difficulty becoming pregnant. My mother, like Hannah, the mother of Samuel, prayed that if God would give her a son, she would give her son to God.[12] This is well and good, but did she have to tell me of that bargain? It resulted in my dedicating my life to the ministry one night after we had sung "I Surrender All" for the twenty-fourth time during the altar call. I knew I was supposed to get saved, but it just did not happen, and I did not think you should fake it. So instead I dedicated my life to the ministry, thinking that if God was not going to save me, at least I could make him indebted to me by becoming a minister. Fortunately for God's church, that has never come to pass.

11. For many summers we made the obligatory trip back to Mississippi to visit kin. I remember as a boy of ten sitting on the front porch with Uncle John Andrew and his son, Thadius, and listening to them discuss whether Lula Jean, who had just driven down the red clay road in front of the house (we waved, of course) was our second cousin fifth or sixth removed. I was also asked to read the Scripture in the Sunday service at the Baptist church that the family attended, only to discover by the embossing on the front that it was a gift of the KKK. I have even grappled for catfish in Mud Creek, scared to death that I would end up grappling a water moccasin. My mother, moreover, never failed to remind me that her great-grandmother was Choctaw.

12. In *Forty Acres and a Goat*, Campbell reports that he had always wanted to be a preacher even though a Jungian analyst told him he did so only because his mamma had decided he would be one five months before he was conceived (2). Will believes that he was called to be a preacher, and I believe his life confirms that call. I was clearly not called to be ordained, though I do preach.

I tried to get smart and sophisticated enough to avoid being a
Christian. I went to college because I was told that if you were going
into the ministry, you should go to college. But I had already decided by
the time I got to college that I had had enough Christianity, so I became
the philosophy major at Southwestern University in Georgetown, Texas.
However, in the process of studying philosophy, I learned just enough to
recognize that I did not know enough to be an atheist. I was in college
from 1958 to 1962, which meant that I learned I should be for integration. I certainly identified with the civil rights movement—I did after all
read *Motive* magazine—but I suspect my liberalism had as much to do
with my identification with a class different from my parents'. After all,
not until college did I recognize that I had come from a poor family.

Somewhere along the way, I recognized that being Christian and
facing the "tragedy of the South" were inseparable. Will confesses that he
realized the inescapability of being Southern, of having to inherit a past
that seemed irredeemable, after reading Howard Fast's *Freedom Road*.
Just as he said coming to terms with that past would occupy him "the
remainder of his days," so my past has occupied me.[13] I too had to learn,

13. Campbell, *Brother to a Dragonfly*, 98. For Campbell's most poignant reflections
on how the South was "marked" by slavery, see Campbell, *Providence*, 125–29. There
he asks, "Why are we still North and South? Was it not the prophet Amos who gave us
the answer a long time ago? Hearts can become so hardened that even repentance is
impossible. But it was not the war of which we could not repent. That was a barbarous
error that could have been so easily avoided, though many still revere it. It is, I believe,
the event of slavery that continues to stalk and haunt the land, and bear the bitter fruit
of which all of us, black and white, North and South, East and West, continue to partake
in ever-escalating portions. Is it because we who are white just don't seem to be able to
forgive people for being black?" (128). I am sure that Campbell would also acknowledge
that the "white problem" involves the presumption that we have a status that makes us
the "forgivers" rather than those who need forgiveness.

For what remains the best account of the relation between being Christian and
Southern, see Walker Percy, "The Failure and the Hope," 13–28. Percy argues, like
Campbell, that the sickness of Christendom lies in the fact that Christians are judged by
the world, as well as by themselves, about whether they have become a group that can
have a good impact on society. As a result, according to Percy, the one advantage the
South has is that it is the only region left in which theological habits of speech persist that
make possible a theological response to slavery and race. For the secular consciousness
of those who came to the South to change the South—"the Berkeley-Cambridge axis,"
(who certainly did much good)—fails to provide the language and practice necessary for
racial reconciliation. Of course, Campbell never lets us forget Thomas Merton's remark:
"To reconcile man with man and not with God is to reconcile no one at all" (quoted in
the foreword to Campbell and Holloway, *Failure and the Hope*, 7).

as Will did, that our identification with the black struggle against racism was right. But such an identification was false if it led me to forget that my people—poor white people—also suffered from a kind of slavery made all the more pernicious because their enslavement could not be recognized as such, because they were white and because whites, by definition, were free.[14]

I did not have a soul sufficient for such recognition as I made my way to Yale. I did not go to Yale to train to be a minister but rather to try to decide if I would be a Christian. I was sure that if I were to be a Christian, I would be a liberal, but I also thought that the Christian complicity with the destruction of the Jews was the clearest indication that Christianity was a false faith. I was stunned to discover, therefore, that it was Karl Barth, not the Protestant liberals, who saw clearly the demonic character of the Nazis.[15] Thus, much to my surprise, I discovered, as Will did, that when all is said and done, it is all about God.[16] This finally brings me to why I think that what Will Campbell has to teach us about the "lot more" of race that is so important.

14. Campbell says that he came to this insight in his encounter with P. D. East, in which he was forced to acknowledge that Jesus had also died for Thomas Coleman, the killer of Jonathan Daniel. Campbell, *Brother to a Dragonfly*, 221–26. In *And Also With You*, Campbell describes the way Duncan Gray exemplified the pain of being a Southern priest because he understood the nature of the tragedy of the South; that is, "he could love, and not reject, his segregationist people because he knew humankind was fallen. All of it. And because he knew the problem was a systemic one, not confined to the Mississippi Delta. But he was a Mississippian. And that was where he chose to wrestle with the principalities and powers diseasing the national body" (150).

15. Will Campbell, good Baptist that he is, has more reason to have been led to the Anabaptists than I have. He was raised Baptist, and I am quite happy that I was not. I suspect, however, that Barth's influence on us led each of us to have great sympathy with the Anabaptists.

16. I love the exchange in *The Glad River* between Model T, Doops, and Kingston. While they are standing in, as well as shoveling, shit, Kingston asks Doops why he and his mamma fight about religion.

"That's what religion is," Doops replied. "Somebody told me a man's religion is what he'll get mad enough to fight about."

"I thought religion was about God," Kingston said. "God is about God," Doops said. "Religion is all about us." All of them had stopped working and were sitting on the tailgate of the pickup.

"Thick cream, Model T. Did you hear what ole Doops said? He said, 'God is about God.' Wonder what that's supposed to mean." When no one answered he said, "The nun told us God is love. But I reckon I never understood that either." (189–90)

WILL CAMPBELL ON RACE

"You know, there's a lot more to this race thing than just segregation."[17] The judgment that there is more to this race thing than segregation was made by Horace Germany, a minister in the Church of God, who had wanted to start a school to train anyone, black or white, to preach. Refusing to give in to the threats of a mob, Germany was savagely beaten. He was beaten unconscious because he refused to fight back. As he reported to Will, "I don't believe in violence. I don't want to hurt anybody."[18] Yet the beating was sufficient to end his ambition to build the school. Instead he sold his property and building to the biggest bootlegger in the county.

Will Campbell has spent a lifetime helping us discover the "lot more" there is to this "race thing." I am convinced, moreover, that the "lot more" Campbell describes is as important today as it was in the early days of the civil rights struggle. My way of putting the matter is that we currently confront the failure of the success of the civil rights movement. Americans believe that Martin Luther King Jr. won the battle against segregation and racism. Thus many Americans assume that we no longer have a race problem in America.[19] We now live in a world in which African Americans can move to the suburbs, have two cars and three TVs, and worry about poor whites moving in. As a result, we (that is, we whites) can say to anyone that thinks we still have a problem: "Look, things have worked out well. You have enough money to buy what you want. Leave the past to the past. What was a little slavery between friends?"

17. Campbell, *Brother to a Dragonfly*, 159. Campbell will often retell a story in another venue. For example, this line and story he first told in an article in *Katallagete* and collected in his and James Y. Holloway's *Up to Our Steeples in Politics*, 46–49. Like all Southern writers, Campbell sometimes expresses an uneasiness about being described as a Southern writer. He is rightly uneasy with such descriptions to just the extent that they are meant to "place" the writer in order to avoid having to take seriously what one has to say. However, Campbell well knows he is Southern for no other reason than he knows there is no escaping the past. More important, he knows as a Southerner that he does not want to escape the past.

18. Campbell, *Brother to a Dragonfly*, 159.

19. For confirmation of how racism continues to exist though few think of themselves as racist, see Bonilla-Silva, *Racism Without Racists*. In particular, Bonilla-Silva locates the "frames" that conceal from whites the persistence of racism (that is, abstract liberalism, naturalization, cultural racism, and the minimization of racism). He thinks that abstract liberalism is the deepest challenge, just to the extent that it hides from whites that "white" is a form of racism.

In an extraordinary essay, "Our Grade is 'F,'" which is the last essay in *Up to Our Steeples in Politics*, a collection of essays from the 1960s that first appeared in his and Holloway's magazine, *Katallagete*, Campbell clearly saw that the battle for civil rights could have the outcome I have just described. Thus, he argued, we have no reason to celebrate the successes associated with the civil rights campaign, for what have been taken as victories hide from us our failure to confront the deeper pathologies of racism.[20] Consequently, Will observes, many who were engaged in the civil rights struggle moved on to other "causes," such as the antiwar movement, because they assumed that particular battle was won.[21] Indeed, many of that era had to move from one cause to another, because without a cause they had no moral compass.

Yet if things are really not all that better when it comes to race in America today, what happened to make the problem of race seem less urgent to so many? At least one of the reasons is that the problem turned out to be less black and white than it first appeared.[22] For example,

20. In many ways, *Forty Acres and a Goat* is Campbell's attempt to come to terms with the "failure" of the movement. For example, he quotes Kelly Miller Smith, a courageous African American pastor, who said as he lay dying, "The civil rights gains we have made are largely cosmetic." Campbell protested by giving a roll call of improvements that Smith had accomplished, yet Smith replied, "But they still don't respect us." This leads Campbell to acknowledge the truth of Smith's words, because "*Freedom* is respect. *Freedom* is reconciliation. *Freedom* is love" (269–70).

21. Campbell and Holloway, *Up to our Steeples in Politics*, 129. For an account of the tensions between liberal confidence and the prophetic religious traditions of the black southerners, see Chappell, *Stone of Hope*. Chappell argues that the history of Protestantism and secular alternatives has been full of surprises, not the least of which is that "the irrational traditions of prophetic, revivalistic religion served the liberal goals of freedom and equality. The flip side of that is that those traditions did not help the allegedly backward, conservative, southern opponents of liberty and equality. Civil rights activists drew from illiberal sources to supply the determination that liberals lacked, but needed to achieve the greatest post–World War II victory of American liberalism. Their opponents failed to draw anything similar from similar sources" (179). What Chappell, an avid atheist (thus the adjective "irrational") "discovered," Campbell knew in every bone of his body. Campbell, moreover, understood earlier than most that the "liberal story" that shaped how the story of the civil rights struggle would be told would not be sufficient for helping us negotiate the continuing challenge of race. Campbell was quite active in the antiwar movement, helping young men get to Canada. See his account in *Forty Acres and a Goat*, 119–42.

22. At least part of the complexity is that whites cannot accept the forgiveness necessary to be free from their sin. In *Forty Acres and a Goat*, Campbell quotes John Ross's observation about Andrew Jackson's Indian removal strategy; that is, "The perpetrator of

Campbell reports that he and a handful of folk who walked to school in Little Rock with nine black children "felt fresh and clean inside. But today we would hesitate to take that same walk, not for fear of a governor's National Guard, but for fear of meeting the jeers of 'Honky, go home!'"[23]

One of the things that happened to the civil rights movement was the increasing recognition by African Americans that when you have presidents and southern mayors joining hands and singing "We Shall Overcome," you had better think twice about what it means to be "integrated." African Americans, according to Campbell, rightly began to see that while good liberal white Americans were open to integration, there was a condition to it. That is, whites

> were willing, yes, even eager to receive blacks into *our* schools, *our* neighborhoods, *our* jobs, families and bedrooms. But they also saw that our understanding of the end of segregation was usually identified with that kind of acceptance which presupposes, among other things, that there are two cultures, two races, two types of men, a hierarchy of creation. "Integration" came to mean the active perusal of a course allowing the two races to encounter each other in such a way that the white partner could forgive his black brother for being black and permit him to become an honorary white man. Nothing more was required of blacks other than that they learn their lessons: keep their yards clean, keep their voices down, wash themselves at least once a day, enjoy the treasures of higher culture, stabilize their courtship and marriage customs, just as the white man is alleged to have done. The beginning of genocide is not ovens and concentration camps. The beginning of genocide is the beginning of integration: the expectation of the majority that the minority will become like the majority.[24]

a wrong never forgives his victims."). That insight makes clear why Campbell has rightly understood that the challenge of race is not something you easily get over.

23. Campbell, *Up to our Steeples in Politics*, 130.

24. Ibid., 131. In a wonderful scene in *Providence*, Campbell reports his attempt to get an African American to tell him about the fire that destroyed the Providence plantation. To do so, he promises he will not use the informant's name. During the interview, the elderly African American and Will share their grief concerning the death of their fathers. Campbell observes:

> In that moment I knew something I had never known before. Death is *that*. Friend is *friend*. And macho is a *goddamn lie*. I had never thought of "integration" as being something one felt. Now I was learning that is all integration is.
> When we gained our composure, each one taking an identical red bandanna from his pocket and fiercely blowing his nose, my new friend quickly bowed his

We should like to believe that Campbell has got to be wrong. Surely it is an exaggeration bordering on irresponsibility to suggest that integration and genocide might be connected? Yet we also know that subsequent developments surrounding race in America make what he said in 1970 ring true. The problem of race, it seems, is that it is by no means easy to say what the problem of race is. In the early days of the civil rights struggle it seemed clear what needed to be done as well as who the enemy was, but now it is more difficult to name the challenge or to locate the enemy. This means we should have recognized that, from the beginning, the battle was not "against flesh and blood, but against principalities and powers" (cf. Eph 6:12).[25]

Campbell uses the language of "principalities and powers" because he learned that the "lot more" to this "race thing" is sin and redemption. But if that is true, then race is not a problem you can "solve" through state power or social engineering. From Campbell's perspective, the problem with the way the problem of race has been understood is that Christians have allowed the problem to be described in humanistic terms. Christians, in the name of Christian love, rightly resisted those who refused to employ people on the basis of race, or who threatened and who taunted mothers taking their children to school. Campbell acknowledges that these humanitarian and egalitarian concerns lie within the province of Christian witness; but when they constitute all that Christians have to say about race, they are not enough. They are not enough because God, not the human, is the only point of reference that matters.

The sin therefore is that the whole issue of race is an effort to deny the sovereignty of God, to negate the absolute supremacy of God. Once a person has truly seen this truth, that person can no longer be a racist, and can no longer grovel in the agonies of self-pity. From that point on, the racist logic and desire for self-justification are terrifying. The racist is now afraid to call anyone unclean, to discriminate against anyone, to stand in judgment over any group or individual, or to set himself above any of

---

head. "Amen," I heard him say, his voice firm and clear. He had let his father go, as I had let mine go. The communing had introduced a sluggishness in both of us and I knew the story about the Providence House fire would have to wait for another day. As I started to drive away, he came and opened the car door, shook my hand again, and said, "You can use my name if you want to." *Integration is trust.* I told him, no, I had made him a promise. Integration is promises kept. (213)

25. Ibid., 130.

God's human creatures. From the moment either the segregationist or the integrationist really accepts the absolute sovereignty of God, either is forever thereafter terrified to usurp that authority or to claim any part of it for him- or herself. And this usurping is precisely what one does when one determines a pattern of behavior by classifications of race or class, or thinks that God is obliged to conform reality to one's own notion of what ought to be.[26]

In other words, the categories of race, or the classification of people by color, do not exist in the new creation enacted in Jesus Christ. The Christian message on race is quite simply the gospel: that is, "while we were yet sinners, Christ died for us" (Rom 5:8). "That something has been done for us something free, something with which we had nothing to do, something undeserved and unearned. In this 'new creation' (2 Cor 5:17); we are neither Caucasian, African, Asian, male nor female, bond or free. We are a third race" (cf. Gal 3:28).[27] How then did Christians begin to think of race as a natural category? According to Campbell, they did so when the emphasis in Christian theology began to be on humans rather than God. Nothing is more indicative of such an emphasis than the presumption by modern liberal Christians that the race problem can be solved politically. Such a presumption serves to legitimate the modern nation-state, which, ironically, has been the primary agent for the categorization of people by race.[28]

Christians have quite simply confused humanism with the gospel. Thus, Campbell's judgment that theological liberalism "probably did more to impede progress in race relations in America by keeping man at the center of thought and action than did even fundamentalism."[29] For under the influence of liberalism, "the church tried to effect reconciliation where there already *is* reconciliation, while the *only* thing that God

26. Campbell, *Race and the Renewal of the Church*, 53–54.

27. Ibid., 39.

28. One often finds in Campbell insights worthy of Foucault. Campbell's understanding of the disciplinary function of modern state formations in regard to race, for example, has been substantiated by Goldberg in *Racial State*. Goldberg argues that the necessary homogenizing logic of the modern liberal bureaucratic state cannot help but reproduce states in which racial distinctions are necessary to contain the threat of hybridity (30–34). For Campbell's account of the bureaucratic nature of the modern state, see *Up to Our Steeples in Politics*, 104–5.

29. Campbell, *Race and the Renewal of the Church*, 57.

has asked from the Church was to *live* thanksgiving for others and so express thanksgiving for what he has done for us."[30]

Will Campbell always describes himself as a preacher, and that he surely is. He disavows having any theological sophistication, often observing that he was an indifferent student at Yale Divinity School. Yet, interestingly enough, I suspect there is no better representative of the "Yale School," a problematic designation itself, than Will Campbell. For as early as *Race and the Renewal of the Church* as well as the essays in *Up to Our Steeples in Politics*, Will Campbell has taught us how theological descriptions should work if we are to better understand why racism is a matter of sin and reconciliation.[31] That he has done so I take to be an enduring gift for the continuing struggle to overcome the stubborn reality of race.

WHAT ARE WE GOING TO DO NOW?

Of course, it is one thing to describe race as a theological problem. It is quite another to ask, how does that help us? Campbell and Holloway end *Up to our Steeples in Politics* with the question, "what are we going to do now?" They describe the various things that might be done—voter-registration drives, petitions, protest marches against anything, getting middle-class church leaders involved in politics, conducting seminars and consultations on "next steps" in race relations, doubling existing staff, and, above all, doing a survey. Campbell and Holloway note that all of the things are what Christians do and are expected to do, but they wonder if this kind of "doing" has anything to do with Jesus's account of who the neighbor is, or with Jesus's refusal to become obsessed with Herod's influence or with what it would take to overthrow Caesar.

Campbell and Holloway observe that the question, "what can we, as Christians, do to help?" is the question the oppressor demands of his victim. So rather than providing the above list, they quote their friend Thomas Merton's response to the question of what to do: "Before you

---

30. Campbell, *Up to our Steeples in Politics*, 3.

31. For example, consider his redescription of what it means to be a segregationist: "The truth is that 'segregationist' means most of us in one form or to one degree. It does not mean only the rabid and lunatic fringe that expends all of its energy in race hatred. For the Christian, it must also mean anyone who regards people 'from a human point of view,' and who classifies and categorizes members within the body of Christ" (*Race and the Renewal of the Church*, 16).

do a damned thing, just *be* what you say you are, a Christian; then no one will have to tell you what to do. You'll know."[32] Campbell adds, "Do? *Nothing.* Be? What you are—*reconciled,* to God and man."[33] Surely that is the last word, but because it is a word, it means there is more to be said. And that is what Will Campbell has done. He has told us stories, wonderful stories of Bishop Duncan Gray, who simply lived the integrity demanded by the language of the *Book of Common Prayer*; painful stories of Joe Campbell, whose suffering is the suffering of the South; the story of his friendship with Thomas Jefferson Eaves: and through these stories, we catch glimpses of the story of Will Campbell, and we know that we are not without hope. So let me end with another story told by a master storyteller.

The story is about the promise and demise of SNCC in Mississippi in the 1960s. It is a story told by Charles Payne in his book, *I've Got the Light of Freedom: The Organizing Tradition and the Mississippi Freedom Struggle*. At the end of his book, Payne observes that the roots of SNCC's early style of celebrating the potential of ordinary men and women, the desire to valorize as many voices as possible, its striving for consensus and the disdain for credentials and hierarchy, reflected the SNCC axiom "that everybody is as valuable as everyone else." Payne notes that this axiom had its roots in the black South's rituals of courtesy; rituals that contemporary Black youth might, and do, associate with symbols of servility.

Payne argues, however, that to so understand courtesy is to think only of what courtesy might have meant for relations between the races rather than to think also of the question of what courtesy meant inside the race. As a result, Payne observes, the critics of courtesy are

> not likely to understand it as one part of a code of conduct which helped an oppressed people give back to one another some of the self-respect the racial system was trying to squeeze out of them, a profoundly democratic tradition holding that every man and woman, merely by virtue of being that, is entitled to some regard. Similarly, the expansive sense of family, the predisposition to see whatever is positive in people, the emphasis on character rather than wealth, are all egalitarian traditions, as empowering as anything SNCC ever devised. The ability to affirm the moral worth of even the most hateful, to look at the oppressor and think without

---

32. Quoted in Campbell, *Up to our Steeples in Politics*, 152–53.
33. Ibid., 153.

irony "There but for the grace of God go I" affirms our ultimate equivalent moral status, even in the face of evidence that seems to contradict it. . . . The young activists of the 1960s trying to work within the organizing tradition were bringing back to the rural Black South a refined, codified version of something that had begun there, an expression of the historical vision of ex-slaves, men and women who understood that, for them, maintaining a deep sense of community was itself an act of resistance.[34]

That, I think, is as good a description as one could want of the life and work of Will D. Campbell, a gentle warrior, who has fought and continues to fight the good fight by telling us stories of lives constituted by the courtesy and courage unintelligible if God is not the One found in the death and resurrection of Jesus.

34. Payne, *I've Got the Light of Freedom*, 404–5. In his essay, "The Failure and the Hope," Walker Percy makes a similar point about the importance of manners in the South. He distinguishes manners from courtesy, because courtesy is more concerned with gestures than with the recognition by one Christian to another of the "infinite value he assigns to the other's person." Nonetheless, while acknowledging the harm that manners may do, Percy argues that it would be a loss "if the ordinary everyday good manners of Southerners, black and white, should be overturned by the present revolution" (24). According to Percy, what would be lost would be the conditions for deepening the personal relationships that must exist if the interior resources for community are to be present.

CHAPTER 5

Letter of April 16, 2007

Stanley Hauerwas

Dear Rom,

> With an edge, one could wonder, what and how does Hauerwas
> learn from radical democrats if what he learns is that Christians
> have always been, in so far as they were Christians, what could
> be called radical democrats, if that is useful? One could wonder
> this precise question without any edge, too. I'm curious what you
> mean to say here.
>
> Similarly, by "haunting," I mean—as I think the word means—
> something profoundly discomforting, even if one can certainly
> want a ghost's presence, as one might wish for a time for the ghost
> of a passed friend or relative. Yoder is profoundly discomforting
> to me, because he raises a number of challenges to which radical
> democrats of several non-Christian varieties have not yet suffi-
> ciently responded, and there are no certainties that we can, even
> if I have more than a little faith we *might*. Is there any analogous
> type of haunting in your relation to radical democrats? Maybe
> not? Cultivating a capacity to be haunted, or rather a capacity
> not to deny being haunted, is integral to what I think of as ten-
> sion dwelling. . . . So, what do you mean by haunting? What role
> might it play generally in Christian communities? What might
> be some of its very specific manifestations in relation to radical
> democrats?[1]

I am not going to begin by trying to directly respond to your question,
"what do you mean by haunting?" I tried that tactic, and it only resulted

---

1. See above, chapter 2, "Letter of July 17, 2006," 31–44.

in my assuming a defensive posture that did nothing to advance our work. You suggested that rather than responding in a self-justifying mode, I should say what inspires and excites me. I wish I had thought of that in the beginning. So here is what inspires me.

I have recently returned from the L'Arche community at Trosly-Breuil in France. There I was able to see the world that Jean Vanier discovered and in which he lives. I was in France to take part in a seminar sponsored by the Templeton Foundation, which was to explore the question, "what can we learn from the mentally disabled?" Being at L'Arche makes clear that such a question is malformed. It is so because the very way a L'Arche home is organized is meant to defeat the idea that a "we" exists that does things for the mentally handicapped. Assistants live with and learn to be loved by the mentally handicapped. The mentally handicapped live with and learn to be loved by the assistants. This is hard but gratifying work. I suspect that many coming from the "outside" would find the world of L'Arche profoundly discomforting.

During the seminar, Vanier was asked how the work of L'Arche is sustained over time. He replied without hesitation: "Celebration." According to Vanier, celebration names the regard for each member of L'Arche, made concrete, for example, in the birthday parties that seem always to be happening. Celebration is Patrick (an elderly core member who has been at L'Arche for thirty years) being the center of attention as we celebrated St. Patrick's Day. Celebration is funerals in which the body is touched and stories told of the one who has died, so that the community can remember how this person, often a quite difficult person, has made the world of L'Arche what it is.

All these celebrations climax with the community's Mass on Sunday evening. The assistants and core members gather. Many are in wheelchairs. I sit next to a gentleman who greets each person entering with a handshake or touch to assure them that they are welcome. Jean Vanier sits at the end of a pew, his arm around an elderly woman who is in a wheelchair. He does not move throughout the Mass. It is an image I shall never forget.

The Mass begins. During the homily, a young women with Down syndrome begins to circle the altar. No one tries to stop her. After a time, she sits, fascinated by the eternal light. There is no hurry. We have all the time we need for everyone to receive the body and blood of Christ. If I have ever come close to seeing what the communion of saints might look like, I believe I may have seen it at Trosly-Breuil during that Mass. The celebration of the Eucharist made us one body for the world—a body united by joy.

If I am haunted, I am haunted by Vanier. I am haunted by Vanier because my strident polemics on behalf of the church seem so hollow when juxtaposed against the confident, joyful work L'Arche represents. I suspect Vanier would remind me, however, that such confidence is but the overflow of the love found through the worship of the Father, Son, and Holy Spirit. To worship such a Lord, a King who rules from a cross, is to learn to live by surprise, because you never know where or how such a God is going to show up.

In an odd way you and I are haunted in quite similar ways. You claim that you are haunted by John Yoder, but John would not have wanted you to be haunted by John Yoder. He would have wanted you to have been haunted by Jesus. And remember the Jesus he would have wanted to haunt you was the Jesus who has been raised from the dead. The only difference between us is that I try to put my body in positions in which I cannot avoid being haunted by that Jesus. This means I go to church. Indeed going to church is one of the most exciting things I do.

That I go to church does not mean I think that Jesus is only to be found there. It just means that he has promised to show up there in a manner that can help us discern how he shows up in other places. Thus, my claim that the first task of the church is not to make the world more just but to make the world the world, is not meant to restrict God's care of us to the church. Rather, it is a way to remind us that whatever we mean by politics, justice, or democracy will be determined by how we have learned to celebrate, that is, to worship. That is why I often call attention to Augustine's claim in the *City of God* (19.23):

> It is we ourselves—we, his City—who are his best, his most glorious sacrifice.
>
> The mystic symbol of this sacrifice we celebrate in our oblations, familiar to the faithful. Justice is to be found where God, the one supreme God, rules an obedient City according to his grace, forbidding sacrifice to any being save himself alone; and where in consequence the soul rules the body in all men who belong to this City and obey God, and the reason faithfully rules the vices in a lawful system of subordination; so that just as the individual righteous man lives on the basis of faith which is active in love,

the love with which a man loves God as God ought to be loved, and loves his neighbor as himself. But where this justice does not exist, there is no "association of men united by a common sense of right and by a community of interest." Therefore there is no commonwealth; for where there is no "people," there is no "weal of the people."

So when Stout suggests, "in issuing its critique of any people, the church, particularly the form of the church Hauerwas defends, must make articulate a conception of justice that includes principled opposition to the arbitrary exercise of power by any group of human beings over any other," I worry that such a conception may tempt me to forget that justice gains its intelligibility from the worship of God.[2] I think the reason I am so attracted to people like Ella Baker and Bob Moses is that their work is celebratory. They do not need a "conception of justice," because they have something better, namely, a way of being with the poor that is celebratory.

That worship (i.e., celebration) is at the heart of justice no doubt will strike many as an extraordinary claim. However, let me try to make such a claim more concrete by interposing a sermon I recently had the opportunity to preach in the chapel at Duke Divinity School.

∼

THE APPEAL OF JUDAS
Duke Divinity School
March 28, 2007

Isaiah 43:16–21
Psalm 126
Philippians 3:4b–14
John 12:1–8

We are well-schooled Christians. We know we are not to identify with Judas. Yet we cannot help but think, thief though he was, Judas was right—the costly perfume should have been sold and the money given to the poor. If we are honest, we cannot resist the conclusion—Judas is appealing.

---

2. Stout, "Spirit of Democracy and the Rhetoric of Excess," 13.

Moreover, if any conviction characterizes what it means to be a Christian in our day, it is surely the presumption that we ought to be on the side of the poor. No longer sure that we know what it means to believe that Jesus is the Son of God, we at least take comfort that to be a Christian requires that we care about those less well off. Of course what it means for us, that is, for the moderately well off, to care for the poor usually extends no farther than our attempt to make the poor like us, that is, moderately well off.

Moreover, given the world in which we find ourselves—a world that thinks that what Christians believe must make us doubtful allies in the struggle for justice—the Christian concern for the poor can win us some respect. The cultural despisers of the church at least have to acknowledge that Christians do some good in spite of our reactionary convictions. So it is good that we burn with a passion for justice. The only problem with such a passion is that it can put us on Judas's side.

This means we are profoundly troubled, if not offended, by Jesus' response to Judas: "Leave her alone. She bought it so that she might keep it for the day of my burial. You will always have the poor with you, but you will not always have me." Jesus, we wish Jesus had not said that. If you needed a text to confirm Marx's contention that Christianity is the opiate of the masses, you need look no further than, "You always have the poor with you."

Yet note: the one who said, "You always have the poor with you," was poor. That Mary saw fit to bestow a lavish gift on a poor person, a poor person who was soon to die, is surely to be celebrated—particularly by the poor. One of their own receives a lavish gift. One of their own is celebrated. So, if you are poor, what Mary does is a good.

It is, of course, true that Christians have used this text to teach the poor to accept their status by suggesting that if they do so, they will ultimately receive a greater reward than those well off. The church has also glossed over Jesus' response to Judas by not asking, "*what if we did more than cared for the poor?*" or, "*what if we celebrated with the poor?*"

That such questions are not asked reflects a church that has forgotten that Christianity is determinatively the faith of the poor. That is why we, the moderately well off, are puzzled by the undeniable reality that the church across time and space has been constituted by the poor. We, the moderately well off, are tempted to think, in response to Mary's gift, "What a waste." Surely a more utilitarian gift would have been more appropriate? But the poor know that this is Jesus, the one who shares their lot, so what could be more appropriate than this lavish gift, bestowed on this man to prepare his body for death?

It is crucial that we notice that this is a dinner where death is as present as those feasting. Lazarus, who had been raised from the dead, is present. Lazarus was raised from the dead, but that only delayed the inevitable. Lazarus, like you and me, will die. Moreover, Mary's anointing presages Jesus' death. Mary had bought the perfume for the day of his death, but it seems she could not wait. And so she anoints him in order to prepare him for death.

I think it is not accidental that death and poverty are connected at this dinner. Death, after all, creates an economy of scarcity. We only have a few years to live. We cannot do everything we would like to do before we die. That some of us have been given more than others is just the way things have worked out. We do not necessarily want to be selfish, but there is just so much that one can do in a world of limited resources.

Mary seems, however, to have caught a glimpse of a different world through her encounter with Jesus when he raised Lazarus from the dead. Mary's gift—her outrageous gesture of love—indicates that she has been drawn into the abundance of God's kingdom enacted by the life and death of the one who has said he is the resurrection and the life. She knows there is always "enough" because we cannot use Jesus up.

From the *Book of Common Prayer*, we pray this prayer for a monk:

> O God, whose blessed Son became poor that we through his poverty might be rich: Deliver us from an inordinate love of this world, that we, inspired by the devotion of your servant may serve you with singleness of heart, and attain to the riches of the age to come; through Jesus Christ our Lord, who lives and reigns with you, in the unity of the Holy Spirit, one God, now and for ever.

You know you are in a different world than the world of scarcity when you are part of a people who can call monks rich.

The grammar of this prayer, a grammar that must be written on the habits of our hearts, is crucial if we are to resist the appeal of Judas. We are Jesus' people, who have been freed from the economy of death. Mary's extravagant gesture turns out to be what God has done for us, that is, to lavish us with a love we cannot use up. But even more startling, we turn out to be the gift God would give the world through the work of the Holy Spirit.

That is why we must think of the wealth of the church as the wealth of the poor. The beauty of a cathedral is a beauty for the poor. The church's liturgy, her music and hymns, is a beauty of and for the poor. The literature of the church, her theology and philosophy, are distorted if they do not contribute to a common life determined by the worship of a Savior who was poor. The church's wealth, Mary's precious ointment, can never be used up or wasted on the poor. Thus after Jesus is dead, Nicodemus will use almost a hundred times the amount of Mary's gift to care for Jesus's body.

No doubt such an account of the church's wealth can be an invitation to self-deception as well as a justification for us, the moderately well off, not to hear the call of those in need. Yet "the poor you will always have with you" is not a description to legitimate a lack of concern for the poor. Rather, it is a description of a church that has learned that, "insofar as you do it to the least of these, you do it unto me" (Matt 25:40). Mary the sister of Lazarus has done for Jesus what the church must always be for the world, that is, a lavish gift poured out for the poor by the poor.

Prudentius, a Christian poet and contemporary of Ambrose, celebrated the life of Saint Lawrence. Lawrence was a deacon in the church of Rome in the middle of the third century. Lawrence was responsible for caring for the treasury of the church of San Lorenzo. The prefect of Rome had heard that Christian priests offered sacrifices in vessels of gold and silver, and commanded Lawrence to place before him the church's wealth. According to Prudentius, Lawrence replied:

> Our church is rich.
> I deny it not.
> Much wealth and gold it has
> No one in the world has more.[3]

Accordingly, Lawrence promised to bring forth all the "precious possessions of Christ" if the prefect would give him three days to gather the church's wealth. Given the three days, Lawrence used them to gather the sick and the poor:

3. Quoted in Wilken, *Spirit of Early Christian Thought*, 225.

> The people he collected included a man with two eyeless sockets, a cripple with a broken knee, a one-legged man, a person with one leg shorter than the other, and others with grave infirmities. He writes down their names and lines them up at the entrance of the church. Only then does he seek out the prefect to bring him to the church. When the prefect enters the doors of the church, Lawrence points to the ragged company and says, "These are the church's riches, take them." Enraged at being mocked, the prefect orders Lawrence to be executed slowly by being roasted on a gridiron.[4]

Lawrence exemplifies what it means for the church always to have the poor with us. To have the poor with us, to have Jesus with us, does not mean our task is to make the poor rich. Of course, rich and poor Christians alike are called to serve one another. Rich and poor alike are called to feed the hungry and to clothe the naked. But the church, if it is the church of the poor, must refuse the bargain with death that tempts us to live as if life is a zero-sum game of winners and losers. We are, after all, Mary's people who have touched and have been touched by Jesus. We know, therefore, that we live in a world of abundance, because you cannot use up the one who has been raised from the dead.

I am quite aware that some may well find what I have said to be "idealistic." Yet in a moment we will again eat and drink with the poor person who has invited us to share his body and blood. This is the gift we cannot use up. This is the gift that makes possible a people capable of sharing food with one another. This is the gift that makes possible a people who have time for one another. This is the gift that challenges presumptions of power, prestige, and status that we think necessary to be of service to the poor. This is the reality that makes it possible to resist the appeal of Judas. So come and receive this lavish gift, and by receiving may we become poor, so that the world might see what it means to be rich.

~

I find being asked to preach to be one of most intellectually demanding as well as satisfying things I get to do. When I preach, I am under authority, which means, to the best of my ability I am obedient to the texts. Preaching is praise. Preaching is celebration. In particular, this sermon was preached for the students and faculty of the Divinity School at Duke

---

4. Ibid., 225–26.

University. But that the sermon was preached in the Divinity School Chapel means there were no poor people present, or, at least, there were no obviously poor people present. Accordingly, some may rightly wonder if such a sermon is not an exercise in false consciousness. That danger can never be eliminated. It would be a danger even if poor people were present.

This is a reminder of why the stories of Ella Baker and Bob Moses are so important for the church. It is not as if Christians have our act together, making it possible for us to support the work of Baker and Moses. Much more important is our ability to see that the work they did is work that needs to be done in the church itself if we are to celebrate with the poor. For I take it that this is what radical democracy is first and foremost about: namely, learning to celebrate with the poor by learning to listen.

Yet I hope it is the case that the church, which makes it possible to recognize Jesus as a poor person, also has something to contribute to the work of radical democracy. Of course, what the church most importantly has to give is *people*, but they are not just any people: they are people formed by a particular language learned through worship. That language matters is why I think that the witness of Will Campbell is so important. For I take it to be the case that his growing alienation from the civil rights movement was largely the result of the displacement of the language of sin and reconciliation in the interest of political gains. In short, Campbell was insisting that the "race problem" required a more complex narrative than one about "winners" and "losers." I think the subsequent history of race in America is increasingly confirming Campbell's point.

So Campbell is a crucial test case for me. Attracted as I am to radical-democratic process, I worry that it can become an end in itself, an end to which God becomes an afterthought. Of course, the only assurance that this will not happen is the people who are radical democrats. This is why I think my emphasis on the centrality of the church is so important. For people do not drop from the sky but rather become who they are through training in practices that form the habits of their hearts and tongues.

That I seem so "churchy," that I write first and foremost about the church, is not because I have no interest in the "world." Rather I emphasize the significance of the church because I fear that the devastated character of the church in our time will be unable to produce the Will Campbells, the Ella Bakers, the Martin Luther Kings, the Bob Moseses. But it is never a question of church or world. Rather it is a question of having a people so captured by the worship of God that they can be for the world what the world so desperately needs.

If I have a basic political conviction, it is that people matter. Politics names for me the practices required for the formation of a people in the virtues necessary for conversations and conflicts to take place if goods in common are to be discovered. These goods are not abstract but draw on the stories of failures and successes that make a people recognizable to one another. Vulnerability must be at the heart of such a politics just to the extent that living well requires readiness to learn from the stranger. I should like to think that vulnerability is at the heart of what it means to be Christians, because through worship we are trained to have our lives disrupted by that strangest of strangers—God.

CHAPTER 6

Democracy and the Radical Ordinary:
Wolin and the Epical Emergence of Democratic Theory

Romand Coles

I

Democracy is a notion at once too obvious and too impossible. It is too
obvious insofar as it is an integral and rarely considered element in a
political rhetoric that is invoked, as Sheldon Wolin puts it, because of
"its utility in supporting a myth that legitimates the very formations of
power which have enfeebled it"—such as the hegemony of global capital,
the megastate in pursuit of militarized empire, and cultural matrixes that
are increasingly produced in ways that fall into line with both.[1] In this
context, democracy is too obvious neither merely because it is frequently
reduced to "free markets," nor simply because it is assumed to be identical
with constitutional representative institutions and rights (thereby eclips-
ing questions of democratic modes of engagement that necessarily exceed
these forms), but also because these forms have themselves come to be
(un)thought in an increasingly fetishized manner. Hence, even questions
about whether representation is working on its own terms, tend to be
diminished and dissipated in the face of mythic presentations of the sheer
existence of "representative" institutions that incant a virtually unquestionable "yes" to "democracy." As such, both the practice and the rhetoric
of representative democracy have often become integral components of

1. Wolin, *Politics and Vision*, 601.

modes of power that are anti-democratic even when measured by the limited representative sense of this word.

Democracy is, relatedly, a concept that is too impossible because when perchance it is drawn into the foreground (usually as it is preceded by terms like "radical," because it has become so impotent alone) it leaves many with almost no idea of what it could possibly mean, or even how it might be interesting. It becomes a concept too vitiated to solicit and provide some traction for serious questioning. In spite of the myriad democratic gatherings, practices, and struggles that have been waged on many fronts for centuries and continue today, we find ourselves so often with a concept that disappears before it can call or enchant us.

"Democracy" seems prone to dispossession: to being lost in the "too obvious" or the "too impossible." I take it that the above forms of dispossession are antithetical to the flourishing of democracy. And yet democracy, as I have argued at length elsewhere, hinges on not being in complete possession of itself: it must not know too well what it is, but rather remain significantly a question to itself so that it can be opened to others and a future that is neither yet known nor yet realized in being.[2] We have just seen some examples of this in relation to early SNCC organizing.[3] The question becomes, then, in what ways might dispossession be a good thing for democracy and in what ways might it not? And might there be better ways to remember, engage, and theorize these virtues and vices of dispossession, so that rather than lend ourselves to those who would mobilize and take our powers for devastating purposes, we might rather begin to enhance our capacities to resist such formations and be inspirited to more hopeful democratic initiatives? Perhaps even inspirited to unwonted intensifications, accumulations, and strange constructions of democracy?

I want to suggest that Sheldon Wolin's writing is one of the richest places from which to reflect upon these questions. Hence, in this chapter I shall journey toward the question of radical democracy in dialogue with his work. Wolin offers us a distinctively illuminating vision of radical democratic theory, judgment, virtues, power, and practice that is at once synoptic, nuanced, and ordinary in the most profound senses. Moreover, he offers us an account of democracy's disappearance—stretching across

2. See *Beyond Gated Politics*.

3. See chapter 4 above.

centuries—that is invaluable for interpreting the challenges, character, and requirements of democratic striving in theory and practice. Reanimating democracy at this historical juncture requires profound efforts to grasp the depth and scope of the modes of de-vitalization that have hitherto often rendered it too obvious and too impossible. Yet this is not simply a *critical* task, but also something akin to recovering a sense of democratic grace—a sense of the world as immanently shot through with fugitive democratic possibilities, gifts, scattered shards of light calling us to receive, gather, and carefully engage each other in relationships that slip beyond the oblivion of anti-democratic cages to initiate better things.

Wolin's work in this light has epical character in two senses: First, it seeks to overcome radical democracy's own profound reluctance—across the centuries and up to the present—to generate theory. This reluctance renders democracy too inarticulate at key junctures, such that it tends to become too vulnerable in some bad ways and not vulnerable enough in some ways that are key to the vitality of democracy. Second, Wolin's work seeks to overcome the anti-democratic thrust of most of the canon of political theory and, directly related to this, the male heroic epic performance at the heart of the tradition of grand theorizing. In this sense, I shall argue that his theory is epical in a manner that we might call "heroinic"—marking both a debt to Ella Baker and the de-centered character of radical-democratic theory's origins and aims that is markedly at odds with what Wolin takes to be the male hero upon whom epic theorists model themselves.

II

Wolin's biography does not stand outside or above the myriad ways in which democracy is disappeared and devitalized for the sake of established powers. Rather he alludes to the pre-1960s decades of his life as a time when he was ensconced in some of the central modes of political de-vitalization and disappearance that he later devotes himself to criticizing and transcending. Not unlike Augustine, his life might be viewed as the work of conversion (even if Wolin generally refrains from writing of it in personal terms): it is an unending struggle to turn toward that to which he had been largely blind and maybe even fearful. Hence, in the "Preface to the Expanded Edition" of *Politics and Vision*, Wolin writes of an "evolution" of his "understandings and political commitments"—a "journey from liberalism to democracy." Again, not unlike Augustine, whose conversion is significantly born with and in response to many around him, Wolin's journey is initiated—or at minimum inflected and intensified—in relation to others: "the public events and my own experiences of the intervening decades [since the first edition of *Politics and Vision* in 1960] have substantially affected my thinking about politics and political theory."[4] Finally, again not unlike Augustine, Wolin understands the shift in the trajectory of his life journey to be something of an epical endeavor, even and especially as the character of the "heroic" is turned inside out and upside down along the way.

III

To what and to whom did Wolin respond? What and who provoked, inspired, and informed this endeavor to shift toward a notion of democracy at once so powerful and so elusive? Re-enter Ella Baker, Bob Moses, and hundreds of others in SNCC who were organizing and practicing lived theory across the South. Wolin did not himself directly engage in this endeavor, but the radical-democratic trajectory of his thinking and experience as a politically active member of the Berkeley faculty was ignited and profoundly oriented by what he and John Schaar referred to as the "heroic age" of the Free Speech Movement (beginning in December 1964, a few months after Mississippi Freedom Summer) and the wider student rebellion on the Berkeley campus and across the U.S.[5] The student radicalism "reminded us of some basic values that were disappearing in the thoughtless rush for the future. Very much of what they did had to be done before anyone would listen."[6] It is likely that Wolin included himself in the "anyone" who needed the theatrical and dynamic political performances to begin to listen to the possibilities of radical-democratic modes of being. On Wolin's account, the most profound and radical aspect of what the students did was not to be found in the concrete objectives of the Free Speech Movement, the very name of which was an "accurate indicator of the limited nature of their aims." Rather, "their radicalism was . . . *in their appetite for politics* . . . several of them had acquired it . . . in Selma and the civil rights movement. . . . What was truly radical about the

4. Wolin, *Politics and Vision* (2004), xv. The brackets are mine.

5. Wolin and Schaar, *Berkeley Rebellion and Beyond*, 19.

6. Ibid., 42.

students—and the faculty—was the transformation from an apolitical to a political mode of being."[7] From his earliest reflections on the Berkeley rebellion, Wolin marks where this came from: "Berkeley in particular, and the San Francisco Bay Area in general, have sent more young people to the South [including student leader Mario Savio] in the struggle for racial justice than any other place except New York."[8] Tom Hayden similarly extends this observation in relation to the radical-democratic impulse of the wider student movement. Speaking of the radical-democratic vision and practice of SNCC that I discussed earlier, Hayden says: "And this was how SDS was born as well, much of SDS. I started in the South, not in Ann Arbor; I spent two years in the South."[9] Written in Ann Arbor by Hayden among others, many of the profoundest suggestions of the Port Huron Statement (which in turn spawned numerous other radical-democratic ventures across a vast swath of everyday life) came directly from the lived prophetic theory of people like Baker and the traditions of struggle they worked to extend (even as it is relatively unreflective about its roots in these traditions).

Hence I am suggesting that Wolin's radical-democratic theory was engendered through his engagement with the receptive arts of political insurgency that had long been struggling to create some warmth and power in the "iceberg" (as Moses called it) of American racism. It was precisely in resistance to racism—which from the beginning both inflected and undermined the deepest elements of "democracy" in the U.S.—that radical democracy was brewing in theory and practice: liturgies of beloved community struggles fired the radical democratic political imagination of Wolin and many of those indebted to him.[10] If we miss this fact, we miss the ways in which widespread democratic insurgency was born of this wound at the heart of U.S. democracy, and was itself an integral event giving birth to the "lived experience"—the emotions, perceptions, imaginations, performances, tacit and explicit knowledges—through which Wolin's thinking was fashioned, inspired, and informed. He has devoted his life and his reflective powers to an effort to elaborate, extend, and shape what he takes to be most promising directions of this insurgency. Insofar

7. Wolin, "Destructive Sixties and Postmodern Conservatism," 148.

8. *The Berkeley Rebellion and Beyond*, 39. The brackets are mine.

9. Greenberg, *Circle of Trust*, 32.

10. Wolin acknowledges this. I underscore it.

as we misread Wolin in ways that ignore these wellsprings and confine him to a scholarly context, we would—in the very form of our reading, pull Wolin into a professionalized matrix that is de-democratizing. In "The Destructive Sixties and Postmodern Conservatism," Wolin himself expresses a strong sense of being swept up in an ecstatic democratic upsurge in the midst of a history in which democracy has been continually disappeared (even as his own omission here of countless other struggles in the intervening years participates in the disappearing of democracy)—when he writes:

> The sixties were the first great attempt . . . at a democratic revival of American political life since the Populist revolts of the last quarter of the nineteenth century. . . . The sixties converted democracy *from a rhetorical to a working proposition*, not just about equal rights [for African Americans, Hispanics, Asian Americans, gays and lesbians, women, students], but about new models of action and access to power in workplaces, schools, neighborhoods, and local communities.[11]

Thinking in relation to the opening paragraph of this essay, the sixties pulled democracy beyond the "too obvious" and the "too impossible" to become a practiced direction and a compelling question to us. They raised the hope for "the revival of a sense of shared destiny, of some *common fate which can bind us into a people we have never been*." Such a hope lay in resistance to the idolatrous deployments of technology in warfare, deadening work, the destruction of nature, and communications that "obliterate the last traces of the varied cultures which have been the inheritance of all but the most benighted societies." The sense of a "common fate which can bind us into a people we have never been" lay precisely in a "new politics devoted to nurturing life and work . . . a politics which seeks to discover what men can share—and how what they can share can be enlarged and yet rise beyond the banal."[12] At the heart of the hope and question of a shared political destiny attentive to differences, was cultivating an acknowledgement of "being in a political situation—talking on a plane of equality and acting in a spirit of generosity with other parties."[13] Wolin and Schaar perceived intimations of these things in the

11. Wolin, "Destructive Sixties," 144. My emphasis and brackets.

12. Wolin, *Berkeley Rebellion*, 95. My emphasis.

13. Ibid., 91.

best moments of the struggles around People's Park, in which people in Berkeley took up a political mode of being in relation to these hopes and fears. Yet the best was imperiled from nearly all sides.

The democratic initiative that traveled up from the South and ignited myriad struggles in the coming decades around a host of issues from the most ordinary to the most sublime, *lost itself to a great extent during the sixties—as it had repeatedly before and has repeatedly since.* One aspect of this, on Wolin's reading, is the fact that, "the New Left failed to create the new radical theory beyond both liberalism and socialism which the Port Huron Statement had called for." Echoing some of the sorts of critique raised at the end of my discussion of SNCC in chapter 3, Wolin saw a growing "revulsion and rage" that was "increasingly impatient with theory."[14] What had at the outset tended more toward non-ideological opening in a constellation of nonviolence and in an "ethic of sincerity and personal encounter," hardened into "anti-intellectualism."[15] What began as a compelling questioning of malignant modes of authority shifted toward a rejection of the question of authority altogether. On Wolin and Schaar's reading, the New Left was not "able to develop a conception of political action coherent and effective enough, over the long pull, to sustain its members in a political vocation—to answer the questions: What does a radical look like in American politics, and how does he define himself in action which goes beyond the episodic and theatrical?"[16] Lacking a rich and variegated language, many lacked vision—even in relation to the practices in which they themselves were engaged. And lacking vision, they participated in their own disappearance and assimilation to subjugative modes of power and counter-power.

This apparent incapacity of radical democracy to generate theoretical voice (which we have already begun to critically interrogate in relation to early SNCC) is far from unique to the 1960s. One of the very striking claims Wolin will make about democracy in ancient Athens for example (as I will discuss below) is that over one hundred years of feisty insurgent democracy failed to produce a single radical-democratic theorist. Perhaps radical democracy is so swept up in insurgent efforts either to take power, or to receive others in ways that might cultivate new modes of power and

14. Ibid., 121.

15. Ibid., 40 and 121.

16. Ibid., 121.

voice, or both, that it is preoccupied with remaining at the liminal edge
of the not yet speakable in ways that greatly impede theoretical work.
Insofar as Wolin's work seeks to venture beyond this lack and theorize
this edge, it would in a sense be epical in a history of radical-democratic
politics that has mostly eschewed theory. He thus would be working for
radical democracy—in ways he (and I) think to be critically important,
by moving against the grain of some of its own deepest tendencies. Yet
precisely what "epical" can mean in the context of radical-democratic
politics and theory is something that is not at all clear and to which I
shall return shortly.

Beyond the anti-intellectualism and wariness of authority, however,
sixties radical democracy faced trouble developing theoretical vision for
reasons that were deeply enmeshed in the growing character and constraints of most universities (especially public ones) in the context of a
technological society articulated around the imperatives of the bureaucratic state, the mega-corporation, and the military-industrial complex.
Such a society "has no need (save ornamental) for modes of knowledge
built on lived experience ordered by disciplined reflection and extended
by moral and aesthetic sensibility."[17] Yet it is precisely reflective attention to lived experience—as well as the cultivation of moral and aesthetic
sensibilities capable of tending dynamically to its complexity in radically
democratic ways—that was lacking in the techno-university and the cult
of spontaneity that became prominent in reaction to it. At the heart of
the problem was what Wolin perceived to be an ethos of productivity
associated with an anti-democratic tempo that not only ground down the
myriad practices, traditions, and goods beyond the walls of the academy,
but also generated a "new pace of academic life . . . racing to the frontiers
where the future beckons. . . . Forgetting and destroying are necessary
preconditions for productivity: he travels fastest who travels lightest: he
travels lightest who sheds civility, tradition, and care for the common
culture of the intellect."[18]

Radical-democratic initiatives were themselves profoundly limited
by the civilization of forgetfulness they sought to resist. In absence of sustained commitments to cultivating vision, theory, sensibilities, practices
of tending, authority, and memory, democracy frequently disappeared

17. Ibid., 9.
18. Ibid., 67.

from the eyes and imaginations even of those who sought to cultivate it. Unable to function as something "like a Sorelian myth, a unifying image [or "shared political destiny"] that fortified the will to act and lent coherence to what were otherwise disconnected, heterogeneous, and random "happenings," what remained in future decades "were a Myth Manque and a heap of disaggregated events that made it possible to select the sixties of one's choice." Yet as "Myth Manque, an exhausted narrative," the radical democracy of the sixties was increasingly "unable to say why its story is relevant to the present or the future, and [it is thus] fated to shuffle off into nostalgia, a memorial service at Woodstock for pudgy yuppies."[19]

Wolin is not wholly pessimistic here, even if he is profoundly disappointed. Indeed, the essay that conjures up "pudgy yuppies" ends by proclaiming that: "The sixties may lack their myth, but its ideal of re-democratization is not dead. It forms a part of a recurrent aspiration: to find room in which people can join freely with others to take responsibility for solving their common problems and thereby sharing the modest fate that is the lot of mortals."[20] Nevertheless, democracy's lack of a sense of itself—as both a vision and as a question—leaves it relatively fragmented and anemic in the face of destructive forces that are neither.

Still, the question remains: How do we resist the manifold tendencies to forget democracy, without, in so doing, remembering it too well; without theorizing it in ways that make it too obvious and thus another technique oblivious—if not hostile—to the manifold and emergent character of "lived experience" that is such an integral medium and focus of democracy's care for life? Wolin spends his life with this question. In an essay written at the close of the twentieth century, when Wolin was nearing eighty, he writes: "My formative experiences are: a child during the Great Depression, a flier in World War II, a Jew during the era of the Holocaust, and an activist during the sixties—all, except the last, experiences dominated by loss." If the sixties were not dominated by loss, if they called him toward a generative journey of theoretically articulating democratic hope, the journey nevertheless was tightly connected to loss: "the loss of liberal innocence."[21] In other words, one could say that radi-

19. Wolin, "Destructive Sixties," 142–43. Brackets mine.

20. Ibid., 154.

21. Wolin, "Political Theory: From Vocation to Invocation," 3.

cal democracy's hope hinges on the loss of liberal democracy's innocent sense of possibility as zooming-toward-the-new, traveling lightly on the cutting edge of the temporal frontier. Remembering radical democracy's hope would hinge on remembering that it is born/e in relation to the presence of the past and to that which is emerging beneath the intentions of a methodically self-conscious present moving into the future. What might it mean to cultivate democratic vision that refuses to "get over" the losses implied in all—even the most democratic—thinking, seeing, and acting? What would it mean to cultivate a democratic theory that refuses to get over the hopes stationed and emerging in the ordinary lived experience that exceeds it?

IV

By the end of the 1960s Wolin wrote "Political Theory as a Vocation," in which he sought both to resist the micro-logical contours of anti-democratic discursive practices in the corner of the university that he experienced most (i.e., political science), and simultaneously to register a response to the decade's democratic upsurge that had significantly extended and reworked his sensibility and political-theoretical imagination. On Wolin's reading the anti-democratic technological imperatives of the wider society took the form of what he called methodism in the social sciences, which was tightly entwined with the injunction to get over the past as both a source of wisdom and haunting remorse. Lodged in his account of the vocation of political theory was an initial articulation of an alternative radical-democratic ethos and pedagogy that would inform his work for decades to come.

By "methodism," Wolin had in mind the behavioral paradigm that was concerned primarily with stipulating techniques for gathering and evaluating empirical facts in a manner seeking to be objective, detached, and pragmatic, with an "animus against tradition." The aim of methodism was to provide the "speediest discourse"—the straightest and shortest path—to the most parsimonious explanations in terms of ahistorical, lawful regularities governing political life. Yet through and beyond these basic features of political science, what is most remarkable about Wolin's account is that it treats political science as a disciplinary practice that constitutes selves well-conformed to the requirements and limits of the political and economic order. Beneath and entwined with rules and techniques, methodism engenders an ethos. In part, Wolin addresses ways in which qualities of cognition are shaped by methodism, with its single-minded search for regularity, its definition and constraint of legitimate questions in terms of their conformity with methodological limits and available techniques, its studied if unstated assumption that the "fundamental purposes and arrangements" of society were settled, etc. In this sense, methodism is an uncritical "ideological paradigm reflective of the same political community which the normal scientists are investigating."[22] Yet this is the tip of the iceberg.

At a more profound level, methodism is a technology for producing selves and sensibilities—*an emotional-perceptual opening toward the world*—suited for a technological society. "What is the human significance of choosing a theory?," Wolin asks. "It initiates new ways of thinking, evaluating, intuiting, and feeling; and it demands a substantial sacrifice in the existing forms of these same human processes."[23] Beyond the explicit cognitive commitments involved, it shapes "the way in which the initiates will look upon the world and feel it."[24] Indeed it shapes the ways our senses and bodies will move about the world, where and how they will invest their time, as—in the case of methodism—it insists on the Middle Ages's "shortcut," Descartes's "straight road," the "beaten path rather than 'blazing' a trail." Methodism, as Wolin recounts Petrus Ramus arguing, is fundamental to "every discipline and every dispute," "a shortening of the highway." Methodism, as a radically reductive theoretical mode, doesn't wonder about or wander toward peasants, beggars, wilderness, or dark women beyond the highways—at least not as part of their pent up "journey toward truth." Starting at least with Descartes, methodism far exceeded "the more narrowly intellectualistic connotations of the 'mind,'" and was rather a mode of reeducation, or "regimen" for "conversion," "for conditioning and disciplining" the "nature, character, and temperament" of the novice.[25] Methodists were, Descartes writes, to "train ourselves first in those easier matters. . . . Thereby we shall accustom ourselves to proceed by easy and familiar paths, and so, as easily as though we were at

22. Wolin, "Political Theory as a Vocation," 28.

23. Ibid., 57.

24. Ibid., 28.

25. Ibid., 34–36.

play, to penetrate ever more deeply into the truth of things."[26] It accomplishes this partly through explicit training, including systematic doubt aimed at purging habits and customs. Yet equally important is the mode in which selves are to be swept up in and enveloped by time: the way extensive methodological training necessary to be "qualified and certified," "preempts a substantial portion of [students'] energy and time" in which other kinds of knowledge, experience, and practice might lead one to wonder, wander, or move deliberately in other directions.

At the level of affect, the singular pursuit and practice of being thus preoccupied with regularity, logical consistency, and compact testable hypotheses becomes productively entwined with the production of a "fear of disorder."[27] The animus against tradition is entwined with a relation to the present order that is at once hubristic (viewing it as the most advanced edge of progress) and "submissive" (submitting all ideas to the test of conformability to the present order of things and its supporting methods). Secure in resolute adherence to the techniques of progress, the methodist may err, but with Descartes, "will be relieved from all repentings and feelings of remorse which are wont to disturb the consciences of those who vacillate."[28] All told, Wolin renders methodism as a mode of emotional-perceptual-cognitive constitution of selves through repetitions that constitute a deep ethical layer beneath the diversity and dynamism of specific methodologies. Indeed, erring in explicit technique itself is of less concern than orthodox adhering to the disciplinary modes and character of methodism. The truth of Wolin's claim can often be glimpsed in political *science* faculty meetings, where those of lesser (or "outdated") methodological proficiency frequently try to compensate by offering the most intense, ostentatious, and exemplary performances of the ethos—accompanied by the most intense demands for conformity to it—in deliberations over hiring, curricula, and so forth. Wolin echoes Kuhn's sentiment that this mode of pedagogical practice and performance is "narrow and rigid . . . probably more so than any other except perhaps orthodox theology." And "an impoverished mind . . . sees an impover-

26. Quoted in ibid., 36.
27. Ibid., 38.
28. Ibid., 39.

ished world"²⁹—an emotionally impoverished eye is the desiccated root of an impoverished mind.

In contrast to such impoverished vision and reflection, Wolin's critical sensibility and analysis of the affective-perceptual vocation of methodism was significantly indebted to his experiences of radical democracy in the sixties, which practiced and fomented a very different mode of being in the world; and his critique only becomes thoroughly vivid when placed in this context and juxtaposed with his account of the vocation of political theory, which is everywhere marked by these experiences.

The extent of the effects of the sixties' radical-democratic imaginary on Wolin can be seen when one compares his discussion in the introductory chapter on "Political Philosophy and Philosophy" in *Politics and Vision* (1960) with "Political Theory as a Vocation" (1969). The former text is remarkable for its sharp sense of how the tradition of political theory provides "forms of seeing" related to "where one stands" immanently in a political field, so that no single philosopher can ever express "the whole" of politics or political philosophy as such. Rather political philosophy is "an activity whose characteristics are most clearly revealed over time," and hence one of its most vital qualities is inextricably attached to its unfolding as "a varied and complex tradition" through which we might cultivate more subtle and expansive visions by engaging juxtapositions.³⁰ While Wolin is deeply critical of the reifying and transcendent elements of the "architectonic vision" of so many political theorists beginning with Plato, he affirms what he takes to be a widespread sense in the tradition, "that fancy, exaggeration, even extravagance, sometimes permit us to see things that are not otherwise apparent." "Fancy seeks to illuminate," and though every effort conceals and reduces even as it reveals, myriad efforts taken together afford a more cultivated and nuanced sense of the "varied and complex" character of political life.³¹ At its best, theory seeks by spurring action to reduce the gap between imagined future possibilities and the constraints of the present, while recognizing that the action it might spur always needs the exaggerated horizon-defying dimension of theory.

29. Ibid., 49 and 51.
30. Wolin, *Politics and Vision* (1960), 3.
31. Ibid., 18.

Yet for all the richness, astonishing nuance, and simmering radical-democratic elements just below the surface of explicit theorization in Wolin's account in *Politics and Vision*, perhaps he is not wrong when he reflects later that it remained largely within a liberal frame. Condensing the *telos* of a wide-ranging tradition, he writes sympathetically that: *"the subject-matter of political philosophy has consisted in large measure of the attempt to render politics compatible with the requirements of order."*[32] The question is how to have order without extinguishing politics and politics without neglecting order. The question is how we might—on political terrain—conceive of and practically move toward a "common public order" that best realizes justice and the good life, while acknowledging the need for "constant readjustments" in the midst of political life understood as the "quest for competitive advantage," under conditions of "scarcity," such that significant shifts of the whole occur as different groups gain and lose.[33] The tradition of political theory itself, for all the extreme variations that Wolin interprets, plays an important role as "a powerful constraint," as it

> preserv[es] the insights, experience, and refinements of the past, and compel[s] those who would participate in the Western political dialogue to abide by certain rules and usages. . . . It gives [us] a sense of traveling in a familiar world where the landscape has already been explored; and where it has not, there exists a wide variety of suggestions concerning alternative routes. . . . [It] contributes to the endless task of accommodating new political experience to the existing scheme of things.[34]

When Wolin writes "Political Theory as a Vocation" at the end of the decade, most of the tensional motifs sketched in *Politics and Vision* remain. Yet it is as if they have been reoriented, restrung, magnetized along a different axis, accented in significantly different tones and dialects. There is still a strong and finely articulated affirmation of the ways in which carefully engaging a "varied and complex tradition" cultivates beings whose cognition and judgment may be more nuanced and attentive to the manifold character of political life, more capable of moving be-

32. Ibid., 12. My emphasis.
33. Ibid., 10 and 11.
34. Ibid., 22.

yond the debilitating effects of a fetishized parsimony,[35] and more likely to make discriminations that torture less the richness of the world. Yet the accent is no longer toward making politics compatible with the order (contra "organization" that *kills* politics in the name of order), accommodating new political experience to existing schemes, or giving us a sense that we travel in a familiar world. Rather, there is a shift that emphasizes engaging past theories "not because they are familiar . . . but because they are strange and therefore provocative."[36] Order must now become subordinate to an ethos of tending more fluid differences of human beings and collectivities by means of more difficult memories.

Why? Not simply because the world is complex and manifold in excess of any theoretical rendering, but moreover because Wolin had gained a heightened sense of the tremendous extent to which political life and the world more generally is dynamically infused with still-inchoate possibilities beneath the official scripts of anti-democratic vocations. Engaging the substance and intensity of efforts of the past might enliven and empower our sense of these tacit potentials as well as our capacity for activities required to engage and nurture them. One phrase Wolin uses to evoke this quality of our political and social world (and my favorite) is "emergent irregularities," which are so at odds with the methodological expectation of and insistence upon regularity.[37] Emergent irregularities are more likely to be witnessed and engendered in the world, when our mode of being and sensibility become not only "mindful of logic, but more so of the incoherence and contradictoriness of experience" that is beyond all formulation[38]; when we "believe that because facts are richer than theories it is the task of theoretical imagination to restate new possibilities."[39] Part of what engenders this sense of incoherence and contradictoriness, which might heighten our sense for emergent irregularities, is the *theoretical traveling* from allusive vision to discordant allusive vision. If regimens of methodist repetitions and highway-travel dull such capacities, disciplined regimens of repeatedly moving to and

35. It should not be forgotten that Ockham, who formulated the most parsimonious parsimony in the form of a "razor," also formulated history's most severe conceptualization of sovereignty. The two are profoundly related.

36. Wolin, "Political Theory as a Vocation," 63.

37. Ibid., 29.

38. Ibid., 45.

39. Ibid., 75.

fro between discrepant political visions nourish—in the very exercise of moving among and across differences—nuanced emotional sensibilities that are greater and deeper than any of the explicit theoretical articulations involved. Hence we see the continued yet modulated pertinence of the vocation of political theory.

Wolin's heightened sense of the mind, imagination, body, and world as reciprocally provocative potentials emerges significantly in response to the struggles of the 1960s, which he at once describes as a "world coming apart" and a world of gatherings such that it "is beginning to voice demands and hopes that are 'unreasonably high'" to the methodists seeking to maintain a polity of order and regularity.[40] Of course, it seems more than likely that part of what engendered Wolin's receptivity to these voices beyond the liberal order was precisely the comparatively dynamic richness of a mind deeply steeped in and attuned to the complexity and variety of historical political thought as he interpreted it. Yet his engaged receptivity during the sixties as a faculty member deeply involved in the dialogues and democratic struggles at Berkeley—his travels across the boundaries of more "proper" scholarly contexts, from the emergent public spaces of Sproul Plaza and People's Park abuzz with radical-democratic transgressive intensities, to more deliberative democratic forums such as Faculty Senate meetings—seems in turn to have had profound effects on his political sensibility, energy, imagination, and theorizing. Remembering this experience a few decades later, Wolin writes: "The intensity of the experience . . . changed everyone involved. For many of us it was the experience of moving from an apolitical to a deeply political existence, from a protected status with known boundaries to a condition that was risky and unfamiliar."[41] It was risky and unfamiliar in large part because it involved precisely receptive bodily movement (which we see Wolin seeking to articulate also as theoretical travel among complex, various, and dynamic spaces) across boundaries and differences through which people might more democratically tend to and also engender tacit knowledges and emergent irregularities.

Wolin's deepening appreciation for democratic attentiveness to and care for a protean and emergent world required a pedagogy for cultivating sensibilities that might animate selves and collectivities beyond

40. Ibid., 73 and 75.

41. Wolin, "A Look Back." I wish to thank Nicholas Xenos for alerting me to this article. See his related thoughtful discussion in "Momentary Democracy."

their theoretical, imaginative, emotional, and institutional more-settled presumptions and toward receptive engagements with a world exceeding any of these. Though Wolin called this the vocation of political theory, he could have called it the vocation of radical democracy, as the latter calls us to question the categorical-perceptual-emotional subjection of the world, which Wolin increasingly recognized as integral to anti-democratic modes of power. It is in relation to such a radically democratic pedagogy that the disciplinary project of methodism came to the fore, and he increasingly cultivated the former as a potent alternative to the latter.

Contra methodism's compact suitcase, Wolin advocates a pedagogy attached to a "diverse and ill-assorted baggage," a "complex framework of sensibilities built up *unpremeditatively*" through engaging in practices of tending to the manifold character of a historical world with its variegated traditions of thinking and becoming in specific sites such as neighborhoods, churches, schools, unions, watersheds, cities, and so forth. Through such performances one might develop a richer appreciation of the "allusive and intimative" knowledges necessary to engage these with care—a sense and taste for engaging "tacit knowledge" inhering in oneself, surrounding traditions, and their emergent struggles. A significant part of a pedagogy in tacit knowledges and sensibilities concerned learning "how to make one's way about the subject field," patiently cultivating a sense of "appropriateness" that is receptive to its everyday "supporting lore."[42]

Relatedly, and in marked contrast to methodical rigidity, such education would strive to cultivate a "meditative culture" that better enables us to be open to the abundance of a world that in turn solicits and nurtures a mobility of imagination and theorizing more suited to it: "playfulness, concern, the juxtaposition of contraries, and astonishment at the variety and subtle interconnections of things."[43] What was required were beings attuned to both the vital importance and the "*drama* of offering a theory that couldn't be accommodated within the prevailing values and perceptions of the world"[44]—something akin to what Yoder calls a "readiness for

42. Wolin, "Political Theory as Vocation," 45–46. Emphasis mine.
43. Ibid., 51. Emphasis mine.
44. Ibid., 58.

radical reformation."[45] One key way to engender such a sensibility was to *"preserve a memory of agonizing efforts of intellect to restate the possibilities and threats posed by political dilemmas of the past"* in ways that "sharpen our sense" not of the identity of thought and world, but of the "subtle, complex interplay between political experience and thought."[46] I think Wolin is suggesting here that preserving a memory of agonizing efforts must go beyond simply articulating the moves that were explicitly made to also portraying the experience of theoretical struggling—such that it might in turn vivify our responses to the kinds of energies and emotions involved.[47] Increasingly this task would involve preserving memories of the agonizing efforts of radical democrats to practically and theoretically restate the possibilities and vivify the spirit of political imagination—like those bracing historical and contemporary discussions of democratic struggles by Lawrence Goodwyn and Harry Boyte in the first volumes of *Democracy: A Journal of Political Renewal and Radical Change* (the journal Wolin began editing in 1981).

Wolin envisioned a meditative culture with theoretical and political capacities to become "sensitive to the claims and characters of many ["interrelated and interpenetrating"] provinces" and simultaneously attentive to questions of "rendering what is proper to a civil community."[48] This involved becoming more receptive beings who were animated and desirous of engaging in the agonizingly dramatic yet playful work of political tending to "emergent irregularities"—*both old and new*—with "varied forms of knowledge for which there is no limit"[49]: Beings with a taste for the dynamic epical requirements of engaging our political life, from the largest issues—like racial oppression, decaying urban areas, and global capitalism—to the smallest—like how to care for a tiny patch of earth called People's Park. The slight accent on order, in the order-politics tension depicted in *Politics and Vision,* shifts in the sixties toward a sense that political orders must be subordinated to the service of the diverse

45. Yoder, *Priestly Kingdom*, 5.

46. Wolin, "Political Theory as Vocation," 62. Emphasis mine.

47. Perhaps Wolin's best effort to evoke the drama of theory with such mimetic effects is to be found in *Hobbes and the Epic Tradition of Political Theory.* This is of course ironic, as Hobbes's *Leviathan* would extinguish such theoretical ventures in the future it affirmed.

48. Wolin, "Political Theory as Vocation," 60–61.

49. Ibid., 60.

tacit forms of life and experience that are the stuff of nonsubjugated human being, democratic political wisdom, and ethical flourishing. The tension between care for forms of life that already exist and a dynamic engagement that transgresses such forms is (as I will discuss more below) rooted in the very manifold character of these forms themselves, each with purposes, times, and spaces that both enable and encroach upon each other—requiring endless dynamic renegotiations and reformations under even the best of circumstances. Dynamism in such cases is immanent to tending to what already exists. In times when a narrow set of purposes or a single form ripped itself free from—and sought to impose hegemony over—the manifold provinces of being, "political renewal" would increasingly involve more "radical change" than seeking a world farther beyond what already exists.

If we recall some of the language Wolin and Schaar used in their essays on *The Berkeley Rebellion* and elsewhere, the debts of Wolin's shifting understanding of political theory to radical-democratic organizing practices indebted to SNCC are clear: At its most compelling moments they saw in these efforts a "plenitude of spirit, open and vital," "an ethic of sincerity and personal encounter" (40), "good-natured, ironical, and humorous" (46–47), "a spirit of generosity with the other parties" that accompanied their "appetite" for political modes of being and epically serious tasks (91). As we have seen, this was "impure" from the start (how could it be otherwise?), the seeds of its destruction were present from the beginning, and it did not last long. The Berkeley faculty on the whole never went so deep as to seriously engage questions concerning "a redefinition of the faculty vocation" in relation to students and the broader community. They drew back from "heavy civic commitments" involved in transformatively reorganizing the university such that it might shift away from techno-statist-corporate modes of being and toward complex, varied, and dynamic pedagogies of tending to "emergent irregularities." These tasks, and the energies and dispositions they might require, were deemed "incompatible with research."[50] Hence, by the late sixties, the thinking, imagination, emotions, and energy Wolin developed in relation to these performative efforts were increasingly channeled into essays such as the one we have been discussing, with its suggested epical overturning of methodist social sciences. If part of what defeated radical democracy in

50. Wolin, "Destructive Sixties," 147, 150–51.

the sixties was an anti-intellectualism that inhibited the emergence of the requisite theoretical work on political ethos (and political crisis)—work that might have better oriented a more genuinely democratic political culture—Wolin responded by beginning to turn his practiced imagination to addressing this deficit. In essence, the task became an epical envisioning of a radical-democratic theorizing, a politics of tending a very different vision of the world. Yet as he turned to the tradition of political theory in order to do so, he discovered a task far more epical than he had earlier imagined—and epical in different ways.

V

Epic theory, Wolin tells us, "marks a break" of great magnitude from previous ways of "looking at," thinking about, feeling, and judging the world. It generally emerges in response to crises—"derangements"—and seeks radical change in relation to questions of public concern.[51] Wolin's most dramatic account of epic theory is found in his discussion of Hobbes, in which he attempts to "recapture . . . the human excitement which moves the theorist."[52] Wolin uses epic to evoke a "heroic" tradition in which political theorizing—much like political action on Arendt's account—is indebted to the Homeric epics, in which the hero is a "doer of great deeds and a speaker of great words." "For the heroes of political theory, the great deed *is* the great word," which might draw awe and remembrance for its achievements (5). For the tradition of political theory, the epical competition for recognition is not just with contemporaries, but a "contest over intellectual and cultural mastery" that occurs in relation to others "throughout the centuries." It is a struggle to provide the best comprehensive illumination of our political condition in the hope that this illumination might one day be joined with action to change the world (8). With "boldness and daring" theorists have sought and achieved "nothing less than the reduction of the political world, with all of its buzzing confusion, its mysterious forces, and its sacral overtones, to a rational manageable, intellectual order" (10–11). For example, Hobbes sought "glory" (albeit a glory connected to an estimation of the public good) by "seeking to dislodge the reigning 'heroes' and to establish his own supremacy" (15).

51. Wolin, "Political Theory as Vocation," 65ff.

52. Wolin, *Hobbes and the Epic Tradition of Political Theory*, 4. Hereafter indicated in this paragraph by page numbers.

Like many others, he sought "immortality by going beyond the highest mark set by others," by rendering an immortal architecture for politics. Yet unlike his sense of those who preceded him, he sought this immortality in "right method," which would guarantee "general, eternal, and immutable truth" (22). Intensifying an impulse of many epic theorists, Hobbes sought to envision and build a world in which there could be no future epic theorists. It was an "anti-hero's utopia," in which people would be both relieved and disallowed of the contingencies, risks, complicities, responsibilities, guilt, and hopeful possibilities of the political (50). He would be not only the greatest but also the *last*—all who followed being reduced to "supporting cast" (28). The "passionless plodding" of today's methodists exemplifies this imaginationless cast, though not the fanciful playwright. Hobbes's utopia becomes "an attempted epitaph to politics, another denial of the ancient hope of a public setting where men may act nobly in the furtherance of the common good" (50).

Until and probably beyond the end of the 1960s Wolin maintained a sense that the canon of political theory contained a number of sharp, nuanced, and affirmative discussions of "the political." Yet as the years roll along, his thinking begins to shift quite radically on this question, and he comes to see in canonical theorists one assault after another on the political and democracy—not just in modernity but all the way back to some of those he had previously thought of as bearers of "ancient hopes." Increasingly the canon becomes a record of the suppression and containment of democratic hope. Hope could be found in the vast portion of the canon only in the negative traces of the democratic adversary that lurked in the margins of primarily anti-democratic texts and theorists. This meant that Wolin's project of envisioning democracy as the exemplary form of the political would require a theoretical effort and achievement that was itself as epical as anything he had described in Hobbes and other theorists.

Indeed, in important senses Wolin's project was perhaps much *more* epical, even if this "more" profoundly transformed the very term— epic—that it expands. Wolin's project would require a *synoptic critique of the anti-political* character of virtually the entire canon (Spinoza and Tocqueville are among the few major exceptions—and only in part), as well as an alternative paradoxically *anti-synoptic vision of the political* that gives expression to a dramatically different "way of looking" at the world. Note that "way" is the most important word between these quotation marks, and in the context of Wolin's radical-democratic theory this word would mean not a static form, but a dynamic mode of thinking and perceiving.

As we have already seen, the world that Wolin senses teems with "emergent irregularities" calling for our attention. In the midst of and embracing such a world, visions of the political would no longer be able to take as their primary task articulating (or at least evoking, or progressing toward) forms, regularities, norms, paradigms, methods, or synoptic patterns of political human being. On Wolin's reading, this mode of aspiring itself has been the *way* that virtually all previous political theory has proceeded—a way that has generally culminated in visions of order that would tightly confine if not entirely eliminate political life. For Wolin, the epic challenge was no longer to offer a new paradigm higher than the rest in the sense that it afforded better "handles on history" (Yoder's phrase).[53] Rather, the question of politics and vision in a protean world becomes one of evoking new ways—both theoretically and politically— of animating the "subtle, complex interplay between political experience and thought"[54] that remain forever and generatively nonidentical. The question concerns more *how* radical democrats ought to perceive, articulate, and nurture this interplay at the heart of democratic political thought and action, and less *what* form it ought to ultimately take. Though as Adorno and Wolin both knew, careful attention to what and who we are facing is an absolutely integral part, though not the singular *telos*, of a politics that places its heavier emphasis on nurturing modes of coexistence more capable of dynamically tending to beings and forms of life that are forever elusive, surprising, and changing. Hence Wolin's distinctive epical task is to change profoundly very questions and aims of thousands of years of political theorizing. Hobbes, of course, thought (or at least said) he was doing this with the introduction of methodism into political philosophy. Yet as he remains within the horizon of containment and form in a manner that Wolin does not, his mode of theorizing evades questioning a certain formalism of thinking that variously characterizes so many canonical theorists.[55] Indeed, as suggested above, Hobbes might

53. See Yoder's chapter, "The War of the Lamb," in *Politics of Jesus*.

54. Wolin, "Political Theory as Vocation," 62.

55. At least as Wolin reads them, even as he acknowledges subdominant themes consciously or unconsciously at work in ways that problematize and set in troubling motion many of the dominant anti-political motifs. It is beyond the scope of the present discus-

be read in no small part as seeking to reduce thought itself to form in order to master the world—even as his own imagination is far too wild to be thus reduced.

Before delving into a more thorough account of these claims, it is important to note at the outset that Wolin's epic effort performs a certain *reversal of the heroic*, even as his project is in some senses mimetically inspired by the drama of transgressive endeavors to articulate a public good that is so characteristic of epic theory. If Wolin opposes the confinement of radical democracy in most epic theorists, he nevertheless views their *striving itself*—with all its drama, agonism, risk-taking, fancy, exaggeration, and life-staking concerned engagement with questions of public good—as paradoxical exemplifications of the very "political" that they fear, loathe, and seek to suppress. He is animated from the beginning to emulate the theoretical intensity of such efforts and sees their vast differences of vision as a profound illumination of precisely the complex protean political world that calls him to theorize and tend to what their theses deny. Yet where epic theory had sought to achieve a *higher* manifestation of heroic form-giving force—a more successful mastery—Wolin's articulation of radical democracy seeks responsive engagements with the textures of political modes initiated by or in relation to those who repeatedly resist and radically transgress the unquestionable hegemony of such orders. With Yoder, he seeks to "unhandle history." The epic envisioning of politics Wolin offers moves *beyond the heroic* theorist and toward thinking, imagination, and affect born in, informed and nurtured by modes of receptive tending to a world that exceeds theoretical forms proceeding from "on high." It will, in fact involve cultivating modes of theoretical and practical working *as and with* the lowest, the discarded, the dirt of the order. If "heroic" may still retain an affirmative connotation in this context, it will refer to those initiatives that relax and even weaken traditionally heroic muscle and instead cultivate alternative capacities and powers for multifarious democratic tending *by and to* specificities and emergent irregularities denied by a certain unrelenting flexing.

To mark this difference of a new epic striving, let us call these "heroinic"—and not least in order to mark again the profound debt to Ella Baker, Septima Clarke, Casey Hayden, Jane Stembridge, Fanny Lou

---

sion to assess the accuracy of his account, but vital counterpoints in coming to such a judgment are found in many of the more ironic readings of the canon offered by one of Wolin's best students—Peter Euben.

Hammer, and numerous others with them, including Bob Moses and Amzie Moore. Radical-democratic theorizing will be heroinic precisely—and only—insofar as it disperses our sense of the sources of wisdom, energy, political action, and experience in relation to which it gains orientation, vitality, and even its very existence. Thus, it is heroinic to the extent that it de-professionalizes, de-individualizes, and de-authorizes accounts of itself, and shifts the drama of its origins and its ambitions from the glory of the purported "playwright" to that of the democratic political vitality of the manifold cast that is writing lived theory as it responds to the extraordinary challenges of the ordinary. Beyond the statuesque recognition of the heroic, the epic theorist would join with and call us to the multitude of those remembering and energizing fugitive currents of democratic tending.

VI

"It is curious," Wolin quotes A. H. M. Jones, writing "that in the abundant literature produced in the greatest democracy in Greece there survives no statement of democratic political theory."[56] Is there something about the boundaries and forms that democracy would resist, something about the fugitive character of radical-democratic struggling that makes writing radical-democratic theory difficult, improbable, or perhaps almost impossible? We have seen a similar problem in relation to theorizing democracy in the sixties. How might we better negotiate this difficulty? In what ways might writing be part of democracy's problem and how might writing nevertheless help address the problem of which it is a part—perhaps even play an important role in the vitality of democratic initiatives? The history of political theory is, on Wolin's reading, of as little constructive help here as is the history of radical-democratic politics. Wolin notes that "in the estimation of virtually all the canonical political theorists from Plato to Jean Bodin, democracy was rated either the worst of all forms of government, save for tyranny, or the least objectionable of the worst forms."[57] If democracy is "the worst," perhaps this speaks of a certain way that it erodes and "un-handles" the rigidity thought to be

56. Quoted in Wolin, "Norm and Form," 44.

57. Ibid., 31. Of course, there are many "democratic" theorists in modernity, but Wolin thinks most of these efforts largely obfuscate and undermine that in the name of which they claim to speak.

necessary for the mutually entwined enduring "glories" of both the heroic theorist and the vision of the heroic polis—or empire. Yet Wolin writes and passionately seeks to give expression to democratic theory even as he sees very little to draw on from the canon.

This means that he will have to pursue a very different relationship with the "great texts" (which he illuminates as profoundly as anyone ever has). The dialogue between and among political theorists across the ages is often rendered as a dialogue between great thinkers who author great works. To take up political theory is often construed as a process of being initiated into that dialogue by engaging the truth-claims of authors who variously organize texts with logical and rhetorical skills to offer a vision of the political world. Yet as Wolin develops as a heroinic epic theorist, he increasingly reads history of political thought in a very different manner. To engage in an epic striving toward a world more capable of tending from, with, and to the complex, various, and emergent irregularities of ordinary life that methodical and overarching orders tend to suppress, requires that we enact modes of reading that themselves begin to practice such receptive care in relation to the textual orders of the canon. In a later essay (discussed more below), Wolin aligns himself with Adorno's claim in *Minima Moralia*: "Theory must needs deal with cross-grained, opaque, unassimilated material, which as such admittedly has from the start an anachronistic quality, but is not wholly obsolete since it has outwitted the historical dynamic."[58] This expresses well the art of cross-grained herme-neutics that Wolin deepens as time goes on—both with respect to the political world and to the world of canonical political theory.

Wolin very distinctively reads the canon not to seek the wisdom of its nearly universal propensity to suppress or at least greatly reduce and normalize democracy to a set of constitutional regularities,[59] but rather to consider the traces of radical democracy—or "democracy's surplus"—as it repeatedly finds itself inscribed in the muffled cross-grained margins of these projects. Democracy shows up persistently in anti-democratic texts, Wolin argues, as the opponent that these texts must conjure up in order to defeat and thereby establish modes of anti-democratic suprema-

58. Wolin, "Invocations of Political Theory," 4.

59. Wolin thinks these inscribe "the universal tendency of institutionalized systems of power to advantage the few and exploit the many." Wolin, "Norm and Form," 48. It should be noted that Wolin spent many years artfully engaged in more conventional hermeneutical work, as represented in much of *Politics and Vision*, etc.

cy. Moreover, "democracy comes to us . . . through hostile interpreters . . . because the meaning of the 'people' overlaps that of 'the political', making it virtually impossible to discuss the latter without including the former." Hence, "the politics of the demos has not been lost to memory but is preserved though half-buried in the political theories of democracy's critics" as they invoke aspects of the demos episodically to secure legitimacy that terms like "political" tend to call forth.[60]

Practicing a cross-grained hermeneutics, Wolin lingers with democracy's ghostly appearance as it survives, half-buried, mouth-twisted, in the margins, in order to discern the possible wisdom that might be found there. He writes: "I propose accepting the familiar charges that democracy is inherently unstable, inclined toward anarchy, and identified with revolution and using these traits as the basis for a different *a*constitutional conception of democracy."[61] In other words, he practices a hermeneutics of learning from the traces of what is intentionally defined as excrement, in order to imaginatively theorize democratic modes that radically exceed and oppose the reductive antidemocratic presumptions of virtually all epical theoretical striving.

Re-orienting a magnetic field, Wolin fashions the "familiar charges" into an alternative way of looking in which democracy becomes an "unsettling political movement," "a moment rather than a teleologically completed form."[62] Indeed democracy appears to critics such as Plato, as a "total disrespect" for the forms of antidemocratic power; a "cultural practice that extends to striking changes in the behavior of women, children, and slaves . . . the radical denial that social deference and hierarchy are 'natural'" (50). While Plato sometimes depicts democracy as "amorphous," utterly "inchoate," and "inherently formless," Wolin gives expression to a more nuanced reality by latching on (like a stone-faced trickster) to some of Plato's satirically intended comments about the "bazaar of constitutions" found in democratic cities: democracy is "diverse and colorful" rather than mass and monochromatic: It is "unique in being related to all constitutions: it is not so much amorphous as polymorphous" (50). It is a "fuller representation of the polis and its different kinds of ordinariness" (53).

60. Wolin, "Norm and Form," 55.

61. Ibid., 37. Emphasis is Wolin's.

62. Ibid., 29 and 40. Hereafter in this paragraph referenced page numbers refer to "Norm and Form."

Wolin pursues this path of thinking to qualify his rhetorically provocative (and frequently misunderstood) claim about democracy being *a*constitutional. Democracy is *a*constitutional and *a*morphous in the sense that it repeatedly seeks to transgress constitutions that in design—or effect—would defeat and normalize it. Yet democracy simultaneously aspires to a *different kind* of constitutionalism. While it opposes the containments of "constitutional democracy," it also seeks to engender "democratic constitutionalism," by which he means "the domination of democracy over constitution" that has nothing to do with spontaneous "mob rule."[63] Let me elaborate this claim as it came to be articulated in one specific political context—the democratizing Athenian polis—and then discuss further the vision and principles that Wolin sees entwined with it (39).

Part of what Wolin means by a *democratic* constitutionalism, in which democracy dominates over constitution-as-organized-containment, can be gleaned in his conception of "rational disorganization," which aims in part to construct institutions and practices that disorganize and disperse human and organizational propensities to master the world: "democracy as resistant to . . . rationalizing concepts of power" (37). We might think of this as a very paradoxical effort to make immanent in institutional practices modes of power that are analogous to the kind of power Yahweh employs in the destruction of the Tower of Babel. Democracy is not another form of "ruling over"—or a mere substitution of one or a few leaders by rule of the many, but rather the effort to replace ruling with another kind of power. It is this other kind of power that would seek to dominate constitution-as-rule. Because the propensity to re-establish mastery is highly inventive (and often secreted to varying degrees even by practices that would thwart it), so too the democratic constitutionalism that would help disorganize such mastery must be manifold and improvisational in development.

Wolin's account gives mention to a rich array of institutions that were an integral part of the long democratizing struggle in fifth-century Athens: "cancellation of debts, the elimination of debt bondage for citizens, the division of citizens into four distinct classes according to wealth, allowing the least wealthy of the four access to the Assembly,

---

63. This is not at all to ignore the risks here, but rather to remain tenaciously in pursuit of a certain distinction.

establishing a people's court" (35). Feuding tribes seeking to rule each other were mixed politically. Ultimately a century of struggles—that suffered losses as well as gains—culminated in achieving popular control of the major institutions of power by eliminating "property qualifications for citizenship," establishing "a flourishing system of local institutions [for participation] in the *demes*, where citizens acquired experience and joined in nominating local men to serve in the central institutions," and creating participatory democratic practices in governing institutions such as the Assembly, the Council, and the Courts. Yet as even the (free male) citizens took power and fashioned practices where they could tend to questions of public good, they sought to institutionalize processes that would prevent new forms of organizing the rulership of one group over others: "the system of annual rotation in office, the lot, and the public subsidization of citizen participation" were thus "*the most crucial and revealing* elements in Athenian democracy" (42, my emphasis). These were the most crucial and revealing elements of democracy, because they reflected an ethos that tended beyond the horizon of rule and toward specifically democratic modes of power. It is thus a serious misreading to understand Wolin's claims about democracy's *a*constitutionalism to mean that he thinks questions of constitution—or inscribed forms of life—are irrelevant to democracy. Far from it, they are vital conditions of its possibility. Yet they are most significantly thus insofar as they disorganize and disperse constitution-as-organization and paradoxically help facilitate the disorganization and dispersal of hierarchical tendencies of institutionalization: democratic constitutionalism seeks "institutions that subvert institutionalization" (43). In this way, he argues, the demos is better able to share power and practice modes of receptive tending disallowed by hierarchy. Note that many of the institutional reforms Wolin mentions establish conditions that help create places where the demos can act. They help the demos generate power. Yet for these spaces to be democratic, they must be formed, reformed, and entwined with others such that they increasingly conduce toward sharing power and tending to the world rather than ruling over it (the verbal form here in part reflects the ever-lasting imperfectability of such efforts).

Wolin argues that Aristotle sought to "modify the harshness of th[e] principle [of rule] by stipulating that in a politeia . . . [of] true equals, the citizen should know how to rule and be ruled."[64] Yet, on Wolin's reading this reciprocity of ruling/being ruled remained too much within an imaginary in which the moment of rule was still understood in overly instrumental terms. Wolin neither claims that instrumental action falls out of democratic cooperation, nor denies that there is likely to be a residue of coercion that at least unwittingly creeps into even the most admirable human efforts. Rather his point is that the deepest transformations of the demos are entwined with and oriented by a political imaginary in which "equality (isonomia) can be seen as a protest by the demos against [instrumental-hierarchical] conceptions of rule." Democracy is not about having "a share" of power as rule, but is rather about a mode of sharing power that tends as, with, and to the emergent irregularities we are. Of course, Wolin recognizes how profoundly undemocratic Athens was in relation to women, metics, slaves, etc., but his point (as I develop more fully shortly) is in no small part that the democratic imaginary "was and is the only political ideal that condemns its own denial of equality and inclusion."[65] And hence it must aim at cultivating political capacities for sharing and tending *as such*. It is worth quoting him at length on this point:

> I shall take the *political* to be an expression of the idea that a free society composed of diversities can nonetheless enjoy moments of commonality when, through public deliberations, collective power is used to promote or protect the well-being of the collectivity, . . . Democracy is a project concerned with the political potentialities of ordinary citizens, that is, with the possibilities for becoming political beings through the self-discovery of common concerns and modes of action for realizing them.[66]

VII

However much democracy is *aided* by "institutions that subvert institutionalization," it loses its soul as soon as it *identifies* itself with these. When Wolin quotes Spinoza's "*Determinatio negatio est*" (determination is negation),[67] he seeks not to fetishize pure indeterminate flow, but to

64. Ibid., 45.
65. Wolin, "Transgression, Equality, Voice."
66. Wolin, "Fugitive Democracy," 31.
67. Wolin, "Norm and Form," 48.

signal that when and where the demos reduces itself to a set of institutions and identities—*democracy is not happening*: it ceases to be a process of tending to the world's ordinary emergent irregularity and slips back into new modes of rule over everything and everyone that would question its own reified boundaries.

This thought means that democracy must seek to become a distinctive life form built around a tremendous tension. *On the one hand, democracy cultivates a profound resistance to a certain mode of habitualization.* Wolin notes that in relation to democracy, Aristotle worries that "law depends on the habits of obedience which have been fostered over time. [Yet] a disposition to change the laws, which is one of the most persistent charges leveled against democracy . . . allegedly undermines the power of law and the habits of obedience to government."[68] To a significant extent Wolin again "accepts the charges." The possibility of democracy is indeed integrally linked to defying habits of obedience to government and established constitutions that would suppress and contain it. This is partly a negative claim, linked to his insight in "Political Theory as a Vocation": "because history suggests that all political societies have both endured and employed violence, cruelty, and injustice, and have known the defeat of human aspirations, it is not surprising that the theorist's concern for *res publica* and the commonweal has issued in theories which, for the most part, have been critical and, in a literal sense, radical."[69] A political theory and political practice that fails to keep alive this indeferent sensibility and activity is undemocratic in the senses in which we are, with Wolin, developing this term. Because "no ruling group voluntarily concedes power," dispositions and capacities that facilitate radical challenges to anti-democratic powers—in contrast to the dispositions that accrue from long-term unquestioning obedience—are part and parcel of the formation of a radical-democratic ethos. Indeed, a democratic ethos is deeply entwined with such challenges, insofar as it is significantly through challenges that (e.g., in Athens) "an unusual level of political maturity and self-confidence" develops; "its political skills were refined by the constitutional conflicts of that period." Again, quoting Wolin at length:

> . . . there is always more politics involved than concrete results might suggest. A new statute, a change in the powers of an insti-

68. Ibid., 47–48.
69. Wolin, "Political Theory as a Vocation," 67.

tution, the abolition of certain established practices are all piti-
fully small testimony to the enormous amount of human activity,
interaction, changes in consciousness, and acquisition of skills
that brought about the changes in question. Significant political
changes are the product of transgressive actions. They disturb the
power relations, interests, expectations, and taboos that typically
cluster around all laws and institutions.[70]

Thus good democratic organizing has a certain *trickster quality*: often
people are drawn to work around relatively minor issues precisely in order to generate the activities, relationships, changes, and acquisitions that
are integral to cultivating radical-democratic modes of culture and power.
In other words, to use contemporary terms in a contemporary context:
Radical-democratic organizing centrally involves (even as it does many
other things) strangely playing an "interest group liberal game" with an
eye to cultivating a "radical-democratic game" that is very different. It is
"trickster" insofar as those drawn into the game (in the form of a democratic coalition) often have little or no appreciation for the cultivation of
a radically different ethos and mode of power that is being developed and
yet may only become recognizable retrospectively (this is importantly
true for organizers as well). It is also "trickster" insofar as those playing the interest group liberal game in an effort to *diminish* democratic
advances often neither have nor develop a sense that the deeper game
being played is not the one they imagine but rather a radical-democratic
game—though dramatic changes on all sides are an open question, and
radical democracy is radical only insofar as it does not close these possibilities in the name of dogmatic adversarial politics.[71]

Yet the transformations of consciousness, expectations, emotions,
and skills are not simply magnetized in a negative direction. They are
simultaneously and relatedly linked with cultivating forms of what we
might call "radical-democratic maturity" (drawing on Wolin's language
above). Here I am referring not simply to the development of political
practices of reciprocal accountability, visibility, listening, and so forth—

70. Wolin, "Transgression, Equality, Voice," 79.

71. I discuss the idea of radical-democratic trickster politics more extensively in "Of
Tensions and Tricksters: Grassroots Democracy Between Theory and Practice," a version
of which is included in this volume. Of course, resisting "dogmatic adversarial politics"
does *not* imply resisting politics with strong agonistic and oppositional aspects. What is
at stake in resisting the "dogmatic" is resisting the re-demonization of others that kills
democracy from within as surely as it destroys it from without.

as crucial as these are. At the profoundest level, this generative maturity concerns capacities and dispositions that facilitate receptive "tending" to the manifold world around us. Wolin sometimes thinks of this ethos in terms of "restoration" or "renewal," but not in a nostalgic sense, because it most often (and in some senses always) concerns a call to community that "has never been" (as we have seen above). Democracy as restoration or renewal evokes "the idea that a free society composed of diversities can nonetheless enjoy moments of commonality . . . to promote or protect the well-being of the collectivity." It "draws on the simple fact that ordinary individuals are capable of creating new cultural patterns of commonality at any moment"; they can move beyond the old patterns of indifference, unequal power, and the fear and loathing of difference to "experience a democratic moment and contribute to the discovery, care, and tending of a commonality of shared concerns" in their ordinary lives, concerning a thousand things like housing, wages, health care, the natural environment, work, schools, and so forth.[72]

Renewal and restoration, thus, are moments of tending to that which and those who have been excluded or subjugated by a particular order of things—a particular reified "common"—in ways that transcend these limits, allow us to countenance one another anew, and create fresh patterns of coexistence through these new sensibilities and disclosures. It can be about differences *or* commonality, and is generally about both.[73] Renewal can involve engaging tacit knowledges, relationships, modes of common life "within" a recognized community that are excluded, diminished, or subjugated by dominant political scripts and epistemological forms, or it can be about tending as, with, and to different unacknowledged groups "outside" who have been on the undersides of dominant forms of power. Indeed, the suppression of "outside others" and the suppression "within" an order of tacit democratic knowledges, possibilities, and modes of tending (that is, most especially: the waning of a vibrant receptive democratic culture) are tightly entwined on Wolin's reading. Nowhere is this clearer than in his discussion of the rise and fall of democracy in Athens, in "Norm and Form."

72. Wolin, "Norm and Form," 58.

73. Wolin is critical of fetishizing either difference or commonality, and has tried to articulate the political in ways that resist fetishizing or even accenting one or the other—a point missed by many of his interpreters.

Recall that Wolin attributes the rise of democratic culture and politics to the countless struggles in fifth-century Athens in which the free male demos gradually disrupted anti-democratic hierarchies, took power, and created institutions through which it gained popular control of governing. Yet the paradox, on Wolin's reading, is that it is precisely the "victory" of these democratic struggles that gave birth to the defeat of democracy as a distinct, vital, and dynamic form of tending, receptivity, renewal, and power. Once "in power," a carefully delineated demos gradually ceased actively to tend to, as, and with the emergent irregularities of the world and settled not only into a form of government, but a teleologically completed form of life—"routinization, professionalization, and the loss of spontaneity and of those improvisatory skills that Thucydides singled out as an Athenian trademark. . . . It [institutionalization-fetish and static-careless ritualization] tends to produce internal hierarchies, to restrict experience, and to inject an esoteric element into politics."[74] In modernity, as we have seen, this takes the form of what Wolin refers to as "methodism" and "organization." Such "internal" devitalization of a democratic culture, however, is not just an "internal" affair. And this is not only because radical democracy is always born in relations of tending to that which lies beneath or beyond the methodical enactment of constitutional forms—as, say, tacit knowledges and/or emergent irregularities.

In "Norm and Form," Wolin analyzes the pivotal moment when Athens ceased to be a "dynamic and developing political culture":

> For Athenian democracy to continue to democratize, it would have had to confront itself rather than its enemies. The crucial moment occurred in 403 or 402 B.C. when the restored democracy rejected a proposal to limit the franchise to property owners, thereby preserving its egalitarian conception of citizenship. At the same time, however, it refused to extend citizenship to those slaves who had assisted in the revolution against the Thirty . . . [which was] symptomatic . . . of a conservative temper indicating that democracy had "settled down" and found its constitutional form, its ne plus ultra.[75]

The expression "would have had to confront itself" is key here. In order for "the demos" to have continued to nurture cultures and powers of

74. Ibid., 36. Brackets mine. Aspirations and practices of empire certainly aided the decline.

75. Ibid., 43.

tending it would have had to more searchingly respond not only to the suppressed otherness "within" itself (i.e., among those acknowledged as included), but also (and relatedly) to the others it excluded at its "external borders." Insofar as it settled into these latter exclusions, the demos came to identify with extant forms in a manner that stifled its life as insurgent receptive care and transgressive sharing of power. It began to intensify mobilizations of sensibility, consciousness, and practice around defending (and extending, in the form of empire) these forms over against the others. The exclusion of "external" heterogeneity from the question of commonness was implicated in a relationship to form and limits that was simultaneously a symptom and stifling of the very "internal" democratic culture it had nourished (despite exclusions) as long as it was inventing more democratic modes of power on its own behalf. In *Presence of the Past,* Wolin gives an analogous account of how the mythic "*unum*" in United States history has similarly combined the project of excluding others *and* tacit modes of otherness (such as robust democratic engagement) within the circle of those accorded full citizenship. The exclusions of external and internal otherness reciprocally solicit, and generally feed and intensify, each other.

To summarize: the implications of this discussion are crucial for our understanding of radical democracy and they cut in at least two ways: Radical democratization requires—and manifests, to the extent to which it is happening—both a trajectory of increasing inclusiveness and an intensification of dispositions, capacities, and practices of receptive tending. Inclusion without the development of institutions of "rational disorganization" and an ethos of active tending, likely devolves into mob rule or an organizational totality rather than incarnations of new forms of relational power-sharing. On the other hand, an ethos of tending is quickly undermined when it ceases to question and transgress the modes in which it excludes "others" as unworthy, incapable, dirt, etc. Tending and inclusion are inextricably related and both are crucial dimensions of democracy.

This means that democratic "commonality" for Wolin is not a nostalgic appeal to a lost community—which, again, Wolin repeatedly tells us "never was." Rather it is a quasi-mythic appeal to a *constituent moment* in which inclusion and receptive tending are acknowledged, intensified, extended, rearticulated, enacted—*enhanced*. These moments happen. They happen neither as perfection, nor as enduring continuity across time—but as moments enacting intensifications and enhancements of inclusion and tending that are linked crucially but discontinuously across disparate times through disruptive memories and re-creations of the political that solicit and spur one another into becoming. To appeal to such moments is to seek to re-shape ourselves in relation to a responsibility we inherit with their memory. Democratic commonality refers to a deepening of our propensities to engage (*and be engaged by*) memory and creative work in ways that enhance our capacities both to acknowledge our isonomic being together and to tend receptively to the diversity we are in ways that "contribute to the discovery, care . . . of a commonality of shared concerns."[76]

When Wolin draws on Locke's depiction of a constituent moment as a "homogeneity" that is a "suspension of heterogeneity," he is thinking *not* of the forgetful erasure of difference (which he has, for example, repeatedly criticized with great insight in relation to how liberal social contract theory entrenches inequality through the erasure of difference).[77] Rather he is evoking a posture of opening to the others with whom we are co-implicated to question, discern, and create common goods at the transformative intersection (*inter esse*—between-being) of a multitude of interests, visions, and passions.

> Recall the remarkable phenomenon of Polish Solidarity: a movement composed of highly disparate elements—socialists, artists, teachers, priests, believers, atheists, nationalists, and so on. Yet one of the literal meanings of solidarity is 'community or perfect coincidence of (or between) interests.' Clearly homogeneity was not then and need not now be equated with dreary uniformity, any more than equality need be mere leveling. What it does require is understanding what is truly at stake politically: heterogeneity, diversity, and multiple selves are no match for modern forms of power.[78]

Beyond fetishizing difference or fetishizing unity, Wolin takes fugitive democracy to be the incredibly difficult call to enact moments of transformative care for difference *and* commonality, and this, in the overwhelming face of global corporate power and the megastate. He stakes his

76. Wolin, "Fugitive Democracy," 43.

77. See, e.g., chapters 7 and 8 in *Presence of the Past*, and chapter 15 in *Politics and Vision*.

78. Wolin, "Fugitive Democracy," 44.

claim precisely in a refusal of the alternatives that are frequently hypostatized in contemporary academic debates—even as he is (in my view) sometimes less subtle than he might be about some of the positions he criticizes in a manner that itself risks reinstituting hypostatized alternatives (he has his reasons).

There is no doubt that Wolin thinks fugitive democracy must have deep roots in local political engagements. But there should similarly be little doubt that he persistently criticizes a localism that would become parochial or take itself to be a self-sufficient autonomous alternative. Hence at the conclusion of "Fugitive Democracy" he writes that in addition to cultivating a plethora of local modes of democratic engagement, "renewal must draw on a less simple fact: a range of problems and atrocities exists that a locally confined democracy cannot resolve. Like pluralism, interest group politics, and multicultural politics, localism cannot surmount its limitations except by seeking out the evanescent homogeneity of a broader political."[79]

What is needed, he suggests, is a "*multiple civic self,* one who is required to act as a citizen in diverse settings: national, state, city or town, neighborhood, and voluntary association. It is perhaps the most complex conception of citizenship ever devised and yet we have no coherent conception of it."[80] It draws selves to democratic practices not only on different scales but across different themes and concerns that transcend singular scales.

At the larger level, Wolin views meaningful democracy as linked to efforts to open alternative insurgent democratizing spaces that encroach upon the de-politicizing prerogatives of the megastate and global corporations—whether these be military, ecological, economic, etc. "Democracy stands for an alternative conception of politics, even a standing criticism of and a living opposition to the megastate and to media politics."[81] Yet

---

79. Ibid., 44.

80. Wolin, *Presence of the Past*, 190. My emphasis.

81. Ibid., 191. I suspect there are more opportunities for "media politics" than Wolin may recognize, but clearly the dangers are tremendous, as indicated for example in discussions of SNCC. Nevertheless, it is difficult to see how radical democracy can avoid this sphere; simultaneously radical-democratic deployments of it have largely yet to be invented—though the Zapatista's and Moveon.org are among those who are initiating suggestive possibilities. See also Andrew Szasz's account of the anti-toxic waste movement's use of media imagery in *EcoPopulism: Toxic Waste and the Movement for Environmental Justice.*

though such formations at the national and transnational levels are necessary, they have heightened—even severe—risks of becoming modes
of "representative" democracy that are less and less representative as the
relatively few who can participate in them are cut off from the ordinary
lives, visions, and concerns of those they claim to represent. (The operations of many national and transnational NGOs illuminate the pertinence
of his concern.)

Wolin emphasizes the need for what I have been calling in other
chapters the "liturgical" aspect of democracy. A key character of radical-
democratic liturgical experience is that it *virtually always happens between as well as within* singular settings.

> The value of each of these involvements lies in their coexistence,
> the fact that they place different demands and offer different expe-
> riences. *For what democratic politics is about is not simply discus-
> sion and cooperation among friends and neighbors but deliberation
> about differences, not just differences of opinion and interest, but
> the different modes of being represented in race, culture, ethnicity,
> religion, gender, and class. The encounter with difference is becom-
> ing the most important experience in contemporary America as
> new populations make their homes here.* For difference presents
> a potential anomaly to the politics of the megastate: it upsets the
> passivity that is the essential condition of bureaucratic rule and
> the imagined politics of the mass media.[82]

This sensibility is precisely what I am calling, with Bakhtin, the "border
at the core" of the liturgical dialogical body politics of becoming radical democratic peoples (see especially my discussions in the chapters on
Rowan Williams and L'Arche). When it comes to engaging a tradition that
is largely "other," most people probably can engage no more than one at
any (necessarily quite extended) time, if the engagement of the edge is to
have a depth that transgresses established codes of "diversity." Yet most of
us are "betwixt and between," as MacIntyre acknowledges,[83] in ways that
make transformative encounters with differences in ordinary life very
available to people—if we will engage the difficult work of acknowledging
and tending to them. In Durham, for example, the intersections between
different issues—health, wages, housing, neighborhood, race, immigra-
tion, education, environment, safety, and so forth—very quickly call us

82. Ibid., 191. My emphasis.
83. MacIntyre, *Whose Justice? Which Rationality?*, 397.

to negotiate the entwinements and tensions of a complex and dynamic lifeworld. Moreover the complex mix of Christians, Jews, Muslims, and atheists in Durham CAN is *beginning* to solicit liturgies of the edge that have great potential if they are not marginalized and diminished by bland ecumenical tendencies in the dominant American culture.

For all these reasons, Wolin emphasizes that "democratic possibilities depend upon combining traditional localism and postmodern centrifugalism."[84] Localism and overly centered democratic allegiances and liturgies have historically often tended toward parochialism or—worse—rabid prejudice, even as the local is generally the most accessible site of everyday practices of democratic tending. "Postmodern centrifugalism" checks these tendencies and at its best solicits responsiveness both to the myriad differences that have been articulated by radically inegalitarian modes of power, as well as to "emergent irregularities." Yet on its own, it not infrequently tends to have an allergy toward questions of commonness, the common good, and so forth. A manifold "political ecology of localism"[85] that tends to the complexity of the ordinary "can generate and continuously renew direct political experience." And it is not hopeless when combined with an attentiveness to difference and insurgent publics on a variety of larger scales that oppose the megastate and global capital, and gradually seek institutions of "rational disorganization" that might de-center, disperse, and devolve their gargantuan organizational powers.[86]

But this is easier said than thought—let alone done. And how, more precisely, can Wolin's repeated variation on Locke's constituent moment—evoking renewal as "evanescent homogeneity," as it does—avoid ultimately being conflated with those calls to pure positivity or pure negation that are historically widespread, politically disastrous, and continue to re-emerge—"same as it ever was." To gain a deeper grasp of the heroinic epical democratic political vision Wolin offers, we must turn to a fuller discussion of tending and its relation to his idiosyncratic reading of Montesquieu's constitutionalism.

84. Wolin, *Politics and Vision*, 604.

85. I develop this idea in "The Wild Patience of Radical Democracy: Beyond Zizek and Lack."

86. Ibid.

VIII

Wolin develops the notion of "tending" as an alternative to what he calls the politics of "intending"—which seeks to mobilize and subjugate the archaic and emergent irregularities of the world to antidemocratic modes of power concentrated in nations, states, corporations, and the hybridizing fusions of these that constitute what he calls the contemporary "economic polity." Here are some of the main contours of this mode of being, which we have already discussed in the context of Ella Baker:

> . . . tending: to apply oneself to looking after another, as when we tend a garden or tend to the sick. It implies active care for things close at hand, not mere solicitude. . . . Tendance is tempered by the feeling of concern for objects whose nature requires that they be treated as historical and biographical beings. . . . proper tendance requires attentiveness to differences between beings within the same general class . . . implies respect that is discriminating but not discriminatory. The idea of tending centers politics around practices, that is, around habits of competence or skill that are routinely required if things are to be taken care of. [It involves the entwinement of] 'habits of the heart' . . . and intimate political experience . . . acquired in . . . everyday life.[87]

> Difference signified exception, anomaly, local peculiarities, and a thousand other departures from the uniformity that a certain kind of power prefers. Difference rejects the notion of a single narrative history and unifying single purpose. It favors a pluralistic conception of history, or histories rather than history. Difference is not about a unified collective self but about the biography of a place in which different beings are trying to live.[88]

Tending might be characterized as a conservative radicalism, or radical conservatism. It articulates itself as a peculiar—and sometimes puzzling—tension between the two: Tending is a process of *democratizing* that "wants to conserve, but it is driven to radicalism because there is no way for its conception of life forms to be maintained without opposing a system of power in which change has become routinized."[89] Yet what tending most struggles to preserve are life forms where diverse practices

87. Wolin, *Presence of the Past*, 89.
88. Ibid., 93.
89. Ibid., 88.

of democratic cultivation of and care for differences and common goods have themselves begun to take root and intensify; such as the localities and regions associated in the Articles of Confederation, characterized by "populist tendencies in state politics, and an incipient, though inchoate, democratic ideology" (when has democratic ideology *not* been largely incipient and inchoate, one influenced by Wolin might ask?). It is conservative in the face of future-driven forms of organizational power, yet in the thickets of modes of life more akin to its vision, its politics are less "conservative" or "radical" and more what we might call "discerning," as communities gather around the possibilities and challenges of specific situations and places, and exercise political judgment and action in efforts to nurture life. To get at this, Wolin writes (in a mythic evocation of what was most promising in American life prior to the U.S. Constitution) of a plethora of state and local institutions "and a vast array of spontaneous ad hoc life forms that arose and disappeared according to their usefulness. These were the institutions by which Americans tended to the common concerns of daily life."[90] Note that neither conservation nor transformation are fetishized here, but rather situated in a messy matrix of daily common concerns in response to which democratizing communities utilized and invented "spontaneous and ad hoc" associations that "arose and disappeared."

With this semi-mythic discussion, Wolin offers a vision of radical democracy under (comparatively lucky) conditions in which it is neither engaged in ceaseless intense "tout court" radical struggle against antidemocratic forms of power, on the one hand, nor settled into a reified sense of democracy-as-institutional identification, on the other—the two conditions he generally portrays in ancient Athens. Rather, in relation to pre-Constitutional America he develops a democratic imaginary that projects democracy as sufficiently pervasive and differentiated to provide a multitude of everyday political experiences, and as simultaneously oriented toward tending to the complex "common concerns of daily life," such that it cultivates a sense of its becoming that is not wholly identical with the extant institutions and associational forms it has developed to do so.[91] This is part of what Wolin is getting at in *Politics and Vision*, when

90. Ibid., 87.

91. Note that while this account is drawn from *Presence of the Past* (1989), it is wrong to "periodize" this imagery as something he left behind in his work from the mid-1990s forward. For example, virtually all of it reappears and receives development in his

he writes that "the demos signifies not only citizenry in general but carriers of everyday cultural traditions, a role that was never captured in the narrowly political conception of democracy held by Athenians."[92]

As tending, democracy discerns and articulates itself in efforts to care for, as, and with manifold forms of life—including many that are archaic and emergent irregularities residing significantly beyond the concepts and practices it has ready to hand. Thus it must be spontaneous, inventive, ad hoc, and willing to help move beyond institutions and associations that are no longer responsive to the complexity of the ordinary. Thus, one could say that democracy is *radical* in the sense of being and understanding itself as a politics essentially engaged with and enacting the "not yet," because forms of tending always and as such exceed themselves in caring for inexhaustible ordinariness (an inexhaustibility I call "radical" in the title of this essay). Radical here would concern roots we can never *possess* and relations with *that which exceeds roots*. Nevertheless this image of democracy also has a profoundly conservative sense insofar as it seeks to care for forms of life that already exist in myriad ways that are good. Moreover, democratic practices of tending and enabling these goods are encroached upon (and encroach upon each other) in thousands of ways that violate fragile goods and call for careful political judgment and frequent conservative resistance. Better, again, to speak of a *discerning* body politics that cares not for these terms—conservative and radical—that so often tend to reify political oppositions in ways that block more hopeful democratic possibilities than they illuminate.

Democracy as tending to the complexity of the ordinary thus requires a subtle relationship to questions concerning the cultivation of "habits"—to reflect further upon a theme we have already begun to discuss. On the one hand, we have seen that Wolin rejects Aristotle's emphasis on cultivating the manifold habits associated with deferential obedience to governing laws, arguing that this kills the spirits and acts of transgressive enhancements of inclusion and tending that are the very heart of radical democracy. On the other hand, we have seen that Wolin refers to democratic tending *as* the cultivation of habits of ongoing care for differences and commonalities of persons, communities, practices, and places. Such habits, dispositions, and competences are "routinely

---

Tocqueville: Between Two Worlds.

92. Wolin, *Politics and Vision*, 605.

required if things are to be taken care of." Hence democratic tending
requires cultivating relatively sedimented modes that have histories of
working well in particular contexts. Yet paradoxically and inextricably
entwined with these modes, democratic tending must cultivate habits of
attentiveness to the surprising specificities and inexhaustibility of what
and who is cared for (or with), such that these modes are opened beyond
themselves—given a dynamic quality by the objects of tending, which
resist reifying tendencies that accompany habituation. We might speak
here of a tensional ethos of tending that seeks to interweave both habits in a more traditional sense and "habits of dehabituation," to evoke
this nuanced relation to the cultivation of habits in a world in which the
ordinary is complex and shot through with archaic and emergent irregularities. Perhaps the cultivation of habit in the more traditional sense of
the term gets more play in relation to practices of tending to specific beings and goods, while "habits of dehabituation" are accented more in the
tensional interstices where we are called to exercise judgment between
different configurations of practices, beings, and goods. In all cases, both
are vitally important. Wolin's debt to Aristotle here is as profound and
strange as is his resistance to him.

Clearly this is an *ethos*, but Wolin is profoundly aware that it requires building a "democratic constitutional" context in order to have a
chance of flourishing. In the context of the megastate and superpower he
takes this to be an extremely difficult project whose success should not be
expected any time soon. Nevertheless, Wolin offers a remarkable image
of "democratic constitutionalism"—what we might think of as a radical
democratic *habitus*, in Bourdieu's sense of the term—that might provoke
de-reification and animation of radical-democratic habits and practices
as much as "constitutional democracy" tends to congeal and stifle them.
In other words, Wolin seeks to convey a sense of the shapes and textures
of a political terrain or *habitus* that might help engender "habits of dehabituation," and he does so in terms of an even more intense imaginary of
"rational disorganization" than ancient Athens alone can provide. Though
this theme is further developed in his book on Tocqueville, perhaps its
most vivid and concise portrayal is in his short chapter on Montesquieu
in *Presence of the Past*.

In resistance to a Hamiltonian politics that would constitutionalize
the suppression of democratic tending in order to enhance U.S. empire
through "streams" of power flowing from a governed populous, Wolin

retrieves an archaic democratic imaginary from an idiosyncratic reading of Montesquieu. He is aware of the dangers that accompany this project, so let us start with the closing of his essay in order to resist them from the outset:

> The difficulty in getting a purchase on these problems is that criticism appears as an attack on rationality inspired by an atavistic urge to return to a simpler age. Perhaps, however, the solution to the crisis of reason, as Montesquieu suggested, is not in simplification but in complexity. But how does complexity itself avoid appearing as a simple solution? Perhaps it has to do with treating complexity as signifying diverse claims and life forms so that the marks of a solution are not simplicity or elegance or reduction, as we have been taught, but the creation of conditions which encourage complexities that live by different laws and defy Cartesian solutions.[93]

Wolin seeks to revive the Montesquieuian image of the political and social world as a "labyrinth," in opposition to modernity's more common notions of "system" and "organization," in order "to convey the tortuous character of society, its undesigned, unpremeditated qualities, its opaqueness to linear and univocal reasoning."[94] With Montesquieu, Wolin develops a theory of "law" that is profoundly anti-methodological (in relation to the sense of methodism discussed above) and aims to provide a *habitus* that would solicit rather than stymie democratic habits and virtues of tensional tending. Law in this sense "becomes a subversive notion rather than the sign of a unitary scheme of things," insofar as it adheres to the specificities of the world—and the multiplicitous relationships between specificities—that resist monological universality. "All beings have their laws," and as each being exists in a context consisting of complex relations with myriad different beings and configurations of beings, all beings are subject to a variety of "laws" emerging from the specific relationships and "conditions that enable things and beings to persist." "Yet laws," as Wolin reads Montesquieu to argue, "are not to be understood as commands but as reciprocal relationships expressive of the natures of those to whom the laws apply."[95]

93. Wolin, *Presence of the Past*, 119.
94. Ibid., 107.
95. Ibid., 104–5.

Laws have a fixed character insofar as they express indispensable conditions for beings to endure and flourish. They thus affirm and call us to attend to what Wolin calls, on the last page of *Politics and Vision*, the "value of limits" that is "rooted in the ordinary" and resists violation.[96] Insofar as radical democracy calls us to habituate ourselves to tending in light of such laws (rooted in the specificities of beings and relationships, and in contrast with the laws of overarching structures and dynamics of suppressive governance), it articulates a motif indebted to a subversive re-appropriation of Aristotle. Yet the situation is infinitely more complicated for *human* beings insofar as humans not only have relatively inelastic properties rooted in our physicality, and rather elemental relationships with the world, but we are

> also endowed with a nature that is 'free' and 'intelligent.' [Our] nature leads [us] to 'violate endlessly the laws that God has established and to change those [we] have established [ourselves]. It is, Montesquieu declares, a 'necessary' law of man's nature that he 'must find his own way'. Necessity was thus transformed from a repressive term implying closure to one suggesting openness. . . . [This means] not simply that he is free to make mistakes but that in fact he does . . . a being of limited understanding, prone to err and subject to 'a thousand passions'. It is his nature 'to forget'.[97]

The dynamic character of human beings and their relationships, as well as our forgetfulness and erring, entails that social and political well-being are always swept up in the "emergent"—as well as the extant—complexities of the ordinary. Radical-democratic judgment and action would always have us engaged in processes of "finding our own way." Yet this same *openness* of our being calls for *multifarious encumbrances* that might remind us of—as well as guide and *prod* us toward—modes of existence conducive to various goods developed and discerned in specific contexts and relationships over time. Without such encumbrances—numerous dense practices and narratives of tending—we are especially prone to becoming subjects and objects of simplifying and blind will to power. Yet encumbrance itself, when it is centrally organized and systematized, becomes a tool of such power—interlocking and reifying habits. Hence, radical democracy seeks the encumbrance of a labyrinth. "Transgressive,

96. Wolin, *Politics and Vision*, 606.
97. Wolin, *Presence of the Past*, 105.

changeable, and forgetful man is heteronomous man, the subject of a variety of laws. He is, by nature, not the malleable object of a single and sovereign lawmaker or law-declarer. Instead, he is the object of multiple claims and subject of multiple constitutions."[98] Such multiplicitous encumbrance demands that we cultivate political judgment that is attentive to the specificities of beings, contexts, and goods in ways sensitive to diverse limits and modes relevant to flourishing. This is especially so when these specificities give rise to tensions and discrepancies that reawaken our receptivity to, and responsibility for, the radical complexity of ordinary life.

As Montesquieu puts it: "Good sense consists in large measure of knowing the nuances of things." In Wolin's hands this always demands generative political work involving "new patterns," insofar as we become highly aware that the "social whole" and its constituent parts are "deposited by historical actions and inactions and [are] apt, therefore, to be marked by ignorance, foolishness, and immorality." Thus we must regard the "several structures of relations" while refusing to fetishize any one of them. At the same time, however, the labyrinthine character of this radical-democratic imaginary chastens those acting in the present and resists the will to seek salvation through the establishment of overarching systems. Attentive to specificities of commonality and difference, Wolin's Montesquieu-inspired constitutionalism "stood for the domestication of power by an unplotted conspiracy of difference, that is, the modification of power by several modes of accommodation. . . ."—complex space and time that is recalcitrant to despotisms that would simplify.[99] Yet the domestication of power engendered by this labyrinthine imaginary is concerned to resist not only the encroachment of grand despotisms, but also the myriad encroachments *within* the labyrinth spurred by mini-despotic tendencies of particular beings, modes, goods, and contexts to colonize and subsume others. It is precisely this radically decentered and tensional political situation—or *habitus*—that might best solicit and empower an ethos of agonistic tending, and provide a multitude of sources and practices upon which we might draw in our political efforts to nurture life.

It is helpful to link this thought to Wolin's discussion of Locke's constituent moment that we touched upon earlier. We saw that Wolin con-

98. Ibid.

99. Ibid., 106–7. This complexity resists the "secular" simplification of space and time, as Talal Asad describes it in *Formations of the Secular: Christianity, Islam, Modernity*.

ceives of constituent moments as democratic events where people with different traditions, histories, interests, issues, and so forth, renew a sense of isonomic being-together: an *inter-esse* (interest: literally, between-being) that enables them to create new patterns of commonality (or "homogeneity") that are simultaneously enriched by and transfigurative of their differences in ways that enhance inclusiveness and tending. When Locke's constituent moments are situated in Montesquieu's labyrinth, what emerges is a vision of constituent power that is dispersed across and radiates from specific social places and times. Wolin argues that efforts to engender homogeneity from a spatially and temporally unified center inevitably suppress the populous they would empower by *rendering invisible and hence more operative* histories and powers that rearticulate structures of hierarchy. Yet he suggests that constituent moments that are spatially and temporally complex are far more hopeful. Beyond reified fragments and reified totalities, such moments articulate new connections, relations, and commonalities *from specific complexly differentiated places*: they send charges of enhanced democratic community that radiate from specific relations and run through (or reverberate across) a political terrain as people negotiate different histories, goods, powers, traditions, and problems in transforming efforts toward the "discovery, care, and tending of a commonality of shared concerns."[100] Simultaneously rooted in and emerging from numerous specifically negotiated intersections of a labyrinthine political terrain, such moments contribute to an illumination (and enactment) of radical-democratic community through a commingling of differently refracted hues each one of which is itself complex insofar as it too is generated at the interstice of different practices that have emerged at (and often live according to) different times and coexist in rough accommodations. Informed and inspired by the labyrinthine character of democratic enactments, such moments study and work their hopes in ways that retain particularity even as they endlessly "seek out the evanescent homogeneity of a broader political." This "broader political" in Wolin's sense is not a single totalizing image of "everyone everywhere always," but rather the specifically delimiting idea of all who are (and that which is) significantly co-implicated in the problematics to which we struggle to tend in particular places and times. The broader political undulates—modulating shape, scope, depth, focus, register, and direction—in

---

100. Wolin, "Fugitive Democracy," 43.

relation to a multitude of sites that project and engage it. It is the matrix of these undulations and seeks to transform superpower not through the formation of a singular collective subjectivity that would fatefully reproduce what it would abolish, but rather through the enhancement and intensification of radical-democratic tending powers understood as the trans-temporal construction of an undulating labyrinth. This is akin to what Wolin has in mind when he writes of "encouraging complexities" of "different life forms" that would gradually "domesticate power by an unplotted conspiracy of difference." Radical democracy would thus be a *conspiracy*, insofar as it is guided by an urgent desire to disestablish superpower, the megastate, and global capitalism. It is *unplotted*, insofar as it realizes that the only way out is from within the scattered remnants of and emergent possibilities for labyrinthine political practices of renewal that work outward toward broader political configurations from specific places, problems, and relationships.

Recalling again Locke's constituent moment, Wolin retains from this concept the crucial image and solicitation of radical inclusivity. Yet he resists the forgetful and totalizing characteristics that frequently accompany liberal articulations of it, by dispersing it in a labyrinth of complex space and time. This enjoins us to cultivate not only the normativity but also the *power* of "broader politicals" in ways that resist the disempowering aspects of some forms of multicultural and postmodern fragmentation, while at the same time avoiding the political calls to a new Leninist collectivity that have recently re-emerged in response.[101] A radical democratic politics of the labyrinthine "broader political" displaces revolutionary politics from imaginaries of total rupture (which is existentially terrifying and politically disastrous in ways that rightly contribute to its suppression), and situates transformation and transcendence immanently within specific places, times, and problematics in ways that are at once radical *and* partial in origin and aspiration. They aim to radically transform local and larger political horizons not *tout court*, but through manifold particular cuts and reworkings in the process of tending to specific problems, commonalities, and differences. This radicalism that refuses to constitute itself as the effort to seize imaginary reigns that would control history, avoids the existential terrors associated with the will to

101. For a more extended critique of Zizek's new Leninism, see my "The Wild Patience of Radical Democracy: Beyond Zizek and Lack." For a collection of new Leninist themes, see Budgen et al., *Lenin Reloaded: Towards a Politics of Truth*.

abolish horizons, and instead engenders revolutionary desire in and for the tasks of radically reconfiguring the world through an ongoing series of specific interventions that take shape as an "unplotted conspiracy." *In this sense*, Wolin offers an image of perpetual revolution that might be livable insofar as it calls us not to proceed as a total mobilization (into pure "flow") of everyone, everywhere, always, but rather in a manner that moves about—fugitively, episodically, evanescently—from place to place, from this time to that, energized here where there is a crisis, habituating there where things are working better, flowing with ordinary tempos here, disrupting them there, confining itself here, radiating outward there: performing the patient revolutionary labor of the radical ordinary.

IX

How might we think with more political economic specificity about what I have perhaps too often rendered through a variety of electrical, optical, spatial, and acoustical metaphors? And how might we do so in ways that allow us to imagine the devolution and deconstruction of the economic polity? Let me very briefly list several modes of labyrinthine radical-democratic engagement that seem to me to be among those that suggest some ways forward. Integrally associated with each of the following transformations is the work of what I have elsewhere called "moving democracy," "political ecologies of democratic practice," "trickster politics," "wild patience," and so forth, which is both required for and cultivated by radical-democratic organizing when it is faithful to the motifs we have been discussing.[102] In other words, each of the following transformations requires and cultivates work analogous to that which we have discussed in relation to the receptive liturgical formations of SNCC inspired by Ella Baker and L'Arche communities inspired by Jean Vanier. Such work is the tending to and of the radical-democratic ordinary that draws from and further builds upon Wolin's labyrinthine polity. The most radical registers of radical democracy concern our receptive capacities for becoming footwashed and footwashing peoples (as Hauerwas and I argue elsewhere in this book)—both literally and metaphorically. If I focus on aspects that have a more "policy" ring here, it is not in order to draw radical

---

102. See, e.g., "Moving Democracy"; "The Wild Patience of Radical Democracy"; as well as "Of Tension and Tricksters" and "To Make This Tradition Articulate," chapters 13 and 3 respectively, in the present volume.

democracy back into a reified political universe of settled forms, but in an effort to give more specificity to Wolin's evocations above concerning democratic constitutionalism—the formation of Montesquieuian "laws" that might contribute to a better abode for cultures of tending.

One of the most insightful gatherers and inspirers of such efforts is Gar Alperovitz, who perhaps not coincidently recalls traveling as a Senate aide through Mississippi with Bob Moses, and working with the Mississippi Freedom Democratic Party in 1964, as among his most formative experiences. In *America Beyond Capitalism: Reclaiming Our Wealth, Our Liberty, and Our Democracy*, Alperovitz discusses numerous efforts to create a labyrinthine polity from within the increasingly monolithic dynamic organization dominated by global capital. He envisions the revolutionary work of developing a "new system" in terms of "the steady building of a *mosaic* of entirely different institutions, but in a manner that is peaceful and evolutionary." He finds hope in the fact that below the radar of the megastate and the media there is an "extraordinary range" of new ideas and initiatives being undertaken by ordinary citizens discovering that "what seems radical is often common sense at the grassroots level."[103]

The core ethos that guides Alperovitz is in many ways consonant with the Wolinian themes discussed above: "democracy from the ground up" that is inclusive, egalitarian, pluralizing, and provides a plethora of different sites for people to gather together in formative practices of tending to questions of liberty and the common good. The "pluralist commonwealth" he advocates is being generated by literally thousands of de-centered and decentralizing efforts across the U.S. These include thousands of worker-owned firms, as well as Employee Stock Ownership Plans that—though currently undemocratic—are setting the stage for democratizing "demands for more voice." They also include numerous municipalities that are seeking to democratize wealth through a variety of efforts, from ownership of land that enables cities to better extract surplus from private entities for public goods and the development of the commons, to municipal start-up venture capital programs that retain stock and public power in businesses that provide benefits for local economies, to community land trusts that provide public goods such as low-income housing and open space, to municipally owned utilities, to Community

103. Alperovitz, *America Beyond Capitalism*, viii, 6, 3, ix.

Development Corporations that combine community services with the generation of wealth, to co-ownership and control practices that combine several public and private entities. At the state level he sees hopeful signs in developments such as California's efforts to direct the multibillion-dollar public pension funds toward in-state economic developments that are environmentally sustainable and economically transparent. In many of these efforts Alperovitz identifies a host of undemocratic structures and practices. Yet he argues persuasively that: a) they have often been supported by a broad swath of the political spectrum and provide vital openings for a pluralistic radical democracy that, if combined with b) the rise of insurgent democratic organizing by many groups that is directed toward democratizing these institutions, and c) the development of nationwide efforts to create structural changes more conducive to the flourishing of decentered and decentralized political economies, might d) usher forth radical changes that could provide potent alternatives to capitalism across the continent and beyond. An additional democratizing dimension that should be added to this mix is the democratic cultural change that Harry Boyte discusses in books such as *Everyday Politics*, which traces and theorizes numerous efforts to change the institutional practices and cultures of public and private organizations from within, such that they are democratized internally and cultivate an ethos of "public work" oriented to providing a plethora of public goods in reciprocal relationships with the specific communities they engage—like students organizing in schools, or staff and elderly forming democratic communities in institutions for the care of the elderly.

Each one of these efforts is hopeful but insufficient and easily co-opted if developed in isolation from related efforts and registers of struggle. In my view, then, it is key to combine several elements that are often insufficiently drawn into relation with one another in both the scholarly literature and in "on the ground" efforts: social movement organizing attentive to the liturgies, practices, and institutions through which we might become people more capable of tending across difficult differences; articulations of political vision, ethos, and sensibility that are integral to radical democracy; local structures of democratic political economy; and national and transnational organizations, networks, and institutions that can both work to empower these and facilitate coordination among them where this is deemed desirable, and also fend off large-scale assaults of empire, capital, and hegemonic nation-states. (World Social Forum is a suggestive and hopeful—if highly imperfect and struggling—effort to open these possibilities on a transnational scale.[104])

The work of J. K. Gibson-Graham, in *Postcapitalist Politics*, provides an informative and inspiring example of the effort to think at the creative nexus of transformations in ethos, organizing practices, and institutions. Highly attentive to the ways in which shifts in affect and cognition may contribute to and benefit from alterations of daily micro practices of initiatives that are developing "community economies," Gibson-Graham (a pen name shared by Julie Graham and Catherine Gibson) take important steps toward theorizing elements that are often ignored or separated from one another. They trace numerous efforts that are analogous to initiatives traced by Alperovitz, such as the development of alternative economic enterprise networks that link enhanced community control and community goods to economic development. Their largest scale example is the Mondragon Cooperative in the Basque region of Spain, which consists of many thousands of workers and hundreds of co-ops. At a smaller scale is the Economic Model for Millennium 2000 initiative in western Massachusetts, which consists of a network of those businesses in which 5%–20% of their equity is employee owned and another 5%–20% is held by a community fund administered by a regional economic council consisting of "labor unions, community groups, churches and educational institutions, community development funds and agencies, government, and private business."[105] The aim is to tie capital to a locality, distribute the surplus for strengthening the local community economy, enhancing community engagement, providing social services, and so forth. On a still smaller scale, they point to efforts such as Nuestras Raizes (Our Roots) in the city of Holyoke, Massachusetts, whose membership has many Puerto Rican immigrants, and that consists of a network of community gardens in reclaimed urban spaces that provide food and income for families, job training for youth, workshops on food preparation, organic farming, grassroots leadership development, and includes "a green house, a business incubator, a commercial kitchen, and a restaurant that uses foods produced from the greenhouse."[106] Each of the community economy initiatives Gibson-Graham discuss draws on the economic di-

104. One of the most important discussions of the World Social Forum in relation to the focal themes in this chapter is Santos, *Rise of the Global Left*.

105. Ibid., 182.

106. Ibid., 188.

versity (remnants of the labyrinth) and extant skills of people in order to intensify and proliferate a labyrinthine political economy.

Unlike Alperovitz, Gibson-Graham's attention and examples are not confined to the U.S. but draw from around the world, from Gibson's Australia, to Mexico, to the Philippines, India, and Spain. Moreover their discussion looks at the development of radical-democratic practices of tending and labyrinth formation not only among relatively *rooted* people, but also among those who are *routing* transnationally, such as those associated with the Asian Migrant Centre in the Migrant Savings for Alternative Investments program, in which overseas migrant workers regularly put a portion of their often sub-"living wage" incomes into a co-operatively governed account that fosters the development of alternative enterprises in their home communities. Gibson-Graham suggest some of the ways in which such practices begin to offer not only institutional alternatives but alternative formations of subjectivity as well, as people make connections, envision themselves as working together for democratic, egalitarian, and empowering futures, etc.

A key part of effectively devolving the economic polity in the directions of labyrinthine radical democracy will involve efforts to utilize and construct municipal, state, national, and transnational institutions in ways that facilitate the empowerment of—and connections between—efforts such as those discussed by Alperovitz and Gibson-Graham. Defensively, this will continue to involve efforts (however difficult) to use extant political institutions and invent new ones to "thwart the worst" by organizing grassroots political power to enact restrictive regulations, such as the Citizens Clearing House for Hazardous Waste, which since the 1980s has networked literally thousands of backyard anti-toxics efforts in communities across the U.S. to impact national policy concerning the production and control of hazardous waste.[107] Offensively, it will involve efforts to gain democratic control over economic surplus (in the form of pension funds, taxes, etc.) in ways that promote democratizing political economic initiatives and commonality. If we clip Unger's fetishization of hyper-innovation (criticized earlier) as the basic imperative of democratic redistributions of economic surplus, and rather make innovation a question and one option among several to be deliberated and decided

107. See for example Andrew Szasz's excellent account of the social movement and political economic policy dimensions of these efforts in *EcoPopulism: The Toxic Waste Movement and Environmental Justice.*

by communities of various scales and concerns, his work can be used to open important possibilities. The idea here would be (thinking *with* Unger) to utilize a variety of mechanisms to democratically capture and redistribute economic surplus in ways that nurture community initiatives and public goods developing at a variety of sites: these could range from hyper-speed efforts to spur innovations around alternative energy, recycling, water use and treatment technologies, and so forth, to nurturing the brilliantly archaic efforts of radical slow-time agrarian practices of community propounded by Wendell Berry and others.[108] The labyrinth of radical democracy, as articulated in the spirit of Wolin, is a temporal as well as spatial imaginary, evoking the commingling of a multitude of practices operating according to different traditioned teleologies and different paces of development and/or conservative stewardship. If this strikes you as a rather unsystematic list, that is part of the point.

X

At the turn of the twenty-first century, Wolin writes an essay entitled "Political Theory: From Vocation to Invocation," which constitutes a certain return to questions he addressed in "Vocations of Political Theory." Wolin's new set of reflections occurs at a time when democracy seems to be retreating under the enormous pressures of global capitalism, the megastate, and empire. He contends that, amidst the consolidation and proliferation of these modes of power, elements of the "cross-grained" (that which is variously damaged, marginalized, left behind, and subjugated, by the order) are being produced and incorporated by the order in two senses: First, the system endlessly reproduces dystopias of poverty, environmental destruction, racism, violence, and so forth, as conditions of its own (would-be "end of history") functioning. It enhances itself through increasingly dynamic modes of power that endlessly engender suffering associated with ever-more frequent dislocations that populations are enjoined simply to "get over." Second and more recent, the cries of suffering, discontent, and resistance that are ineliminable responses to these dystopic effects are often managed and contained—sometimes even *produced*—in significant part in relation to the proliferation of "theory" in academic institutions that increasingly fulfills—or threatens to fulfill— functional requirements of the order, even as critical theorists proclaim

108. See for example Berry, *Art of the Commonplace*.

themselves to be "transgressors" who resist it. In a variety of ways, Wolin suggests, the antithesis of superpower is often "neutralized," and for these reasons, "not lost but subsidized."[109] Thus, where Wolin's earlier essay addressed problems of "undertheorization," in which method had displaced theorizing the complex and emergent character of political life, Wolin's later essay addresses "overtheorization," in which theory proliferates innocuousness and assimilation in the name of overwrought critique, and blindness in the name of infinitely subtle illuminations and hyper-specialized abstractions of subalternity.

"How to explain," Wolin asks, "a housing situation in which the most notorious theorists of wrong are not only extended hospitality by a certain community, the academy, and even honored as they are being 'called'? Where . . . the most subversive, dangerous, and deliberately outrageous among them find that despite their best efforts, their market value rises in synch with the Dow Jones, as the most affluent institutions, those most integrated into the same power structures responsible for the wrongs exposed . . . bid for the most celebrated subversives?"[110] Wolin suggests numerous ways in which the accents and (im)balances of many prevalent strands of contemporary theory (which is not to say every letter of every theory[111]) might serve as "normal theory" that inadvertently aligns itself with the current order of things. Here are a few examples: as with privatizing modes of power, much contemporary theory reflects "the crumbling of the language of commonality"[112]; for all Wolin's attention to differences, he worries that a certain rendering of "hyperpluralism" fragments publics ethically, drains their power, and helps generate undesirable, mutually hostile modes of incoherence; theory has become self-referential and enclosed around discussions of its own conditions, "spectatorial . . . in search of distance rather than an intervention driven

109. Wolin, "Invocations of Political Theory," 4.

110. Ibid., 12–13.

111. Still, my sense is that Wolin over-simplifies critical theory and postmodernism in ways that impede as well as disclose important insights. These exaggerations also risk inhibiting political possibilities for collaboration and development, even as they are part of an *ongoing relationship* between Wolin and many "postmoderns" who are—directly or indirectly—his students. Thus his exaggeration is likely intentional and meant to open and contribute to potent political and theoretical possibilities. The questions of an optimal "politics of theory" in this relationship are essentially contestable. My effort in this chapter is crafted as an intervention in this set of affairs among a few others.

112. Ibid., 10.

by urgency. . . . it is theoretical theory rather than political theory" and frequently deflates a sense of urgency[113]; its avant-garde temporality increasingly fits a world in which domination operates in significant measure by accelerating paces of change; its failure to attend to questions of generality too often leaves it relatively silent about systemic crises; the over-use of "heavy" terms like "violence" and "terror" tend to normalize our sense of these conditions in ways that create a certain unresponsiveness to the exceptional; it too often avoids fundamental aspects of contemporary power, such as corruption, that do not have a "focused victim."[114]

How might invocations of political theory move beyond these accommodations? Wolin is not sure, but offers a number of important suggestions throughout his more recent writings. He concludes his essay on political theory as invocation by defining the crisis of our time thus: "'The new is killing us and the old, as yet, is not required to be reborn, but revitalized.' Revitalized, that is, as an element in the unborn theory that will recognize democracy as the dystopia of our time and understand that the opposite is condemned to be oppositional."[115] In a world that insists people "get past" the losses imposed by "ever-accelerating change" (to borrow a trope from Wendell Berry), political theory and democracy must cultivate the project of remembering and revitalizing the "old," the archaic, the cross-grained—not in order for it to be "reborn" as a repetition of a now nostalgic past, but rather as given/giving new life, becoming "revitalized" in "unborn" (not yet) democratic initiatives that would oppose the current order of things and move beyond the impasses of contemporary modes of power and theorizing. Part of "the old" consists of the losses that record the dangers and damages lodged in contemporary dynamics—recollections of which are crucial to cultivating orientations and energies that would genuinely resist them by refusing the "get past" that is integral to the proliferation of hegemonic practices. In negative image, these losses harbor Blochian dreams that are immanent in the ordinary and exceed the limits of the megastate and are a condition of our opposition to it.

113. Ibid., 15.
114. Ibid., 12.
115. Ibid., 21. The internal quote is Wolin's revision of a statement by Gramsci.

The injunction to revitalize the old is also consonant with Wolin's claim concerning democracy as a mode of being that is a "recurrent possibility as long as the memory of the political survives."[116] At the profoundest level, democracy as the occurrence of solidarity among those in a present moment thus hinges upon a certain *solidarity of radical democratic beings and initiatives across time*. If anything could extinguish the possibility of democracy, the utter obliteration of the memory that at other moments the political has *already* transgressed the forms that would suppress it might indeed do so. In other words, as Derrida puts it in several places, the fact that "the impossible has already happened, and we know it has" is an elemental condition of democratic questioning, imagination, and action that is always deemed "impossible" by dominant orders of power.

In one sense, extinguishing the memory of the political is itself impossible. We have seen that even as the tradition of epic political theory has almost always sought to conjure radical democracy *away*, it is nevertheless condemned to conjure democracy *up* in its very efforts to do so. The same might be said for orders of political power. The "memory of the political survives"—if in the form of shards—in spite of and even through the efforts of those who oppose it, because evocations of democracy and the public good that are deployed in order to gain legitimacy for antidemocratic projects almost always dredge up excessive traces of what they would suppress. Thus, as ever-haunting remnants, the memory of the political seems in Wolin's view to be as fated to survive as it is doomed to do so only in forms that are episodic and in need of rebirthing. For these reasons alone, democracy is never patently impossible.

At the same time, however, the memory of the political can be greatly suppressed in ways that render the (re)emergence of democracy much *less* possible—much less probable. Thus Wolin's phrase "as long as" in the sentence under discussion also works as an injunction to remember the past moments in which the political emerged yet which have been suppressed in current configurations of "the past." "As long as" is an injunction that the existence of democracy hinges upon cultivating intergenerational solidarity—a heroinic epic tradition of democracy, even as this is a tradition that (re)connects discontinuous episodes in

116. Wolin, "Norm and Form," 55. This phrase is repeated and further developed in "Fugitive Democracy."

order to be enabled to act in radical-democratic modes on the present and future. "As long as" is an injunction to create communities of democratic theory and practice that are essentially entwined with the arts of invocation. While order traditionally conceived as a form of social space seeks to suppress democratizing as a verbal mode of life, perhaps nothing so threatens democratizing as order based fundamentally on the amnesia of "ever-accelerating change" rushing into the future. Hence a critique of the economic polity quite specifically brings democratic theory as invocation into the foreground.

Yet political theory can never be simply a vocation in Wolin's terms, even under the best of circumstances. The tensional complexity, the emphasis on mobile and emergent tending, as well as the tragic aspects that are inherent to democratic labyrinths prevent it from simply being a vocation as Wolin defines it: a "certain commitment, 'ideal' though not disinterested, to the particular practice in question."[117] It can and must be a commitment to nurture democratic forms of life, but because these have a labyrinthine and emergent character it is always also a commitment to those extant complexities and emergent irregularities that have been denied by the aspects of blindness and encroachment that are an ineliminable aspect of every order of things no matter how radically democratic. Indeed, radical democracy is not simply a resistance to blindness and encroachments that are external and antithetical to its becoming. Rather it *must also* cultivate an acknowledgement and resistance to those forms of blindness and encroachment that its own modes of being harbor and nurture in spite of—and because of—the mode of co-existence it takes to be highest.

Every form of life secretes problematic aspects of limitedness, and this is true in distinct ways, Wolin acknowledges, of those that are called to specificity and place to the degree that democracy must be (even as it is by no means exclusively this). Hence, he writes in one of his most recent essays, "Local democracy's communal virtues are inseparable from the vices of parochialism."[118] Local tending tends to cultivate an attention to a set of specificities that can occlude (and thus remain or become complicit in) a host of other problematic issues. For this reason (echoing his call for the entwinement of "local centrifugals" and "postmodern centripetals"

117. Wolin, "Political Theory: From Vocation to Invocation," 5.

118. Wolin, "Agitated Times," 10.

we discussed above) the multiple civic selves of labyrinthine democracy, are called to also enact and become capacious toward "agitation as mass protest, raucous demonstration, street theater with jarring rhythms, cacophonies that contrast yet complement the slower tempos of parochial politics, directing local attention to broader, more transcending issues of war, peace, environment, and social justice—issues that are beyond the competence of local powers yet demand the attention of citizens who, by definition, are simultaneously local and national [*and clearly transnational!*]."[119] Human beings are called to work across a variety of levels and this can diminish the deleterious effects of each one considered alone. Yet this does not prevent the effects of those specific levels, issues, and problems in which we find our finite selves most invested from engendering the deeply problematic myopias that are "inseparable" from their exercise. Because none of us is nearly infinite enough to rise beyond these limits, we become in spite of ourselves inhospitable to all sorts of important concerns. Hence we are in need of agitations not only emerging from the multiplicities we embrace, but also from *others*, recalling what has been diminished by the finitude of our commitments and affections. Political theory of even a radically democratic polity would thus have always to remain significantly "invocation" as well as "vocation."

This can be seen from another angle in Wolin's allusion to the paradoxical undersides of the principles inherent in any radical-democratic ethos. However much radical democracy seeks to become isonomic inclusion and tending, it can never wholly avoid creating space for and inadvertently nurturing its opposite. Thus democracy partly involves invoking and seeking renewal in the face of the memory of democratic losses that emerged from past democratic moments: "Without necessarily intending it, [ordinary individuals engaged in radical-democratic initiatives] are renewing the political by contesting the forms of unequal power that democratic liberty and equality have made possible and that democracy can eliminate only by betraying its own values."[120] Democracy can never be simply vocation, because some of the values that its vocation will not allow it to betray (e.g., a great space for liberty partly because this is a condition of its own emergent character) nevertheless make possible developments that will themselves betray it. Hence democracy is inher-

119. Ibid. Brackets mine.
120. Wolin, "Fugitive Democracy," 44. Brackets mine.

ently entwined with its own betrayal in a manner that requires it to tend to the world also as invocation: becoming aware and seeking to renew itself in the face of loss from which it can never entirely free itself—losses that give its futurity an ineliminable retrospective dimension even under the best conditions, let alone those conditions that are far more hostile to it.

For all these reasons and more, the radical-democratic ordinary is inherently tensional in a way that not only opposes antidemocratic powers that transcend it, but is endlessly agonistic in relation to itself. The ordinary "affirms the value of limits" in ways that both oppose superpower and impede encroaching aspects of other sites within the multiplicity of the ordinary. Yet every particle of the ordinary, as already intimated above, *is itself in episodic need of interruption.* Hence Wolin theorizes demonstrations as a crucial condition of "unincorporated politics," which as we've seen even in relation to local radical-democratic practices, must "disrupt the ordinary tempos."[121] Democratic time must always be in no small part "agitated time," in the sense that it is the time of vocation *and* invocation, tending retroactively, in part, to wounds it has helped inflict in its own flesh in spite of itself.

And as goes democracy, so goes democratic theory, which similarly has its investments, parochialisms, and liberties that inadvertently nurture damages democratic theory illumines primarily in retrospective light. A world in which democracy has a fugitive character that no refinement of tending and inclusion could *entirely* dispel—a world in which in fact, anyhow, democracy has endured in strangely episodic fashion across centuries that have been largely radically *anti-*democratic—is one in which *theory too is and must be fugitive.* This is implied by the tension between vocation and invocation, by the need for strife between theoretical projects, but also by Wolin's sense of "agitation" that is central not only to his most recent work but also to "Political Theory as a Vocation" and many works in between.

Looking back to "Political Theory as a Vocation," we see the extent to which choosing a theory is an epic endeavor involving significant sacrifice: it involves cultivating perceptions, affections, emotions, habits, relationships, political involvements, cognitions, in ways that are always costly to alternative modes, even as some are far more costly than others.

121. Wolin, "Agitated Times," 2.

"Agitation," thus, is never that which ought to simply occur between different theories lodged within the universe of scholarly activity. When Wolin writes of how particular *political* investments are entwined with "different character, sensibilities, and tempos—'set in [their] ways'" that become "inhospitable to agitation," he could easily be writing of *theory*. Theorists are called to generate agitation within and between themselves. But this will never be enough, given the depth and extent of the existential-political investments with which theory sweeps us up. Hence theory too requires the "jarring rhythms and cacophonies" of political forms of life that are different from the life of the desk, the laptop, the seminar, the conference, etc. This may take many forms, from the ways in which various modes of local political tending jar certain abstracting secretions of theory, to the ways in which literally agitating "mass protest, raucous demonstrations, street theater" and the like, also send reverberations through our bodies that similarly unsettle our frames and commitments. This implies an injunction toward radical-democratic political engagement as a condition of theory's own possibility, and of two kinds: On the one hand, it implies an injunction that political theorists cultivate political practices that facilitate reflective work at the limits of themselves and the political ethos and practices in which they find themselves most deeply invested. On the other hand (and often relatedly) it implies the injunction to cultivate more capacious, receptive, and discerning relations with agitations that come from others—in spite of so much within each of us that resists this. One of Wolin's persistent ideas is that theory, like the political, is so often—perhaps even most often—awakened in no small part from without.

Recall that Wolin concludes "Politics as a Vocation" with a questioning hope regarding the "Panglossian Twilight" of methodism: "Is it possible that . . . Minerva's owl is beginning to falter as it speeds over a real world that is increasingly discordant and is beginning to voice demands and hopes that are 'unreasonably high'? Perhaps it is possible, especially if we remember that in Greek statuary Minerva's pet was a screech-owl, for a screech is the noise both of warning and of pain."[122] Recall again, too, how Wolin writes of *his own* awakening as a radical-democratic *theorist* in the midst of engaging in and witnessing radical-democratic body *politics*: "The intensity of the experience . . . changed everyone involved. For

122. Wolin, "Politics as a Vocation," 75. Brackets mine.

many of us it was the experience of moving from an apolitical to a deeply political existence, from a protected status with known boundaries to a condition that was risky and unfamiliar."[123]

Yet if Wolin calls political theorists toward the indispensability of political engagement—both for radical democracy and for democratic theory—it would be a grave mistake to view this as a *reduction* of theory to the demands of present engagement. Certainly tending to the present is *part* of its vocation. Yet the tragic finitude of these demands calls it endlessly to engage these through strategies of invocation, searching across the centuries for the expression of damages and possibilities that might enable present political initiatives to enhance their awareness of their limits and move with a wild patience beyond what stifles flourishing in the present. Such invocations are fundamentally contested projects, and invocation as such brings it into relations of solidarity that are always difficult and not infrequently unwanted.

Radical-democratic theorists can thus quite often be uneasy and troubling allies in the radical-democratic engagements and tending that are indispensable conditions of possibility for their own thinking—let alone for a world in which they might with others endure and flourish more broadly. Hence, no small part of what is heroinic about the epic theory to which Wolin gives such profound expression is its proclamation of profound and ongoing indebtedness to radical-democratic initiatives that themselves only rarely express more than episodic (often retrospective) appreciation for the agonistic contributions of theorists. Perhaps—difficult as it is—this is precisely as it should be. The uneasiness in this relationship is among the most vital conditions of flourishing radical-democratic formations, even as this uneasiness threatens to damage the relationship in ways that can rip asunder the gifts of receptive generosity such communities can give.

---

123. Wolin, "A Look Back."

CHAPTER 7

The Pregnant Reticence of Rowan Williams:
Letter of February 27, 2006, and May 2007

Romand Coles

February 27, 2006, and May 2007

Dear Stanley,

I see several possibilities and questions emerging in light of Rowan
Williams's work, which I want to explore here in relation to issues of
bodies and edges of engagement that have been a locus of our conversations. I am concerned with questions of how we might better acknowledge and live the edges and overlaps across historical time and space.
Writers like Williams—along with Yoder, Wolin, and others—show us
that our modes of engaging our historical inheritance and our modes
of engaging social spaces are deeply intertwined with and generative of
each other (or mutually *de*generative, as the case may be). I am interested
in ways that Williams's work would have Christians practicing church
and "discovering Christ in one another" (where "one another" includes
discovering Christ in non-Christians as well as Christians) in ways that
deepen themes I find so compelling in Yoder.[1] Indeed, it seems to me
that Williams's reading of Christ's trial, cross, and resurrection addresses
quite profoundly many of the concerns I raised at the end of my essay
on Yoder.[2] In so doing, he offers a set of stories (or *stories of stories* of

1. The phrase "discovering Christ in one another" is, of course, Williams's subtitle to
Where God Happens, which I am intonating toward somewhat different margins than
Williams is generally engaging in that text, even as these are central concerns in many of
his other writings.

2. See Coles, "Wild Patience of John Howard Yoder," chapter 4 in *Beyond Gated*

Jesus) that ought to inspire, animate, and inform non-Christian as well as Christian radical democrats. Or, at any rate, they leave me with the question: *How could they not?* Indeed, might they not do so in a manner that intensifies the haunted experience I evoked in relation to Yoder? Being haunted does not extinguish the spirit of critique. Hence, I am moved *by* Williams perhaps *beyond* some of his formulations that I still find problematic. It seems to me that Jean Vanier offers his light and flesh to these problems in ways that are consonant with and advance further what I think is most compelling in Williams, as I suggest in my reading of Vanier's work on the gospel of John and the practices at L'Arche that are entwined with it.[3] And so, with each critical engagement, I keep rediscovering the ghosts not at a more comfortable distance but in ever more vivid and uncanny proximity.

~

Let me briefly situate this claim about the "vivid and uncanny" (referring to ways in which Williams and Vanier appear to be whispering in my ear and pulling me by the arm in ways that are at once where I am wanting to go and yet at the same time coming from an entirely unexpected direction) in relation to my infatuation with M. M. Bakhtin and the passage of his that I have mentioned many times in our seminar, conversations, and letters:

> One must not . . . imagine the realm of culture as some sort of spatial whole, having boundaries but also having internal territory. The realm of culture has no internal territory; it is entirely distributed along the boundaries, boundaries pass everywhere, through its every aspect, the systematic unity of a culture extends into the very atoms of cultural life, it reflects the sun in each drop of that life. Every cultural act lives essentially on the boundaries: in this is its seriousness and significance; abstracted from boundaries it loses its soil, it becomes empty, arrogant, it degenerates and dies.[4]

I think it is clear that the claims here are *both* normative and descriptive—the normative being especially clear in relation to Bakhtin's discussion of novels (exemplified by Dostoevsky, who refuses to silence

---

Politics, 109–38.

3. See chapter 9 below.

4. Bakhtin, *Problems of Dostoevsky's Poetics*, 301.

or kill off the disagreeable characters who populate his writing, with all their difficult edges). "One must not imagine the realm of culture . . ." expresses Bakhtin's sense of how pivotal our cultural imaginations are in determining the ways in and degrees to which cultures might be generative of life, light, and fullness, and the ways in and degrees to which they might not. Hence he lodges a fundamental injunction in relation to the way we imagine cultural being as such. Bakhtin enjoins us to form our cultures in deepening awareness that if we imagine them as internal territories abstracted from their boundaries, they (and we) will "lose their [and our] soil, become empty, arrogant, degenerate and die" (or live as death-giving). In contrast, those who would take up the task of dwelling vulnerably at the edges—those who would gather in recognition that "boundaries pass everywhere, through every aspect" might engender a tensional "significance" and "seriousness." When he says, "every cultural act lives essentially on the boundaries," I take this literally and prescriptively: where there is life-giving, there is vulnerable exposure to the difficult edges of life. Following the theme of light, we might read Bakhtin's thought that "the systematic unity of culture [as exposed, tensional, and vulnerable edge-dwelling] extends into the very atoms . . . reflects like the sun in each drop of that life" to mean that those who seek light through the imagination of a protected interior will extinguish it. Those who would seek light by renouncing it as an interior, fortressed possession might engage in lighting up "like the sun in each drop of that life."

We know that Bakhtin seems to have gleaned these themes in relation to an idiosyncratic quilting of Eastern Orthodox Christianity and Marxism (explored by the soon-to-be-banned group "Resurrection," to which he belonged in the 1920s), as well as Russian literature, Buber, Kierkegaard, and others.[5] His work is *endlessly suggestive* (but also *merely* so—for reasons that likely had to do with the censorship and punishment to which Bakhtin was subjected) in terms of its ethico-political significance. Yet a powerful case can be made that Williams's reading of Christ's trial, cross, and resurrection provides one of the most compelling—and one might even say *radicalizing*—articulations of a rendering of Christianity in Bakhtinian tones.

≈

5. See Todorov, *Mikhail Bakhtin: The Dialogical Principle.*

I read Williams's *Christ on Trial: How the Gospel Unsettles our Judgment* as one of the most profound, probing, and undeniably *unsettling* accounts of what it might mean to cultivate traditions of association that repeatedly strive toward a vulnerable and generous edge, eschewing interior territory as a locus of transcendent monological control over time and space. Williams renders each of the Gospels in a way that brings to life how Christ's trial, or *experimentum crucis*, undoes or erodes our confidence in, sense of, and most especially our yearning for an inside (of self, of church, of tradition, of group) that would transcend edge-dwelling; an inside where things are assured, unquestionable, pure, where the distinctions between one's "own" and the others are unequivocal, where there is assurance of being right, true, good—in contrast to *them*.

I think this has everything to do with the question of the emergent complexity of the "radical ordinary," and here I see Williams drawing very close to Wolin. It is no coincidence that "ordinary life" finds its way into the very first sentence of *Christ on Trial*, or that it finds important articulation later in the text (to which I return at the end of this chapter). Williams imagines the trials of ordinary life as unsettling situations calling us to seek to "find out the truth" in surprising manifestations.[6] We too often flee these trials. The stories of Christ's extraordinary trials call us to engage our more ordinary trials in the most profound sense, *even as our capacity in turn to see and to understand Christ's trials itself stems largely from how we engage the difficulties in our own ordinary lives from day to day.* "Moral life is a process in which we shall find out truths about ourselves. The difficult, non-negotiable aspects of being human . . . have a capacity to tell us things—often unwelcome things—about who or what we are" (*CT* x). In other words, moral life is elaborated in relation to the complexity of the ordinary, not by fleeing to an imagined interior of, say, a subjectivity, moral law, or revelation, where things are simple and transparent. The gospel calls us to the stations of the cross in ordinary and extraordinary life, and from these stations we are better able to hear the gospel and begin to discern. To put it more strongly: we cannot hear the gospel except by tending to the difficulties and differences of the ordinary—to which it in turn calls us. The ordinary is where we meet up with Jesus, and he is more profoundly nowhere else.

6. Williams, *Christ on Trial*, ix. Hereafter cited in text as *CT*.

The task, then, is to cultivate a community in relation to the memory of Christ's trial, cross, and resurrection such that Christians might gradually conform themselves to his generous and vulnerable cultivation of becoming, at and through the edges of life rather than in a mythic transcendence of them. The task is to become a community and selves seeking strange flourishing in the potentially virtuous circular relations between the ways in which we live *temporal* edges in deepening remembrance of Christ, on the one hand, and the ways we dwell with social *spatial* edges, on the other, as we discover more cruciform possibilities in the present, possibilities that better enable us to see Christ.

When we were reading Williams in our seminar, Stanley, you asked me whether I think Rowan Williams is saying anything that Yoder doesn't also say or think. I think the answer to that question may be "probably not," or, "precious little." But what if we seek the difference Williams makes in a different way? What if we seek it not in what Williams *says* over and beyond what Yoder says, but rather significantly *in what he does not say?* What if, in other words, Williams's distinction rests in a tenacious restraint, a pushing away in relation to what Yoder will more often proclaim? What if Williams's difference is a certain silence?

That silence is a key theme for Williams is clearly indicated by the fact that he begins and frames his discussion in *Christ on Trial* with the Gospel of Mark, in which he reads the central motif to be that "Jesus knows more than he can say; he is like a naturally gifted musician trying to explain to slow or even tone-deaf listeners how basic harmony works. And when the transforming power of his presence breaks through in healing, he hurries to forbid people to talk about it. *It is as if he knows they will only find the wrong words, the wrong categories*" (CT 2, my emphasis). Working toward the radically vulnerable generosity of Christ on trial, Williams writes:

> Throughout the Gospel, Jesus holds back from revealing who he is because, it seems, he cannot believe that there are words that will tell the truth about him in the mouths of others. What will be said of him is bound to be untrue—that he is master of all circumstances; that he can heal where he wills; that he is the expected triumphant deliverer. . . . *There is a kind of truth which, when it is said, becomes untrue . . .* [In a world of demons and suffering and abused power] whatever is said will take on the colouring of the world's insanity; it will be another bid for the world's power,

another identification with the unaccountable tyrannies that decide how things shall be. *Jesus, described in the words of this world, would be a competitor for space in it, part of its untruth.* (*CT* 6, my emphasis)

In other words, our language has been repeatedly forged in a world striving for mastery over space—territorial hegemony in which fortresses are established to defend the illusion of "internal territories" where we would dwell secure, remote from and unaccountable to others at the vulnerable edges that surround us and "pass everywhere, through [our] every aspect." Hence language born of and entwined with such practices (and who would be free of them?) very frequently twists even our best-intentioned proclamations that "another world is possible" in ways that reinscribe the morass we are trying to transform. Let us risk putting it more strongly: It is not merely that with such language we build fortresses to master and defend space; it is that we constitute the illusory spatiality of "world" as fortressed space. It is not just that we misdescribe space with our words. Rather our language and the space of illusion called "world," or "principalities and powers," are born twins. To become more deeply aware of this is to feel the necessity for arts of expressive silence in which other possibilities—which are always and everywhere underway in our places and words—might be acknowledged, nurtured, given expression.

We tenaciously tend to assimilate God's "transcendence" to some notion of "what *we* mean by greatness"—some notion of omnipotence governing, or even saturating, history and topography from a throne on high that would be the condition of this history and space. Thus, Jesus can only really speak (in a way that might be more genuinely heard) in front of the High Priest, where he is utterly bereft of unaccountable power and the categories associated with it: "God's 'I am' can only be heard for what it really is when it has no trace of human power left to it . . . when it is spoken by a captive under sentence of death" (*CT* 7). With unrelenting intensity, Williams writes: "either we see that the whole story of Mark's Gospel leads here, to this restored silence, or we abandon the attempt to make any sense of it" (*CT* 8). Only here can Jesus' words radically refashion our understanding, and after this he falls silent. Precisely in the image of the victim without worldly power, Williams suggests in *Resurrection*, we can see most clearly the shape and possibilities of "creative action."[7]

7. Williams, *Resurrection*, 15. Hereafter cited in the text as *R*.

Far from mastery, it is only by turning toward Jesus' "I am" in the sheer absence of territorial power that we can begin to see salvation in another quality of power characterized by "a willingness to *receive* from those we have imagined have nothing to give" (*R* 17, Williams's emphasis).

Of course, what words could better signify the heart and work of John Howard Yoder? And yet perhaps a certain distinction remains in a certain *not saying*. Yoder frequently employs and thus takes risks with words like "Lordship," "Victory," "Kingdom," "only," and so forth, that perhaps exert a certain pull toward territoriality in spite of Yoder's best efforts to hammer them toward new nonconstantinian meanings. Perhaps even "Lordship of the Lamb" might leave traces of territorial taste? I have heard many (not all) peacemaking "Yoderians" in my classes speak in ways that sometimes raise my suspicions thus, in spite of denials that follow when I voice such concerns. At any rate, Williams wonders whether terms such as these in most contexts might not feed our desire to think of God as the exemplar of our images of grandeur (even if significantly but insufficiently transformed in peacemaking garb): "God becomes the illustration of what is highest or strongest for us," whereas the one who says "I am" appears "neither wise, nor holy, neither admirable nor impressive." Jesus thus calls us to a silence in an awareness that we have had "our careful and exact expectations overturned" (*CT* 9). The challenge is, how to communicate this silence? Williams follows Jesus to suggest that learning arts of silence is an integral aspect of a more hopeful communication that grows through awareness that "*there is a kind of truth which, when it is said, becomes untrue.*" Hence Williams will speak in ways that negate some of the profoundest impulses of even many peacemaking Christians: "*At this moment*, God is *not* and can*not* be what guarantees success or provides a convincing explanation of the strange behaviour of those who refuse the world's ways . . . there can be *no* simple assurance of final victory" (*CT* 12–13, my emphasis).

Of course, Williams in so many places proclaims that the truth of resurrection is that violence and "betrayal is *not* the ultimate fact in the world"—*not* final (*R* 41–42, my emphasis). The negation is crucial both for what it says and for what it does not say. It denies the finality of territorial competitiveness, or that topography *as such* must be constituted through such territoriality. There is another way. Yet what we see in the incarnation of Jesus is not the *object* of our hope (an ordered and secure topography in the form of his resurrected body) but the vulnerable *way* of radical hope (in which his body is disordered in crucifixion and is disordered in new ways with his resurrection). The expressive presence of his resurrected body silently confounds our sense of the objective order of things: he appears when least expected, first to the least; his body has disruptive holes in it into which he calls those who doubt; he gives himself to be eaten; he exits closed tombs and enters rooms with closed doors; he repeatedly confounds our most fundamental senses of temporality. On Williams's reading, we misread Mark if we understand Jesus as assuring us with historical guarantees—even eschatological guarantees, for such assurances self-destruct precisely in being said, *or even in being thought or believed*, in the wrong ways at the wrong times. If *this moment* of Christ's most radical, speechless vulnerability does not reconstitute Christians through and through and even in what they say, they will surely lose the way. And perhaps so will any radical-democratic "we." If victory—even eschatological victory—is imagined as a mode of expressive being in space and time (space and time that would finally pass beyond the vulnerable "border at the core"), Williams seems to be suggesting, then we will have fallen far short of the radical character of Mark's gospel.

Of course, we are tempted through the end of the gospel to forget: to forget that Christ, who says he will save those who believe in him, is calling people to a way of expressive dwelling beyond the competitive modes that would securely constitute space and time by seeking to transcend the immanent vulnerabilities they present. He is not, nor is he calling people to be, a body-object that would rise invulnerably above these. This way is beyond our concept of an *object* that has been *made* by a fixed law. Rather "Jesus grants us a solid identity, yet refuses us the power to 'seal' or finalize it, and obliges us to realize that this identity only exists in an endless responsiveness to new encounters with him in a world of unredeemed relationships" (*R* 84). Beyond territorial spatiality, in Jesus' life, "the human map is being redrawn, the world turned upside down" (*CT* 52). Jesus' good news is that he "interrupts and reorganizes the landscape in ways that are not predictable" (*CT* 40). He does so not as a simple reversal; rather, he "threatens because he does not compete . . . and because it is that whole world of rivalry and defense which is in question"(*CT* 69). In this sense, the "unworldliness" of Christ's kingdom is "a way of saying 'yes' to the world by refusing the world's own skewed and destructive account of itself" (*CT* 88). To "let the world be the world," then, would be to aspire to participate in engendering histories and places that cohere as gift through the ligatures of undulating receptive relationships rather than the immutability of law. This is a torn, but by no means hopeless, call.

If Williams sometimes moves beyond Yoder here, it is perhaps only in the way that he infuses mission with a certain silence, evangelism with recursive turns. Perhaps in the weight and also the buoyancy of a quietude, the radical curvatures and pregnant reticence of his rhetorical paths. The crucial theme in Williams's chapter on Mark is that how, when, and where things are *not* said, or said negatively, is every bit as (or more) important to the meaning and import of the Gospel as what is said affirmatively. "Either we see that the whole story of [Coles's reading of Williams's reading of] Mark's Gospel leads here, to this restored silence, or we abandon the attempt to make any sense of it" (*CT* 8).

In a wonderful passage in *Resurrection*, Williams contends that what most compels trust is how Christian contemplatives

> constantly bring before us the fact that Christian speech is *for ever* entering into and re-emerging from inarticulacy. This is not one moment of dumbness or loss followed by fluency, but an unending flow back and forth between speech and silence; and if at each stage the silence and the loss and emptiness become deeper and more painful, so at each stage the recovered language is both more spare and more richly charged, . . . When Christian speech is healthy, it does not allow itself an over-familiarity with a taking for granted of its images—its Scriptures, its art, its liturgy; it is prepared to draw back to allow them to be "strange," questioning and questionable. (*R* 73)[8]

Perfect. Yet let us explore the fluency—the spare and richly charged speech—side of this oscillation in order to gain a fuller sense of Williams's evocation of the transformation of the world announced and performed by Jesus. For this we must turn to Williams's reading of Matthew's Jesus, which overflows with talking and telling (as do significant portions of his readings of Luke and John). Matthew relentlessly makes abundant connections: "seeing whole what most people see in fragments" (*CT* 26). Yet the whole is not akin to the highest or the greatest human expectations that Williams warns us about in his reading of Mark. Rather, his connec-

8. One finds a more extended meditation on this theme in Williams, *Wound of Knowledge*. For an enactment in response to 9/11, see Williams, *Writing in the Dust*.

tions are unfathomably strange, starting from the family tree, which is interrupted "four times by allusion to the unimpressive or disreputable outsiders—namely the women . . . either foreign, immoral or both" (*CT* 27). God's work appears precisely through this interruption of the patriarchical order—an "enormous divine joke: this is not a family tree at all, because Mary's child is of God, not Joseph the son of David" (*CT* 28). Matthew's connections will rarely if ever bolster the security and assurance of insiders but rather call them to question what they thought was theirs. The questioning in Matthew, however, takes less the form of showing how *little* truth is within and before a people, and more a form of *how much*: how much has been right under our noses and yet utterly unacknowledged. If Mark might emphasize a certain lack, Matthew emphasizes abundance. Hence "the ability to *recognize*, which is crucial to living in Wisdom, is likely to show itself most clearly when connections are made between improbable things and persons" (*CT* 41). Fragmented wisdom, *Shekhinah*, is teeming right before us, "the most fundamental thing, yet hardest to recognize" (*CT* 44).[9]

This theme receives a most powerful discussion in Williams's analysis of Luke, an analysis throughout which rings the pivotal insight that, "*God is in the connections we cannot make*" (*CT* 56, my emphasis): the outsiders, remainders, those who do not belong officially to our order yet are everywhere swarming—in the garden, on the road, on the border at the core. Now if Mark is concerned about how language profoundly risks and conceals what it would reveal, Matthew develops this insight in terms of social practices, traditions, hierarchies, and identities that systematize such oblivion in order to secure a sense of boundaries: "What if I became incapable of telling truth from falsehood? What if the maintenance of my religious identity became a weapon against God?" (*CT* 35). "Matthew's narrative does not allow the believer—in particular the articulate and educated believer, the teacher, the expert—any fixed answer to the question of how I might know that I am still with Jesus rather than with Caiaphas. As soon as there seems to be an answer to such a question, it becomes part of just that system of religious words and religious fluency that helps to make possible the exclusion of Jesus" (*CT* 36). The objective of the

9. From Jewish mysticism: "The *Shekhinah*, the presence of God, which is identified with God's wisdom, is fragmented at the creation of the world. Broken into scattered sparks of living truth, it is buried deep in the texture of the material order, hidden in the lives of surprising people, buried deep" (*CT* 43).

church community should rather be to free ourselves "from an attitude ... of *ownership* where the words and images of faith are concerned" (*CT* 40, Williams's emphasis).

Exemplary of this dispossessive maneuver is Williams's reading of Acts 4:12, where "only in Jesus is there salvation" often has been tragically taken as a consummate expression of a Christian monopoly on truth (odd, given that Acts 4 is a text on dispossession if ever there was one). Instead Williams emphasizes that far from being a "justification of fierce Christian exclusivism" that would legitimate condemning unbelievers, these words are said to those in the court who *condemned Christ as un-faithful.* The apostles are saying that the condemners can *only* find reconciliation in difficult relation with their specific victim (thus the word *only* is turned inside out). The dispossessive truth is that there is no salvation that can "bypass the history and memory of guilt [inflicted by those seeking mastery over a community they take as their exclusive possession], but rather builds upon and from it" (*R* 12, brackets mine).

Beyond our sense of the "true world" as a secure possession, Williams enjoins that we cultivate dispositions for sensing that Wisdom "interrupts and reorganizes the landscape in ways that are not predictable" (*CT* 40); that the "ability to *recognize*, which is so crucial to living Wisdom, is likely to show itself most clearly when connections are made between improbable things and persons" (*CT* 41). In contrast to those who worry that Williams may be entirely jettisoning order here, I think his point is that beyond reified order we can participate in fragile yet rich order-as-becoming, through receptivity and generosity that is the very substance and movement of the triune God. It is *our* sense of order, not God's, that Williams is rendering problematic. Williams describes the alternative possibility for understanding and participating in the ongoing event of (re)creation like this:

> [Resurrection] is an event which is not describable, because it is precisely there that there occurs the transfiguring expansion of Jesus's humanity which is the heart of the resurrection encounters. It is an event on the frontier of any possible language, because it is the moment in which our speech is both left behind and opened to new possibilities. It is as indescribable as the process of imaginative fusion which produces any metaphor; and the evangelists withdraw as well they might. (*R* 97)

I have been arguing that Williams reads Jesus to suggest a new socio-political possibility beyond historical and spatial territoriality. Williams argues that at least insofar as friends of Jesus would follow his way, they would "inhabit that kingdom with no defenses, the kingdom which does not derive from the world." They would aspire to move beyond territoriality and become like "God [who] loves the world because that is God's nature—self-bestowal, self-sharing. The world's refusal and nonrecognition of this establishes the boundary that makes the world an enclosed system hostile to God and hostile to anyone who does not play by the rules of rivalry" (*CT* 88, my emphasis). Easy to say. Yet nearly impossible to think or begin to imagine what it might call us to do, this "way of saying 'yes' to the world by refusing the world's own skewed and destructive account of itself" (*CT* 88). And insofar as this "yes" is unimaginable, would it not continually be drawn up and deployed as an excuse, a ticket to lord it over those others who are wholly responsible for "rivalry," with their alien "no's"? And how is a "refusal" to be distinguished from a "no" that would lord it over those who and that which it "negates"?

Let me intensify this questioning by returning to a passage from the introduction of this book:

> "Not competitors for space in this world" is a difficult aspiration for human beings, not simply because we are fallible or fallen but also because an ineliminable aspect of what we think it means to live well in this world is to have enemies, to name and struggle against the bad and sometimes the evil. This does not mean "demonizing," nor should "enemy" be ascribed as an immutable label. Nevertheless, insofar as a person or group struggles against particular practices or persons, there is a profound sense in which we are always competitors *against* particular patterns of territoriality. Yet does it follow from this that competitors *against* must be competitors *for* new modes of dominating space in this world? With Williams we would *aspire* toward new modes of becoming communities that at once oppose territoriality and aim toward more receptive and generous practices of coexistence. This is a never perfectly achieved and never-ending task which will frequently err and always be in need of rethinking, reorganizing, and new beginnings informed by histories of such efforts in the past. It is a fine line—a fine edge—this distinction between competing against and struggling for something that is beyond the logic of competition. We frequently (and, to some extent, likely always)

confuse one side of the line with the other, and often we even become invested in and systematize such confusions to the benefit
of new conquests.[10]

How might we resist this?

There are no abstract ways to entirely avoid the delusions that
swarm the aspiration toward a "yes" beyond competitive territoriality.
Yet there are a number of specific ethical and political practices that
Williams suggests, and I think they go a good distance to (dis)orienting
any communities striving to resist such delusions. First, middle, and last,
Williams enjoins us to keep alive penitent senses of our histories. Our
histories are *not* that of the "pure victim Christ": we should not locate *our*
identity there. We should not story ourselves primarily as an excluded
minority church or other group, while marginalizing the myriad ways
we ourselves—whoever we are—have been implicated as perpetrators
of as yet unreconciled violence.[11] Again and again, Williams writes
that "Christ will always be in exile, a refugee, in a world constrained by
endless struggles for advantage, where success lies always in establishing
your position at the expense of another's" (*CT* 45). Those who struggle
to remain with Jesus depart from him exactly to the extent that they
forget the ways he is an exile and refugee from *their* communities and
efforts, as well as from those communities from whom they themselves
have suffered. Such forgetting is the beginning of rivalry. The kenotic self-
forgetting, self-emptying—but also new wealth—to which Jesus would
call us hinges on not possessing him in whose name we would move
beyond being competitors in this world. We must maintain penitent
memories of ourselves and our communities in order to engender the
capacities for self-emptying requisite for *caritas*.

Related to this, Williams provides two images of church practice that
I think are particularly powerful for their evocation of what a nonterritorial mode of becoming community might look like. The first image concerns what could be described in terms of the character of those explicitly
committed to belonging to and associating as the body of Christ:

10. See pages 15–16 above. My emphasis.

11. Joseph Wiebe makes an insightful case for this in his reading of Rowan Williams
in Wiebe, "Inheriting John Howard Yoder: A New Generation Examines his Thought."
Wiebe contends that Williams pushes this idea and practice farther and more consistently than did Yoder and many Mennonites.

The late Dom Hubert van Zeller of Downside Abbey told the delightful story of a North Welsh convent where the garden gate had at some point in a chequered career been reversed—so that the side facing inward now read "Private" in large letters. The cloister was being warned to keep its distance from the privacy of the world. This reversal is no bad symbol of the necessary revisions in our understanding of peace. The "world," the unregenerate, uncritical life of most human societies, is the place of private, isolated existence, fear of facing the cost of decision and involvement—haunted by the fantasy of "peace" . . . withdrawal . . . shrink from tension. . . . In contrast, the cloister abandons privacy for a solitude which forces people to confront their fear and evasiveness and so equips them for involvement by stripping-down of the will. . . . It is a lifestyle which at one level *invites* conflict [beyond self-protection and self-gratification], the conflict of which the rest of society is afraid, in order to allow a more truthful and courageous humanity to emerge. And the peace of the cloister lies in and through this particular battle.[12]

In this light, the church would seek ways beyond the illusions of territoriality not only by refusing conquest of "peace" through empire but also by refusing strategies to secure "peace" by withdrawing from tension (or what Yoder might have called miniconstantinianisms). Church would thus be the practice of becoming a people equipped for generous involvement not only by becoming vulnerable but moreover *hospitable* to conflict. It would be a more genuinely "public" space, in which differences would be neither obliterated nor avoided but rather engaged as a tensional and generative source for learning how to live better together. This image suggests a divine "yes" to the world that involves not simply harmonies beyond the world's rivalries but also dissonances and tensions beyond such rivalries.

Of course, one way of conceptualizing the dissonances and tensions beyond the world's rivalries is to think of these tensions as a prelude to a more thoroughgoing peace-beyond-conflict, where there would be pure harmony, pure resolution of all dissonant differences. Only harmonious differences would thus remain. Yet why should Christians assume *that*? Since when and how did anyone come to know so much about God as to preclude dissonance-beyond-rivalry as part of God's deepest peace? Perhaps the will to imagine a final peace entirely beyond dissonance is

12. Williams, *Truce of God*, 63.

largely a projection by competitors for space in this world who yearn for freedom from tension? Williams offers us many reasons to suspect that this may be so. What if, beyond both competitive yearning for control and the competitive yearning for peace as pure harmony, Williams is suggesting the *possibility* that a more thoroughly Godlike peace might involve generative conflict and tension—but conflict and tension forged in generous receptivity among differences whose difficult divergences are part of their ongoing and evolving yet never-resolving gift to one another and to the world? What if this is a part of the gloriousness of God's creation? Perhaps the providential sign on the gate of the convent suggests precisely this possibility, and perhaps the practices of engaging tensional difference within the gates—that is, engaging the "borders at the core"—are not simply "transitional goods," if you will, but an aspect of Christ's eternal "yes," his ultimate reorganization of the world, his gift, his "conflict beyond competition"?

This distinction between generous tension and competitive territorial tension would be supremely difficult to discern, to be sure. Yet perhaps honing our judgment toward this edge might prove more fruitful than the likely more reductive and dangerous distinction between dissonance and harmony? I see no better image of community practices for cultivating such judgment in the day-to-day than the one Williams evokes in the name of a gate calling it to resist withdrawing from the tensions of difference into the security of a private "peace."

There is no doubt that Rowan Williams thinks that tension lived generously is the basic shape of all Christlike communities in history. Whether he has intended to raise the *question* (as I am perhaps stretching him to do?), whether this might not be a possible eschatological form of peace, of the "world upside down," I do not know. Yet given that eschatology is as such beyond all horizons of imagination, I do not see any reason to exclude, nay, even any reason not to *entertain* the possibility that this may be an aspect of peace in the deepest and highest senses? Perhaps this question might keep a more genuine faith with the "inarticulacy" from which and towards which all language discovers itself? Is it closer or farther from God to wonder this question and seek to live within it? Perhaps only those closer than I might judge well? Nevertheless, I would suggest that holding this open as a magnetic possibility might be crucial, at any rate, for living well in history precisely insofar as the yearning for peace beyond tension—even when couched as a vague eschatological fantasy—threatens to erode the very peacemaking-as-tension that is at the heart of the body of Christ recollected in a providential sign that radically transfigures the meaning of "gate" as well as what lies on either side.[13]

Williams's "gate"—his gated politics—is a gate that I could love. I could love Williams's "gate," significantly, because the difference that it nurtures engenders an excess beyond the gate that recalls Ani DiFranco's line that "enough is not enough without more."[14] And it is Williams himself who offers a profoundly suggestive vision of what this "more" might entail, which brings me to his second image of noncompetitive community. Williams's affirmation of tension-dwelling within the gates of the church leads him to proclaim that "the church is always renewed from the edges rather than from the center."[15] This affirmation in turn is

13. I think Williams's reading of the Trinity, in "Trinity and Pluralism" in *On Christian Theology* points in the direction suggested in these paragraphs. Drawing on Raimundo Panikkar's work, Williams conceives of the Trinitarian structure as "a source, inexhaustibly generative and *always* generative, from which arises form and determination . . . the source of all does not and cannot exhaust itself simply in producing shape and structure; it also produces that which dissolves and re-forms all structures in endless and undetermined movement" (167). From this Trinitarian vantage point, Williams argues that there can be no perspective outside plurality nor any legitimacy for fetishizing any particular state of unorganized plurality. Rather it calls Christians to "work on the basis of a 'christic' vision for the human good, engaging with adherents of other traditions without anxiety, defensiveness or proselytism" (170). As Williams unfolds the meaning of this further, he writes of cooperation, analogical perception, mutual nurture, and other harmonious tropes. *And* as he elaborates a "hopeful and creative pluralism," he writes of "mutual challenge" (174) and mutual "critical responsibility." This critical responsibility often takes the form of penitent "negations" (such as those discussed above), yet the critical eye toward "waste, cruelty or disorder" is mobile and challenges non-Christian others as well. Ultimately, that tension is a constitutive part of Trinitarian becoming is signaled not only in the relation between different groups but in the unfolding of Christianity in the midst of a heterogeneous world where Christians must, Williams maintains, "find God in the present tension between tradition and unforeseen possibilities . . . this endlessly self-corrective movement" (179). All this leads to a radical suspension of eschatological imaging that is proximate, though perhaps not identical, with that which I seek to hold open in a specific and ethically important way with the question I raise above. Williams affirmatively quotes Panikkar that beyond the present patterns of Trinitarian christic practice: "What it *will* finally be is not something theory will tell us, but something only discoverable in the expanding circles of encounter with what is not the Church" (180).

14. Ani DiFranco, "Whatall is Nice." *Reveling/Reckoning*, Righteous Babe Records, 2001.

15. Williams, *Where God Happens*, 111. I take it that the deeper call in this sentence is to realize that there is no "center" of tension-free church space but rather "border at the core," in Bakhtin's sense.

entwined with a sense that for the reverse-signed gate not to undermine the church, a more genuine polis, it must acquire a porosity, perhaps even a mobility that acquires a certain power of its own. I am almost tempted to imagine something like a turnstile that somewhat unpredictably spins people out and pulls people in, in ways that make possible cooperation, pluralized hopes, and unwonted relations—and further undulate the "exterior" edges of the church. Williams argues that the church must be "a life endlessly sensitive, contemplatively alert to human personal and cultural diversity, tirelessly seeking new horizons in its own experience and understanding by engaging with this diversity" (R 63). He is clear that within the reverse-gated church there must be liturgies for believers that deepen the possibility of the church's becoming a polis in the senses we have been discussing. Yet alongside and related to these senses of polis, Williams calls for church experimentation that aims to "develop what have been clumsily dubbed 'para-liturgies'—corporate symbolic actions which do not so deeply presuppose the kind of symbolic identification involved in the Eucharist, yet still open up some of the resources of Christian imagination to the uncommitted." In so doing, the church might not dilute the life of the resurrection gospel, but show itself more deeply to be "the Church of *Jesus*" (R 68–69). I think the language of "corporate" and the emphasis on *Jesus* are key here.

In other words, Williams is suggesting that the edge between the church and nonbelievers has an essentially ambiguous character. On the one hand, there are liturgies for the committed, which form the more typically recognized body of Christ. Yet it is the character of *this body* to form as well more "penumbral" edges *with* outsiders: an edge that is of indeterminate width (formed through various corporeal symbolic relations with nonbelievers such that the flesh of Jesus extends beyond the committed and is *realized* rather than *corrupted* in so doing) and more indeterminate lighting. Like the penumbral light of a partial solar eclipse—where some of the sun's rays are blocked by the moon while some light arrives on earth to form a distinctly muted and surreal illumination—some of the light of the church extends beyond the body of believers into the penumbral edge in varying ways and degrees, mixing with other lights and with shadow. As the sun's penumbral illumination of the earth during a partial eclipse is not well-described as "lesser," so Williams suggests it is possible to imagine and practice intercorporeal illumination between the church "proper" and nonbelievers, such that there is actually a supplemental *en-*

hancement of the light breaking forth from the church of *Jesus*. Rather than a rare episodic event however, penumbral flesh would be elemental and constitutive of the body of Christ. In this sense, it might perhaps be better to speak of the "Christ*ec*centric" more than the Christocentric, the "Christ*a*logical" more than the Christological, and the "Cruc*a*form" more than the Cruciform. Or so it would seem to one who knows little of such things.

Williams explores this theme further in *The Truce of God*, where he joins Metropolitan Paulos Gregorios in suggesting the need for

> the stimulus of some quite new kinds of community. . . . There is today an urgent need for an interdisciplinary, intercultural, inter-religious community of mature, capable, charismatic people who will live together . . . participate in the struggles of the community around them . . . ; evolve a way of life, a style of living in com-munity, with simplicity and spontaneity, not averse to produc-tive manual labour, not closed to the world outside, not afraid of poverty . . . not closed to the religious and cultural sensitivities of others in the community at large . . . embody a new spiritu-ality—*askesis*—based on prayer, meditation, worship, and sacra-mental life. . . .[16]

Williams concludes his discussion by again suggesting that the "truce of God" requires bodies that willfully blur their boundaries in order to become more, not less, cruciform: "If a community or communities like this came into being it would indeed—whatever its interreligious charac-ter—be a 'Church-like' phenomenon, suggesting models for the Christian future in particular as well as the human future in general."[17] Returning to the theme of the radical ordinary, Williams suggests that "a church which could depend upon and look to centres like this would be a far more effectively nourished body than one surviving only on a diet of hopes, statements, vaguely outlined visions (like this book)."[18]

A nourished body of Christ, like Christ, requires an extremely thick yet flexible, modulating, vulnerable, filamented, and porous (maybe even gelatinous?) membrane as the flesh that at once joins with and distin-guishes it from the world. It is a reflectively practiced incarnation of flesh

16. Williams, *Truce of God*, 126–27.

17. Ibid., 128.

18. Ibid.

as pregnant depth, which I have discussed elsewhere.[19] Such a flesh shows up unexpectedly, according to nonlinear times, a crucified and resurrected body with holes, seeking unlikely relations with the least and with the others well before the high priests who maintain religious identity as a "weapon against God."[20] Ultimately, the church is flesh through and through. The distinction we have made between the gated church and the paraliturgical church is itself an event of a flesh, which must precede the distinction, necessary though it is.

I have said that I could love the gate that Williams describes, the flesh that it is—flesh of turnstiles, flesh of porosity. Would not the turnstile—would not being *stuck* in the turnstile—revolving in and out on the threshold between the church and the other, the church *as* this relation to the other, the other *as* this relation to church—would not spinning here be the locus of a breathless—hyphenated—revolution with a distinct and important attraction? Perhaps. But such a location would be no less prone to the dangers of violence and oblivion than locations on either side. Neil Young gives penetrating expression of something akin to this danger in "For the Turnstiles":

> All the bushleague batters
> Are left to die
> On the diamond.[21]

Yet the hometown fans head "for the turnstiles." The turnstiles—these easy gates spinning people in and out—these are places where it is entirely too easy to exit whatever is damaging; too easy to exit whatever becomes difficult, and this ease includes even the difficult liturgical practices in which we might better learn to dwell in action or in stillness with difficulty.[22] Turnstiles can be an excuse to avoid tension as easily as they can be places where tastes and powers for living tension generously might be cultivated. The instant the turnstile becomes a fetish, a competitor for space, it probably becomes too little of anything—or too much of a

19. See my chapter on Merleau-Ponty, in Coles, *Self/Power/Other*, 99–169.

20. It is hard to fathom how profoundly transformative this statement is—especially coming from the archbishop of Canterbury. Williams wrote this prior to becoming archbishop, but his tune has not changed in this respect.

21. From *On the Beach*, 1974.

22. Most of the issues I raise about "turnstiles" here could be raised with respect to porosity, penumbra, and numerous other metaphors I have tossed into the mix.

"thing" to facilitate the traveling that it might otherwise help enable. The turnstile, too, requires a negative theology, or at least a negative dialectic. *Listening to Rowan Williams calling us to be still and to act with more wisdom in the midst of the radical ordinary is, for me, precisely such an effort.*

There is no theoretical way to "get this right." The only way to negotiate the multiple dangers and reap the possible harvests is to "make an art of ordinary living" (*CT* 108). At the heart of this art, Williams tells us, is learning to live without fear of the radical ordinary, learning a strange freedom from our relentless efforts to exit the challenges and gifts of the present by deepening the vortex of "the busy and frantic ego, trying to impose an individual will on the world" (*CT* 111). "Real life in Christ requires us to look death in the face—the little deaths of dishonesty and evasion as much as the great risks faith may run" (*CT* 116). And Thich Nhat Hanh would add: Real life in Buddha. And I would add: Real life in radical democracy. What converges here would be that "at the centre there is a displacement" of the frantic ego, and "that displacement is freedom" (*CT* 111). Yet "the hardest thing in the world is to be where we are." "Being where we are requires a formidable amount of switching off—of those very systems and stimuli that purport to make sense of the environment" (*CT* 89). We are called to learn at this station of the cross one day at a time, in pools of specific and often unexpected relationships.

And yet we are *also* called to struggle against large systems of organized cruelty in ways that could not be more urgent. Any urgent struggles that are not deeply informed by people engaged in the arts of the ordinary quickly go crazy. Yet all arts of the ordinary that read patience as an invitation to escape from the tasks of large struggles against the gargantuan and fast-moving whirls of destruction are likewise highways of delusion. It is among our most essential challenges to learn how better to combine these twin yet agonistic necessities. I suspect that whatever success we achieve will be fragile and temporary, for this intense edge is not a place any of us can inhabit for long. Among the things we need, then, is a special appreciation of and deep listening to all those prone to fall (but also to rise) from this edge in an opposite direction from those persons closer to us in orientation, practice, and strategy. Thus some other-than-Christian radical democrats have a deep stake in the words and example of the archbishop. Thus, may we join with such Christians in forming the shape-shifting trickster body of radical democracy, expecting that some of the most vital shapes, energies, and modes of this body will come from the work they may do better than the narrower "we." Maybe, I suggest, toward a polymorphous hope.

Wild Peace,

Rom

CHAPTER 8

The Politics of Gentleness:
Random Thoughts for a Conversation with Jean Vanier

Stanley Hauerwas

THE GENTLENESS OF JEAN VANIER

"Love doesn't mean doing extraordinary or heroic things. It means knowing how to do ordinary things with tenderness."[1] Tenderness and gentleness characterize the life and work of Jean Vanier, as well as the L'Arche
movement. Vanier observes that "community is made of the gentle concern that people show each other every day. It is made up of the small
gestures, of services and sacrifices which say 'I love you' and I am happy
to be with you.' It is letting the other go in front of you, not trying to prove
that you are in the right in a discussion; it is taking the small burdens
from the other" (25–26). Gentle. The world of L'Arche is gentle, and I
want to use this occasion to explore the politics of gentleness—that is,
why gentleness is constitutive of any politics that would be just.[2]

　　Gentleness is usually the last thing most of us would associate with
the rough-and-tumble world of politics. Politics, we assume, is either
about conflict or about getting your interests satisfied, or both. Gentleness
is a characteristic of personal relationships having little to do with questions of power or rule. This assumed dichotomy is, of course, exactly

---

　　1. Jean Vanier, *Community and Growth*, 220. Page references to *Community and
Growth* will appear in the text.

　　2. "This occasion" was a two-day "Conversation with Jean Vanier and Stanley
Hauerwas" at the University of Aberdeen in September 2006. I am extremely grateful to
Professor John Swinton for making this conversation happen.

what I want to challenge by calling attention to the role of gentleness in L'Arche.

This puts me in my usual stance: that is, drawing on Vanier and the work of L'Arche to develop a critique of current assumptions about ethics and politics. So I am "using" Vanier and his friends yet one more time; but thanks to Hans Reinders, I am not going to apologize for writing "about" the intellectually disabled.[3] Rather I am going to make the most from being drawn into the world of L'Arche and try as best I can to say why I think that world has so much to teach us about how we should live to enhance the moral and political character of our lives.

To focus on gentleness does create a rhetorical problem. My style is polemical, and many, I suspect, would not characterize my work as gentle or tender. Accordingly, I worry that my attempt to argue for the significance of gentleness for Vanier and L'Arche may betray what he and L'Arche are about. My only defense is that God has given us different tasks. My task has been to put Vanier's wisdom into conversation with philosophical and political positions that I fear are antithetical—if not outright threats—to those we call intellectually disabled. That has meant, however, that my writing style is aggressive and confrontational.

However, I do not want the way that I argue to belie the significance of gentleness, which means, I hope, that I will prove to be an adequate listener, because learning to listen is basic to the gentle character of life in L'Arche. But I am an academic, and academics are notoriously bad listeners. We always think we know what someone is going to say before they say anything, and we have a response to what we thought they would say, in spite of what they may have actually said. To learn to listen well, it turns out, may require learning to be a gentle person.

That is particularly true if Vanier is right that to learn to listen can be quite painful. For example, Vanier observes:

> Communities which start by serving the poor must gradually discover the gifts that those poor people bring. The communities start in generosity; they must grow to listen. In the end, the most important thing is not to do things for people who are poor and in distress, but to help them to have confidence in themselves. . . . Some communities grow by listening to their members' needs for formation and well-being. This growth is usually material: the communities go for the best and most comfortable buildings,

3. Reinders, "Virtue of Writing Appropriately," 53–70.

where everyone has their own room. These communities will
die fairly quickly. Other communities will grow by listening to
the cry of the poor. Most of the time, this leads them to become
poorer themselves, so that they can be closer to the poor people.
(97–98)

"Most of the time this leads them to become poorer themselves."
What might that mean if I am to listen to Vanier? I do not want to become
poorer. I want to remain the academic who can pretend to defend those
with mental disability by being more articulate than those I am criticizing. In short, I do not want to learn to be gentle. I want to be a warrior on
behalf of Vanier, doing battle against the politics that threaten to destroy
his gentle communities. Vanier, of course, is no less a warrior, but where I
see an enemy to be defeated, he sees a wound that needs healing.[4]

According to Vanier, we all carry a deep wound, that is, the wound
of our loneliness. That is why we find it hard to be alone, trying to heal
our aloneness by joining a community. But to belong cannot help but
lead to disappointment. What we must realize is that "this wound is inherent in the human condition and that what we have to do is walk with
it instead of fleeing from it. We cannot accept it until we discover that we
are loved by God just as we are, and that the Holy Spirit, in a mysterious
way, is living at the centre of the wound" (94).

This is the radical insight I take to be at the heart of Vanier and
L'Arche, making possible the gentleness that heals. The stories Vanier tells
of the handicapped are often stories of loneliness not easily overcome.
For example, he tells the story of Daniel whose disabilities were so severe that his parents did not want him, which meant that after being put
in one institution after another, he ended up in a psychiatric hospital.
Vanier observes that even at L'Arche he would now and again flip out of

---

4. I suspect that the gentle character of Vanier's work tempts some to miss his quite
critical and biting comments. For example, he observes in *Community and Growth*:
"Marxist philosophers take the struggle against injustice and class warfare as their starting point, rather than an attitude of trust and wonder. That is why there are no Marxist
communities, but only groupings of militants. If people come together just to fight, there
is no love for or trust in the other; there is no thanksgiving. A community must always
remain a community of children—but children who are intellectually conscious and
have a vision" (69). Vanier can be quite critical, moreover, of Christian communities.
For example, he notes that at one time religious orders may have been too closed in on
themselves and rightly recognized that they must be more open to society, but they often
threw off their traditions in a way that resulted in the loss of identity (75).

reality, "hiding his anguish and himself behind hallucinations. He had constructed thick walls around his heart that prevented him from being who he was. He felt guilty for existing, because nobody wanted him as he was."[5] Vanier observes that the heart of a child is so easily hurt, and the hurt becomes a wound around which we build walls of protection. Walls so constructed can only be breached by gentleness.

THE POLITICS OF GENTLENESS

But what does this have to do with politics? I think it helps illumine why, as Hans Reinders has argued, liberal political theory has found it difficult to provide moral standing for people with mental disabilities. According to Reinders, at the heart of liberal political arrangements is the assumption that "individuals are free to live their own lives as they prefer, provided that they allow other people equal freedom to do the same, and provided that they accept and receive a fair share in the burden and benefits of the social cooperation."[6] But people with mental disabilities, from a liberal perspective, are judged to lack

> to a greater or lesser extent the powers of reasons and free will. Since these are powers that bring substance to the core values of the liberal view of public morality, mentally disabled people never acquire full moral standing in this view. This is because its moral community is constituted by "persons" and these, in turn, are constituted by the powers of reason and free will. This conception of the person is particularly problematic with respect to the inclusion of severely mentally disabled citizens, since on the liberal view only persons in the sense of rational moral agents can be recipients of equal concern and respect.[7]

I fear it may sound overly dramatic, but what Reinders describes is what I take to be the wound that animates liberal political theory and practice—a wound, moreover, that is well protected by walls not easily breached because they seem so reasonable. It is to Martha Nussbaum's great credit that she has acknowledged that liberal political theory, as exemplified in the work of John Rawls, has difficulty in recognizing the status of the mentally disabled. In her book *Frontiers of Justice: Disability,*

---

5. Vanier, *Drawn into the Mystery*, 145.

6. Reinders, *Future of the Disabled*, 14.

7. Ibid., 15–16.

Nationality, Species Membership, Nussbaum observes, as Reinders argued, that the parties assumed to have the status necessary to negotiate the conditions of a just society "are human beings possessed of no serious mental or physical impairments."[8]

Nussbaum takes as her task to remedy the failure of liberal political theory and practice to include the disabled without abandoning the fundamental insights of liberalism. She does so in the name of three mentally disabled people: Sesha, the daughter of philosopher Eva Kittay and her husband Jeffrey, who will never walk, talk, or read because of her cerebral palsy and mental retardation; Nussbaum's nephew Arthur, who is without any social skills because of Asperger's syndrome and is unable to learn in school but is mechanically adept; and Jamie Bérubé, who was born with Down syndrome, and who is the son of Michael Bérubé and Janet Lyon, literary critics.[9] That Nussbaum names real people I take to be an indication that this is not just a theoretical exercise for her.

According to Nussbaum, at the heart of liberal political theory is the attempt to secure social cooperation on the basis of mutual advantage for the contracting parties. A "strong rationalism" informs the liberal project, in the hope that an account of political life can be justified that avoids as much as possible appeals to intuitions and prejudices.[10] Therefore, liberalism seeks to provide an account of justice that does not depend on the presumption of altruism but rather assumes an admittedly fictive bargaining process that establishes fundamental principles of mutual advantage.

Nussbaum does not call into question these fundamental presuppositions of the liberal political project. Yet she acknowledges that to so understand the character of justice leads to the result that people with disabilities are omitted from consideration. This is at least partly the result of conflating the question, "by whom are society's basic principles designed?" with the question, "for whom are society's basic principles designed?"[11] Nussbaum thinks that because these questions are conflated, liberal political theory ends with a counterintuitive result—those with

8. Nussbaum, *Frontiers of Justice*, 17.

9. Ibid., 96–98. For my discussion of Jamie Bérubé, see my chapter, "Timeful Friends: Living with the Handicapped," 11–25; and Michael Berube's response: Bérubé, "Making Yourself Useful," 31–43.

10. Nussbaum, *Frontiers of Justice*, 53.

11. Ibid., 16.

mental disabilities are excluded. Such a result is counterintuitive because, at least in our time,

> the issue of justice for people with disabilities is prominent on the agenda of every decent society, the omission of all of them from participation in the situation of basic political choice looks problematic, given the evident capacity of many if not all of them for choice; and their omission from the group of persons *for whom* society's most basic principles are chosen is more problematic still.[12]

It would seem all Rawls, or other like-minded liberal theorists, needs to do to respond to Nussbaum's concern for the disabled is to let the parties that participate in the original bargaining game know that some of them may have disabilities for which provision will need to be made. But Rawls is unable to accept this suggestion, Nussbaum argues, because if he did so, he "would lose a simple and straightforward way of measuring who is the least well-off in society, a determination that he needs to make for purposes of thinking about material distribution and redistribution, and which he makes with reference to income and wealth alone."[13] It is also the case that Rawls, like the social-contract tradition in general, simply does not take into consideration impairments that are relatively rare.

Nussbaum argues, therefore, that rather than focusing on income and wealth as Rawls does, a capabilities approach is necessary if the mentally handicapped are not to be unfairly excluded. According to Nussbaum, to focus on capabilities means that we are fundamentally bodily beings whose rationality is but one aspect of our animality. Therefore our "bodily need, including our need for care, is a feature of our rationality and our sociability."[14] To focus on capabilities means the variation of needs can be respected, making possible discriminations such as why children need

12. Ibid., 18. Nussbaum's appeal to "the agenda of every decent society" looks very much like an appeal to an intuition. She defends her "intuitions" by arguing that her account is no more or no less dependent on intuitions than Rawls's account of "justice as fairness." She argues that, like Rawls, her account will depend on how the background of "considered judgments" is open to revision (173–76). I am sympathetic to Nussbaum's defense of her intuitions, but I remain unconvinced that her account is consistent with the "strong rationalism" at the heart of Rawls's theory of justice.

13. Ibid., 113–14.

14. Ibid., 160.

more protein than adults or, more generally, why it is often the case that some need more care than others, and why that care must be individualized.[15] Nussbaum thinks, moreover, that such care is rightly understood to be a matter of justice.

One cannot help but be sympathetic with Nussbaum's attempt to help us better appreciate the needs of the disabled. However, as Alan Ryan points out, it is not clear that the concept of capabilities advances the concept of justice. For the very notion of capabilities depends on close analysis of practices that allow correlations to be made between the needs of a particular person and what will satisfy those needs. But that kind of concreteness is not available as long as Nussbaum is determined to maintain the Rawls's liberal framework.[16]

Ryan quite rightly observes that it is not as if Nussbaum is not persuasive about the needs and capacities of the disabled, but it is not clear why our (by which I assume he means those of us who are not disabled) relation to the disabled is a matter of injustice. What, Ryan asks,

> would be lost by saying that the duties are stringent, inescapable, and urgent, but not duties of justice? Nussbaum shows—over and over—that no theory that explains justice as a contract for mutual advantage will show that these duties toward the disabled are a matter of justice. There may be little mutual advantage for the person who helps Arthur. Do we need a different theory of justice or should we say that many duties are grounded directly in the needs of beings to whom duties are owed, but are not a matter of justice? What difference does it make which we say?[17]

Nussbaum might well say in response that it makes all the difference what we say, because if we do not understand what is done in the care of Sesha, Arthur, and Jamie, we may abandon them to a world that cannot be trusted to care for them. They are lucky because they had parents who cared, but what happens if you do not have parents who care? Yet the problem with Nussbaum's attempt to provide a theory to ensure that Sesha, Arthur, and Jamie be cared for is that it is just that—a theory. It is a theory, moreover, in which the wound of loneliness is made a necessity in order that we might be protected from one another.

15. Ibid.,170.
16. Ryan, "Cosmopolitans," 48–49.
17. Ibid., 49.

In contrast to Nussbaum, Reinders argues that there is no point to try to argue with someone who is a skeptical spectator that they should care about the disabled. Rather, crucial for a liberal society is that people exist who are willing to be engaged in the practice of caring for the disabled. According to Reinders, no public policy or theory can resolve the problem of what appears to be the burden of the lives of the disabled unless "it can tap resources that motivate citizens to value the commitment that it requires."[18] For whatever significance can be found in sharing one's life with another person (a significance that will usually come as a surprise) cannot be found outside the activity itself.

This finally brings me back to the gentleness that characterizes the work of L'Arche. In an early essay, "L'Arche: Its History and Vision," Vanier provides an account of how he became Jean Vanier. He first met people with mental handicaps in 1963. Father Thomas Phillipe, a Dominican priest, was a chaplain for a home of thirty men in a small village called Trosly-Breuil.[19] Vanier was teaching philosophy at St. Michaels College at the University of Toronto, but through Father Thomas he met and began to live with Philippe and Raphael in Trosly-Breuil. Vanier reports:

> We began living together, buying food, cooking, cleaning, working in the garden, etc. I knew really nothing about the needs of handicapped people. All I wanted to do was to create community with them. Of course, I did have a tendency to tell them what to do; I organized and planned the day without asking their opinion or desire. I suppose this was necessary in some ways for we did not know each other and they came from a very structured situation. But I had a lot to learn about listening to the needs of handicapped people; I had a lot to discover about their capacity to grow.[20]

18. Reinders, *Future of the Disabled*, 207.

19. In his commentary on the Gospel of John, *Drawn into the Mystery*, Vanier compares the effect Pére Thomas Philippe had on him to Jesus' calling the disciples. Vanier notes that on leaving the navy in 1950, he went to the community funded by Pére Thomas, and "his presence changed my life—or rather orientated my life in a new way. By his very presence, Pére Thomas seemed to communicate a presence of God that filled me with inner peace and silence and drew new life from within me. I knew very quickly that I was called to become his disciple, or spiritual son" (41).

20. Vanier, "L'Arche: Its History and Vision," 52. The story of L'Arche and Vanier has now been told by Kathryn Spink in her book *The Miracle, The Message, The Story: Jean Vanier and L'Arche*.

In short, Vanier had to be taught how to be gentle. It is not easy to learn to be gentle with the mentally disabled, for, as was indicated above, they also suffer from the wound of loneliness, which means they too can ask for too much, which in turn means that gentleness requires the slow and patient work necessary to create trust. Crucial for the development of trust is that assistants discover the darkness, brokenness, and selfishness shaped by their loneliness. According to Vanier, through the struggle required for us to discover that we are like the mentally handicapped—wounded—we discover how much "we need Jesus, and his Paraclete. For without them, we cannot enter into this life of compassion and communion with our weaker brothers and sisters."[21]

In case anyone wonders if Vanier recognized the political implications of what he was learning, he tells us that through his contact with men and women with intellectual disabilities,

> I discovered then how divided and fragmented our societies are. On the one hand are those who are healthy and well integrated into society; on the other are those who are excluded, on its margins. As in Aristotle's day, there are still masters and slaves. I realized that peace could not prevail while no attempt was made to span the gulf separating different cultures, different religions, and even different individuals.[22]

Jean Vanier wrote his dissertation on Aristotle. He knows well that Aristotle thought the test of any good polity was revealed by its ability to sustain friendship between people of virtue. Aristotle, however, would not have thought it possible for a friendship to exist between those who are mentally handicapped and those who are not. Yet Vanier believes that friendship is what L'Arche is about. That he believes this is not only a challenge to Aristotle's understanding of friendship but to the presupposition of liberal political theory and practice, which tries to envision a politics in which friendship is an afterthought.

That is why I am bold to suggest that the gentle character of the practices that constitute the work of L'Arche are not peculiar to that work, but rather are necessary for any polity that would be good. For gentleness is a virtue that, as Hans Reinders observes, depends on our learning to see that

21. Vanier, "L'Arche: Its History and Vision," 59.
22. Vanier, *Made for Happiness*, xiii.

the other person is "given" to us in the sense that, prior to rules and principles of social morality, the presence of the other in our lives constitutes our responsibility. Moral responsibility arises neither from contractual relationships nor from the cooperative exchange between independent individuals. Instead it arises from the nature of the moral self that discovers itself within a network of social relationships. . . . The benefits bestowed by love and friendship are consequential rather than conditional, which explains why human life that is constituted by these relationships is appropriately experienced as a gift. A society that accepts responsibility for dependent others such as the mentally disabled will do so because there are sufficient people who accept something like this account as true.[23]

These are not small matters. Sharon Snyder and David Mitchell, in their book *Cultural Locations of Disability*, advocate a cultural model of disability and hope "to theorize a political act of renaming that designates disability as a site of resistance and a source of cultural agency previously suppressed—at least to the extent that groups can successfully rewrite their own definition in view of a damaging material and linguistic heritage."[24] Such resistance is necessary because, they argue, the very designation of disability in modernity represented a scourge and a promise: "its very presence signaled a debauched present of cultural degeneration that was tending to regress toward a prior state of primitivism, while at the same time it seemed to promise that its absence would mark the completion of modernity as a cultural project."[25] Still, I confess that I am not convinced a cultural-studies model of disability will provide the resistance Snyder and Mitchell so desire.

Rather, I think that Vanier, through the witness of L'Arche, has given us the kind of gift we need to help us overwhelm the wound of loneliness that grips our lives in the name of freedom. Such a gift Vanier rightly thinks to be political. For without examples like L'Arche, we will assume that there is no alternative to the politics of distrust that derives from the wound of our loneliness.[26] I fear many of us, like Daniel, feel guilty for

23. Reinders, *Future of the Disabled*, 17.

24. Snyder and Mitchell, *Cultural Locations of Disability*, 10.

25. Ibid., 31.

26. In his book on the work of Alasdair MacIntyre, *Tradition in the ethics of Alasdair MacIntyre: Relativism, Thomism, and Philosophy*, Christopher Stephen Lutz calls attention to an extremely interesting example MacIntyre gives in his essay "Can Medicine

existing and as a result seek to protect ourselves with walls thickened by our refusal to acknowledge our vulnerability. Vanier exemplifies a way to be with one another, a way to overcome our walls of protection, which we could not "think up." We do well, therefore, to attend to the lessons of L'Arche on how to be (even in the most difficult relationships) gentle.

GOD AND GENTLENESS

To try to suggest the political significance of gentleness seems quite enough a task for any one paper, but I cannot conclude without exploring what may be an even greater challenge. Put simply, I wonder if the kind of gentleness constitutive of L'Arche is possible without God. Vanier's written work is suffused with his unmistakable Catholic convictions and piety. Indeed, in many of the quotations from his work already cited, he makes clear that without Jesus and the Holy Spirit, the work of L'Arche would be impossible.

Yet in *Made for Happiness* Vanier observes that though many people today have no religious faith, it remains important for us to be able to communicate with them at a rational level in order to reflect upon things human. He rightly says that many of Aristotle's insights are valid for any ethics. For according to Vanier, being human does not consist in obeying laws, but rather "becoming as perfectly accomplished as possible. If we do not become fully accomplished, something is lost to the whole of humanity. For Aristotle, this accomplishment derives from the exercise of the most perfect activity: seeking the truth in all things, shunning lies and illusions, acting in accordance with justice, transcending oneself to act for the good of others in society."[27]

I have no reason to question Vanier's use of Aristotle as a way to sustain a conversation with those who do not share his Christian convictions.

Dispense with a Theological Perspective on Human Nature?" that illumines the political significance of the virtue of gentleness. MacIntyre quotes a German physician, Dr. F Holzel, who said about the euthanasia program in 1940, "The new measures are so convincing that I had hoped to be able to discard all personal considerations. But it is one thing to approve state measures with conviction, and another to carry them out yourself down to the last consequences . . . If this leads you to put the children's home in other hands, it would mean a painful loss for me. However, I prefer to see clearly and to recognize that I am too gentle for this work . . . Heil Hitler!" (103). Lutz remarks that such a comment reveals that though real virtues can appear as vices, they nonetheless function as virtues.

27. Vanier, *Made for Happiness*, xiv.

With Charles Pinches I have explored some of the same resources that Aristotle provides for helping Christians understand what it means to be Christian.[28] With Vanier I believe we were created for happiness, which turns out, as Aquinas suggests, to be nothing less than to be befriended by God. But to be befriended by God is surely to require a transformation of self not unlike learning to be gentled into being by being befriended by a person as unlike me as the mentally disabled. Accordingly, Aristotle can help us make connections with those who do not share our faith; but it remains the case that what we believe as Christians may finally "explode" Aristotle's categories.

This means, I think, that if gentleness is a virtue constitutive of politics, then Christians cannot help but be in tension with liberal political arrangements. For one of the reasons Nussbaum finds a Rawlsian account attractive in spite of the exclusion of the disabled is that such an account

> is articulated in terms of free-standing ethical ideas only, without reliance on metaphysical and epistemological doctrines (such as those of the soul, or revelation, or the denial of either of these) that would divide citizens along lines of religion or comprehensive ethical doctrine. It is therefore hoped that this conception can be the object of an *overlapping consensus* among citizens who otherwise have different comprehensive views.[29]

This makes all the more important that L'Arche not hide its lamp under a bushel basket. If L'Arche loses its theological voice, I think it will be a loss not only for L'Arche, but for any politics—and in particular for those determined by liberal political arrangements—in which L'Arche exists. All I am asking is for Vanier to be willing to wash the feet of those who do not share his faith. In his commentary on the Gospel of John, Vanier reflects on the problem of power by commenting on Jesus's washing of the feet of his disciples (John 13:1–17). He notes that all societies are built on the model of a pyramid with the powerful, the rich, and the intelligent at the top. Yet Jesus takes the place of the slave by washing his disciples' feet. Vanier confesses that he is deeply moved when someone with disabilities washes his feet. That someone with disabilities should

---

28. Hauerwas and Pinches, *Christians among the Virtues*, 3–51.

29. Nussbaum, *Frontiers of Justice*, 163.

wash the feet of Vanier is the reason that the politics of the gospel, as Vanier puts it, is of a "world upside down."[30]

Vanier observes that it is tempting for those who would wash the feet of the disabled to assume the model of the pyramid of power in the name of the service they perform. For example, he suggests that after the conversion of Constantine in 313 CE, church and state became intertwined, with the result that many bishops and abbots acted as if they were princes and lords. The dominant habits of the society became the habits of the church, corrupting it. Yet Francis of Assisi came along, refusing to attack the institution of the church, which included many good people, yet choosing another way through his commitment to the poor.[31]

Reflecting on Francis's Admonitions to the heads of his fraternities, Vanier notes,

> Followers of Jesus will continually be caught up in the paradox. Shepherds, teachers and leaders are necessary. They have power, but how should they exercise that power in the spirit of the gospels? How should they give a clear message about the truth of Jesus' message? How should they speak out against the powers of wealth? How should they be servant-leaders who humbly give their lives?[32]

Vanier answers: "When the poor and weak are present, they prevent us from falling into the trap of power—even the power to do good—of thinking that it is we who are the good ones, who must save the Savior and his church."[33] This means that the politics of gentleness cannot be a triumphalistic politics. That is why it is crucial that the theological voice of L'Arche not be silenced: it is not for us as Christians to regret the loss of Christendom. But that makes it all the more important that the care—the gentle care exemplified by Jesus in washing his disciples' feet, that gentleness exemplified in L'Arche—be an unapologetic witness to the One who would save us through the cross. Otherwise, how would the world know—the world as described by Rawls and Nussbaum—that our loneliness has been overwhelmed?

30. Vanier, *Drawn into the Mystery*, 228.
31. Ibid., 236–37.
32. Ibid., 237–38.
33. Ibid., 238.

CHAPTER 9

"Gentled Into Being"

Romand Coles

OPENING REFLECTIONS ON GENTLENESS
AND CRITICAL BITING.

"Tenderness and gentleness characterize the life and work of Jean Vanier as well as L'Arche movement," writes Stanley Hauerwas.[1] I take claims like "gentleness is constitutive of any politics that would be just" to exemplify Hauerwas at his most profound. That Hauerwas reaches his deepest waters in relation to people with disabilities is ultimately the best reason to listen to what he has to say. Moreover, I think that the theme of gentleness is one of the deepest currents in much of his writing, which often ventures toward possibilities of church and politics that would be more capable of engendering friendship by becoming, with Vanier, "friends of time"—friends with God. (Truth be told, Vanier is probably just as important as John Howard Yoder in the constellation of figures who inform Hauerwas's political sensibility.[2]) This current is sometimes obscured as Hauerwas wrestles against the institutions, practices, and ethos of the secular theology of the "economic polity" (in Sheldon Wolin's terms). For Wolin, the economic polity constitutes time as forgetfulness, as efficiency, and as salvation-as-progress through the nation-state and markets—all of which engender a radical impatience that cuts deeply into possibilities for

1. See page 195 above.
2. These connections are most explicit and clear in the collection of his essays on theology and disability, edited by John Swinton: *Critical Reflections on Stanley Hauerwas' Theology of Disability*.

becoming communities through which we might learn better to befriend time and enact a politics of gentleness. When Hauerwas senses that the church is starting to internalize these motifs, it quite simply infuriates him—and he has never said gentleness somehow implies that one should not have and identify enemies.

Yet the arts of "critical biting" (to borrow Hauerwas's language in the previous essay) and the arts of gentleness—each one so difficult on its own terms—are infinitely labyrinthine and trying when they are entwined with one other, as Hauerwas and I both think they must be. Readers—and writers—can lose their bearings in these efforts. I certainly have.

I embrace the greater part of what Hauerwas is calling the politics of gentleness (though I do not understand it in terms of becoming friends of God—so, many will ask, *do I?*), and I share with him a sense that intense struggle with enemies is *also* profoundly important. Yet there are some important differences between our understandings of these arts and their entwinement, and in this essay I want to explore some of these differences. My suspicion is that in some ways I am in search of more vulnerable renderings of Stanley's wonderful phrase, "learning to be gentled into being," and that (relatedly, but in tension) I seek an explicitly more rhizomatic sense of political struggle. I think that Jean Vanier offers a very rich exemplification and articulation of liturgies of receptive gentleness, and in what follows I want to think with and perhaps beyond Hauerwas in order to suggest more precisely some of what this might entail. I am using "liturgy" in this essay *not* (as I am often prone to use it these days) in the broader radical-democratic sense of the regular practices through which we might engender capacities to be people(s) capable of reciprocally responsive relationships that are the mode and substance of more genuine publics; I think that the liturgical work I discuss below in connection with Vanier does indeed provide an exemplification of liturgy as public work in this sense. Yet I want to think here by cleaving to the edge of a *Christian* corporeality, especially to the edge of Vanier's reading of the Gospel of John. I want to do so in order to question and nudge what I take to be problematic about the "liturgical turn" as it tends to be given expression in Hauerwas's work, and particularly in his "big book" that "his friends have written . . . for him," namely, *The Blackwell Companion to Christian Ethics.*[3] I want to apply this pressure in the very intimate proximity of the practice of footwashing. Let me begin with a brief discussion of what makes me uneasy—in spite of so much that is compelling—about the liturgical turn articulated in *The Blackwell Companion to Christian Ethics* before I discuss a footwashed political response to it.

Some Things That Trouble Me About Some Things I Admire.

The Blackwell Companion to Christian Ethics charts a direction with which I sense many affinities, even at the immeasurable distance in which I find myself from the God with whom the writers seek friendship. The "liturgical turn" to textured body practices in Christian ethics has much to contribute to the practice and theory of radical democracy, and something similar is at work in the reflective practices cultivated by the IAF, the early SNCC, and so forth. Moreover, beyond "usefulness," there is much in the volume that is simply astounding, like Emmanuel Katongole's thick descriptions of Christian worship as "wild space," exemplified by a church in Kampung, Malaysia, where the practice of greeting stretches on for a long time and in which each "ha[s] a chance to touch, kiss, shake the hands, and look into the eyes of everyone else in the congregation," and thereby unlearns hegemonic articulations of race and ethnicity in this diverse community.[4] Throughout the book, concrete practices of economic sharing, justice, reconciliation, and peacemaking find expression in communities of worship in ways that I want to join in praise, celebration, and struggle. And I want to do so in a manner that greatly exceeds the inexorable limits of a paragraph that is structurally a preface to my worries.

But alas, here are some worries. At the outset of chapter 2, "The Gift of the Church and the Gifts God Gives It," Hauerwas and Wells write, "God gives his people everything they need to follow him."[5] Of course, what Christian could *not* believe this to be true? Yet I worry that this claim is often inflected in ways that risk more than it should, by projecting an imaginary of the church, ethics, and discipleship primarily as an

3. These phrases are from the "Preface" to Hauerwas and Wells, *The Blackwell Companion to Christian Ethics*, xiii.

4. Katangole, "Greeting: Beyond Racial Reconciliation," 75.

5. Hauerwas and Wells, "Gift of the Church," 13. This is also a dominant motif throughout Wells, *God's Companions: Reimagining Christian Ethics*.

interior volume, a prior preparatory space (separated from the world) that is the most elemental space-time of the formation of peoplehood. I worry that this risks tacitly reinscribing some dominant motifs of the "principalities and powers" that undermine the kingdom to which Jesus calls people. I worry that this imaginary of the liturgical turn risks getting Jesus wrong.

I am *not* worried that the church imagined and practiced in these pages is in its accent on the interiority and separateness of its space, a "sect." These pages lean with passion toward hospitable engagement with and service for the world beyond the church. Many of the essays end with nods toward something akin to receptive generosity toward non-Christians. Yet the liturgical imaginary on these pages threatens to establish a sense of the church in a manner that may *at least* vitiate the possibilities for such receptivity, and that may possibly steer Christians in markedly different directions—directions that render such relations with others less likely and less fruit-bearing.

> The Eucharist offers a model of this companionship [with God]. Disciples gather and greet; are reconciled with God and one another; hear and share their common story; offer their needs and resources; remember Jesus and invoke his Spirit; and then share communion, before being sent out. Through worship—preparation, performance, repetition—God gives his people the resources they need to live in his presence.[6]

Maybe. But what I find largely missing are practices of Eucharist that inhabit the *decentering* that I take to be the heart and soul of the practices to which Jesus calls people. Here I am thinking of something beyond the contestation over identity-marking "closed communion" and hospitality-marking "open-communion" that Gerald W. Schlabach discusses. Rather, my worry concerns the (anti-Bakhtinian) imaginary of "concentric circles" that Schlabach embraces.

> The Eucharist is at the very center of the Church's life . . . and thus constitutes the Church as the very body of Christ. Cantalamessa asks readers to envision three concentric circles. The outer one is the entire universe, the smaller is the Church, and the smallest is the "host" or Eucharistic bread. Just as the Eucharist leavens

6. Ibid., 13.

and makes the Church into bread for the world, the Church is to
leaven and nourish the world. [7]

My sense is that this imaginary constitutes the borders between church
and world in a way that *makes the border secondary to an interior volume* that is at the center and that *only prepares for* rather than *is itself
partly constituted by the borders themselves.* This accents in turn the voice
of the church, *its* service to the world that it "leavens and nourishes":
The church construes itself as the footwash*er* (but not also in need of
being foot-*washed* by non-Christians), as Eucharistic *host* (but not also
in need of following Jesus's call to non-Christian tables and of sitting at
the lowest spot), and as *server* more generally (but not also in need of
being *served* by others beyond church walls in order to be able itself to
serve). In other words (in a point I will develop below), I suspect that this
concentric imaginary that governs most of the essays in this Blackwell
volume's incarnation of Hauerwasian motifs reconstitutes what I would
call the "heroic" *precisely where Jesus calls for a mode of service radically
other than this mode, and this mode of service can only* become *in departure from the heroic.* It is as if there is a people called and gathered *prior*
to encountering others, rather than a people equiprimordially gathered
and formed precisely at the borders of the encounter. This emphasis on
gathering prior to an encounter engenders an intense focus of energy
around the practices of the interior circle of the church, and then, for the
most part, a focus on secondary calls to work and learn in relations with
those beyond the church. It is not that such relations with those beyond
are not important to the writers, but rather that they are construed as
somehow less pivotal to the very *formation* of peoplehood to which Jesus
calls people. It is as if (impossibly!) the form is prior to the edge and prior
to the edgework that it is said to make possible. Yet if this is so, I worry
that the form will always have privilege in a manner that undermines the
very *caritas* it would strive to incarnate.

The "evidence" that nurtures this worry is found precisely *in the textual practices* predominant throughout this volume. The essays virtually
never articulate practices of learning from or with non-Christians. Far
from the liturgical turn, at the very moments when they consider such
possibilities, they become incredibly abstract, gesture-ish, and extremely

---

7. Schlabach, "Breaking Bread: Peace and War," 369. See my discussion of Bakhtin in
the essay on Rowan Williams above, 175–76.

brief.[8] Is this textual practice not itself a manifestation of the paucity of receptive engagement that I fear to be an outcome of this concentric imaginary of the liturgical turn? Might this not inscribe and inadvertently bear witness to a flaw that is likely articulated in the politics of churches that practice themselves into being thus? This is my worry.

Even though I do not much care for the subtitle ("Preparation for Service"[9]), Mark Nation's essay ("Washing Feet") touched me, swept me up in a whirl where the world turned upside down—sent me on a journey. Far more than any other essay in the volume, perhaps, Nation discusses liturgy in a way that comes closest to placing equal accents on both the "receiving" and the "giving" aspects of footwashing. His remark that the difficult endurance of receiving is "an aspect . . . we often miss," signifies to me something I have suggested is missing from (or underdeveloped in) the accounts of so many liturgies in this volume.[10] Nation's lingering with the receptive aspects is exemplary. We must not refuse our feet to Jesus, and Jesus is the spatially and temporally displaced stranger, if there ever was one, in John's account. We must feel the pressure of his touch, the touch of the stranger. This is something akin to what Rowan Williams calls, in his "Afterword" to the volume, "a God, the 'pressure' of whose being is toward the other, so intensely that the eternal divine life itself is a pattern of interweaving difference that then animates a world of time, change, differentiation, in which the unifying call for all things and persons is to show forth God in the way each one is uniquely capable of doing." Williams calls Christians to the experience of being foot-washed by "unbelievers" (even though he does not refer to this liturgy here): becoming aware through their touch of the "pressure of God," or of "the

---

8. Scott Bader-Saye's essay ("Listening: Authority and Obedience") is one of the better ones in relation to my concern, but it still textually performs the problem beyond which, with Barthes, it thematically moves in the last section. Phillip Kenneson similarly calls, in the final paragraphs of his essay ("Gathering: Worship, Imagination, and Formation"), for a church that "becomes visible and addressable, opening itself up to being probed and criticized, not only by God, but also by the world" (66). Having evidenced vulnerability, Kenneson then quickly reasserts a heroic motif by assuring readers that "the *ekklesia* has its own reasons, internal to its own story and vocation, for carefully examining and critiquing the shape of its own embodied life" (66). This is surely true (though the surface has barely been scratched in the essay), but perhaps the equally important point is that the *other* reasons may be just as important.

9. It is the *pre* of "preparation" that bothers me for reasons that will become clear in what follows.

10. Nation, "Washing Feet: Preparation for Service," 443.

theological challenge that is posed by the experience of *seeing* in a life that is not conventionally a life of faith more than the liver of that life sees, seeing something of epiphany, response to the wanting-to-be-in-us of God."[11] All this suggests a corporeal imaginary of liturgical practice that moves beyond the concentricity that I find vitiating. Spurred by Nation and Williams, I found myself seeking to join and incarnate "embodied grace" at the de-centering edges where Christians feel and see the "wanting to be" beyond the walls of the church. And so I find myself in the strange position of tracing a Christian liturgical ethics that I found largely underdeveloped in the Blackwell volume—even as my own efforts below are deeply indebted to it. And so I found myself learning from and with new and strange friends.

Toward a Footwashed Politics of Footwashing.

As much as anyone I have read, Jean Vanier imagines, thinks, reads, and writes from his body. He bears witness to Jesus through a body practiced in relationships of gentle friendship with the "least of these" (who are among the most). And he is deeply suspicious of those who would believe it possible to think or imagine or bear witness to God in absence of gently befriending the least, even as he affirms manifold ways of engaging in such relationships, and many other things it is crucial to do as well. Breaking bread and footwashing, and loving the neighbor and the stranger—these are not metaphors for Vanier; they are the painstaking liturgies of daily life through which we can learn together what it means to become accomplished human beings made for happiness. These are the ways in which we can learn, in Hauerwas's terms, "that our loneliness has been *overwhelmed*."[12]

Hauerwas warned me, before I had read Vanier, that I might find his writing "too pious." But I did not. And I think the reason I didn't is that Vanier manages, in his best writing, quite simply to lay *flesh* on the page, wounded and glorious flesh. What often rings as repulsively "pious" to my ears when it sounds like disincarnate preaching has a way of resonating deep into the soles of my feet when expressed through the flesh-pen of Vanier. Those who read Vanier primarily as a theologian of pen and ink will most likely miss the profundity of his thinking.

11. Williams, "Afterword," 498.
12. See page 207 above. My emphasis.

While Hauerwas appreciates in Vanier's *Made for Happiness* some of the motifs in Vanier's effort to employ Aristotle to "communicate with [the many people today who have no religious faith] at a rational level," Hauerwas is wary that this could become part of an effort to "hide the lamp under a bushel basket."[13] He is far more compelled by those writings in which Vanier proclaims that the "the gentle care exemplified by Jesus in washing his disciples' feet, that gentleness exemplified in L'Arche, [is] unapologetically a witness to the One who would save us through the cross."[14] His hunch is that the liturgical union of word and deed should not be broken, for Hauerwas is being modest when he writes, "I *wonder* if the kind of gentleness constitutive of L'Arche is possible without God"[15]—rather, he *doubts* it (which is not to say he *dismisses* it).

Thus Hauerwas urges Vanier to continue on with motifs of "unapologetic witness to the One" by continuing to give explicit expression to Jesus the footwasher: "All I am asking is for Vanier to be willing to wash the feet of those who do not share his faith."[16] Hauerwas wants Vanier to continue to bear witness in word and deed to Jesus, who "takes the place of the slave by washing his disciples' feet."[17] What an "*overwhelming*" liturgy of formation and witness! Such could only be conceived in the flesh—no disembodied imagination could ever have conjured it up.

Yet it is precisely the motif of "overwhelming" that I wish to explore in relation to the liturgy of footwashing, because witness is for Vanier so fundamentally an *overwhelming* practice. And overwhelming moves uncontrollably in many ways, often splashing surprise and unexpected good news in the face of the one bearing witness. Hence in the vortex of overwhelming liturgies, one may perhaps find a path beyond some of the still too monological and too borderless renderings of liturgy that I suggested were problematic. This path beyond might help to render openness, receptivity, and vulnerability to non-Christian others not in abstract terms, but at the core of Christian *liturgical* practice itself, as Vanier profoundly expresses it. *Overwhelming at the core. Border at the core.* One can glean a hint of this when Hauerwas writes: "Vanier con-

13. See page 206 above.
14. See page 207 above.
15. See page 205 above. My emphasis.
16. See page 206 above.
17. See page 207 above.

fesses that he is deeply moved when someone with disabilities washes his feet. That someone with disabilities should wash the feet of Vanier is why the politics of the gospel is, as Vanier puts it, of a 'world upside down.'"[18] Yet, does Hauerwas embrace *how* upside down Vanier suggests that Jesus calls our world to be? Does he want to? I believe he should, and that to do so might inflect his witness in subtle yet decisive ways.

Hauerwas asks Vanier to wash—in word and deed—the feet of un-believers. And he notes that Vanier confesses being deeply moved when his feet are washed. There is a *difference* in these two related moments—in footwashing and in being foot-washed—a difference easy to overlook by too quickly subsuming a footwash*ed* politics within the frame of a foot-wash*ing* politics. Yet Vanier's writing warns us that to do so is to miss some of the deepest truths in John 13 and the ethics and politics of Jesus more generally. Indeed, he thinks it is to risk turning again right-side-up the world that should be "upside down."

In Vanier's *The Scandal of Service: Jesus Washes our Feet*, he dwells not only on footwashing, but on *undergoing* having one's feet washed.[19] Jesus arises, removes his outer garments, girds himself with a towel, and kneels before each of his disciples in the middle of the meal, not before (as Jewish tradition had it). Hence from the beginning, the disciples are thrown radically "out of joint"; they experience both the unexpected nature of Jesus's action (disrobing, assuming the place of the slave or intimate other[20]) and a radical disruption of temporal flow as well.[21] Vanier reads this through his body: "it is always very moving for me when someone with disabilities washes my feet. . . . It is the world turned upside down."[22] He knows this experience of difficult undergoing and pleasure well, and he knows it is at the heart of the matter. He stays with the experience, draws us to it, and calls people to stay with it: "Imagine

18. See page 207 above.

19. In Vanier, *Scandal of Service*, this theme is even more striking than in his *Drawn into the Mystery of Jesus through the Gospel of John*, where similar motifs resound but in somewhat less poignant form.

20. It should be added that Jesus took a place of less status than even a Jewish slave had, as slaves were prohibited from washing feet. See, Duke, "John 13:1–17, 31b–35," 399.

21. For the "interruptive" character of Jesus' action, see Thomas, "Footwashing within the Context of the Lord's Supper," 176.

22. Vanier, *Drawn into the Mystery*, 230.

the disciples' surprise when they saw Jesus [begin to do this]. . . . They must have looked at each other in amazement: 'What is he doing now?' It was such a strange action!"[23] Vanier returns repeatedly to the specificity of facing this strange upside-down experience of *undergoing*—of having one's feet washed: "The disciples resist. Peter reacts strongly. He expresses what is probably in the heart of each of the disciples. This same resistance is perhaps in each one of us."[24]

In a wonderful essay on footwashing, worth quoting at length, Paul D. Duke develops and dramatizes it this way:

> You can feel them squirming. Their embarrassment is palpable, as enacted by Peter. But the dread is not so much centered in how menial an act Jesus has undertaken for them, as in how painfully intimate it is. . . . The indignity for the disciples resides in their teacher's disarming initiative to touch them in this way, to bring himself so near and naked to their need, to apply himself to their private rankness, to cleanse for them what they would prefer almost anyone else to cleanse. No wonder Peter resists. He has signed up to follow Jesus, not to have the unpleasantness at the foot of his life exposed and handled for him. He prefers the dignity of self-reliance, the fantasy of being heroic. . . .Who can blame him? Who wants to be so powerless, so humbled?[25]

Many commentators pass relatively quickly over this undergoing, this experience of the foot-*washed* in order to move to the more active *washing* side of this liturgical practice.[26] And to be sure, Jesus commands his disciples: "So if I your Lord and Teacher, have washed your feet, you also ought to wash one another's feet. For I have set you an example,

23. Vanier, *Scandal of Service*, 16.

24. Ibid., 21.

25. Duke, "John 13," 400.

26. The washing side can be accented a second time, not only by subsuming being "footwashed" within the rhetoric of "footwashing" (which still evokes—even if it does not linger with—the fact that wherever a community engages such practices reciprocally, being footwashed must be an integral part of the practice), but by using the more active verbal structure "washing feet" to depict the practice, further obscuring the overwhelming undergoing aspect. Within *God's Companions: Reimagining Christian Ethics*, Samuel Wells titles the section in which he discusses this practice of footwashing simply "Washing Feet," and the section avoids discussion of undergoing. I find this book to be engaging and illuminating yet problematic in ways very similar to those I discussed in a letter to Hauerwas in the summer of 2006 (see above, 40–43), a letter in which I discussed Wells's *Improvisation: The Drama of Christian Ethics*.

that you also should do as I have done to you" (John 13:13–15). But *Jesus*, like Vanier and Duke who follow him, *does not pass quickly to the commanded act.* Indeed, before commanding his disciples to wash each other's feet, he dwells upon and indeed *commands* this difficult *undergoing*: "Unless I wash you, you have no share with me" (John 13:8). And the command takes a most radical form: It is commanded *as an undergoing.* This will not be something you author or even coauthor with Jesus, *even in the minimal sense of understanding the act you must undergo.* Jesus is very clear about this: "You do not know what I am doing, but later you will understand" (John 13:7). One goes under and endures the opacity of being foot-washed in the hope of a promised future understanding. Vanier might call this "understanding to come," that of "the world upside down," thinking of themes in Rowan Williams that I explored in chapter 7 above.

Exactly how are we to understand this "upside down"? Let us examine a few aspects. Of course, there are all the very familiar and absolutely important motifs: the Lord as servant assuming the position of the least; service beyond being served as the highest end; humility; radical hospitality; cleansing; discipleship; forgiveness; reconciliation, just to name a few. Vanier brings these to life in his readings of John. Yet each of these practices, which are so "upside down" in relation to the dominant values of most political orders, has a strange and persistent tendency to turn itself "right side up." These practices tend to reconform to the patterns of the "principalities and powers," *especially when rendered in ways that accent the intentional and active dimensions.* One can already glean this when Duke writes that the disciples would "prefer the dignity of self-reliance, the fantasy of being heroic."[27] As foot-*washers*, they can find ways to maintain this posture; they can turn humility and service back around toward will to power.

This can take overt forms, such as happened for centuries when "the practice became used by members of the ecclesiastical and political hierarchy for coronations of kings and emperors, and installations of popes and other leaders."[28] Martin Luther was keenly aware of the way *this* ceremonial humility could be used to establish a power hierarchy legitimated by the self-claimed superiority of the "humble," when he wrote: "the

27. Duke, "John 13," 400.
28. Graber-Miller, "Mennonite Footwashing," 158.

superior washes the feet of his inferior, who, the ceremony over, will have to act all the more humbly towards him"[29] Vanier is very clear that power, even the power of "servant-leaders," can "quickly corrupt," as the history of the church from at least Constantine forward amply illustrates.[30]

Yet Vanier suggests that the corruption can be (and often is) more insidious, more in the soles of our feet, than this. For Jesus realizes that even those who do not wish to turn humility into a tool of their own will to power, even those who wish to live lives that serve the poor and the stranger "will always be tempted to imitate the 'kings of the Gentiles'. . . to exercise authority and help the poor from 'on top', as someone superior, out of pity or even a certain disdain."[31] Moreover, even if they escape *this* hierarchical imaginary, they will likely be caught by another: even if they do not position *themselves* "on top," they may likely live lives that evade generous receptivity toward others by *clutching overly tightly to an intelligible order that first and foremost provides them security by conforming continuously to their expectations.* Vanier suggests that this is the root of Peter's resistance to Jesus:

> Peter is so human, like us all. He has his culture and his own ways of doing things. Jesus is superior, the Lord and Master. He should never wash the feet of his lowly disciples. It is they who should wash the feet of Jesus, while those inferior to the disciples should wash their feet. . . . Peter cannot understand the meaning of this gesture. He needs Jesus above him, not below him. Jesus gives him security. Jesus obviously has authority and power. . . . But Jesus wants to enter into a new relationship with Peter.[32]

We can say that Jesus wants Peter to realize that in his kingdom, "the weakest and the most humble are given the most prominent place," and of course this is true. [33] But it is, as we have seen, a truth that is easily thinned to nearly nothing and easily turned "right side up." Peter could hold tightly—too tightly—to *both* Jesus's *and* Peter's kingdoms in the act of footwashing. Indeed, the act itself could be the bond. But Jesus "wants

29. From *Sämtliche Schriften, pt. xiii (Magdeburg 1743)* col. 680. Quoted in Graber-Miller, ibid.

30. Vanier, *Drawn into the Mystery*, 234–36.

31. Vanier, *Scandal of Service*, 32.

32. Vanier, *Drawn Into the Mystery*, 226–27.

33. Vanier, *Scandal of Service*, 32.

a new relationship" with Peter. He wants Peter to *endure* a footwashing from Jesus; he wants Peter to endure what seems so out of order, so out of time, so incomprehensible that it can only be understood *later*. Perhaps at the deepest level Jesus wants to teach Peter that at the heart of his discipleship is learning the capacity to enter relationships that one can only understand *later*, *after* one has leaned into them with vulnerable receptivity—patiently and perhaps only after a long time. *Maybe "leaning" is already to say too much?* Perhaps Jesus insists that Peter *lend* precisely this weakness at the soles of his feet to the relationship, not just his intending hands and his towel—though surely he wants these too. *This weakness: what if this weakness would be the hinge upon which the door to the kingdom (that gives prominence of place to the weakest) would open—what if this would be the very meaning of new life?* "In order to show the radical newness of life in his kingdom, Jesus washes the feet of his disciples. This shocks and scandalizes them. They find his gesture unacceptable, they cannot understand, and so this becomes a moment of painful testing for them."[34] Perhaps this *enduring* is the very becoming of *agape, caritas?* "That is why to have one's feet washed by Jesus is not optional, but a vital, necessary part of discipleship. It means entering a new world."[35] Thus Vanier takes pains to specify some of the many ways that this entrance may be subverted and the sort of enduring through which such subversion might be less easy.

Of course, this enduring too could be woven into yet another heroic tale of self-reliance—with Jesus now stepping forth to take the heroic throne. But Vanier will not have it. How did Jesus himself acquire this sense of *agape*? *From the others* from whom he received it: "Jesus had already had his own feet washed by a woman's tears (Luke 7:36) and by the precious nard or perfumed ointment of Mary of Bethany (John 12). He must have felt in his own heart all the love contained in this gesture and been moved by this expression of love and the relationship it established. He wanted to express his love for his disciples in the same way."[36] When Jesus speaks harshly to Peter, Vanier conjures, his words hide not only an urgency, but an ongoing "great vulnerability."[37] Vanier's Jesus, like

34. Ibid., 33.
35. Ibid, 34.
36. Ibid., 35.
37. Ibid., 23.

Rowan Williams's Jesus, is born and dies not as a self-reliant hero but as a being whose "new life" is found in ongoing and entangled dependencies through which he opens (and calls us to open) to others. It is these *entanglements all the way down* that keep turning the world "upside down," that help resist our persistent tendencies to try to put it "right side up" and "back in joint."

Jesus, refusing the place of the hero, is ceaselessly strange, ushering an "authority at the heart of community in a totally new way, a way that is humanly incomprehensible and impossible."[38] What is impossible to grasp, and can only be worked and unworked, is the way the high and the low, the familiar and the strange, ceaselessly imbue and transform each other. At the Last Supper, as at so many times before, Jesus the leader, thought to be recognizable, stoops and becomes incomprehensible, when such a gesture is least expected. He becomes not only a slave but the *strangest of strangers*, and he is asking to touch you intimately where the rankness lies at the foot of your life. He cannot presently tell you why, but he insists that you *must* endure this (from the strangest of strangers), and that such endurance is the door and the way to be with him, whom you love and (only) thought you knew, but whom you will only know (and then only somewhat) *later*. The world whirls, in resistance, in acceptance, and it does not stop.

Vanier is still whirling, with Raphael Simi, with Philippe Seux, with a Jesus calling him and them to the impossibly strange in the flesh of the world.[39] And who is more strange than Jesus to the disciples, when he stoops to wash their feet in the middle of supper? This is a *living question* for Vanier:

> It is not surprising that Jesus comes under the guise of a stranger: "I was a stranger and you welcomed me." The stranger is a person who is different, from another culture or another faith: the stranger disturbs because he or she cannot enter into our patterns of thought or our ways of doing things. . . . It is always a risk to welcome anyone and particularly the stranger. It is always disturbing. But didn't Jesus come precisely to disturb our routines, comforts, and apathy?[40]

38. Ibid., 44.

39. Simi and Seux are the first companions with disabilities with whom Vanier began living in a small house, the first L'Arche community, in 1964, in Trosly-Breuil, France.

40. Vanier, *Community and Growth*, revised edition, 266.

And this question again whirls the world upside down: *If Jesus is the stranger, and if the stranger is among other strange things a person of another faith, then what exactly does it mean when Jesus calls people to follow Him?* What would it mean to speak of a "monotheism" *here, in this way*? What would it mean to speak of *his victory* in the midst of *this* whirling? Jesus says he is the Son of God, but of the God who addresses all Jews by saying "you are gods" (John 10:34). What does God mean when his Son, the only path, quotes him as saying to the Jews, "You are gods" and then situates God as the kneeling foreigner? I do not presume to be able to answer these questions. Yet it seems to me that they are precisely the inextinguishable questions in the midst of which whatever it might mean to touch and to be touched by the flesh of the Word-world could possibly take any shape that has anything to do with him. Vanier learns this as his feet are touched; and as his hands touch the feet of others.

And all *this*—neither some happy ecumenism, nor some easy, lazy reason ob(li)vious to all—is why Vanier again and again offers variations on a theme in the face of border-guard Christians: "At times, my own journey to openness was quite difficult. We in L'Arche were not always understood as we welcomed people from different traditions into our communities. Some people could not see or understand that we were not losing faith in our tradition, but were being called to go deeper into it, to be more firmly rooted in it."[41] Vanier is driven deeper and becomes more firmly rooted by and through welcoming others from traditions that are strange to him—traditions that he does *not yet* understand but hopefully might *later*—precisely by the footwashing forces that *whirl* him with Jesus, calling him to great vulnerability, patience, radical receptivity. He is opened by *this* liturgical turning, where *borders* are *overwhelming* at the *core*.

A presupposed shared sensibility *may* set the tone of some L'Arche communities, such as one I am aware of, which has drafted a Spiritual Life Statement that refers to "the underlying unity of all faith traditions."[42] Yet Vanier's radical hospitality and relationship building is ever aware that

41. Vanier, *Drawn into the Mystery*, 216.

42. I do not know enough about this particular community (which will remain anonymous) to know how to interpret this phrase and the statement more generally. Is it naïvete or an expression of studied and working hope hard wrought in ongoing relationships, or both, or something else entirely?

the call to being footwashed by other traditions is among the most trying works: "It is never easy to remain firmly rooted in one's own traditions and at the same time to be open to people of other traditions, to receive from them the gift of their tradition and all that they are living."[43] Indeed, Vanier is emphatic on this point: "There is nothing more prejudicial to community life than to mask tensions and pretend they do not exist, or to hide them behind a polite façade and flee from reality and dialogue. A tension or difficulty can signal the approach of a new grace of God."[44]

In the deepest moments in *Made For Happiness*, Vanier seeks to move beyond an Aristotle who "was enclosed behind city walls," not by imagining an edgeless cosmopolis to which we always already belong, but rather precisely through the edgework of a "compassion [that] engages the body . . . [for] it is through the body that we draw nearer to others. We discover that the fragile person can help us to accept ourselves with our own frailties and we undergo an inner transformation. We become more human, more welcoming, and more open to others."[45] Such edgework in interfaith settings is the site of "pain and hope." Vanier is at pains to chasten the beautiful soul in the 1989 preface to *Community and Growth*: "This growth means a continual and deeper listening to God, to people, and communities as they grow and live through crises and tensions, as they bear fruit and give life."[46] "Community life . . . needs a certain discipline and particular forms of nourishment,"[47] such as footwashing and being footwashed across communities of different faiths, as happened between the Muslims and Christians who worked to serve (and, for Vanier, also fundamentally to be *served by*) people with handicaps in a L'Arche community in Bethany;[48] and as happened between Christians and Hindus in L'Arche communities in India.[49] Hopeful, for Vanier, is

---

43. Vanier, *Drawn Into the Mystery*, 216.

44. Vanier, *Community and Growth*, 121; cf. 124. In contrast to such flights from reality, Vanier solicits "a realism born of a willingness to listen and a desire for truth even if it is challenging and hurts" (123).

45. Vanier, *Made for Happiness*, 188.

46. Vanier, *Community and Growth* (revised edition), xiv.

47. Ibid., 12.

48. Vanier, *Scandal of Service*, 63–64.

49. For more on this, see Spink, *Miracle, the Message, the Story*. Spink's stories about interfaith practices, promises, and difficulties (particularly in India) draw attention to, but really only touch upon, complexities clearly worthy of an entire book.

that the growth of interfaith dialogue and understanding is not a *departure* from Jesus but a *deepening* with him: "The more we are called to be open to others and encourage the gift of God in them, the more we must be rooted in our own faith, growing in a personal relationship with Jesus. And the more we become one with Jesus, the more we open up to others and begin to see and love them as Jesus loves them."[50] Where the flesh of the hand meets the flesh of the foot, we relearn "a deeper purification" in relation to the others: how to "die to the selfishness" of our own cultures and religious traditions, and discover gifts in others.[51]

These liturgies of patient learning and relearning are the doorway and the way of *caritas*. And paradoxically, the doorway and way move too quickly to be caught at rest. Vanier's thoughts shift in the whirl: Communities and traditions have to be built, and take form, and know each other, in order to develop disciplines and practices that make radical welcoming possible: "There is a time for everything." Yet we shouldn't fixate on this priority lest we destroy it: "The second period doesn't necessarily follow the first: they are bound up in each other: A community will always need times of intimacy, just as it will always need times of openness. If it has only one or the other it will die."[52] Vanier is whirling but not frantic. Each of these tensional tasks must be pursued with time-full care and intricately intertwined. Magnificent, they are nonetheless unfolded through the arts of "living littleness" rather than with an accent on grandiose schemes.[53] Yet littleness does not mean isolation from the larger world: Echoing the Bakhtinian insight (from my essay on Rowan Williams) that animates nearly every reflection I have brought to these dialogues, Vanier writes: "A community that isolates itself will wither and die; a community in communion with others will receive and give life."[54]

Yet there are many ways for a community to "isolate itself," to refuse the "great vulnerability" enjoined by the Footwasher. If Keith Graber-Miller is right, it was common that Mennonites began to so isolate themselves in the sixteenth century by "the simple *performance* of a ritual such as footwashing [that] serves as a boundary-defining function, reflecting

50. Vanier, *Drawn Into the Mystery*, 215.

51. Ibid., 215, 213, 210–11.

52. Vanier, *Community and Growth* (revised edition), 266–67.

53. Ibid., 307.

54. Ibid., 103.

a group's self-identity and conferring identity. . . . drawing boundaries between insiders and outsiders."[55] The "world turned upside down" by a liturgy that involved undergoing an informative touch from strangers became in part an act of separation through purification. In the past century, on Graber-Miller's account, many Mennonites have shifted "toward engagement with [the surrounding] world rather than withdrawal into pure communities," and as they have, there has been "a nuanced shift away from *agent*-centeredness in the ritual and toward *other-* or *act*-centeredness.[56] Yet in light of questions that emerge in Vanier's account, one wonders: Is *act-centeredness*—at least if it is accented significantly at the expense of undergoing—really primarily "other-centered"? Or may act-centeredness (also) at least tacitly reinsinuate the acting-hero-as-server, for whom enduring and being served by the informing touch of strangers would vanish as a locus of serving the other. Insofar as this were so, it would appear that the current liturgical practice-interpretation of footwashing among such Mennonites may to some degree contribute to undercutting the very profound receptive practices that seem integral to work being done by the Mennonite Central Committee and other exemplary Mennonite organizations. Could it be that such receptivity is among the most vital liturgical practices in Mennonite communities—the engagements where the border is at the core?

At any rate, this seems to be the thrust of Jesus and Vanier. I have written elsewhere about liturgies of "tabling" as among the concrete practices in which radical democrats are rebeginning to form receptive communities across myriad differences in the midst of adversities.[57] One obvious Christian analogue is evoked by Rowan Williams in *Resurrection*, where he writes of a "shared table" where people gather as material extensions of Jesus's "embodied grace" in "circumstances remote in space and time." Williams conjures a radically inclusive table where *"relinquishing what is ours* is crucial in the Eucharistic process"; where "men and women turn to their victims and receive back their lost hearts."[58] As I have argued in an earlier essay, there is so much to be commended in this vision, and we must always be powerfully drawn by it. Yet perhaps it must be juxta-

55. Graber-Miller, "Mennonite Footwashing," 151–55.

56. Ibid, 165.

57. See chapter 7, "Moving Democracy," in *Beyond Gated Politics*, 213–39.

58. Williams, *Resurrection*, 111.

posed with and supplemented by an image and practice of another sort
of tabling in order to keep whirling the world upside down—in a spirit of
Williams and Vanier that comes closest to that of radical democracy.

In *The Scandal of Service*, Vanier draws on the Gospel of Luke in
his discussion of the meaning of a kingdom of servanthood: "The kings
of the Gentiles exercise lordship over them; and those in authority are
called benefactors. But this must not be so with you; rather let the greatest among you become as the youngest, and the leader as one who serves.
For which is greater, the one who sits at table or the one who serves? Is
it not the one who sits at table? But I am among you as one who serves"
(Luke 22:25–27).[59] Jesus here seems to be cultivating a disposition to seek
the greatest—the ones to whom we ought most strenuously bend our
ears and most enduringly offer our vulnerable yet seeking feet and gentle
hands—among those who are *not at the table*. For those who live lives in
unacknowledged service to the table (where one always finds some who
betray "the least of these" with whom Jesus identifies himself) often have
a perspective that illuminates the insidious ways in which even the more
inclusive and generous tables participate in sabotaging the "world turned
upside down." Solidarity with them is a crucial practice for resisting
these tendencies. Of course, one form that solidarity can and must take
is inviting them to the table. Jesus makes this case many times. But Jesus
seems to imply that another form of solidarity is crucial as well. In Luke
14:7–11, Jesus discusses not whom to *invite*, but rather *where one ought
to sit*: "do not sit down at the place of honor. . . . But when you are invited,
go and sit down at the lowest place. . . . For all who exalt themselves
will be humbled, and those who humble themselves will be exalted." I
understand Jesus in this parable to be speaking not only about where
one ought to seek to sit at the table, but also about what tables one ought
most to seek in the first place. He is saying, become one whom those who
are the lowest in—or most excluded from—the hierarchies of power that
emerge at *any* table would invite to the place where *they* eat and discern.
Then, when invited, take the lowest place at these places, and sit *there*. In
this way you may be "raised up," because there will be no knowledge of
what is highest (of what is just, good, beautiful, or sublime) that has not
formed in relations of *both* including and being included by "the least."

59. Quoted in Vanier, *Scandal of Service*, 32.

If this is so, as I think it is, then Jesus is saying something about the "Eucharistic process" that is profound and often overlooked. For if Jesus is remote from the seats at the table and "among us as one who serves" (and how could he possibly put this more graphically than by *leaving the table, insisting on this radically displaced and stooped location, removing his outer garments, and washing the feet of those at the table?*), then to join Jesus, and I mean literally—to become an extension of his "embodied grace" in "circumstances remote in time and space"—must mean somehow to partake in *communion* with others at "tables" and "places" that are at a distance from those of greater stature, at greater distance from those where one feels belonging, security and (at least in these senses) power. And since Jesus is as a stranger, this must mean sitting receptively and generously at the tables of those of other traditions when invited, as well as calling them to join the body of Christ. And seeking to become worthy of being thus invited. Otherwise, we would forever have as little idea about what it would mean to live well as those vying among themselves in Luke's parable "about who should be reckoned the greatest." In other words, insofar as we (this goes for any *we*, but I am speaking here to those who would listen carefully to Jesus) would understand liturgy exclusively or primarily in terms of interior spaces of formation (even radically inclusive and service-preparing spaces), we would largely *be fooling ourselves* into thinking we were forming an extension of the body of Jesus. Such spaces are *part* of the "Eucharistic process," but must be joined with practices of becoming worthy of being invited by, and of sitting in the lowest places with, those who are not part of this part. It is because Williams and Vanier hear this infinitely difficult call to works that must remain without definitive names (even though they and we have plenty of struggling examples) that they repeatedly evoke the ineffable, which, as we have seen, Williams sometimes calls "paraliturgy," with all appropriate discomfort.

Along with Jean Vanier and Rowan Williams, Ella Baker and Ernie Cortez are among the many exemplifications of radical democrats and Christians struggling to form such "paraliturgies" among different communities of faith, and between such communities and a broader radical-democratic tradition that includes many who are something other than believers in God (though surely we are people of faith). The proof of the gospel message that I have explored here lies in the "good works" and "good being-worked" that it has helped into being, a few stories to which we are drawn in this book.

In these stories, one has to squint oneself stupid not to see that the streams of the most exemplary radical democracy and radical *ecclesia* are fed by multiple sources beyond the limits of what any single tradition can call its "own." The proof of the wealth of this gospel message is that it has engendered some people who realized that they were sufficiently poor to not want more than such a place in the "victory"; a place such as Norman Maclean evokes:

> *Eventually, all things merge into one, and a river runs through it.*
> *The river was cut by the world's great flood and runs over rocks from*
> *the basement of time. On some of the rocks are timeless raindrops.*
> *Under the rocks are words, and some of the words are theirs.*
> *I am haunted by the waters.*[60]

I am haunted by the touch of words.

Words of touch.

Timeless raindrops on rocks.

60. Maclean, *River Runs Through It*, 104.

CHAPTER 10

To Love God, the Poor, and Learning:
Lessons Learned from Saint Gregory of Nazianzus

Stanley Hauerwas

"It is the poor who tell us what the *polis* is."
   —Oscar Romero[1]

THE POOR AND THE UNIVERSITY

"Woe is me," wrote Gregory of Nazianzus when he was delayed from leaving Constantinople to return to Nazianzus and retirement.[2] His words exactly express my sentiments, given that I am faced with the task of writing on Gregory of Nazianzus. I am without eloquence, yet I must write about the most eloquent theologian in the Christian tradition—Gregory of Nazianzus. My plight is even more deplorable. I am not a scholar or the son of a scholar. Even less can I count myself a patristics scholar. Alas, I am but a theologian, which means that I live in fear that someday someone will say in response to a paper such as this, "You really do not know what you are talking about, do you?" To this I can only reply, "Of course I do not know what I am talking about because it is my duty to talk of God." This is a self-justifying response that may indicate how theologians live in a permanent state of self-deception.

That I am in such a woeful state is the fault of Frederick Norris. He told me that I would be a natural for writing on Gregory of Nazianzus.

1. Quoted Holman, *Hungry Are Dying*, 107.
2. Letter 182 in Barrois, *Fathers Speak*, 71.

So I have read the *Orations* of Gregory of Nazianzus that Norris told me I should read. I have also read the extraordinary scholarly work on Gregory by Frederick Norris, John McGuckin, and Susan Holman. But my reading has only made me aware of my inadequacy. At best, I can be no more than a reporter of their work. I can only ask you not to judge me harshly, for I am only doing what Norris asked me to do.

I must now report, however, that this opening gambit exemplifies the rhetorical device known as the "Southern con," that is, a feigned incompetence to secure the listener's sympathy. As far as I know, the scholarly study necessary to trace the origin and development of the "Southern con" has not been done, but I suspect that we (that is, those of us lucky to be born Southern) learned to use it on the Yankees, who assumed that if you talked with a drawl, you must be stupid. It is a great advantage for your enemy to assume that you are not all that bright.

My use of the "Southern con," however, is meant to pay homage to Gregory, who, McGuckin observes, often disparaged "rhetoric" as "superficial decoration and verbosity." Yet McGuckin notes that if we look closely, we will see that Gregory is "merely using a carefully crafted rhetorical device to persuade his audience to lay aside their resistance to the craft he is employing to convince them of his argument's merit."[3] It turns out that the Greeks must have had roots in the South.

The only problem is that this time, the con happens to be true. God only knows what I am doing writing a paper on Gregory of Nazianzus and, in particular, on his Oration "On the Love for the Poor."[4] It has been years since I originally read Gregory of Nazianzus. As a Wesleyan, I have always held the Cappadocians in high regard; *theosis*, we Methodist's believe, was but an early anticipation of Wesley's understanding of perfection. Moreover, reading Gregory again reminded me how deeply I admire Gregory's theology and style. Yet it remains true that I have nothing new to say about Gregory's theology and, in particular, about Oration Fourteen, "On Love for the Poor."

But I do want to put before us Gregory's reflections on poverty, and in particular, on lepers, to show why Christians have a stake in sustaining the work of the university. You may well wonder what lepers have to do

3. McGuckin, *Saint Gregory*, 41.

4. Saint Gregory of Nazianzus, "On Love for the Poor," 39–71. All references to "On Love for the Poor" will appear in the text using the usual format of the number of the Oration followed by the paragraph number.

with universities, but I take it that Frederick Norris's lifework has been to make unlikely connections. After all, Norris is a self-declared Anabaptist who has spent his life trying to teach anti-Catholic Protestants why they cannot make sense of their ecclesial practices unless they attend to the theologians who did their work in the wake of the Constantinian settlement.[5] I lack Norris's erudition, but like him I want to be a free-church Catholic who refuses to leave behind the institutions of Christendom, institutions like the university, simply because they too often are in service to Caesar rather than to the poor.

Universities, moreover, are institutions that depend on, as well as serve, wealth. Gregory of Nazianzus was able to develop his remarkable rhetorical skills because he came from a family of wealth and power. Gregory's years in Athens made him one of the most educated persons of his time, but he used his rhetorical power to serve the poor.[6] So it is not impossible to connect the university and the poor. Gregory's life and work, I hope to show, not only exemplify this connection between the university and the poor. Gregory's life and work can help us to rethink as Christians what we ought to be about as people committed to a love of learning and to the poor. That connection, moreover, entails a politics that I need first to make explicit.

GREGORY THE PHILOSOPHICAL RHETORICIAN

According to Frederick Norris, Gregory of Nazianzus "was a philosophical rhetorician."[7] Norris's description has the advantage of making clear that Gregory, though he desired to be a monk, could not avoid being drawn into the rough-and-tumble world in which Christians began to create an alternative political reality. To be a "philosophical rhetorician"

5. For Norris's self-description as an Anabaptist, see Norris, *Apostolic Faith*. xiii. Not to be missed is his wonderful account of his family and of the religious background that they represented.

6. Prior to going to Athens, Gregory had studied at Caesarea Maritima, which McGuckin describes as "the closest thing in the fourth century to a Christian university town" (*Saint Gregory*, 36–37). Gregory's decision to study in Athens and to study rhetoric seems not to have pleased his mother, because Athens, according to McGuckin, was widely known for its devotion to the gods and even exceeded Rome in its devotion to pagan cults (ibid., 48). Gregory, however, unlike Basil, loved Athens and excelled not only in his study of the Bible but in the Hellenistic classics. His father basically forced him to leave Athens by cutting off his money.

7. Norris, introduction to *Faith Gives Fullness*, 25.

was to take on the task (a political task) of establishing a Christian commonwealth through speech. It is only against that background that we can appropriately appreciate the significance of Gregory's great Oration, "On Love for the Poor."

Gregory was indebted to Hellenistic culture for his rhetorical skill. Gregory thought that Christians must use the resources and gifts of Hellenism to sustain the work of the church. But his commitment to Hellenism was always disciplined by his Christian convictions. Gregory was in fact baptized in Athens, but he knew, according to McGuckin, that his baptism meant that he was radically committed to Christian disciplines that might create tensions with his intellectual ambitions.[8] Yet under the influence of Prohaeresios, Gregory stood in the tradition of Origen, believing that there could be no disparity between the works of the Logos and the best developments of human culture.[9]

McGuckin, however, reminds us that Gregory's commitment to literature and learning was but a correlative of his desire to live as an ascetic. For Gregory, to live as an ascetic was not in tension with his learning because he understood the discipline of thought to be one of the forms that asceticism must take. Gregory did not follow the pattern of the idle rich, but rather he was "someone who wanted to follow the demands of intellect in a serious spiritual quest. The tools of his *ascesis* were books, enquiring conversation, and reflection in simple solitude. He is certainly an early and serious witness to the physical asceticism of vigils, and simplicity of lifestyle, and in this followed the intellectual tradition of simplicity of lifestyle as advocated by his intellectual hero Origen."[10]

In the Hellenistic world, to become a philosopher was to be identified with a way of life and politics. Gregory wanted to be a rhetor, but he understood that vocation to be a contribution to the establishment of a

---

8. McGuckin, *Saint Gregory*, 55.

9. Ibid.

10. McGuckin *Saint Gregory*, 97. McGuckin notes that as the son of a very wealthy landowning bishop, Gregory spent much of his career reflecting on the moral value of wealth. He came to the conclusion that the only attitude one could take toward wealth was to assume that material goods are only temporary. As we shall see in Oration 14, he comes to the conclusion that, in McGuckin's words, "only almsgiving can restore to a human being that condition of freedom that humanity lost in the ancient fall from grace, since it renders us liberal in the image of God rather than cramped in cupidity which is the mark of oppression" (152–53).

Christian polis.[11] Like the Hellenistic polis, the city that Gregory served was a city of words. According to Brian Daley, SJ, the Hellenistic city was one

> supported by the power of words, of rhetoric, and embodying
> what might be called a philosophy. . . . Basil and the two Gregories
> sought to move the heart by the incantation of words, cunningly
> arranged, and by the power of the imagination to elicit new re-
> solve for action; they invited their hearers to enter into and know
> themselves, by what Pierre Hadot has called an ancient variety of
> "spiritual exercises," as well as to reflect on the universal charac-
> teristics of human nature; their aim was not simply to promote a
> way of living successfully in the city, but of living well—of real-
> izing human excellence and perfection in self-mastery and social
> responsibility, of acting before others in the city in such a way as
> to win their admiration and even their envy.[12]

The significance of the Cappadocians' commitment to learning, to rhetorical beauty, can be best appreciated against the background of Emperor Julian's policy of prohibiting Christians from holding the office of teacher. According to Julian's *Edictum de Professoribus* (June 17, 362), "it is dishonest to think one thing and teach another. No professor, therefore, who does not believe in the gods must expound the ancient

11. Gregory was a rhetor, but he had no use for rhetoric to secure personal power. With his usual candor, in a letter to Gregory of Nyssa, Gregory of Nazianzus accuses Nyssa of desiring glory by pushing away Scripture for pagan literature: "You have taken in hand dried-up, insipid writings, and the name of rhetor is more pleasant to your ear than the name Christian. But we prefer the latter, and all thanks to God! No my dear, do not suffer this any longer; sober up at last, come back into yourself, defend us before the faithful, defend yourself before God and before the mysteries from which you have estranged yourself! And do not serve me captious arguments in the manner of rhetors, saying: 'What then? Was I not a Christian, while I was a rhetor?' No, my dear, you were not! Forgive if I make you sad, it is out of friendship; or if I flare up for your own good, the good of the entire priestly order and, I should add, of all Christians. And since we ought to pray with you or for you, let God assist your weakness, He who brings the dead back to life" (Barrois, *Fathers Speak*, 37–38).

12. Daley, "Building the New City," 459. Daley argues that Basil's great social and monastic enterprise, the large and complex welfare institution that became known as "Basileias," "represented a new and increasingly intentional drive on the part of these highly cultivated bishops and some of their Christian contemporaries to reconstruct Greek culture and society alone Christian lines, in a way that both absorbed its traditional shape and radically reoriented it" (432).

writers."[13] Julian argued that a culture cannot be divorced from its religious heritage without being damaged. Constantine had tried to replace the gods with Christianity, but that project, from Julian's perspective, had to fail. Rome could not survive without the gods.

Gregory of Nazianzus rightly understood Julian's edict to be a challenge to his rhetorical vocation. Accordingly, he gave himself the task of exploring the nature of a Christian alternative to Julian. He therefore composed rhetorical texts for the classroom to be used by Christians, because he was convinced "of the importance of providing a body of didactic material for Christian training."[14] At the end of his life, he sold his books to give the money to the poor, but he also desired that his Letters and Orations be collected because he thought them important for the use of those charged to lead the church.

For Gregory, good Hellenist that he was, rhetoric was intrinsic to the formation of a good society necessary for training of good people. He held himself accountable for what he said as well as for the way he said what he had to say. To speak the truth required that the speaker be truthful. Susan Holman observes that in the Hellenistic world, a leader's moral standing "was judged on the basis of his class, his education, and his consequent ability to verbally express himself with eloquence within a given rhetorical structure. Words in this culture were *spoken*—even when they were (also) written down."[15] Through words and actions, which, for Gregory of Nazianzus, were the same thing, he sought to build a world that would be an alternative to the world that Julian had tried to reestablish.

The significance of Gregory's Oration "On Love for the Poor," must be understood against this background. For Gregory is not simply urging those not afflicted by poverty or leprosy to aid those so afflicted. Rather, the rhetorical power of his descriptions of the afflicted seeks to make them unavoidable citizens of the new politics coming to birth, called Christian. In "On Love for the Poor," Gregory seeks to make the poor seen, to make the poor part of the community, because unless they are seen to be integral to the community, we will fail to see Christ. Gregory, the great Christian rhetor, in the words of Susan Holman,

---

13. McGuckin, *Saint Gregory*, 117.
14. Ibid., 118.
15. Holman, *Hungry Are Dying*, 22.

expresses moral excellence by his physical style in oral declamation, so he also points his audience to Christ, the word made flesh. . . . The poor and destitute who had no rhetorical voice of their own—the incarnation of the Word takes on meaning by the rhetor's (that is, the bishop's) verbal identification of these poor with the body of Christ. As the Cappadocians use traditional New Testament images to identify the poor with Christ, the body of the poor—in its most literal, mutable sense—gains social meaning. The rhetorical expression of this body gains a language and a voice of its own as it is viewed as the body of the Logos. The theology of the incarnation takes on meaning relative to the culture in which it is defined, and this culture profoundly influences the way the theology is understood.[16]

"On Love for the Poor"

Hopefully, we are now in a position to appreciate Gregory's argument in his Oration "On Love for the Poor."[17] The date or the reason for Gregory's Oration cannot be established with certainty. It seems reasonable to associate Gregory's Oration with Basil's building of his hospice for the poor and lepers in Caesarea in response to a famine. McGuckin suggests quite reasonably that "On Love for the Poor" was written in 366 and 367 to raise money for Basil's leprosarium.[18] That Gregory's Oration was connected to Basil's building for the poor is significant because such a connection makes clear that the building and the Oration should be understood "liturgically."

Leitourgia in the ancient world was understood as any "public service performed by private citizens at their own expense."[19] Julian had called

16. Ibid., 22.

17. Some might dispute the description "argument" for "On Love for the Poor." For a good defense of Gregory's "method" as argument see Norris, introduction to *Faith Gives Fullness*, 35–39.

18. McGuckin, *Saint Gregory*, 145–46. Holman provides a very good overview of the various arguments for when and why Gregory wrote Oration 14 in Holman, *Hungry Are Dying*, 144–46. McGuckin thinks that "On Love for the Poor" was "conceived as a general fund raiser, that also served as an important discourse setting out the terms for the Christian imperium's policy of *philanthropia*. As such it is an keynote piece of political oratory, as well as a decisive theological essay in which Gregory sets out his mind on the social altruism that characterizes the inner spirit of the religion of Christ" (*Saint Gregory*, 147).

19. Holman, *Hungry Are Dying*, 21.

attention to Christian philanthropy for the poor in order to shame his pagan priests to do more for the poor than the Christians were doing. Julian argued, without much evidence, that the physical care of the poor—as an act of piety—was required by Hellenistic religion. Basil's building and Gregory's Oration were, therefore, a counterpolitics to Julian's. Care of the poor constituted the center of the work that Basil and Gregory understood was necessary for the constitution of the community they were intent to establish.

Basil's Sermon on behalf of the poor and Gregory's Oration "On Love for the Poor" exemplified Hellenistic *leitourgia*. The Greeks assumed it was the obligation of well-off citizens to contribute to the well-being of the city. What is different, Holman argues (drawing on the work of Evelyne Patlagean), is the rise of a new type of donor. The donor who had been an eminent citizen now renounces the identities of such citizenship—that is, marriage, family, and property—"to choose poverty, celibacy, and ascetic generosity."[20] The *leitourgia* system was a patronage system, but the character of the patron was now transformed.

Gregory therefore begins "On Love for the Poor" by making himself one with the poor: "My brothers and fellow paupers—for we are all poor and needy where divine grace is concerned, even though measured by our paltry standards one many may seem to have more than another—give ear to my sermon on loving the poor" (14, 1). Throughout the Oration, Gregory emphasizes that those who are better off should never be tempted to think that because they are so, they are fundamentally different than the poor and the leper. After all, we all share the "affable enemy and scheming friend," that is, the body, which has been given to us to remind us of our weakness and true worth (14, 7).

That some are poor and some are rich is but a reminder that we are all subject to fickle fortune: "Our fortunes run in a cyclical pattern that brings changes one after another, frequently within the space of a single day and sometimes even an hour, and one may rather count on the shifting winds, or the wake of a sea-faring ship, or the illusory dreams of night with their brief respite, or the lines that children at play trace in the sand, than on human prosperity. The wise are those who because of their distrust of the present save for themselves the world to come" (14, 19). Gregory asks us to ponder how abandoned we would be if we were

20. Ibid., 17.

allowed to think our prosperity was permanent. How fortunate it is that misfortune befalls us, given how attached we become to what we have, how addicted we are to our possessions, how firmly enthralled by our riches we are (14, 20). [21]

Accordingly, Gregory refuses to speculate whether affliction actually comes from God: "Who really knows whether one man is punished for his misdeeds while another is exalted for praiseworthy behavior, or whether the opposite is true: one man is placed on a pedestal because of his wickedness while another is tested because of his goodness, the one raised the higher that he may fall the harder, the other persecuted for no discernible reason in order that any impurity he has, even if scant, may be smelted out?" (14, 30). No one is free of corruption, making it impossible to attribute every instance of hardship to moral turpitude or to a reprieve from piety (14, 31).

The reason that some are favored and some afflicted is often unintelligible to us, and that unintelligibility is itself a gift. For our difficulty of comprehending the reason behind favor or affliction points us to the "reason that transcends all things. For everything that is easily grasped is easily despised, but what is beyond us increases our admiration in proportion to our difficulty in apprehending it; and everything that exceeds our reach whets our desire" (14, 33). That is why we should neither admire health nor loathe disease "indiscriminately," but rather we should "both cultivate contempt for the benighted health whose fruit is sin and respect for that disease that bears the badge of saintliness by showing reverence toward those who have triumphed through suffering" (14, 34).

21. Gregory says, "Let us not struggle to amass and hoard fortunes while others struggle in poverty, lest from one direction the divine Amos reproach us with these harsh and ominous words, Come now, you who say, 'When will the new moon be over,' that we may sell' . . . May we avoid the same fate in our day; may we not be so addicted to luxury as actually to scorn the compassion of a God who condemn this behavior, even though he does not turn his wrath upon sinners at the moment of their transgression or immediately after it" (14, 24). In Oration 17 Gregory observes that "prudent men" declare that it is good to be afflicted. That is why we should "relinquish neither anxiety in time of happiness nor confidence in time of sorrow. Even in fair weather let us not forget the gale, nor in the storm the pilot; yes, let us not lose heart in the midst of afflictions or become wicked servants who acknowledge their master only when he treats them well and repudiate him when he tries to correct them. Yet there are times when pain is preferable to health, patience to relief, visitation to neglect, punishment to forgiveness. In a word, we must neither let our troubles lay us low nor a glut of good fortune give us airs" (17, 5).

The disease that bears the badge of saintliness Gregory identifies as leprosy—the "sacred disease," which devours flesh and bones and marrow (14, 6).[22] His "respect" for the "disease that bears the badge of saintliness" is witnessed by his profound identification with those who bear the disease. His description of their suffering is devoid of sentimentality. He understands, therefore, that the leper's physical disfigurement is but the outward sign of a deeper disfigurement; namely, they become unrecognizable to themselves. As a result, they call out the names of their mothers and fathers in hope that they might be identified from the way they used to look. Yet even the fathers and mothers of those so afflicted drive them away, in fear of those they once loved. The mother, this poor woman, "wants to embrace her child's flesh but shrinks from it in hostile fear" (14, 11).

The affliction of leprosy is horrid enough, but even worse is the knowledge of those so afflicted that they are hated for their misfortune (14, 9). They are driven away, not only because of the irrational fear that they may infect us, but because we refuse to comprehend their suffering: "So they wander about night and day, helpless, naked, homeless, exposing their sores for all to see, dwelling on their former state, invoking the Creator, leaning on each other's limbs in place of those they have lost, devising songs that tug at the heartstrings, begging for a crust of bread or a bit of food or some tattered rag to hide their shame or provide relief for their wounds" (14, 12). [23] Yet there is no comfort even in their common

22. Some may think that Gregory's focus on leprosy makes his case too easy. Little can be done to cure the leper, but we think much can be done to alleviate poverty. Gregory certainly thought, as we should think, that poverty should not exist, but he did not think that being poor was the worst thing that could happen to a person. Indeed, he thought there might be some distinct advantages to being poor if we are to follow Christ. From Gregory's perspective, the rich, not the poor, are the most burdened. Samuel Wells recently stated this reality when he remarked, "The rich, if we are Christians, need the poor in a manner the poor do not need the rich."

23. Gregory tells his hearers that they should at least help those suffering from leprosy by offering encouragement and keeping them company: "You will not demean yourself in the process; you will not catch their malady even if the squeamish deceive themselves into believing such nonsense; or rather, this is how they justify their, call it over-cautious or sacrilegious, behavior; in point of fact, they are taking refuge in cowardice as though it were a truly worthwhile and wise course of action. On this score accept the evidence of science as well as of the doctors and nurses who look after these people. Not one of them has every yet endangered his health through contact with these patients. You, then, servant of Christ, who are devoted to God and your fellow man, let compassion overcome your misgivings, the fear of God your fastidiousness" (14, 27).

suffering: "They lie beside one another, a wretched union born of disease, each contributing his own misfortune to the common fund of misery, thus heightening each other's distress; pitiful in their affliction, more so in the sharing of it" (14, 13).

Gregory fears that his detailed descriptions of those who suffer from leprosy may alienate his listeners' festal spirits. Yet he tells them that he speaks with such detail because he seeks to persuade them "that sometimes anguish is of more value than pleasure, sadness than celebration, meritorious tears than unseemly laughter" (14, 13). For whether his hearers like it or not, the lepers he describes are formed from the same clay as his listeners; the lepers are knit together with bones and sinews as they are; and, more importantly, the lepers "have the same portion as the image of God just as we do and who keep it perhaps better, wasted though their bodies may be; whose inner nature has put on the same Christ and who have been entrusted with the same guarantee of the Spirit as we" (14, 14).

It is not the leper but the well off who walk by and neglect those so afflicted who are in greatest peril. Gregory's depiction of the rich is as uncompromising as his portrait of those who suffer from poverty and leprosy: "As for us" (he addresses the rich as "us"),

> we magnificently ensconce ourselves on high and lofty beds amid exquisite and delicate coverlets and are put out of temper if we so much hear the sound of begging. Our floors must be scented with flowers—even out of season—and our tables drizzled with perfumes—so that we might coddle ourselves all the more. We eat from a table lavished with meats arranged in a manner to pander to our indecent and ungrateful belly. Wine is rejected and praised in an effort to gain the reputation of being extravagant voluptuaries, as if it is shameful not to be considered depraved (14, 17).

Why, Gregory asks, are we so sick in our souls with a sickness worse than any that affects the body? The body's illness is, after all, involuntary, but the sickness of wealth is deliberate. Why do the rich revel amid the misfortune of their brothers? Surely it is because we fail to see that we can only "gain our lives by acts of charity."[24] To so give is to imitate the

---

24. Gregory began "On Love for the Poor" with a description of twenty virtues that might be considered primary but concludes that charity is the first and greatest of the commandments. For "nothing so serves God as mercy because no other thing is more proper to God, whose mercy and truth go before, and to whom we must demonstrate

character of God. Gregory reminds his hearers that no matter how much they give, "you will never surpass God's generosity even if you hand over your entire substance and yourself in the bargain. Indeed, to receive in the truest sense is to give oneself to God" (14, 22).

Gregory ends "On Love for the Poor" urging his hearers to "appropriate the beatitude" that blesses those who are the merciful (14, 38). He concludes:

> If, then, you place any credence in what I say, servants of Christ and brothers and fellow heirs, while we may, let us visit Christ, let us heal Christ, let us feed Christ, let us clothe Christ, let us welcome Christ, let us honor Christ, not with food alone, like some; nor with ointments, like Mary; nor with tomb alone, like Joseph of Arimathea; nor with obsequies, like Nicodemus, who loved Christ in half measure; nor with gold and frankincense and myrrh as the Magi did before these others. Rather, since the Lord of all will have "mercy, and not sacrifice" (Mt. 9:13) and since a kind heart is worth more than myriads "of fat sheep," (Dn. 3:39) this let us offer to him through the poor who are today downtrodden, so that when we depart this world they may receive us into the eternal habitations (Lk.16:9) in Christ himself, our Lord, to whom be the glory forever. Amen. (14, 40)[25]

---

our capacity for mercy rather than condemnation; and by nothing else more than by showing compassion to our fellow man do we receive compassionate treatment in turn at the hands of him who weighs mercy in his scale and balance and gives just recompense" (14, 5).

25. Holman raises the interesting question of whether the effectiveness of Gregory's identification of the poor with Christ depends upon Cappadocian Christology being specifically Arian or Nicene. She observes that none of the texts by Basil, Nyssa, or Nazianzus on the poor are theological treatises, but, she says, their "elevated view of the poor as they relate to transcendent and incarnate deity in the Cappadocian texts is different from implications that logically attend Eunomius's Arian view of Christ, at least as the Cappadocians understood that view, as one in which the Son differed from the Father in hypostasis and substance precisely because of the Son's generate nature. A 'Eunomian' identification of the poor with Christ would most logically, in theory at least, maintain a certain unbroachable divide between generate (be it Christ or the poor) and transcendent. None of the three Cappadocians recognizes any such barrier. The religious power of the poor in fact rests on the belief that they hold a direct line of access to the highest realm of deity; their generate nature in no way limits this access and is in fact one of its most characteristic features" (181). Gregory's rhetoric, as this quotation makes clear, is suffused with biblical allusions. I have obviously not done justice to his use of Scripture as integral to the rhetorical power of his argument.

A University of the Poor

Gregory's "On Love for the Poor" was a liturgical action in which the poor and the leper, through the power of beautiful words, were made the center of a city ruled by Christ. Lepers are not recipients of charity, but rather they *are* God's charity for a community that is formed by as well as formed to be charity. Gregory "entitles" the poor, but as Holman observes, "the power of the poor depends on their place of primary honor in the kingdom of God. It depends on their revisionist identity as kin. The rights of these poor depend on their constructed religious role: as patrons, engaging in civic gift exchanges by receiving alms and effecting redemption."[26] Gregory's great gift, a gift made possible by his classical education, was to make his words work. Norris beautifully describes the way Gregory's words work this way:

> When Gregory looked outside his own life to the lives of others, he found it easier to describe how any Christian ought to look at the poor and the lepers by speaking of the situations in picturesque language. He focused the attention of the Constantinopolitan community on such problems by rhetorically connecting the death of Christ for human sins and the Christian treatment of those economically less fortunate or those so pitifully diseased. He made his appeals through strong rhetorical arguments, images that convinced. Here, as a contemplative who painted the ugliness of poverty and leprosy contrasted with the beautiful life created by Christ, he empowered his congregation to recognize that the saved, sinners nursed to health, should assist those whose condition was so grave. Contemplation was good but so was action. He described the afflicted in poignant terms. Those with no voice, no breath, no hands and no feet gave thanks that they had no eyes to see their ravaged bodies. Not even the misery of human life in itself could be detailed without the use of images and carefully crafted phrases. Ugliness would have to be presented with the same attention to detail that the contemplation of beauty demanded for speaking of magnificence. The contrast would only be properly strong if the same approach were employed in discussing each.[27]

26. Homan, *Hungry Are Dying*, 151.

27. Norris, "Gregory Contemplating the Beautiful," 11.

Gregory had been born rich, but he had learned to live as one born poor. Gregory had received the best education available, but that education had not alienated him from the poor. Yet that is exactly what happens to most who receive university educations in our time. At best, the modern university produces people (even some who may have come to the university from poverty) who, after being at the university, want to "do something for the poor." The university cannot produce people capable, as Gregory was capable, of seeing and describing the poor as beautiful. He was able to see the beauty of the poor because, schooled by Christ, he had no reason to deny them or wish they did not exist. His descriptions of those who suffered from leprosy were loving because he had learned to love Christ, and, therefore he could not help but love the afflicted, even those afflicted with leprosy.

Yet love of the poor and the leper is a profound challenge for those schooled by the presumptions of the modern university. In her extraordinary book, *Politics of Piety: The Islamic Revival and the Feminist Subject*, Saba Mahmood observes that the scholarship surrounding the poor and oppressed sponsored by the modern university robs them of agency. Mahmood's subject is Islamic women determined to learn to live lives of submissive modesty through prayer and the veil. Mahmood observes that such women are usually described in scholarly studies as deprived of the ability to enact the ethics of freedom "founded on their capacity to distinguish their own (true) desires from (external) religious and cultural demands."[28] Yet Mahmood observes: "If we recognize that the desire for freedom from, or subversion of, norms is not an innate desire that motivates all beings at all times, but is also profoundly mediated by cultural and historical conditions, then the question arises: how do we analyze operations of power that construct different kinds of bodies, knowledges, and subjectivities whose trajectories do not follow the entelechy of liberatory politics?"[29]

28. Mahmood, *Politics of Piety*, 148.

29. Ibid., 14. Mahood observes that even subaltern studies, which intend to show that the oppressed are not without agency through subversion or resistance, nonetheless continue to presume that a category of actions exists shaped by the universal desire for freedom. In contrast, Mahmood notes that even though her study focuses "on the practices of the mosque participants, this does not mean that their activities and operations they perform on themselves are products of their independent wills; rather my argument is that these activities are the products of authoritative discursive traditions whose logic and power far exceeds the consciousness of the subjects they enable. The kind of agency I

Mahmood notes that there is a politics assumed and legitimated by the scholarship that describes Islamic women as devoid of agency. It is the politics of secular liberalism that assumes the task is to privatize religious convictions in the interest of a progressive realization of freedom.[30] The university has been a crucial legitimating institution for such a politics, underwriting the state as the agent of liberation. Claims of and for rights, goods, and services made on the basis of identities shaped by liberal understandings of agency fall on the state as the source of their fulfillment. As a result, all aspects of human life (such as those associated with he family, education, worship, welfare, commercial transactions, birth and death) are now "brought under the regulatory apparatus of the state."[31]

The privileged place of the sciences in the modern university, particularly of the sciences associated with medicine, reflects this ethos of freedom and subsequent legitimation of the state. The sciences are often justified as having special status, because scientific knowledge is, allegedly, less arbitrary than the knowledges associated with the humanities. However, the prestige of science in the contemporary university has less to do with its assumed epistic status than with the assumption that science promises to give us the power to be freed from the limits of the body. Accordingly, science enjoys governmental support because governments in modernity legitimate themselves by promising to save us from illness and death.

In such a world, Gregory of Nazianzus's Oration "For the Love of the Poor" is unintelligible. Indeed, "For the Love of the Poor" challenges the

---

am exploring here does not belong to the women themselves, but is a product of the historically discursive traditions in which they are located" (32). That, I believe, is almost an exact description of what Gregory Oration "On Love for the Poor" performs for lepers.

30. I am hesitant to use the descriptor "liberalism," but Mahmood uses that term to describe "the belief that all human beings have an innate desire for freedom, that we all somehow seek to assert our autonomy when allowed to do so, that human agency primarily consists of acts that challenge social norms and not those that uphold them" (5). This view, which she also identifies as secular, is not simply a view of the state (though it is that); rather Mahmood identifies a "form of life" (191). I think she quite reasonably calls this position "liberal."

31. Mahmood, *Politics of Piety*, 193. It is important, however, to note that, to the credit of the modern university, someone such as Mahmood has been produced. The liberal formation of knowledges characteristic of the university as we know it is capable of self-correction. That this is so indicates that Christians cannot (nor should we want to) disparage the work of the liberal university. There is no "going back," only a going forward in the world as we find it.

deepest presuppositions of the politics of our day—a politics that gains its legitimacy by promising to eliminate suffering. Christians would be fortunate if the political challenge to Gregory was a Julian, but our problem is more complex. We are now the enemy unable to sustain educational alternatives capable of producing people who, like Gregory, through the gift of speech create community in which the loneliness of suffering is overwhelmed. Shaped by the rhetorical habits of the modern university, Christian and non-Christian alike cannot help but read Gregory's "On Love for the Poor" as reactionary.

Of course some may well ask, why do Christians need universities at all if they are institutions antithetical to Gregory's call for us to love the poor? The answer to such a challenge is that Christians need places of study where works such as Gregory's "On Love for the Poor" will continue to be studied and, hopefully, imitated.[32] As Gregory did in the fourth century, Christians today must continue to learn from Hellenism (which will no doubt come in surprising forms) if we are to say for ourselves and for the world that an eloquence learned from patient endurance is crucial for us to love and to be loved by the poor.[33]

Crucial for such an enterprise is that people like Gregory of Nazianzus exist. "No monks, no Christianity" is, I think, a generalization that is true for the very existence of the church. But I also think that any university that would form people who can love the poor will need those present

32. Harry Huebner ("Learning Made Strange," 303) argues that the church needs to challenge the university to place on its agenda the claim that a people's faith can be sustained only when its people are trained to negotiate economics, politics, science, sociology, and philosophy of the biblical faith in a world of competing claims: "The church needs an educated people to present a more complexified view of human nature—of violence, sin, peace, and love—than most people have, given their somewhat distorted view of things learned from popular culture. The church needs and educated people to present alternative answers to questions of justice, international relations, and power to present alternative models for how people can live together in ways that liberate and heal brokenness. The church needs an educated people to promote structures that foster the art of welcoming the stranger in a culture of protectionism; to promote that truth is not a possession but a gift in a age of capitalism; to promote that forgiveness in a viable strategy of social reconstruction in a culture of fear." Bruce Kaye, however, reminds me that the study of Gregory could take place in the church if necessary.

33. Mahmood, *Politics of Piety*, has an extraordinary account of the virtue *sabr*, which is akin to Christian patience, but means "to persevere in the face of difficulty without complaint" (171). Mahmood notes that the justification of *sabr* is neither the ability to reduce suffering, nor the achievement of self-directed choices, but rather the way that such a virtue as *sabr* makes one subservient to God (173).

who, by living with the poor, have learned to live as the poor live. It may well be that universities desiring their teaching to be disciplined by the gospel have at the center of their work, for example, a L'Arche home or a Catholic Worker house.[34]

Gregory drew on Hellenism to learn to be a rhetor, but he would not have been able to write an Oration like "On Love for the Poor" without having been baptized into Christ. To produce Gregories in our day, we will need the gifts of the university, but we will equally need people who do not need to attend the university to live lives faithful to their baptism. For Gregory knew—great rhetor that he was—that a people must exist with ears trained by the worship of the true God if the beauty of words like those in "On Love for the Poor" are to persuade. Our task as Christians (and the particular task for us Christians privileged to serve in the university) is to be, as well as to train, a people capable of reading and receiving a Gregory. Frederick Norris has spent his life trying to help us listen to Gregory, which is why it is so appropriate that we honor him on this occasion.[35]

34. Moreover, it should not be forgotten that because of universities, the Catholic Worker—and Dorothy Day and Peter Maurin—were formed, and that they in turn have formed ways of understanding the world. See, for example, Zwick and Zwick, *Catholic Worker Movement*. Jean Vanier, the founder of L'Arche, wrote his dissertation on Aristotle on friendship. His book *Made for Happiness: Discovering the Meaning of Life with Aristotle* is a wonderful exemplification of his ability to transform Aristotle's understanding of happiness and friendship through what he has learned living in the L'Arche community. Drawing on the work of Ernst Bloch, Romand Coles argues that the hunger of the belly and the hunger of the mind cannot be separated. The intellectual task will fall short, Coles suggests, if it seeks to proceed without engaging the questions of hunger with the hungry. See his "Hunger, Ethics, and the University: A Radical Democratic Good in Ten Pieces, " 253–76.

35. I am indebted to Sheila McCarthy for pressing me to try to articulate the relation between the university and the poor.

CHAPTER 11

Letter of January 8, 2005

Romand Coles

January 8, 2005

Dear Stanley,

I just read your fascinating paper on Gregory of Nazianzus. I think the Romero quote, "it is the poor who tell us what the polis is," and your condensation of Gregory's insight that the poor and the lepers are "God's charity for a community formed by charity in order to be charity," are about as pivotal beginning points for a semester on Christianity and radical democracy as I can imagine.

I take it that the solicitation to think and form communities *with* the poor, the lepers, the marginalized—in search of these truths—is at the heart of radical-democratic practice and distinguishes it from tepid notions of Christian charity as "helping," on the one hand, and from bureaucratic modes of welfare-state politics, on the other. It isn't that either of the latter two might have no role to play in response to suffering, but that all efforts that take them as central are wide of the mark. Wide of the mark both in missing the kind of enduring relational power that is necessary to transform odious systems of power, and in missing the infinite that is immanent (you would say, I think, "incarnate") in the ethical work of constructing such relationships. Put more strongly (because what would it mean to rein in vision and say it less so?): *truth* is in the difficult work of forming receptive relationships with the world's suffering-dreaming *as paradoxical and pregnant gifts*, in order to become communities that pronounce potent alternatives to that which is odious about "the principalities and the powers."

A *radical* democracy—whatever larger structural alternatives it comes to advocate—understands itself first and foremost as rooted in this liturgical project (drawing upon the Hellenistic *leitourgia*, or public service, but where the reciprocal work of being in relationship and of forming generous and receptive publics *is*, most profoundly, the public service that we might do with each other, above and beyond the instrumentalities in which we ought and must *also* be engaged). I suspect I may be more sympathetic to Walter Rauschenbusch than you are; but if I understand you, the deepest registers of your critique of him aim to illuminate ways in which he forgot and concealed much of this: the ways in which he was insufficiently radical in this sense, or insufficiently cruciform in this sense. One of the points where I believe that our thinking converges is in the recognition that all politics and church practice that shifts its heavy foot from the liturgical to the instrumental will be, in the words of Ani DiFranco, "built like an avalanche."[1]

Of course, as soon as one speaks of forming alternative relationships and communities of vulnerable generosity in relation to subjugated others as gifts, one sounds sappy and impossibly romantic—and one does violence. A certain impossibility infuses such words and makes one fear writing them the nanosecond they hit the page. Your statement of this impossibility in *Naming the Silences* strikes me as exactly right.

Last week, in conversation with you, I said that in spite of all the incredible work being done by the L'Arche communities of which Jean Vanier is a founding member, I found Vanier's contribution to the discussion of your work in the *Journal of Religion, Disability, and Health* to be somewhat underwhelming.[2] Your response, quite rightly I think, was that his words have a difficult time being heard outside the community of practices and relationships in which he is involved—difficult because outside of this context they can appear to fall quite short of the depth of the work being performed; or, alternatively, they sound sappy. Outside of L'Arche, Vanier's witness is difficult to give and difficult to receive. I don't say impossible, but very difficult.

This problem seems deeply related to some of the questions and themes that emerge in the section of your paper on the university and the

1. Ani Difranco, "Tamburitza Lingua."

2. At the time I wrote this letter I had not read any Vanier beyond his short interventions in the mentioned volume. As my chapter "Gentled into Being" makes clear, my understanding of Vanier was radically reformed after reading more of his work.

poor. I mean, think of the difficulties of hearing a statement like, "Lepers are not recipients of charity, but rather they are God's charity for a community formed by charity in order to be charity"! Think how impossibly romantic that can sound in a place as stingy and myopically constrained as the American university! And think of how much more so this must be the case if one tries to speak of them as a difficult gift from the mysterious radical contingency of becoming—a becoming lacking central or even Trinitarian agency. (You may say that the difficulties here are not only contextual but inherent in the unintelligibility of the articulation itself. I will agree with you then. [You should now be sniffing a Northern con!] But I am attracted to and even enthralled [as well as repelled] by the difficulties. They seem to me to provide a certain strange wealth [as well as a strange poverty], and I seek to cultivate the arts and works and words that articulate and intensify the attraction. I bracket this for now, as it is not my central concern here. . . .)

As you say, "The university is not able to produce people, as Gregory was able, to see and describe the poor as beautiful." And a bit later, "We are now the enemy unable to sustain educational alternatives capable of producing people like Gregory who through the gift of speech create community in which the loneliness of suffering is overwhelmed. Shaped by the rhetorical habits of the modern university, Christian and non-Christian alike, one cannot help but read Gregory's 'On Love for the Poor' as reactionary."

If I understand you and Gregory, the rhetorical city of words in which the poor are redescribed as beautiful is an opportunity to question and transform (in vulnerable relationship with the poor) our sense and practices of wealth-making and wealth-giving, not to legitimate and perpetuate structures of exploitation that reproduce poverty, but in fact is the condition of an alternative community that abolishes such exploitation.

Yet two things are crucial here in the supplement from Nazianzus: First, that this abolition does not aim simply to realize—now for *all* people—the acquisition of wealth as it was defined in the situation of exploitation itself. Second, that this abolition is neither possible nor desirable as an anonymous redistributive mechanism that would enable people to go about their lives pursuing myopic self-interest in their everyday lives, assured with good conscience that the basic structure will take care of the necessary adjustments for justice (as Rawls puts it).[3] In short, truly responding to poverty is to radically transform the world by profoundly questioning the meaning of wealth and poverty and (if one is not among those suffering material poverty) by taking up enduring relationships with those who are poor—and recognizing that one stands to receive far more than we can give in such relationships. *This* is also the condition of power for structural change that would abolish capitalist (and other) productions of poverty.[4]

Yet how to create a university community in which such thoughts are not dismissed as hopelessly romantic, on the one hand, or as reactionary, on the other (or both at the same time)? I think your idea that "universities desiring their teaching to be disciplined by the gospel have at the center of their work, for example, a L'Arche home or a Catholic Worker house" is crucial.[5] More generally, I take it that a precondition for a community of inquiry capable of voicing or hearing well the liturgies of which you are writing, or the ones I broadly gesture toward in this book and elsewhere, is serious relationships with the poor and marginalized in our midst. This was part of what I was getting at in the essay on physical and intellectual hunger that I presented at the Kenan Ethics Institute's "Debating Moral Education" conference in Spring 2004 (a significantly expanded version of which is included in this book as "Hunger, Ethics, and the University").[6] It is not only that these relationships and practices are an elemental part of engendering the requisite sensibilities, but moreover that their *absence* requires an enormous quantum of energy, sensibility, and scholarship of *denial* (of, e.g., systemic hunger). Hence, people come not simply to *lack* the requisite sensibilities, imaginations,

3. I articulate this critique of Rawls in "Feminists of Color and the Torn Virtues of Democratic Engagement," in *Beyond Gated Politics*.

4. I take it as obvious and in no need of elaboration that this is by no means a blanket critique of all institutions and practices of the welfare state, but a critique of several of their bases, formative practices, and many of their purposes. Hence in the present context (and especially in contestation to the "global race to the bottom"), I strongly support "universal health care," and I see an important role for state enablement of such; but the questions concern how we understand health and illness, how we fashion political, economic, and social practices of responsibility in relation to these, whether we seek these purposes and responsibilities through the construction of bureaucracies and cultures of deaf expertise or through dialogical communities of caregivers and patients, the relations between larger scale and more local initiatives, etc.

5. See page 245 above.

6. See chapter 12, pages 253–76.

and capacities but also come to be constituted as *resistant* to the presentation and growth of such sensibilities, imaginations, and relational capacities. Evil is not simply an absence but a produced presence that is positively resistant to the presence of poor, or (also) that *produces them as absent* (the poor as *those to be helped* can be a modality of the latter) as Boa Santos puts it.[7] The challenges are severe.

In *Beyond Gated Politics*, I focused on moving beyond the physical and imaginary walls that constitute so much of the present world (and the imaginary is unlikely to budge without reinvented corporeal performances in concert with others). At the Kenan conference, I focused on the need to leave that sterile conference room and engage those beyond the university walls, as a condition of the possibility of thinking. But I now think there was a real lacuna in those ways of putting things. For every university is full of the poor within our walls, within our midst, circulating in and out of our offices, cleaning the bathrooms and moving through hallways where we pass daily, serving us food and drink, maintaining the buildings and grounds in which we try to think, ceaselessly and ironically repairing the walls around East Campus on a regular basis as students and faculty stroll on by. In the first instance, it now seems to me that an elemental condition of the university as an institution that might enhance our capacities for voicing and hearing significant alternatives to the present would be the initiation of attentive, reciprocal, and cooperative relationships with the working poor on campus—*relationships* that are cultivated both as *ends in themselves* and as *avenues for transforming* practices and knowledge productions that have hitherto maintained poverty, disrespect, invisibility, etc. (Insofar as I would explore maintaining the Kantian language of *ends in themselves*, I would shift the imaginative emphasis here toward relationships, rather than unreceptive subjectivities.) Relationships that do not assume the inevitability of the present functional dichotomies (regarding who gets to teach and learn at the university and who doesn't, e.g.). Out of the bottomless poverties and impossibilities of our own lives—and also out of an insatiable sense of yearning for something better—many of us (students, teachers, workers, nonacademic members of the Durham community) are striving to create a community on and off campus in which we might rearticulate better lines of visibility, friendship, and hope. In these relationships, we might

7. Santos, "World Social Forum."

begin to invent a community more capable of voicing and hearing well the utopic spirits of Gregory and Bloch—a community in which these would seem neither romantic nor reactionary, a community in which it might again become possible to think. A community of practice to call forth and carry the weight of words that call forth and carry the weight of the community of practice. We started as a living-wage effort, then deinstrumentalized toward being a livable-jobs/living-wage effort, and now are deinstrumentalizing further toward being a livable-community endeavor. It is not that we are dropping the instrumental aims of last year (far from it), but rather that as *relationships* have begun to form, many of us have begun to realize that *they are the thing*. All our instrumental goals are supports, perhaps urgent and crucial, yet not the real thing unless connected to, ushering from, and nourishing the relationships that infinitely exceed whatever purposes we discern at present.

This raises the question of time, which I think is at the heart of our seminars. How do we become "friends of time," how do we relearn delight in our new solidarities and differences, as you and Vanier put it? This seems to me to be the question that is at the heart of being with the mentally disabled, being a new church, a new democracy. It is taking the time for the question that has drawn our conversation thus far and gives it a future. Without any question, I can tell you that my favorite page in Marsh's *Beloved Community* is 93, where he writes:

> It is easy to forget that so much of a civil rights life involved sitting around freedom houses, community centers, and front porches with no immediate plan of action. The discipline of waiting required uncommon patience even as it sustained humility and perspective, resisting the cultural paradigm of efficiency. SNCC's genius was its ability to demonstrate to black southerners the strategies available to social progress within an unhurried and sometimes languorous emotional environment. As such, a condition for achieving beloved community was a certain kind of stillness in a nation of frenetic activity and noisy distractions, learning to move at a different pace. . . . More than a few left the south out of boredom. Yet most who pursued a movement life understood the quality of their life together as an attempt to live into a new and distinct kind of time. . . . Being revolutionary meant learning how to act out of the deepest silence.[8]

8. Marsh, *Beloved Community*, 93.

In a nutshell, to proliferate words, practices, and powers in response to the authoritative question of *that* time is at the heart of what I understand to be radical democracy. Talk to you later this afternoon.

Hopeful peace,

rom

CHAPTER 12

Hunger, Ethics, and the University:
A Radical-Democratic Goad in Ten Pieces

Romand Coles

This is an immoderate paper, forged at once in the flames of a radical-democratic ethos and a deep suspicion regarding a substantial portion of what is called "moral education." Hunger, that aching in the gut, is at once a prism, a call bell, and potentially a blinder. Hunger is among the most urgent of situations. This urgency at once demands an ethical-political response and critically illuminates many contemporary efforts at moral education. Yet the urgency of hunger can also harbor its own blindness if it is construed only as a call to satiation. If universities are to adopt ethical-political stances toward the world, stances that serve as more than ideologies or as more than new modes of disciplinary power or as more than feel-good exercises that leave most of what is unjust in place, or as more than knee-jerk radicalism, then I suspect we will have to invent arts of negotiating between and entwining responsibilities for the hunger of the belly and the hunger of the mind. This is a small gesture toward that end.

~

Each year at the beginning of the twenty-first century, over 11 percent of the people—about 34 million—in the richest country in the world were "food insecure," which means that they found themselves skipping meals, facing hunger, taking drastic steps to avoid it because they could not afford to eat. (Additionally, tens of millions live with the knowledge that they are never more than a couple of paychecks or a job-dismissal notice away from this situation in which they see some of their friends, relatives, and neighbors.) Even at the end of the extended economic boom during the 1990s, the number of food insecure stood at 31 million people—lots of them kids—living with the proximate specter of hunger. Food insecurity and hunger are not merely problems that we have not yet successfully tackled. They are *systematically produced* by the political economy in which we live. Most people earning minimum wages and supporting households are food insecure, as are vast numbers of those at the official federal "poverty" level. And this urgent metonym of class power and poverty intersects with other modes of power such that the rates of food insecurity increase about threefold for households headed by women, blacks, and Hispanics (all statistics from USDA).

What might it mean to talk about moral education in the context of such systemically engendered *corruption*? I emphasize this word to evoke both the bodily suffering and the systemic core of the problem. The corruption to which I refer is not addressed by fine-tuning mechanisms of oversight and accountability to make the system work as it should. My point is that even when the system—not only its mechanisms of exchange and administration but also its patterns of knowledge production and pedagogy—are working "well," so too is the production of hunger and widespread oblivion to it. Corruption speaks not only of the moral debasement of a situation in which, as Rabbi Abraham Heschel framed the message of the Jewish prophets, "few are guilty, but all are responsible"; corruption speaks also of the literal bodily degeneration of those millions who are born hungry and who die young because of hunger and related ills, and of the degeneration of a collective body that produces this situation.[1] What does teaching "values" mean when many of these values are often articulated in ways complicit with this system of power and suffering, or in ways that are relatively silent about it, or incapable of disturbing the production of deafening indifference? What does it mean to teach values when teaching values leads only to the occasional charitable trip to the soup kitchen on the way to the oblivious high-paying job in the corporate firm?

~

At one time, hunger talk was honest, blunt, and central for many intellectuals. And it is clear that *talk of hunger* was closely linked to the emergence of a new political economic morality—a new moral education. According

1. Heschel, *Prophets*, 16.

to Karl Polanyi, these themes received their earliest articulation in 1786, in William Townscend's *Dissertation on the Poor Laws by A Well-Wisher of Mankind*, which proclaimed:

> Hunger will tame the fiercest animals, it will teach decency and civility, obedience and subjection, to the most perverse. In general it is only hunger which can spur and goad them [the poor] on to labor. . . . Legal constraint [to work] is attended with much trouble . . . whereas hunger is not only peaceable, silent, unremitting pressure, but, as the most natural motive to industry and labor, it calls forth the most powerful exertions; and, when satisfied by the free bounty of another, lays lasting and sure foundations for good will and gratitude.[2]

In a world where some and not others are confined to dirty and servile work, the specter of an aching in the gut is to spur and mold people into the norms of labor and to constitute a morality of docility, acceptance, deference, and thankful allegiance to the powerful. In the first decade of the nineteenth century, Townscend's discourse was taken up across a wide ideological spectrum. This spectrum includes not only Malthusians but traditionalists such as Burke, who affirmed economic liberalism and its constitutive relation to hunger in part as a persistent and detailed mode of governing the poor (without "government") for purposes of public security; and utilitarians like Bentham, who argued that hunger would be both a vital and sufficient force to drive the poor into his panoptic "industry houses"—nightmare utopias of moral betterment and productivity where the poor could be subjected to minute and continuous "inspectability" and administration—a "mill to grind rogues honest and idle men industrious."[3] As Polanyi and Foucault have argued quite convincingly, the panopticon exemplifies a type of moral administrative power and pedagogy that begins to circulate widely in the nineteenth century.

Hence at the same time that Kant theorizes a kingdom of persons as "ends in themselves," Townscend inaugurates a political economic morality that has at its heart the need for working-class people to feel in their gut the *specter of their own end itself*—the prospect of their death—in order to be taught the life of hard work (at miserable pay), civility, and

2. Quoted in Polanyi, *Great Transformation*, 113.
3. Sir L. Stephen, quoted in ibid., 121.

obedience; in order to be taught their true value in market society. Michel Foucault provides a more penetrating account of panoptic power than Polanyi, for he details the ways in which it isolates people (architecturally separating them in more rigid ways from broader social and historical contexts, and also separating them from each other within the new disciplinary cellular spaces) and reconstructs their relations wholly in terms of the objectives of narrowly construed productivity. These separations and disciplined connections then become the new imaginary, which simultaneously produces material goods, class power, and hunger, while minimizing the solidarities, modes of witness, and questioning that might resist these in the name of other alternatives. Yet what Foucault omits is the extent to which the urgency of feeling one's end in hunger was central to the beginning of the "new man" made into commodified, socially and temporally detached labor (detached from places, communities, traditions, unwonted solidarities), a commodity well constituted to conform to the needs of an increasingly mobile political economy of productivity—and incapacitated when it came to initiating anything beyond these requirements. The way that this feeling of death abstracts and reconstitutes selves resonates (albeit very paradoxically and only partly) with those aspects of Kant's moral thought that constitute us as the most abstracted ends, and thereby that also inhibit our capacity for beginning historically specific ethical and political action that might challenge the limits of the given modes of "rationality."[4] What I mean is that our ethical capacities to see, feel, and actively respond to suffering, and to generate social and political alternatives, are profoundly rooted in multifarious and textured human *relationships* that exceed the dominant scripts in manifold ways. Our ethical capacities degenerate insofar as our economic, political, and moral experiences and vocabularies reflect and reinforce, on the one hand, abstract isolation, and, on the other, interactions that are increasingly disciplined on the microlevel in homogenizing ways. I think Polanyi shows that facing the prospect of one's end in hunger played a role driving people into new disciplinary modes of power. Unwittingly, Kant's morality correlates with—and provides too little to effectively resist—the damages associated with selves thus abstracted in the everyday functioning of new systems of productivity.

4. For a detailed analysis of Kant on this score, see Coles, *Rethinking Generosity*.

The widespread experience of hunger played a vital role both in detaching commodified people from their various local contexts and traditions, and in articulating a new metaphysics with profound implications for ethical enquiry and political agency. Polanyi's history captures this tenor repeatedly, as he writes of a new "evangelical fervor" for the self-regulating market, a "fanaticism of sectarians" with a "blind faith in spontaneous progress," "an emotional faith in spontaneity . . . a mystical readiness," and "uncritical reliance on the alleged self-healing virtues of unconscious growth."[5] Connected to a political-economic process enabled by a visceral fear of one's early *end* was the birth of a new temporality, in which the present was understood to be already animated by a future that, as "self-healing," permitted no interruption, no regulation. Pure futurity is the "end of history." A future that might feature a necessary and radical transformation of the present is precluded by the very way the present defines itself as eternally self-correcting in an unlimited way: As the present is always already the future, which always already contains the principle of its own "self-healing" correction still further into the future, every ethical-political initiation toward another world is declared in advance to be impossible. History as the movement of time in which human formations come and go is replaced by a notion of time governed forever by the present formation. And all this is linked to the widespread specter of an aching in the gut, which our society has proved quite skilled at producing, for all its capacity to generate wealth.

∼

This brief sketch is, I think, extremely pertinent to any discussion of ethics and higher education. Hunger is among the most urgent of situations. Yet it is integrally connected to modes of power that—from the microproduction of selves to the macroproduction of theodicies of history and political economy—simultaneously produce this urgency and sever it from ethical and political reflection and action that might transform the world in response. Indeed, as time goes by in the end of history, we no longer hear the Towncsends, Malthuses, Burkes, and Benthams of the world openly articulating the links between hunger, the moral education of the masses, and our political economy. They still dominate the conversation, but they have mastered the arts of esoteric speech, rarely mentioning hunger and speaking instead simply of necessary unemployment, of

5. Ibid., 135, 76, 33.

keeping the minimum wage very low if keeping it at all, of disciplinary reconstitutions of the moral fiber of the poor, of inflationary dangers, and so forth. The theodicy of capitalist political economy has learned to disclose its wounds primarily in softer light—in a light that renders hunger and its urgency publicly invisible and largely unthought about, while capitalist political economy absorbs within itself, and in advance, the domain of legitimate responses to a situation that is, as the familiar refrain goes, "improving though we have more to do." We have become mostly indifferent to the urgency of hunger. That its widespread presence should pose no challenge to our basic frameworks in fundament is a *doxa* that "goes without saying, because it comes without saying."[6]

Two things in this context strike me about so many well-meaning liberal academics who are concerned about the unethical character of the contemporary world and of higher education: First, they rarely mention hunger, and I wonder if this is not one important factor contributing to a certain lack of urgency that pervades too many such discourses (while the right wing has mastered the rhetoric of urgency for disciplinary schemes to secure the order). Second, the discussions tend to focus on renderings of honesty, courage, character, respect, fairness, generosity, and so forth, that are framed as if they could be achieved without doing much at all to question and change the basic parameters of our political-economic relationships and practices or the associated theodicy of history that has bound our ethical-political imaginations. It is as though, if we just walk our paths with moral rectitude and perhaps a little bit of tinkering at the edges of things, this might be enough. But what if many of these sanctioned paths are directly corrupt for the evil they do, or indirectly corrupt for the responsibilities they deny? What if we would have to *walk very different paths in very different ways* in order for ethics and ethical education to have much sense at all? What if a *world* of different paths and modes were necessary, and what if they were necessary *now*—because our situation is as urgent as an aching in the gut? What if ethical education (in absence of the pressure of these questions) might share much more than it would like to with the "Well-Wisher of Mankind," who formulated a pedagogy of "decency and civility, obedience and subjection, gratitude

6. Here I am thinking of Pierre Bourdieu's understanding of deeply inscribed meanings through which we fundamentally perceive the world, and in relation to which we have great trouble becoming conscious. See Bourdieu, *Outline of a Theory of Practice*, 167.

and good will," and who thus laid the foundations for a political economy of hunger?

~

The pain of hunger indissociably gives rise to a most visceral questioning: how then will I feed myself, my child, this friend, this stranger in a context that denies us? This same pain can also demand answers that are, on both personal and macropolitical scales, dead ends—potentially inscribed within either the matrix of egoism or the current framework of alternatives. So the ethical-political issue, it seems, is how to receive the urgency (and the system-questioning pressure it brings) without killing the space of this opening by knowing "too well" what justice entails. How might we avoid the traps of teaching ethics to undergraduates in ways that presume that we professors know what and how they must learn? How might we avoid the traps of "service learning" forms, which assume that students know about the communities to which they are sent: that students know what these communities must learn and how these communities must function? How might we avoid the traps of an ethics education that uncritically accepts conceptions of the self and of the order in our efforts to engender ethical sensibilities? It is precisely here that the hunger of universities concerned with ethical-political education *might* play an important role beyond the confines they often reinforce.

The hunger for knowledge has taken many different forms, not all of them desirable by any means. Yet the forms of hunger that seem to me most promising are those concerned with questions that probe the possibilities for transcending in desirable ways the limits of present orders of knowing and doing. Such questions have a hunger for that which is beyond present "truths" and "necessities" implicated in unfreedom and suffering. I think universities, at their best moments, can be places where this hunger is cultivated, nurtured, and engaged with the world beyond its walls. Kant, who contributed significantly to theorizing the modern university, theorized enlightenment precisely as "an exit," a "way out," an "escape" (*Ausgang*) from humans' "inability to use [their] own understanding without guidance from another." By this last turn of phrase, at his most insightful, he meant not that we should ignore others' thoughts in our thinking, but that we should work to release the "ball and chain" of a lazy reason that accepts the dogmas of the current order as necessary and universal.[7] Radicalizing this formulation with and against Kant, Foucault wrote of an enlightenment ethos as a "limit attitude," "at the frontiers," questioning "in what is given to us as universal, necessary, obligatory, what place is occupied by whatever is singular, contingent, and the product of arbitrary constraints . . . a critique that takes the form of a possible transgression."[8] This hunger for other ways of thinking and being—which Foucault described not as a devouring curiosity but as a curiosity consumed by the "question of knowing if one can think differently than one thinks, and perceive differently than one sees"—is an absolutely vital aspect of the university, and is vital as well to imagining and pursuing ways of eliminating both hunger and the system of commodified labor, disciplinary power, and theodicies of history with which it is entwined. These systems are nearly two hundred years old, and they live on in most efforts to critique and transcend them. Animated by the urgency of hunger, we will have to work hard at the limits of our knowing if we are to move beyond "solutions" that reproduce the very hunger, power, and theodicy they were meant to escape. In other words, the ethical and political hunger of the university is *empty* if divorced from the aching in the gut of millions, but efforts to abolish the hunger will likely be *blind* if divorced from the hunger of the university at the frontiers of knowledge.

∾

Yet there are many ways to be blind. Drawing upon Aristotle's discussion in *De anima*, Derrida notes that bees lack eyelids and thus *always* see. They know a lot but can't learn. They lack the ability not only to hear but also to close off sight (that shutting of the eye at regular intervals), which Derrida links to being able to listen better; whereas "man can lower the sheath, adjust the diaphragm, narrow his sight, the better to listen, remember, and learn."[9] Playfully deflecting an imaginary suggestion that he seeks "to cultivate an art of blinking," Derrida nevertheless proclaims that the university "must not be a sclerophthalmic [dry-eyed and unblinking] animal." Derrida argues that we must relax our teleological energies periodically, rhythmically, like blinking our eyes, so that we might practice an

7. Kant, "An Answer to the Question: 'What is Enlightenment?,'" 54–55.

8. Foucault, "What is Enlightenment?," 45. I develop the dialogical ethic in Foucault's conception of enlightenment in Coles, *Self/Power/Other*.

9. See Derrida, "Principle of Reason," 5.

Enlightenment more infused with "listening." He evocatively seeks this possibility "'in the twilight of an eye', for it is in the most crepuscular . . . situations of the Western university that the chances for this 'twinkling' of thought are multiplied."[10]

One way of remaining sclerophthalmic and blind is linked to the way we often conceive of "frontiers of knowledge," which today many so often interpret as a cutting edge in time: according to the temporal matrix of the neoliberal theodicy, which sees (as we have already noted in relation to Polanyi) the present as the cutting edge of history animated by a self-healing future. Within this frame, traditions of "the past" are to be discarded from contemporary ethical-political dialogues and struggles, as are insurgent efforts that would lean into the future against the grain of "history." (Or, where "tradition" is not to be discarded, it is to be *deployed* for the functional requirements of the present order, but not as a set of sources and ghosts that might radically contest the imperatives of this order.) If the university seeks a chance to make a contribution to transforming a world that produces hunger, it will have to nurture much better than it has spaces for different, not infrequently *rival*, modes of enquiry. This is especially the case as it seems that our political economy is relatively unique—according to economic anthropologists—in its systematic deployment of the threat of hunger. The time is ripe for listening to traditions and to emerging groups that have done or are doing better in this regard.

I think this means that the notion of "frontiers of knowledge" will have to shift from being the edge inhabited by the most advanced "moderns" to being the spaces of scholarly and practical engagement at the edges *between* different groups. With MacIntyre and Mignolo, I think this calls for *universities that create more space to cultivate ethical-political modes of enquiry and pedagogy*—e.g., of neo-Thomists, Jews, indigenous peoples, liberals, Islamic traditions, and radical-democratic genealogists.[11] It will take multiple efforts to think differently, each with some

10. Ibid., 20.

11. See MacIntyre's proposal in *Three Rival Versions of Moral Enquiry: Encyclopedia, Genealogy and Tradition*; and Mignolo's work on the recent genesis of Indigenous universities in Central and South America. See, for example, Mignolo, *Idea of Latin America*. I discuss the question of enquiry and political practice across different traditions in relation to liberalism, MacIntyre, Derrida, education, and urban grassroots political organizing in Coles, *Beyond Gated Politics*.

organizational autonomy and a will to engage at the intersections of myriad efforts.

~

Yet I suspect that this blinking and pluralized hunger for knowledge, the university's hunger, will amount to very little ethically if it does not simultaneously pursue myriad forms of engagement at another frontier, namely, that border between itself and those who live beyond its walls (or who slave within its walls) in or more proximate to hunger and poverty. If, as I have briefly suggested, the hunger of the belly and the hunger of the mind must be entwined in new ways that interweave urgency and reflection concerning the suffering of the present order, then a crucial aspect of this project must involve political modes of engagement with communities struggling with poverty. Such political modes of engagement cannot be limited only to charity or "service" but must involve receptive efforts to learn from and with those who are struggling politically in the neighborhoods and regions of the world that "always get dumped on and never get plowed."[12] We need to move our inquiring and collaborative work to those places. I think we need to do this not only as a central part of exploring and inventing radical-democratic possibilities for transforming the present order, but also because of a sense that our imaginations are as starved and constrained as are the bellies of millions of people. As Adorno liked to quote Benjamin, "While there is a beggar, there is a myth."[13] It may well be that one vital condition of possibility for *thinking* differently hinges very much upon *seeing, being, and doing* differently— receptively engaging other lives, dwelling in the forbidden zones of our cities, inventing other modes of ethical-political relationship and power across the lines that confine both bellies and imaginations. The urgency of ethics and politics springs from both places. Undoubtedly, such efforts will take many agonistic and contested forms. This multiplicity is both necessary and good. But where such efforts are entirely absent, I worry that much ethics talk in the university will be little but a sham.

~

12. This line is from Ani DiFranco, "Not So Soft," *Like I Said,* Righteous Babe Records, 1993.

13. Adorno, *Negative Dialectics,* 203.

Blasphemy! Is not the above suggestion diametrically opposed to one of the most sacred foundations of the life of the mind (and of the institutions devoted to it), namely the presumption that the task of thinking requires disinterest, distance, spaces walled off from the immediacies of everyday life—and most especially from the urgency of hunger—in order to thrive? Would not crossing the lines and confusing the distinct purposes that delineate these spaces lead to the destruction of precisely what is most precious about higher education? This danger is not to be taken lightly. It is real and requires constant renegotiation. Yet not crossing these lines is a real danger as well (not to mention the danger of powerful corporate imperatives that ceaselessly colonize the spaces of higher education today with such ease, I think, in part because of the political and economic blindness engendered by naive "liberal humanist" assumptions about sharp lines between knowledge and power). Our assessments of and responses to relative dangers always hinge on the terms in which we construe and by which we measure them. Here I want to suggest that rethinking hunger in relation to human becoming, thinking, and imagining can help us reconsider the dangers and possibilities at hand. And no one has done so more profoundly than the German thinker Ernst Bloch.

～

Bloch is an extremely complicated and difficult thinker. At times, perhaps, he exaggerates his claims, offers insufficient support for them, and minimizes other elements of the human situation that put pressure on central themes that he pursues. In the present context, I am interested in him as an *evocative* thinker, one who opens windows for us to begin to see ways beyond some of the impasses sketched above; one who opens doors through which we might move in tentative exploration. Reading Bloch as an evocative thinker here (which is generally how I think he should be read), I am less concerned to defend or elaborate his claims in detail than I am to show how they might spur reflection on the thematic of our twin hungers of belly and mind. Bloch suggests ways beyond reified understandings of humans, the present order, and "the end of history," and he helps advance paths for understanding the politics and production of knowledge—paths that might shift our sense of ethics and higher education in more promising ways. As an evocation, this reading of Bloch is intended as an invitation to urgent conversation rather than as a foundation or a conclusion. The question I bring to my reading of Bloch (which is similar to the question he brings to the world) is not so much, is this true? as it is, what might it be possible to see, become, and do in a better way than the way that we are currently seeing, becoming, and doing? How might Bloch challenge our turning away from the hungry, our aversion to hunger, our abstraction from the body, and our sense of a present beyond which there are no alternatives?

Many thinkers follow Hobbes's rendering of hunger as egoistic appetite, which, unchecked, tends toward a war of all against all that is "nasty, brutish, and short." Another major path of modern thinking follows Locke in locating the most profound aspect of the self *beyond hunger* in rational self-possession. For Bloch, in contrast to Locke, human life is most deeply that which "does not have what belongs to it, but rather searches for it and intends it outside, i.e., . . . [that which] is hungry."[14] Yet far from ensconcing us in egoism, this fact is what *might* draw us into relations of differential solidarity with others, as well as into a longing and hope for more adequate thinking and for a better world.

In a manner that profoundly illuminates the issues at hand, Bloch *reads* hungering as pivotal to ethical-political life, to the life of the mind, and to the relation between the two. Bloch's claim, as I read him, is not that our hungering tends inexorably to give birth to his rendering of it, but, nevertheless, that it solicits and lends itself to such an interpretation, and that this interpretation suggests a vision of and mode of participating in the human condition that is compelling precisely insofar as it transcends many of the problems engendered by alternative understandings. If Hobbes sometimes writes of himself as an eye doctor whose task is to improve our ethico-political vision, Bloch might be read as one who accepts this ophthalmological identity as central to the theorist's task and then offers a radically different reading. Reading, or interpreting the human condition, becomes for Bloch something that is *engendered by the very hunger it seeks to interpret*—in a manner that propels a circle that is essentially never transparent and cannot be finished. The status of Bloch's claims can only be assessed in relation to alternative interpretations, in light of what they illuminate, the responsiveness they nurture, and the modes of life they thus facilitate or impede. Of course, I am interested in

---

14. Bloch, *Principle of Hope*, 1:287–88. Hereafter cited in text with page number in this section.

them in relation to the failures that I have identified through the lens of Polanyi's critical reading of market society.

For Bloch, hunger, *like* all of the human condition, is not a fact that is simply present. Rather it is infused with what he calls "forward dawning" or "not yet"—hope for a fullness that is not yet present. Hunger *shares* this character of opening to the future, but it is also *exemplary* of human being as hopeful, insofar as its relation to the not-yet has a particular poignancy and intensity, even with many other possible ways of living and interpreting it. How hopeful our hunger may be, and how hopeful we humans may become, depends, however, not simply on the presence of hunger but on how well we acknowledge and interpret its futurity (one could say, on how well we hunger for our hunger), on how well we respond to it and act in light of it.[15]

Bloch suggests that we are beings who hunger for situations less degrading and more conducive to thriving; we thirst for well-being, knowledge, and a better world; we feel ourselves searching from an empty place toward a world beyond ourselves and beyond its present configuration. Hence, he writes, "'longing' [is] the only honest state in all men" (45). This longing comes from an empty place—first and most literally the gut, but it is simultaneously entwined with and generative of an unfolding abundance of wishing, imagining, and experimentation that is distinctively human. For Bloch, to acknowledge hungering as elemental is to situate theory and ethics (including his own) within this ongoing movement that none can "possess," yet that all can sense and evoke in ways that inform politics with hope.

Our hunger emerges from deep within our bellies as a drive to stay alive. Yet far from locking us in a state of solipsism, the universality of hungering can open us to others and the world beyond. Bloch argues that "the unemployed person on the verge of collapse, who has not eaten for days, has really been led to the oldest needy place of our existence and makes it visible. In any case, sympathy with the starving is the only widespread sympathy there is, in fact the only one that is widely possible. . . . [T]he cry of the hungry is probably the strongest single cry that can be directly presented" (65). Though the exaggerated form of this statement seems to marginalize other deep streams of compassion, his over-

---

15. As I read things, hunger is a certain pregnancy in human being, and Bloch is a midwife. There are other ways to read Bloch, and Bloch is not entirely consistent.

all point seems important: The sight of others in hunger opens lines of elemental responsiveness—corporeal communication beyond the limits of our individual flesh. We can and do, of course, resist this radically discomforting sense of flesh-crossing vulnerability and suffering, but Bloch contends that face to face with another hungry person, we have great difficulty doing so for long. Interesting is that this difficulty would partly explain the proliferation of ordinances, geographical constructions and practices, highly policed relational taboos, and energetic mobilizations of ideological discourses that impede such witness. Thus, this most basic drive engenders and illuminates *both* our own vulnerable neediness *and* harbors a compassionate call. It *both* harbors an urge that calls our unjust order deeply into question, *and* it can fuel a security-seeking fear of such questioning, which can engender the reactive policing that perpetuates and intensifies unjust orders. This suggests (in a way that perhaps exceeds Bloch's own understanding) that hunger lends itself to radically opposed possibilities. Bloch's project is to seize the more promising *potentia* that is "not yet conscious" and render some of its possibilities more explicit in order to participate in their realization.

Hunger, Bloch argues, is not a static human drive but rather is always *becoming* in historically variable relations with the perceived world, with other needs, and with others. And sometimes our hunger transforms in ways that seek not simply different objects, but more radical renewals in which our vulnerability and longing tend beyond extant horizons: "Hunger cannot help continually renewing itself. But if it increases uninterrupted, satisfied by no certain bread, then it suddenly changes . . . becomes rebellious, does not go out in search of food merely within the old framework. It seeks to change the situation which caused its empty stomach, its hanging head" (75). As nagging and persistent, our longing sometimes solicits critical reflexivity concerning ourselves, our structural situation, and the relations with others that generate and sustain our experiences of deprivation. In this process, our hungering can stimulate our imaginations of and efforts to experiment (with a "revolutionary interest") toward alternative situations that would transcend unjust ills of the present. Vital to such transformations is the emergence of solidarities and collaborations nourished in part by sympathetic communications among hungering and hunger-prone bodies.

On Bloch's account (contra Hannah Arendt), this hunger-related solidarity with others need not develop toward a community that would devour human difference in the in-distinction of our basic neediness. Rather, such compassion and communication *can* (but doesn't necessarily) provide a dynamic opening toward others, through which we might come to acknowledge them as *distinct relational centers* of hunger, dynamic longing, and imagining. Indeed, this hunger-related solidarity is an indispensable condition of such acknowledgement, if there is to be any. The self as a *reflective* hungering being (reflective significantly *because* it hungers), then, comes to understand itself as a being beyond the self's and others' possession—a being *essentially drawn outside itself*. Such reflective hunger, hungers to be responsive to a world of others that it comes to know and desire *as others*, whom it cannot and should not seek to consume—lest it proliferate the contradictions and deprivations of all efforts to do so, and simultaneously deny the abundant richness of human plurality. As we reflect deeply upon our becoming as hungering beings *as such*, Bloch suggests, the character of our hunger shifts from a consumptive focus toward efforts to valorize and create conditions conducive to the generative dimension of our coexistence as plural hungering creatures. We then increasingly hunger to participate with others in the articulation of and struggle toward a community that better enables diverse hungering and hoping selves to flourish together. We become, quite literally, *eccentric*, drawn into "external orbits" in relation to other beings (91).

Nowhere is this clearer than in Bloch's rendering of *utopia* through the lens of hunger—where, I think, Bloch is profoundly suggestive for considerations of ethics, politics, and ultimately higher education. Hungering, Bloch suggests, is paradoxically an emblematic root of *both* the desire to satiate human neediness *and* the infinite fecundity of our insatiable hopeful longing. Utopia must be wrought in response to tensions between *both* of these dimensions of our becoming at once.

On the one hand, the struggle to address our hunger appears to harbor a *telos* of urgent and radical *satiation*. Hunger stimulates wishes, visions, and fantasies of a world of *fulfillment* beyond all deprivation (including, of course, beyond situations constitutive of self-defeating longings that perpetuate experiences of deprivation). Our daydreams beyond deprivation "journey to the end," as Bloch puts it. Beyond "world-improving roaming," or endless striving—which can be a hellish vertigo always threatened with Nothing—hunger endlessly stimulates humans toward fantasies of "arrival"; the imagination of unimaginable conditions beyond want, where all our needs and all the potentials of our own, of others', and of the world's being would be fully realized (95). We imagine and strive toward a world where all potentials for flourishing that are not yet conscious and that have not yet become would be fully manifest. The teleology that surges forth here—animating and orienting our striving—aims in a profound sense toward an absolute, an "*anticipated keeping still*" (289, Bloch's emphasis) in an astonished state beyond need, an immanent leap toward a *summum bonum*. Human experimentation thus driven manifests hunger as a "force of production" in history. Bloch, as we see below, finds this yearning problematic and simultaneously irresistible. In the midst of an endless proliferation of ideologies justifying various modes of suffering and deprivation, these images of "All" energize a radical demythologizing resistance and an imaginative struggle toward alternatives, in the face of powers that seek to abort the fecundity of the human yearning and possibility. Would not an ethics education deprived of this energetic, urgent hope for a perfect flourishing sell short our critical and generative capacities?

Nevertheless, the image of and demand for fulfilled utopic hope can be as detrimental to our flourishing as it may be conducive to it. While our hungering strives beyond hunger toward satiated fullness, simultaneously, as we reflect upon ourselves as hungering beings, we discover the presence of an equally grand and *inexhaustible potential in us that yearns critically and imaginatively beyond every present that claims to encompass satiation and fullness.* As we examine this *insatiable longing* retrospectively, we discover that time after time it discloses detrimental aspects of given orders as well as alternative possibilities. A close look at our hungering discloses that we harbor a tremendous latency that is "not yet conscious" (or "has not yet become") and is precisely a crucial wellspring of our vitality and ethico-political engagement. We thus come to valorize this latent unquenchability within and between us, such that we project it onto our hopeful imaginings of utopian futures. In so doing, we help free the future from our possessive grasp. Beyond a hope for the future as a satiated fully realized "all," we come to appreciate that "it cannot be so because the future dimension . . . itself contains *unmastered* Now, i.e. darkness, just as the Now itself still contains *unopened* future, i.e. newness, and surges forward to meet it" (297).[16] In other words, even

16. In this sense Bloch writes of a "crack" in every utopic imagining—a "blind spot,"

as our hungering suggests that we must strive politically toward conditions conducive to the satiated fulfillment of human potential, it *also* calls us to recognize, respond to, and nurture humans as essentially hungering, striving, imagining beings harboring dynamic, abundant, and unpredictable aspects "opening out on to the as yet unarrived" (139). This "unarrived" is paradoxically a constitutive aspect of hope. Any ethical pedagogy or politics that seeks simply to free us of *this* poverty and its related abundance would be a travesty.

Let me elaborate a few of the interrelated ethical, political, and pedagogical stakes of this brief (and thus sketchy) excursus on Bloch's evocation of hunger-born hope. First, I hope to have gestured toward some of the ways in which the hunger of the belly and the hunger of our imagination might be—contra some prevalent assumptions—not only compatible but also intrinsically and informatively connected with one another. Bloch's interpretation of our hunger(ing) can shed light on some of the *purposes* of human inquiry and political life (i.e., ideal satiation and pregnant latency) as well as on the centrality of *modes* (i.e., urgency and tensional complexity) of opening onto unexpected newness, through which these purposes might at once be sought and unsettled. Far from engendering a simple-minded dogmatism (though the drive for satiation always *risks* this), careful reflection upon our hungering being calls us beyond our complacency with the present *as well as* beyond our complacency with alternative static ideals and arrangements in light of which we would transform the present. These lessons strike me as utterly crucial to a dialogical ethics of higher education *and* of politics, albeit in ways that are not identical.[17]

---

the "unrealized." Hence, Bloch writes (in a very difficult but important passage) of a "*melancholy of fulfillment*: no earthly paradise remains on entry without the shadow which the entry still casts over it. . . . A trace in Realizing itself is even still felt and is present where appropriate goals have been Realized or where monumental dream-images appear to have entered reality with skin and hair, with body and soul. There is a realizing which disregards the deed of the realizers themselves and does not contain it; there are ideals which pretend to be elevated, remote from tendency, abstractly fixed, and thus also suppress the unfinished, unrealized aspect of their realizers. Precisely in the melancholy of fulfillment this most profoundly not yet fulfilled aspect in the subject announces itself in exactly the same way as the insufficient aspect in the fixed material of the ideal criticizes itself within it. *It is therefore also necessary increasingly to set free the element of realizing simultaneously with the element of the future society*" (299, Bloch's emphasis).

17. In a related vein, negotiating the tensions of hunger-born hope might illuminate central questions of ethical pedagogy: relations between vision and receptive listening,

Second, and related to the first point, Bloch sharply illuminates ways in which the highest pursuits of philosophical, theological, and political inquiry are deeply connected with our relation to the hunger of the "least of these" among us. The absence of the pressures of hunger and of the voices of the hungry in our practices of knowledge production at once enable and require a broad array of ideological concealments (such as those Polanyi discusses) that have repercussions that undermine many of the more rarified pursuits of ethical and theoretical inquiry. For if Bloch is right, the denial of transformative witness to the hungry (and the conditions that make them so) requires an intense mobilization of mystifying energy that tends to instigate other sorts of denials and misrepresentations of hunger(ing) as an elemental aspect of human becoming.

In contemporary political and economic discourses, this myopia frequently takes the form of pronouncements concerning the "end of history," as well as ethical visions of the human self as essentially autonomous, independent, and in possession of relatively static forms of ethical reason. Hunger, vulnerability, dependence, and tragic finitude—even in many humane discourses such as political liberalism—primarily appear as deviations from this basic condition rather than as constitutive aspects of humans that are profoundly generative as well as a poverty (or, in a sense, generative *in relation to* our poverty).[18] The ideological insistence upon the sharp lines separating academic inquiry from the pressures of everyday life like hunger manifests itself, in turn, even in many efforts to cross these lines. This can be seen in relatively deaf (albeit in well-intentioned) versions of "service learning," and in relatively deaf projects such as the UN Millennium Development project. Though these latter projects bring academic knowledge into contact with real-world people and problems, they do so in manners that greatly marginalize the importance of *receptive* engagements and relationships with those who will

---

between idealism and relentless critique, between form and openness, between authority and insurgency, between expert knowledge and wider publics, between the hunger of the mind and the hunger of the belly.

18. For a fuller critique of political liberalism on this score, see Coles, *Beyond Gated Politics*; and Alasdair MacIntyre, *Dependent Rational Animals: Why Human Beings Need the Virtues*. Bloch saw similar manifestations of such power-laden cognitive cramping throughout the history of philosophies that privileged static being over becoming. He argued that the complex ideological energies of class power constrained the optics of transformation in the psychoanalytic discourses of his day in relation to the fact that "no matter how loud hunger bellows, it is seldom mentioned by the doctors here"(65).

otherwise be reduced to targets of presupposed ideals. Hence the hungry and impoverished become more objects than subjects of knowledge—in ways that secure the very knowledge brought to bear upon them from dynamics that might transform it "from below." Bloch's work illuminates this vicious circle and incites us to decommission it in the name of more hopeful practice and ethico-political theory.

Third, these points suggest that ways beyond these modes of mis-construal and political containment will have to begin, in no small part, by engaging the question of hunger *with the hungry and with those more proximate to hunger than most of us in ivory towers*. This is both an in-tellectual and a political task, and each aspect will likely fall short if it seeks to proceed very far in absence of the other. Bloch's work suggests that wall-crossing and purpose-confusing relationships and pedagogical practices *with* the poor are essential to *invigorating* a sense of ethical ur-gency—an *energetic hungering*—that seems to disappear wherever such relationships and engagements are lacking. In other words, the problem is not only (as suggested above) that the *thematics* of hunger are actively "disappeared" when such relationships are absent, but that the *energy and urgency of hungering*—for ethical and political change, and for knowl-edge that would provoke and enable change—themselves disappear from discourses born in and carried along by constructed distances from those on the undersides of history. I think this connection between relation-ships and hungering holds true in discourses produced in academically remote locations *across the political spectrum*. Perhaps the *most* unethi-cal and antipolitical effect of these constructed distances lies precisely in the dissipation of urgency—above and beyond the content mystification that such distances also produce.[19] While I am deeply sympathetic with critiques of moralism, these critiques take a wrong turn if they are con-strued to condone the lack of urgency that is already all too pervasive.

Inquiries and pedagogies that move in the suggested alternative di-rections will by no means be easy or without great dangers. The hungry and the poor are—in different ways—as damaged and indifferent as most academics, and we know little about how to form relationships across the

19. My point here is not to condemn distances as such, for myriad types of peri-odic distance may be conducive to thinking and practice. Rather, I seek to critique the construction of particular distancing practices that are too uniform, unmodulating, impervious, and totalizing insofar as they resist juxtaposition with and learning from knowledges and practices born of counter-proximities.

walls and power lines of indifference that saturate our lived geographies. Nearly everything remains to be invented. In closing, I gesture toward a couple of forums that seem promising in this regard.

~

In scores of cities across the United States, the Industrial Areas Foundation (IAF) and other groups are organizing grassroots democracy coalitions across lines of race, ethnicity, religion, nationality, class, and ideology to address myriad forms of suffering in our society and to build radical-democratic countercultures and counterpowers. Associated with some such efforts are organized gatherings for intellectual engagement that mix things up by drawing together students and faculty in universities, along with those outside the academy involved in grassroots leadership in ways that are beginning to inform ethico-political understanding and to generate some of the urgency to which I have alluded. Ernesto Cortez and others in the IAF Southwest region regularly host such meetings in the Interfaith Educational Network (IEN); and Southeast regional IAF organizer Gerald Taylor, along with several organizers and academics (including me), has organized a similar forum called the Third Reconstruction Institute (TRI). The IEN developed in an effort to gather organizers and leaders together every couple months to benefit from seminar discussions with scholars on themes such as race, political economy, religion, civil society, democracy, and so forth.[20] Such seminars provide an opportunity for those engaged in the urgencies of everyday political organizing to *step back* from these immediacies and reflect more broadly. Yet many of the academics who have participated in these events attest to the power of these gatherings in a different way. For many academics, the experience of having our work seriously and critically addressed by people engaged in related daily specific struggles is a powerful and transformative experience. Not only do many academics learn a great deal from everyday knowledges and approaches, but they also find themselves infected by a sense of urgency in relation to their work—an urgency that is often lacking in strictly academic settings. At the intersection between grassroots activists and academics, new modes of knowledge, new types of energy and urgency, and new senses of possibility are generated: all of

20. Stanley Hauerwas and I participated together in one such gathering in August 2005. The exchanges were as invigorating, challenging, and edifying as either of us has experienced in any setting.

these, many are coming to believe, are crucial for reconfiguring practices of higher education in ways at once critical and energized toward public questions and purposes.

The TRI emerged recently, more than a decade after the IEN, and the academics who participated in its founding seek to provide a forum where the meaning and practices of scholarship and pedagogy can undergo transformations through dialogue with nonacademic grassroots leaders. We academics have a distinct interest in this conversation that exceeds the interests of the organizers—even as our diverse interests overlap in ways that facilitate common work. Typically about a dozen academics[21] in the TRI engage in discussion with about three dozen people active in grassroots democracy across the Southeast. These discussions have been by no means easy, but at some point during each two-day seminar significant and enduring epiphanies have happened for many of us. In each seminar conversation, we have had to negotiate fruitful connections between the more theoretical propensities of most academics involved, and the more specific, narrative, and immediately pragmatic orientations of many of the grassroots activists. Given that no set genres exist for such engagements, those in each meeting are drawn to *invent* modes of interaction in ways that are far less necessary when, say, academics meet in typical established settings. This new setting and need for invention creates a certain edginess in the room that is often energizing and theoretically rich in unexpected ways, as numerous specific stories of experiences of racism, for example, mingle with theoretical efforts to theorize race. Though we are still very much in a formative stage, most involved are encouraged by the possibilities that appear to be powerful even if they are still rather inchoate.

Yet these gatherings that cross the lines and confuse the purposes of mainstream academia are frustrating in lots of ways too, and I suspect that this frustration is significantly a good thing. Sometimes academics are frustrated by what they take to be the lack of sufficient theoretical concern and subtlety on the part of some of the nonacademics as we discuss theories of race, democracy, or labor law. This lack of attention to theory on the part of some seems to leave certain frameworks insufficiently interrogated. Analogously, some grassroots participants find

21. We are mostly from Duke at present, though our plan is to build a consortium of universities that will host this institute.

more theoretical emphases in the conversations too abstract, irrelevant, and "pie-in-the-sky." The nagging question—*What the hell are we trying to do here?*—is never too far away from many of us. Moreover, those who are most literally hungry and very poor are not yet present—and the least educated people in the room sometimes express difficulty and frustration in following conversations that many academics thought were pitched at a widely accessible level.

Why do I think this frustration is "significantly a good thing"? First, because it tends to keep us on our toes, and spurs our creative efforts within the seminars to reinvent our modes of engagement, our focus, our senses of purpose—our relationships. Perhaps it helps open us to one another other and to aspects of truth that would otherwise be harder to come by. Second, the frustration of the seminars is "significantly a good thing" because I think the frustration has effects that one could call *pluralizing* and *permeating*. By "pluralizing," I mean that the frustrations *also* generate a sense of the need for other kinds of conversations and engagements, which exceed this grouping. I leave these seminars grateful for what has happened in them and also with a renewed gratitude for other contexts for ethical and political inquiry and practice: undergraduate classes, graduate seminars, interdisciplinary faculty seminars, intimate conversations with other political theorists, and conversations as an activist with other activists. I leave with a renewed sense of the scholarly and political value of the coexistence of *different spaces*, and of the value of *moving to and fro* among them. I also leave knowing that many of the least well off were not present, and this animates my appreciation for and involvement toward efforts to organize in ways that extend the range of participants in the conversation—in churches, soup kitchens, neighborhood organizations, and so forth.

By "permeating," I mean that the frustrations and the epiphanies in the TRI move into and inform my creative efforts in other spaces, into which I bring new stories, insights, questions, modes of participation, urgent energies, possibilities, and a sense that, say, an advanced graduate seminar on philosophies of "self and other" allows us to do valuable and specific kinds of work, but that this work must be transformed in ways that respond to what has been gained and to what has not yet been gained in TRI. It is a question of *translating* the questions, insights, and energies from one space to another—and back. Each space of learning overflows its bounds, and energizes and inflects the transformative work in the others—even as each space highlights the value of their distinction. *Hopefully, in some modest ways, the discrepant sections of the present essay are partially emblematic of the plurality and permeation of modes of engagement, energy, and thematic work that I am suggesting here.*

I suspect that this plurality of related spaces for inquiry, pedagogy, and struggle might provide some initial intimations of possible shapes and flows for more intelligent, ethical, and democratic relationships between those at work in universities and those focused elsewhere and in other ways, including those presently hungry. The point of criticizing the prevalent fabrications of structural, geographical, and ideological oblivion in dominant practices of higher education is not to suggest alternatively that we should collapse distinct spaces into a universalized proximity. This would neither satiate nor be conducive to the ongoing articulation of our hunger-driven hopes. The idea, rather, is to urge that we inhabit a variety of reciprocally informed, inspired, and inflected spaces that draw us into multiple reflective and political relationships (directly and indirectly) with the "least of these" among us, in order to discern and struggle toward a radically better world.[22] Further, the idea is to encourage our receptivity toward those in our reflective spaces who have regular engagements with those who are not *yet* engaged in these conversational spaces (e.g., receptivity to pastors who regularly engage with the very poor in their churches or soup kitchens).

If scholars in universities lack this affirmation of plurality and permeation, I suspect that the complacency of most academics toward the hungering and suffering of the least well off will remain profoundly ideological, apathetic, and self-serving. No amount of discourse on moral education will change this. Everything hinges on our efforts to constitute creative spaces of inquiry and pedagogy that are ethical and political insofar as they do not flee from witnessing and transformative engagement with the hunger in the depths of human bellies—a hunger that is inextricably entwined with the hunger driving our aspirations to ever-new heights.

~

22. Elsewhere I have written at length about receptive modes of democratic engagement. I think encouraging students to learn through involvement in such practices provides an important alternative to some more traditional forms of "service learning." See my chapter, "Moving Democracy," in *Beyond Gated Politics*.

Yet for all the pluralism, tension, difficult translating, patience, and obliqueness so crucial for our struggles toward justice, truth, and democracy (and for all our legitimate concerns about the dangers of moralism), still, as the bumper sticker says: "if you're not outraged, you're not paying attention." The point, as I see it, is not to fashion a politics or moral education beyond outrage, but to invent ways of mobilizing, chilling, and refracting it toward thoughtful, revolutionary change.

CHAPTER 13

Of Tensions and Tricksters:
Grassroots Democracy between Theory and Practice[1]

Romand Coles

INTRODUCTION

These are not easy times for democracy. In the face of multinational corporations, an increasingly corrupt and deceitful political system, megamedia conglomerates, and militaristic televangelists, it is easy to understand how some radical democrats succumb to a politics of the bullhorn. The objective of such politics is to hone the correct line and to strategize ways to project it clearly, loudly, and righteously into the public arena. Yet the success of politics thus framed has been marginal in recent decades, and its democratic credentials questionable—if by *democratic* we mean a politics that engages a manifold people in the difficult reciprocities of active critical judgment, of organizing, of action toward common goods, of more egalitarian distributions, and of deepening acknowledgments of plural modes of being. Most Americans are Teflon to it.

Numerous constituencies have experimented with a variety of political modes in efforts to contest power, to redistribute wealth, and to articulate more democratic relationships. Among these constituencies, the Industrial Areas Foundation (IAF) has staged one of the more impressive efforts of organizing durable grassroots democratic practices across a

1. This review essay details Warren, *Dry Bones Rattling*; Boyte, *Everyday Politics*; Gecan, *Going Public*; Chambers, *Roots for Radicals*. The author wishes to acknowledge helpful comments and criticisms from Susan Bickford, Kimberley Curtis, Jeffrey Isaac, Sanford Schram, and anonymous reviewers for *Perspectives on Politics*, where the essay first appeared.

wide cross-section of people, and of effecting modest but significant re-distributions of power in cities across the United States. After remaining beneath the academic radar, in the past several years a growing literature by IAF organizers and attentive scholars sheds important light on the vision, practices, challenges, successes, and limits of this project. This chapter engages central themes in several of these recent contributions.

At the heart of what seems most promising in this mode of insurgent democracy is the ability to craft vision, practice, and power by sustaining a series of important tensions. This construction of democracy-in-tension promises a responsiveness, suppleness, and mobility that just might develop the power to help bring forth a significantly better world. It is also key to engaging in what I refer to below as "trickster politics," by which I mean a politics that plays one game (i.e., interest-group co-alition politics aimed at redistributions that address pressing issues) in order, more importantly, to enhance another game (i.e., building radical-democratic relationships, counter-culture, and power). In this chapter, I explore some of the cultivated tensions that characterize IAF politics at its best: tensions between voice and listening, between idealism and pragmatism, between commonality and difference, between cooperation and disturbance, between immediate goals and deeper transformation, between interest-group politics and more radical trickster politics, and between authority and grassroots initiative. Before turning to the recent literature on the IAF, I situate this politics in the context of some of the pivotal debates on the left about how best to struggle against the enormous powers that thwart democracy and justice. My concern throughout this essay is to illuminate how the IAF's articulation of these tensions suggests ways that grassroots democrats might work to surmount a number of important shortcomings all too common in progressive politics. At the same time, I suggest that the IAF's explicit and energetic opposition to many modes of progressive activism sometimes draws it toward certain accents that threaten the tensions it postulates at its most penetrating moments. Hence, for example, the IAF risks succumbing, with deleterious consequences, to a politics that overplays cooperation at the expense of disturbance; the IAF risks subscribing to a pragmatic politics of immediacy rather than to a politics that cultivates deeper critique and farther-ranging alternative horizons; the IAF risks falling into a politics that emphasizes authority rather than a politics that prizes more open and radically democratic initiatives. This essay seeks to work a tensional edge between indebted insight and criticism.

EDGY DEBATES AND CONTEXTS

As a most exuberant period of radical-democratic experimentation in the 1960s and early 1970s waned, and as hopes for broad and deep democratic transformations of culture and political economic power diminished, many scholars and activists began to reflect upon the causes of this decline and possibilities for renewal. The critical analyses and political directions that subsequently emerged were manifold, contesting the character of power operating in progressive movements and in the broader society along entwined matrixes of race, class, gender, ethnicity, ecology, religion, sexuality, organizational modes, and strategic action. Some of the most significant efforts to rethink possibilities for transforming antidemocratic political-economic structures engaged the question of organizing: How to organize broad and intense democratic movements that might alter widespread cultural patterns of deferential quiescence and of grossly unjust distributions of goods and productive capacities?

A landmark in this reflective process was Piven and Cloward's *Poor People's Movements.*[2] Questioning pervasive progressive assumptions embodied in organizing efforts like the labor and welfare rights movements, Piven and Cloward argued against seeking transformation by establishing formal mass-membership organizations insofar as such organizations tend toward internal oligarchy, toward bureaucratic rigidity (at odds with the mobility conducive to more successful struggles), and toward increasing cooptation stemming from the need to privilege cooperative relations with external elites (from whom symbolic and material recognition is needed for such organizations' survival). Such organizations tend to erode grassroots democracy and are generally short-lived. The concessions that formal organizations are able to win, Piven and Cloward argued, stem not from their political efficacy but from the initial disruptive insurgency that provokes a delegitimation crisis for political elites. The concessions that elites will make diminish quickly as the insurgency declines or is co-opted. Lacking these concessions from elites,

2. See Block et al., "Symposium," for insightful contemporary assessments of this work.

poor people have no incentives to participate regularly, and they retreat from the organization.

Piven and Cloward argued that the limitations facing efforts to change entrenched powers of contemporary political economy in more democratic and just directions are "large and unyielding." The key to a more effective progressive politics was "to understand these limitations, and to exploit whatever latitude remains to enlarge the potential influence of the lower class."[3] Thus rather than trying to create formal mass-based organizations in the midst of political upheaval generated by people's taking to the streets, it was wiser to intensify the political defiance that foments delegitimation crises from which significant elite concessions most often stem, especially during times of instability. We should seek to "escalate the momentum and impact of disruptive protest at each stage in its emergence and evolution."[4] Though such efforts would themselves be relatively short-lived (because they are significantly dependent on systemic disruptions that tend to be temporary and largely beyond the control of social movements), if the opportunities were seized, movements of irregular action might approach the maximal limit of the concessions winnable from the state at a given point in time. This stark sense of limited possibility was far from their ideal, but "to criticize a movement [or theoretical position] for not advocating or reaching this goal or that one without even the most casual appraisal of its political resources is an exercise in self-righteousness"—something they sensed in many of their critics. [5]

Though significantly persuaded by Piven and Cloward's analysis of politics in the United States, Ira Katznelson nevertheless makes the important argument that Piven and Cloward had overgeneralized the claim about the desirability of disruption over organization.[6] In countries where strong social democratic movements provided stable vehicles for progressive reform, redistributive gains far greater than those made in the United States had been won through combinations of struggle *and* organization. Katznelson suggests the need to invent organizational vehicles, even as he also provides an analysis of how class and community

3. Piven and Cloward, *Poor People's Movements*, 37.
4. Ibid.
5. Ibid., xiv
6. Katznelson, *City Trenches*.

issues have been historically separated in the United States and have been channeled into the politically co-opting "trenches" of trade unionism and of urban machine politics in ways that pose major challenges to doing so. Those who would seek by means of community organizing to accomplish an end-run around the problems of either creating a powerful radical organization or settling for the more minimal returns of a politics of irregular disruption are barking up the wrong tree, according to Katznelson: "Community-based strategies for social change in the United States cannot succeed unless they pay attention to the country's split in the practical consciousness of American workers between the language and practice of a politics of work and those of a politics of community."[7] On Katznelson's reading, questions of class power in the workplace and in the broader political economy were crucial to engage simultaneously and in connection with questions facing neighborhoods, schools, housing, environment, and so forth. A narrow focus on the former conceals the manifold implications of class power. A narrow focus on "community" issues, alternatively, conceals central political economic sources of power, the transformation of which is a condition for addressing deeper community issues in the first place.

Katznelson's critique here is partly aimed at another locus of theory and practice that developed in response to the decline of grassroots democratizing efforts and the right-wing backlash in the early 1970s— namely, the myriad community-organizing efforts that were significantly inspired by and developed beyond the political work of Saul Alinsky.[8] Reflecting on the shortcomings of progressive politics in the wake of the 1960s, organizers in Alinsky's IAF became convinced that successful efforts to democratize culture and power hinged upon going back to the institutions of civil society that remained intact, and organizing within each locality an "organization of organizations" able to connect with and cultivate the more radically democratic and pluralist values rooted in the traditions of different communities, congregations, and families. The IAF sought to be radically countercultural (insofar as becoming grassroots democratic political animals *is* countercultural) but in a manner that eschewed ideological posturing and connected to the specificities of main-

7. Ibid., 194.

8. Alinsky, *Reveille for Radicals*; and Alinsky, *Rules for Radicals* articulated this theory of organizing. Chambers, *Organizing for Family* articulated central theses of post-Alinsky IAF organizing.

stream peoples' everyday lives, faiths, issues, angers, and hopes. It sought patiently to develop grassroots democratic relationships and power in order to reconstitute a broad and deep network across many of the pivotal differences that divide people and render them impotent. The concomitant aim was to hold dominant institutions accountable and responsive to a genuinely democratically constituted people. Yet for Katznelson, the IAF's diminished focus on work, class, and scales of contestation sufficient to alter the prerogatives of capital were major shortcomings.

Indebted to Katznelson, a group of scholar-activists critically engaged the "new populism" of IAF-type organizations and suggested that class analysis and systematic critique (including critiques of traditional ideological frames) should be a part of organizing, as well as a focus on ways to move beyond local organizing to address large corporate and state power.[9] These "transformative populists" sought to develop a politics that worked in the tensions between, on the one hand, the new populism's emphasis on "meeting people where they are" in their communities and traditions, and, on the other hand, the introduction of more radical analyses and networks of organizing aimed at contesting larger modes of power. Only by integrating both horns of the dilemma, they argued, was there hope of inventing a politics that might escape the confines of mere resistance or assimilation, and engender deeper cultural and political economic transformations.

Many of the questions and problems posed by these "transformative populists" remain very important for those who would enhance struggles for democratization and justice. Given the extent to which localities in the United States are shaped and limited by global capitalism and the politics of what Sheldon Wolin calls the "super-power," political initiatives that avoid wrestling with these questions will likely fail to democratize culture and power.[10] Moreover, we might risk complicity with antidemocratic forces insofar as we channel political engagement toward blind alleys and minutia, or political modes that lack larger transformative horizons. The question, then, concerns how democratic organizing might begin around small issues that are immediately connected to people's lives and that are winnable (concerning missing street signs, specific abandoned houses, or potholes, for example) yet that are simultaneously linked to broader cri-

9. Kling and Posner, *Dilemmas of Activism*.

10. Wolin, *Politics and Vision*, chapters 16 and 17 (2nd edition).

tiques and to the task of building larger networks—networks that might transform structures of power.

A number of recent historical developments in the United States are striking and pertinent as we consider the range of alternatives that we have briefly sketched above. First, progressive efforts in the United States to cultivate a politics of disruption have met with relatively little success (whether "success" is defined in terms of intensity, relative durability, or pragmatic results). The anti-WTO protests in Seattle made an important splash, but the protests that followed against neoliberal globalization have become increasingly routine, contained, and marginalized in the broader public sphere. The character of political, economic, cultural, and media power in the United States today pose ever-greater questions concerning the efficaciousness of a politics for which such disruptive protest would be the central tool. Second, for myriad reasons the numerous attempts to develop large, powerful, and enduring progressive organizations (e.g., the New Party, the Labor Party) have had little success forming deep and enduring connections with a broad swath of the public. Third—and in marked contrast—in the decades following the criticisms of "new populism" discussed above, it is IAF organizations and others deeply informed by them that have been remarkably successful at broadening and at sustaining broad-based networks of democratic power, cultural change, and significant redistribution at the local level (around housing, living wages, infrastructure, or schools). The track record of "transformative populists" is far less impressive. How and why have IAF-like organizations done as well as they have during a period of dramatic right-wing ascendancy? Are they primarily indicative of a "politics of containment" that fulfills the functional requirements of the dominant order, or is their work better than this in terms of what it has achieved thus far and in terms of its promise? In considering these questions, it is important to note that the "transformative populists'" analyses of the new populists were rather thin and often inaccurate (as the discussion below illustrates). Many IAF-style groups have, for example, sought to enlarge the scales of political contestation, many entertain critiques of capitalism and class, and many acknowledge a relationship to myriad traditions at once deeply indebted to these traditions and also drawing them into democratically transformative dialogues. In this light, it is important that the politics of community organizing be explored with a fresh eye for its possibilities and limits.

Fortunately, activists and scholars are producing a growing literature that engages these political efforts on the part of tens of thousands associated with the IAF, in scores of U.S. cities—efforts to shift power, political culture, and practical policy outcomes toward increasing grassroots political engagement, equality, and inclusion. Two of these, *Going Public*, by Michael Gecan, and *Roots for Radicals: Organizing for Power, Action, and Justice*, by Edward Chambers, are written by long-time IAF organizers. A third, *Dry Bones Rattling: Community Building to Revitalize American Democracy*, is by Mark R. Warren, a political sociologist who studied the IAF as a "participant observer." A fourth, *Everyday Politics: The Power of Public Work,* is by Harry Boyte, who has long worked at the intersection between theory, history, and political engagement. Below I engage some of the most provocative contributions offered in these works in order to explore ways in which they might inform understandings of democratic political engagement in the context of the debates and challenges sketched above. I focus particularly on themes concerning the ethos and practices of organizing; on civic, political, and economic visions of transformation; on modes of addressing questions of race and gender; and on the role of leadership and authority in radical-democratic work. I am interested in the extent to which theses works are rooted in (and in the extent to which they suggest) practices that might push beyond the "trenches of containment" mentioned above; I am also interested in the question of how the politics of tensions that they articulate might be further developed in order to enhance their capacities for doing so.

DEVELOPING AN ETHOS AND PRACTICE OF GRASSROOTS ORGANIZING

Each of these books charts a course both indebted to and critical of central motifs that emerge in the early IAF fashioned by Alinsky. Though Alinsky was effective in the short run around issues of infrastructure, services, schools, jobs, housing, and the like, his organizations frequently perished after several years, organizers often burned out, and sometimes organizations developed in directions that defied the democratic and inclusive spirit of their emergence. In response, following Alinsky's death in 1972, there was a period of intensified critical reflection upon and transformation of IAF practices.

Where Alinsky emphasized late in his life a narrowly pragmatic understanding of organizing, the new generation of leaders has cultivated a practice and philosophy of organizing that extended in two key ways Alinsky's earlier attentiveness to specific community traditions. First, IAF's own philosophy of democratic organizing has become increasingly entwined with teachings of the religious traditions with which it is engaged. (Christianity and Judaism have played a predominant role, though many networks have increasingly sought out and have been informed by Islam, Buddhism, and other traditions.) IAF's philosophy has drawn inspiration from religious teachings emphasizing political perseverance, liberation, solidarity with the least well off, welcoming the stranger, community building across differences, and so forth. Second, each local IAF organization aims to enhance the institutional strength of each of its member associations—diversifying leadership, broadening participation, reorganizing in ways more conducive to the association's flourishing, and finding practical embodiments of vision.

Yet even as IAF is *inflected* by the visions and practices of the traditions with which it engages, it *inflects* these traditions in light of a radical-democratic ethos that accents inclusion, dialogue, receptivity, equality, difference, a taste for ambiguity, patient discernment, and affirmation that political relationships centrally involve ongoing tension, some compromise, and humility in the face of disagreement (including a hesitancy to push for organizational action on issues where widespread agreement has yet to be forged). Rather than calling upon a politically liberal "public reason" that is worked out in advance and would regulate public discourse on basic issues, the discrepant political voices in IAF draw upon a variety of traditions in a process of dialogue that is more pluralizing and open-ended, and that gradually changes in light of particular engagements around specific issues. The wager seems to be that patient discernment in responsive relationships is both sufficient and, in important ways, better than the terms of a preestablished Rawlsian social contract, because patient discernment in responsive relationships is more respectful of differences and more flexible in relation to human contingencies than a social contract would be.

Chambers has played a major role in these reformations of the IAF in recent decades, reflectively gathering the practical knowledge gleaned from decades of organizing, establishing the IAF's national "ten-day training" institute (which regularly trains dozens of new leaders in the arts of political organizing), and helping to develop a life for organizers that is fulfilling over the long term, rather than a burn-out experience. Yet for all the incisive strategic practical wisdom that Chambers offers about the *nuts and bolts* of organizing, one of the more striking things about his book is the extent to which he painstakingly seeks to convey what he takes to be the *existential attitude* most conducive to vibrant, effective, sustainable engagement in the rough-and-tumble of grassroots democratic politics. For Chambers and many IAF organizers, this ethos is integral to the change in political culture that is required for and pro- voked by radical democracy—and central to the way Chambers seeks to rework the term *radical*.

Radical refers to "root," for Chambers, yet not in the sense of an origin that, once revealed, would provide the foundational lens rendering easily intelligible both our historical situation and what is to be done. Rather, *radical* refers to the truth of spirit, which resides in the *permanent tension* between "the world as it is" and "the world as it should be." The search for meaning and for better forms of political community is "fueled by a tension that won't go away";[11] one that is—when artfully acknowl- edged and given generous form—a source of creative political action for radical democracy and justice.[12] Hence we must "step up to the tension" and avoid succumbing to the cynicism and coercion that result when we collapse it either toward the "world as it is," or toward the marginal mor- alizing that ensues when we collapse it to the "world as it should be."[13] This tensional root emerges in proximity to anger and yearning, and it gives birth to "the radical question of this book . . . why should things be this way, rather than another? . . . why not a different world?"[14]

Chambers argues that radical democracy is a project of learning to live artfully when political community is recognized first and foremost as a *question* rather than as a rhetorical device veiling a politics of the ready- made answer. The pragmatic, strategic, and ethical questions that swarm in the interstice between the present world and other better possibilities call radically democratic selves receptively "to gather with others as fel- low citizens to converse, plan, act, and reflect for the well-being of people

11. Chambers, *Roots for Radicals*, 13.

12. Ibid., 22–23.

13. Ibid., 24.

14. Ibid., 14.

as a whole."[15] Chambers calls this capacity our "politicalness," following Wolin, whom Chambers describes as "America's finest political teacher."[16] Rather than by a prerogative of nation-states, citizenship is constituted by our *politicalness*, which Chambers (again following Wolin) takes to be a birthright of each and every person. The citizenship of radical democracy belongs to all those who respond to the call of politicalness. Organizing is largely the practice of repeatedly soliciting politicalness where it has yet to appear, and of listening carefully to and of working with those who actively respond. This is politically crucial because IAF organizing bridges and transfigures not only divides of race, religion, class, and gender, but also *nationality*, as it engages in political work with thousands of newly arrived immigrants lacking officially sanctioned United States citizenship.

The tension and questioning that the IAF calls people to "embrace everyday [as] the destiny of our spirit" draws people into creatively pluralistic modes of politicalness because

> the tension between the two worlds is a tension between interpretations. The world as it is and the world as it should be are not raw facts or simple objective realities. We don't have objective uninterpreted access to either world. People from different histories see the two worlds differently. . . . What you and I can create for our respective groups . . . and the larger community depends on bringing our respective interpretations together in a better reading or our common situation and obligations than we could do alone, one that enables us to act together with power.[17]

IAF politicalness thus follows the Tocquevillian theme of broadening concerns and horizons through political participation. Yet the IAF radicalizes this theme significantly by rooting the potential sources of democratic life in far more heterogeneous and open-ended locations than did Tocqueville, subtly but critically shifting the orientation of democracy from Tocqueville's accent on relatively stable common foundations in the being or mores of a people, to the unpredictable "dialectic between *being* and *becoming*"—the *interaction* between a rich (if often forgotten) legacy of grassroots democratic practices, heterogeneous traditions, and the

15. Ibid., 18.
16. Ibid., 125, following Wolin, *Presence of the Past*.
17. Ibid., 24.

emergent possibilities that arise as people more receptively engage one another.[18] At their best, IAF practices strive to gather sources of receptivity in each tradition and to work these against the stingier elements that also reside everywhere people co-exist.[19]

At the heart of the philosophy of IAF organizing is the necessity to tap into the "self-interests" of diverse constituencies. Yet Chambers interprets this through Arendt's reflections on *"inter esse,"* which locate our interests in the tensional space "in between, with our relationships."[20] Hence at the same time that a focus on self-interest propels the cultivation of self-recognition, respect, and determination, this focus on self-interest also propels us into receptive political relationships with others. Along with virtually all other IAF organizers, Chambers writes that "the most radical thing we do out of that tension starts with what I call the relational meeting": one-on-one conversations that are vital enactments of the political ethos of the IAF.[21] Where IAF organizing is proceeding at its best, relational meetings are ceaselessly occurring—meetings of individuals propelled into dialogues in which they provoke and listen to one another's stories, angers, passionate dreams, specific issues and hopes, and so forth.

Chambers describes these meetings as "an art form. It's one organized spirit going after another person's spirit for connection, confrontation . . . searching for talent, energy, insight, and relationships. It is where public newness begins . . . the telling of stories that open a window in to the passions that animate people to act."[22] Relational meetings are a vital source of information through which issues, strategies, solidarity, and practices of local organizations emerge. Indeed, the IAF performs thousands of these meetings in each city prior to picking issues, instituting formal structures, or going public. A far cry from groups on the

18. Ibid., 27.

19. On radical-democratic engagements between different traditions and practices of receptivity in IAF organizing, see Coles, "Moving Democracy: Industrial Area Foundation Social Movements" (article); and Coles, *Beyond Gated Politics*. My work in those texts—as well as in the current review—emerges at the intersections between being a political philosopher, a student of politics, and an active member (about ten hours a week) of a local IAF grassroots democracy project in Durham, North Carolina.

20. Chambers, *Roots for Radicals*, 38.

21. Ibid., 13.

22. Ibid., 44–45.

left and right that accent modes of "preaching to their ideological clubs, using their own language, their own fabricated theology, and their own single agendas,"²³ the relational meeting practically embodies the idea "that listening to the stories and insights, the memories and struggles, of another is more important than hustling their name . . . the relational meeting is a risky, reciprocal event . . . a two-way street . . . [where one must] be prepared to be vulnerable."²⁴ Each of these encounters seeks to communicate and exemplify that "its agenda has some fluidity, that its tone or strategy might be altered, that newcomers are expected to bring something to the group's agenda."²⁵ In response to those who think that organizers must come into communities with an ethically and politically "correct" vision, the IAF counters not with a blind faith in the everyday traditions that they find already in play, but with a profound sense that the traditions of most communities have multiple sources (including traditions of radical democracy) that can be drawn upon to animate people to engage in more dialogical and receptive practices, through which a democratically deeper and more plural "we" can be engendered.

The aim of IAF organizing—through house meetings, leaders meetings, community-wide assemblies, action teams around specific issues, grassroots actions at public hearings, and the like—is to generate an enduring radical-democratic counter-culture that could dramatically transform power and policy in directions that are more inclusive, egalitarian, and just. Negotiating between ideals and a pragmatic sensibility, Chambers strives toward a world in which civil society would be not a "third sector" but the "first sector" that would "hold [governments] as well as the moguls of the market accountable"; Chambers aims for a world that recognizes that "the state and market came later and exist to support [civil society]."²⁶ In practical terms, states must "put boundaries on the market" but can only do so in the context of pressures from an attentive, organized, and fluidly active democracy working throughout civil society.

Chambers has been engaged long enough in the politics that Weber famously described as "the slow boring of hard boards" to know the tre-

23. Ibid., 52.
24. Ibid., 49.
25. Ibid., 52.
26. Ibid., 63, 61.

mendous challenges facing the IAF's effort to cultivate radical democracy. Crucial to his interpretation of IAF politics is a *trickster sensibility* that he sometimes calls "political jujitsu," which aims to "use the power of the opposition against itself" to change things.[27] Yet "the opposition" is not simple persons in power who are resistant to democratization, but also the systems of antidemocratic power themselves. Hence, more profoundly, like many tricksters, IAF often pretends to play one game while its real focus is on another. In the face of what Chambers takes to be capitalist markets gone wild—in which capitalism itself acts as an antidemocratic trickster, bestowing upon commodities apparent (and thus real) autonomous steering power-value and a seductive character that cultivates consumerist selves, all the while veiling the human power relations at its core—the IAF crafts an antidote trickster that mimics M-C-M′ (Money, Commodity, Money′) toward radical-democratic ends. Chambers crafts the formula as follows: TEP (Talent, Energy, Power)-CA (Collective Action)-TEP′.

For example, those democratic organizers and leaders will discern multiple issues of great importance to a community and will generate a plethora of action with the ostensible aim of winning significant gains around housing, living wages, education, equitable infrastructure, safe neighborhoods, and environmental justice. The redistributive track record of the IAF is substantial in this regard (especially during a period of dramatic national retreat from redistributive politics), including resources for the construction of thousands of houses enabling home ownership for low-income people, many urban living-wage ordinances, a raise in the California minimum wage, and hundreds of millions of dollars of city and state funds toward poor and working-class schools, neighborhoods, and communities. Yet these issues and *ultimately even the game of interest-group liberalism as such* are *secondary* objectives—the *secondary game*—for the best IAF organizations. A key factor in discerning which issues to pursue—as well as how to pursue them and when to compromise, for example—is the extent to which pursuing certain issues might contribute to broadening and deepening durable radical-democratic engagement, relational power, knowledge, and practices (the *primary* goal).

27. Ibid., 109.

Issues grow in proportion to the political capacities of the organization, for the IAF is very careful not to drag people into many losing battles that are demoralizing and politically debilitating. Action, reaction, and reflection are like oxygen for grassroots politics; they draw new people into political engagement and deepen the vitality of those already involved. In a world where deprivation is pressing, where politically deferent consumerism is rampant, and where the rules of the game often favor myopic greed, Chambers knows that the pursuit of radical democracy must often be oblique, and might don a trickster character. Political games that may seem at times to be primarily about issues that appear (like commodities) to acquire a life, power, and value entirely their own are always *more* about soliciting collective actions and reactions that proliferate horizontal relationships, culture, and power (just as the movement of commodities and money is actually primarily rooted in and aims to proliferate relationships of vertical power).

Thus an issue that seems too small, or a compromise that seems to give up too much, when viewed primarily through the redistributive lens of goods desperately needed (but probably unattainable in a present power context), may be crucial to winning what Chambers takes to be the more important game: enhancing a radical-democratic counter-culture and power that is itself partially constitutive of flourishing. The ultimate aim is to *change the game*, or at least make the radical-democratic game more powerful than the interest-group, distributive game. What I am calling trickster politics—*at its best, and it is easy for it to get tricked*—moves back and forth between these two games, carefully trying to play the interest-group distributive game and to avoid getting caught in its frame, a theme to which we will return in discussing Boyte and Warren. As Chambers puts it, "The line in the fight about how the world should be is now drawn between market values and generational ones."[28]

Questions of Critical and Transformative Vision

As Gecan's *Going Public* repeats many themes discussed by Chambers (with whom he has collaborated for decades), I focus upon his subtle differences. Whereas Chambers consistently links organizing themes to deeper questions of practical philosophy, Gecan's work unfolds by presenting provocative exemplifications of modes of democratic organizing

28. Ibid., 111.

and engagement. His text is divided into four parts, each of which articulates a "habit" that is central to the participatory democratic "cultural work" that the IAF seeks to provoke: "the habit of relating," "the habit of action," "the habit of organization," and "the habit of reflection."

Gecan has an wonderful eye for creating—and voice for narrating—public drama, and his stories (e.g., reversing architectures of power by arriving early to a meeting, occupying the central elevated "plush leather" chairs and tables of the uncooperative commissioners, while insisting that the commissioners sit beneath them in little "rickety wooden chairs" for "peons") are often followed by spirited injunctions like, "Don't whine. . . . Take charge. Be irreverent. Test how plastic the world really is. And learn how to enjoy a win."[29] In the midst of story after story of organized people creating significant power, transformation, and political-economic outcomes that benefit their lives, Gecan's claims that there are "entire continents of political reality still undiscovered and unexplored," or that those involved in grassroots democracy can "become refounding brothers and sisters of their country," acquire needed texture and believability.[30]

Nevertheless, Gecan's ruminations about what these farther-reaching possibilities might look like remain mostly limited to democratizing shifts—albeit profound shifts—affecting the terrain of civil society. Moreover, in a subtle but important way, he generally portrays the relations between civil society (or "relational culture"), on the one hand, and "market culture" and government "bureaucratic cultures," on the other, in a manner that is far less agonistic than Chambers. This difference comes through repeatedly in the way Gecan accents the distinctness of civil society less in *contestational relation* to the other culture-powers, and more in terms that emphasize society's distinct capacities to "figure out how to do what the market or state have either shown no interest in doing or have failed to do well . . . especially . . . the growth and development of people and their voluntary institutions."[31] Striking a moderate tone, his discussion of market culture poignantly describes why he "admires the market's energy . . . and appreciates its power" yet generally does quite little to elaborate why he is "concerned about its impact."[32] At his most

29. Gecan, *Going Public*, 59, 69.

30. Ibid., 6, 135.

31. Ibid., 6.

32. Ibid., 153.

radical, Gecan writes of "holding markets accountable" and "keeping them in their place"—if they will not do so themselves—but the spirit of his remarks on markets tenaciously avoids addressing more deeply critical and transformative issues.

Harry Boyte's *Everyday Politics* labors consistently in democratizing directions that are only occasionally suggested by Chambers and Gecan. Boyte has been engaged in scholarship and political relationships with the IAF for many years. Much of his early work theorizes democracy in a manner deeply indebted to this organizing and to the rich related legacy of "commonwealth" political visions and struggles throughout U.S. history. *Everyday Politics* continues to be deeply appreciative of the innovations of groups like the IAF, but its primary ambition is to render a narrative and theoretical account of the innovative democratic experiments in which Boyte has been involved for the past fifteen years that move beyond some of the limits in political organizing that confines itself to the terrain of civil society.

With Gecan and Chambers, Boyte argues for a mode of democracy that moves beyond a "protest politics" that remains too marginal, too episodic, too preachy and moralizing, and too enamored with disruption to the exclusion of constructive engagement. He is similarly unimpressed by establishment nongovernmental organization politics characterized by bureaucratic expert cultures and minimal grassroots engagement. While IAF-style radical democracy is a major advance, if it fails to develop strategies that democratize work and make it "public," it will likely be insufficient in a period when the "world threatens to become entirely privatized and the market to spin out of control, metastasizing into a cancerous growth that turns private wealth-making into an almost religious ritual." Boyte worries that though the IAF model avoids the depoliticized framework that accompanies many discourses of civil society, it nevertheless remains stuck in the civil-society frame when it "separates 'production', which it locates in the 'economic sector', from public life"; this is a frame in which "the actual process of creating the what—our public wealth—disappears."[33]

Yet power is deeply rooted in the construction of work; and the cultural shaping of selves in work is deeply formative as well. Hence, Boyte argues that deep culture-power shifts will require transforming

---

33. Boyte, *Everyday Politics*, 58.

how people engage in and understand their everyday work. Ignoring this task "removes the large institutions of our world from democratic action, organizing, and transformation," and "ignores the power and authority that citizens can gain through [democratized public] work," which has so often been drawn upon by those who have engaged in transformative politics throughout history.[34]   Moreover, much research indicates that bureaucratic, passive, narrow, privatized work practices are a key part of what ails many people. If grassroots organizations are to effectively engage people in the suburbs, they will have to find ways of listening to and engaging these discontents and the aspirations that venture beyond them. Finally, a focus on transforming work holds promise to "democratize the organized knowledge systems"—higher education, communications, culture industries—that are central to contemporary culture-power.[35]

As co-director of the Center for Democracy and Citizenship at the University of Minnesota's Humphrey Institute of Public Affairs, Boyte has creatively collaborated with others in a variety of laboratories for democracy across a wide range of settings that include efforts to democratize public scholarship at the University of Minnesota and elsewhere; Public Achievement (a youth civic-education initiative that engages students in "politics understood as an activity that negotiates diverse interests for the sake of creating things of broad public benefit");[36] the Jane Addams School (which engages new immigrants and citizens in practices of community-based education in order "to free and cultivate the talents, cultures, and interests of people from diverse backgrounds to the commonwealth");[37] the Lazarus Project (which has transformed a large Lutheran nursing home in ways that have introduced principles from broad-based organizing and have drawn the staff, residents, and families into a "public community" of dialogue and work that has led to numerous significant changes).

These projects—and much of the practical wisdom that Boyte formulates in his stories and analyses of them—are significant, informative, and inspiring even as they are relatively modest and still very vulnerable. They contribute to theorizing democratization by exemplifying

34. Ibid, 66.
35. Ibid., 75.
36. Ibid., 80.
37. Ibid., 103.

important kinds of changes in institutions, culture, selves, and power that can indeed ensue as work is made more democratic internally, and as its purposes are reinterpreted and oriented toward democratic public relationships and public goods. Boyte and his co-creators locate and seize present sites of political possibility, engage them responsively rather than self-righteously, and set to "sweaty and muscular" work of the common-wealth tradition that they remember and reenact in opposition to "the cultural and political force of the market [that] is like a tidal wave rolling across the world."[38] Thus, Boyte bolsters the important critical claim that Habermasians often rely on a problematic "static theory of power, ignoring the interplay between large systems and everyday life, collapsing the lumpy, interactive quality of power dynamics even in situations of sharp inequality into granite-like relationships."[39]

Yet even as Boyte's work suggests important directions for democratization, I wonder if some of his debts to IAF organizing theory are not linked to certain limitations in his analysis as well. One of the virtues of the approaches to radical democracy under review is that they take significant strides toward building a more receptive politics that has had significant success at drawing a wide range of people to grassroots democratic practices. While there is much to recommend these changes, they come at a significant cost when they lead to an organizing culture that shies away from articulating more searching systemic criticism and radical reforms, in the name of staying close to "where people are." This problem marks the kernel of truth in the "transformative populist" critique sketched above. This dampening appears to be most dramatic in Gecan, but is also present in Chambers and Boyte as well.[40]

This wariness takes the form of markedly truncated analyses of market/state systemic pressures as they pertain to the durability, enhancement, and portability of the democratic spaces that Boyte so admirably pursues. Some of his public-works narratives end with qualifications that mark the threatening presence of such pressures, but these narratives are followed neither by careful extended analyses of the forces at work

38. Ibid., 224.

39. Ibid., 93. For parallel critical analyses of Habermas on this point, see McCarthy, *Ideals and Illusions*, and Forbath, "Short-Circuit."

40. Perhaps Gecan simply does not find many of the progressive critiques of markets compelling, but if so, he owes his readers an explanation—one that remains unformulated in his book.

or of the challenges they pose, nor by subtle explorations of the kinds of macropolitical and macroeconomic changes that might be necessary to thwart them, nor (most important) by suggestions about ways that various modes of the "everyday politics" with which Boyte is associated might develop and extend themselves in order to begin building the requisite political capacities, democratic coalitions, and larger experimental visions for moving in the direction of larger transformations that might in turn be more conducive to a commonwealth politics of microexperimentation across institutions of civil society, state, and markets.

For example, Boyte concludes his discussion of Public Achievement by noting "large challenges to sustaining and expanding" such efforts, including the challenges of commercialization and technocracy in the schools, and the deleterious pressures related to high stakes academic testing (No Child Left Behind)—which, an evaluating team argues, threaten the very survival of this effort.[41] In passing, Boyte notes that the nursing home that was the site of the Lazarus Project was a nonprofit operation. How does the growing for-profit nursing-care industry impact the prospects for sustaining and expanding similar projects? Toward the end of his penetrating discussion of advancing the democratic power of higher education, Boyte notes that this power "is largely locked up," thanks to intensifying "marketplace thinking that defines students as customers and judges research only by its commercial utility," and thanks to a deepening mythical meritocracy that entwines "growing economic inequalities [with] educational disparities"; furthermore, higher education "is highly unlikely to change itself, from the inside alone."[42] Yet how might we begin to challenge and change the larger constellation of powers that have engendered these characteristics, in order to provide a context more conducive to the democratic experimentation that Boyte and many others are exploring? And if this link is salient, should not proponents of democratization strive to stimulate careful and sharp criticism of the larger deleterious forces, visions for transforming these forces, and place in the foreground of political dialogue questions concerning ways to engender political constituencies, capacities, relationships, powers, strategies, and critical-constructive visions that address these connections—even if this gives such work a more "progressive" stance?

41. Boyte, *Everyday Politics*, 126.
42. Ibid., 221–23.

These criticisms are not to diminish the force of Boyte's theoretical and practical innovations but rather to suggest ways they might be developed to enhance the odds of further democratization. Moreover, my point is decidedly *not* that radical democracy needs a rigid transformative platform to orient all its efforts, or that transformed markets ought to have no place in the mix. It is rather that since virtually every effort to advance democratization immediately faces severe resistance (and occasional support as well) from market pressures working in myriad ways, proponents of radical democracy need to proliferate careful far-reaching criticism and radical alternative horizons and paths of transition in connection with the concrete immediate work we do to increase living wages, to create better job-training programs, or to advance public works.[43] We need to proliferate critiques and constructive alternatives (across a variety of scales and time frames) that are offered *not above* the fray but *in the fray*: affirming contestation; soliciting the work of independent criticism and imaginative reconstruction from those newly drawn to practices of grassroots democracy; relentlessly striving to link far-ranging transformations to more immediate political challenges and engagements. Ultimately, to follow through on *Boyte's own* critique of those who reify systemic power, we must articulate theoretical analyses, practical political work, and local and larger-scale experimentation that demonstrate ways in which the freer spaces it is possible to *open* in the midst of bureaucracies and markets can survive and *proliferate* in ways that transform currently hegemonic practices until the "powers that be"—that render them so vulnerable—are no longer dominant.

Once more searching criticism and alternatives become constitutive aspects of democratic engagement, a more nuanced approach to the politics of protest will probably have to be invented as well. IAF grassroots politics developed significantly in oppositional response to radical-democratic efforts that overplayed the politics of protest, to the detriment of the many valuable insights and practices gleaned in recent decades of community organizing. Yet my sense is that though Chambers

43. In terms of systemic criticism, many of the insights in the concluding chapters of Wolin, *Politics and Vision*, 2nd edition, are highly pertinent. In terms of alternative visions, grassroots democrats would benefit from close engagement with directions and contestations about democratizing institutions in works such as Pateman, *Participation and Democratic Theory*; Carnoy and Shearer, *Economic Democracy*; Cohen and Rogers, *Associations and Democracy*; Fung and Wright, *Deepening Democracy*; Unger, *False Necessity*; and Albert, *Parecon*.

insightfully discusses the need to move to and fro between political po-
larization and depolarization, the IAF's oppositional stance to protest too
often overplays the politics of cooperation and obscures some of what
is valuable in disturbance. When they do, they become especially vulnerable to the vitiating traps of innocuous assimilation that Piven and
Cloward identified. This stance shows up in the rather dismissive rhetorical posture that finds articulation in parts of Gecan's text, and also in
what appears to be an overall trend in IAF politics—away from the more
dramatic modes of contestation in decades past, and towards practices
that greatly favor more cooperative modes. With deeper critiques and
more expansive senses of possibility, political intensity *might* be generated that could in fact enhance the likelihood of a politics of intermittent
political disturbance that *might* in turn (if conducted as *part of a larger
bag of cooperative and relationship-building practices*) enhance political
power (along the lines of some of Piven and Cloward's arguments), solicit
and energize engagement, and enhance the trickster sensibility that can
evade the interest group frames that accompany the games grassroots
democrats are often forced to play. I emphasize "might" twice because
this possibility is promising but very much part of a more nuanced political art still "in progress"—still to be invented.

Looking at the engagement from another angle, the IAF's significant—if struggling—changes in local democratic cultures, their relative
effectiveness at shifting resources and power downward at a time when the
politics of redistribution is mostly shifting resources and power upward,
their nonbureaucratic mode of broad-based organizing, their increasing
(if slow) development of statewide and regional political capacities—all
of these developments merit a searching engagement with this politics on
the part of those oriented toward more traditional modes of "progressive"
politics. At the very least, the future of democratic engagement requires
a more open and reflective conversation than has yet happened between
proponents of IAF politics and those closer to a politics of disturbance.

Responding to Race

Mark R. Warren's *Dry Bones Rattling* provides an insightful theoretically
informed analysis of IAF organizing in Texas. It is exemplary for the way
it probes complexities and dilemmas of grassroots democracy, and for the
new directions it suggests. Those interested in questions of race, power,

social capital, bridging divides, congregations in political action, and grassroots leadership will find Warren's book an engaging read. In the present context, I focus briefly on his discussions of race and leadership. Each is significant in its own right and offers insights that bear indirectly upon the issues at hand.

As Warren compellingly argues, few recent grassroots efforts have been as successful at bringing blacks, Latinos and Latinas, and whites into enduring political relationships—forging respect, trust, dialogue, and collective action around common goods. What seems to facilitate bridging racial divides—as well as drawing creative strength from *differences*—in IAF organizing across the United States appears to be the solidarity nurtured by focusing on work toward *common* goods. This solidarity enables relationships to form that move people beyond the walls of raced communities, in order to listen to and begin to explore the world they share from the vantage points of others—their stories, neighborhoods, religious institutions—situated across the fraught lines that pervade U.S. history. Until the past decade, when the IAF did talk about race, it generally bracketed broad-ranging discussions of the most troubled differences, and focused instead on specific and addressable issues where race is salient: racial gaps in schools, infrastructure allocations, housing, discriminatory bank lending. Remaining with these topics allows the divide to be "segmented" in ways that—combined with common work—make the issue of race less threatening to many, and less intractable as well.[44]

Yet focusing on commonality and segmentation in order to work obliquely on deeper, broader, and affectively saturated problems of difference has problematic limits as well as advantages. For example, Warren recounts that in 1991, the IAF affiliate in Fort Worth initially failed to respond when a white skinhead murdered a black man and was sentenced only to probation, thus angering many African Americans (and also many Whites and Hispanics). Warren argues that among the numerous reasons for this failure of racial understanding in the IAF was fact that the Texas IAF network, up to that point, "seldom discussed issues of race or racism directly. Nor did the organization provide a forum through which Hispanic and Anglo leaders could develop an appreciation for the

---

44. See Warren, *Democracy and Association*, for another insightful analysis along these lines.

historical experiences of the African American community." Thus, when the injustices "forced the issue of racism so directly, [the organization] was not prepared to act."[45]   Warren argues that "by avoiding open discussion of racism both internally and externally, relationship building is likely to remain fairly superficial."[46] In the following decade, responding to Blacks pushing for discussions of race, the Texas network brought in numerous black scholars (many radical, some provoking heated discussions) to bimonthly seminars on race, which most organizers and leaders found useful.

Warren argues that it is too soon to draw firm conclusions, yet he suggests that the key to negotiating race seems to be sustaining (by constantly readjusting) the tension between emphasizing commonality and emphasizing difference (one might make a similar argument concerning protest, on the one hand, and more cooperative engagement, on the other hand). Many leaders in Texas also emphasize the importance of action, for the way it draws different people (with different emphases on commonality and difference) into relations that are productive and enduring, as well as critical. Critically reflective action can facilitate a politically more creative (because reciprocally informative) relation between short-term time horizons pertaining to urgent issues, and vaster time horizons about themes such as race, which stretch from the deep past and threaten the future. Collective action on immediate issues can enact more hopeful relationships across differences and can produce changes that open beyond the intractable yet impotent fury generated when centuries-old racism acquires an aura of immutability. Simultaneously, the vaster temporal frame provides a lens that is often essential for identifying and framing issues, for informing stronger deeper relationships, and for formulating more powerfully responsive political and economic aims.

It is not difficult to discern important resonances between Warren's discussion of the connections between action on specific issues and broader, more searching critical reflection (as well as the connections between short- and long-term horizons, commonality and difference, and cooperation and agonism), on the one hand, and my discussion about the need to open broader and deeper interrogations of politics and economics related to struggles around specific issues, on the other. In each case,

45. Warren, *Dry Bones Rattling.*
46. Ibid., 122.

the issue is how to entwine different elements central to the structure of human historical experience and political possibility, in ways that help nurture durable and powerful democratic relationships that generate— and evolve in light of—careful practical judgments. The aim suggested by Warren is to work beyond "either-or" structures of theory and practice toward creative tensional articulations of "both-and" through which radical-democratic communities might engender futures that respond better to questions about how the world might better become different.

One wishes for a similarly attentive discussion of the ways that gender relations are simultaneously transformed by and problematically at work in IAF democratic practices, but there is unfortunately very little of such discussion in any of these books.[47] This may appear to be an unimportant oversight, given that women frequently take powerful leadership roles in IAF organizations in ways that radically transfigure gender power structures and performances. Yet the lack of attention to gender in these texts—and the parallel lack of serious discussion of gender within IAF organizing—renders less visible and appreciated the powerful transformative potential of such organizing, and simultaneously tends to push to the margins of public inquiry ways that vestiges of gendered power might continue to be operative in these organizations—whether this inquiry takes the form of a relative paucity of collective reflection on gender power compared with reflection on race, class, ethnicity, and religion, or whether this inquiry manifests itself in difficulties having open discussions about elements of a certain "machismo" that sometimes haunt organizing cultures.

The work by explicitly feminist writers and activists about community organizing, such as the collection of essays that is *Community Activism and Feminist Politics*, edited by Nancy A. Naples, contains extended and insightful discussions of ways such activism has contributed to reconceptualizing categories like "mothering," "family," "work," "politics," and so forth.[48] Similarly, such scholarship attends to the dynamic

47. Rogers, *Cold Anger*, briefly discusses the ways in which Hispanic women have frequently become powerful grassroots leaders in ways that gained widespread legitimacy through the transfigurative interpretations of caring for the home (122–23). See Coles, "Feminists of Color," for a discussion of a democratic ethos (articulated particularly by numerous Chicana feminists) that is pertinent to numerous themes in radical-democratic organizing.

48. Naples, *Community Activism and Feminist Politics*. See also Naples, *Grassroots Warriors*.

ways that critical awareness and transformative practice tend to develop among women located on the underside of race, class, and gender power. It seems rather obvious that such reflective work is integral not only to transforming political thinking, but also to organizing more democratically and efficaciously to confront power and powerlessness in everyday life.[49]

LEADERSHIP, AUTHORITY, AND RESPONSIVE GRASSROOTS ENGAGEMENT

Associated with all efforts to engender political futures are questions of leadership and authority. Given the plurality, contestability, unequal capabilities and interest, and finitude of the human condition, what modes of authority might better inform radical-democratic judgment and action? For such action will inevitably fail to achieve consensus; such action will involve some in more frequent participation and in more powerful positions than others (at least for periods of time); such action will harbor little-recognized encroachments and exclusions, and so forth. Warren notes that many discussions of radical democracy conjure away such questions with illusions of "ultra-democracy" that would be so totally egalitarian, participatory, open, consensual, and decentralized that authority, power, and leadership would utterly disappear. Yet in practice, groups that deny the presence of authority and leadership typically become controlled by cliques, which are all the less democratically accountable for being unacknowledged. Moreover, efforts to work in ultrademocratic fashion tend to be ineffective (and thus unattractive to most people) insofar as they fail to cultivate the leadership of those who develop the "skills, knowledge, and abilities" of what the IAF calls the "arts of politics," such as how to "weigh alternatives, negotiate differences, analyze power dynamics, . . . strategize," build relationships, and to solicit new participants and leaders.[50] Generally, these abilities are attained only through long-term practice and reflection. By eschewing all efforts to organize in modes that cultivate, respect, and draw upon the leadership of those who have acquired abilities for radical democracy, groups tend to squander one of their most precious resources, and in so doing greatly

49. Sacks, *Caring by the Hour*, provides an insightful and textured analysis (with broader implications) of ways gender operates to enable and impede organizing in a particular context.

50. M. E. Warren, *Democracy and Association*, 212.

inhibit their ability to develop collective power and vision for vibrant and enduring democratic practice.

For the IAF, in contrast, as Warren illustrates, radical democracy centrally involves developing grassroots leadership and authority, both within their networks and in the relationship between these organizations and their broader communities. The idea is not to create a hierarchy in which some rule over others, but to organize internally so that those with more developed political capacities are *empowered to lead democratically in ways that aim fundamentally at soliciting and developing new participation and leadership for an ever broadening and deepening radical-democratic community*. Thus, Warren argues, the craft of radical-democratic practice hinges upon "the dynamic between authority and participation which provides the driving force behind IAF organizing."[51] Not only is participation explicitly organized in ways that are inflected by leadership and authority, but leadership and authority are being reconfigured such that their *raison dêtre* lies in the enhancement of participatory democratic engagement. Just as commonality and difference, immediacy and longer-term vision, and agon and cooperation must be entwined with and pass through one another in order to cultivate deeper democratic relationships and vision, as IAF would have it, radical-democratic engagement develops best in tensional relation with notions of leadership and authority that are themselves re-oriented toward radical-democratic aspirations.

This theme is crucial to democratic theory. One of the paradoxes of radical democracy thus far (and foreseeably?) is that in each of its insurgent formations it actively involves only a small fraction of the society in and with which it struggles. Radical democracy is *perhaps always* far more aspiration than facticity. (For example, even Chambers's vision of a world in which IAF and other grassroots efforts were to grow *magnificently* so that perhaps 3 to 5 percent of those in the United States would seriously be engaged and beginning to create fundamental changes, still leaves 95 percent much less engaged.) Such considerations led Hannah Arendt to conceptualize engaged political spaces as, at best, "islands in a sea or as oases in a desert" of political inaction.[52] Thus, even under radically democratic circumstances where political spaces were genuinely open to

---

51. Ibid., 214.
52. Arendt, *On Revolution*, 275.

the engagement of all, she imagined, many would not be drawn to political life, and politics would remain the activity of a "self-selecting elite."

Arendt thought that the problem of reconciling equality and authority, which she called "one of the most serious problems of all modern politics," could be addressed *in a limited fashion* (within politics, in terms of those with more authority than others, and between the self-selecting elite and the "self-excluded" who chose to refrain from politics) by a pyramidal council system that would provide numerous real possibilities for political participation for those "from all walks of life who have a real taste for public freedom [and care for the common world beyond their private interests] and cannot be 'happy' without it."[53] Hierarchical authority would be formed not from below or from above but rather through a process in which *politically engaged* equals at each level selected those among them who would be delegated to the next level up.

Whatever the weaknesses of Arendt's analysis and suggestions, she illuminates more honestly than many the probable undemocratic remainder in even the most radically democratic efforts, spaces, and institutions. Rather than seeking salvation from the conflict between democracy and authority in a significantly mythical (because highly manipulative) vision of general suffrage, which would conceal the *tensional* entwinement of equality and authority beneath the veil of authority-constituted-from-the-bottom (the unengaged voter), Arendt suggests a regulative ideal of political authority based on a system of public spaces that are *genuinely open at the bottom,* and that constitute and populate pyramids of authority on the basis of an *equality-based-on-engagement.* Those engaged in such politics have a responsibility to care for the interests of those who are not, but their legitimacy ultimately hinges upon the openness and equality of public spaces and activities that are confessedly elite (and she is rather comfortable with this fact) rather than mythically egalitarian in relation to the whole of society. Indeed, in addition to a *responsibility* toward those unengaged in public life, Arendt theorizes a need to *protect* public spaces from those ensconced in private passions and interests. Thus, democratic politics requires an authority that exceeds equality in relation to the unengaged, even if it populates a pyramidal structure through egalitarian processes.

53. Ibid., 278–79.

Analogously, the IAF, on Warren's reading, grants an element of authority that is simultaneously necessary (at least in the present context) for the flourishing of radical democracy *and yet* in tension with egalitarian ideals. Yet on Warren's account, the distinction between those politically incapacitated by a sea of antipolitical powers (such as global capitalism, corporatized media, the megastate, and consumer culture) and those cultivating capacities requisite for political life is more graduated, porous, and movable than Arendt thinks it is. Therefore, politicalness is a *continuum* that is simultaneously *more endangered and more hopeful* than Arendt theorizes in *On Revolution*. In this light, many in IAF take politicalness to be paradoxically in need of *both* more authoritative protection *and* more receptive activity.

Effective democratic organizing in contemporary times is a difficult, endangered, and nearly lost art. Hence, in order to increase the odds of sustaining vital radical-democratic organizations, most in the IAF believe it is desirable to imbue their networks with "a hierarchy of grass-roots leadership" skilled at negotiating the difficult tasks of cultivating democratic practices in starkly undemocratic times.[54] Typically, the modes of organizing (e.g., relational meetings, house meetings, action teams on various issues, modes of engaging establishment figures, power analyses, basic assembly structure) are disproportionately informed by organizers and local leaders who have developed within the radical-democratic culture of the IAF. Positions of leadership are generally filled through broad, informal networks of consultation in which those who are currently respected leaders have disproportionate authority and weight in the deliberations. (It is important to note that IAF authority concerns *primarily* the modes of democratic organizing: issues and concrete political strategies tend to be determined in a much more grassroots fashion. Yet authority in former domain leaks into the latter.) This is particularly true in the early stages of an organization's development and becomes significantly less so as a large pool of people with political experience develops over time. Warren does an excellent job identifying and analyzing the specific processes, modes of accountability, and dangers of IAF modes of authority in relation to democratic participation. Such authority is partly aimed at *protecting* organizations from the incompetence of those with significantly less democratic experience. Thus, the IAF justifies a demo-

54. Warren, *Dry Bones Rattling*, 213.

cratic culture that acknowledges an element of informal authority and inequality—albeit very dynamic, mutable, decreasing significantly over time, limited to core questions about organizing, and aimed at enhancing equality in practice—even among those engaged.

Yet Warren's account also reveals a radicalized notion of *receptive responsibility* that informs IAF authority. Because most in the IAF are unsatisfied with a mere *openness* in political process, authority itself is centrally oriented around transgressing the boundary between people who are apolitical and those who are not. That is, authority is fundamentally oriented and legitimated in light of ideals of *soliciting, provoking, and receiving* those who are disengaged, and *participating in developing* their political capacities. Thus, from this perspective, the primary purpose of authority—and the locus of politics—is relentlessly to work the limit between those engaged and those who are not, so that it becomes *radically less authoritative* (neither manipulative nor "self-selected"), and more a site of solicitation of new voices, visions, and energies that will creatively alter the course of the IAF's own development over time. Those persons and modes that best integrate the unengaged have more authority, for politics thus interpreted is not simply an activity of engaged equals accountable to one another, but also an activity receptively accountable to the *others,* ceaselessly attempting to practically interrogate and widen the limits of who is involved, of what issues are brought forth, of styles of engagement, etc.

Warren's account provocatively shows that the dynamic tensions between democratic equality and authority, as well as protection and responsiveness, are negotiated in ways both full of promise and fraught with danger. He shows (in detail that cannot be reproduced here) numerous democratic checks on the power of leaders, on the one hand, yet not insignificant possibilities for abuse and obstruction, on the other. Both practically and theoretically, this issue is clearly a work in progress that will likely modulate in light of new political experience. Such authority is *dangerous* insofar as it can always become a pretext for increasingly deaf, immutable, and deleterious modes of power (perhaps it always does, to some extent). More will need to be done to enhance the receptivity of IAF politics to questions and challenges concerning some of its core ideas, particularly in response to some other types of insurgent democracy, in response to modes of political protest, in response to coalitioning with non-IAF groups, and in response to the linkages between specific "issues" and broader "problems." This more dialogical culture will be enhanced to the extent that the IAF deepens its commitment to and capacities for strengthening member organizations in ways that affirm the autonomy (potentially sometimes in tension with the broader organization) of different member organizations' visions and actions. The culture will be further enhanced insofar as the IAF moves in directions more affirmative of coalitional work—in which the IAF is not the center or the umbrella—with other nonmember groups. Moreover, the IAF would do well to create periodic forums where its most authoritative modes and principles of democratic organizing can be discussed, drawn into question, and potentially reformed. With these important caveats, however, I take the spirit of these emergent theories of radical-democratic authority to be *hopeful* insofar as they may be a condition for transgressing power-drenched contexts of depoliticization in ways that solicit and empower the voices and actions of strangers to political engagement. What Warren's work suggests quite compellingly is that the future of radical democracy likely hinges on the ability to face and to dynamically (re)negotiate the tensions between authority and wildly unpredictable grassroots engagement.

Conclusion

But is there a future for radical democracy? And if so, what might it be?

From the perspective of a trickster politics of tensions, the future of democracy must always remain significantly in question. Democratic ethics and politics hinge on not knowing the future of democracy too well. I take this to be a sensibility that many of the best grassroots organizers repeatedly try to cultivate. Our being in common depends on it.

But there is an even more haunting intonation in the questions above: Is there *any* future at all for radical democracy? Sheldon Wolin, the radical-democratic theorist who (along with Arendt) most inspires many IAF organizers, ends the second edition of *Politics and Vision* with great doubts.[55] In the context of a growing imperial megastate that fuses gargantuan governmental and private corporate modes of power, Wolin argues that democracy today can at best be only "fugitive"—episodic, on the run, generally overwhelmed by greater forces. Perhaps this is all it ever has been or can be?

55. Wolin, *Politics and Vision*, 2nd edition.

When I put this question to a leading IAF organizer, Ernesto Cortez, in August 2004, he seemed to brush this conclusion aside, noting a couple of recent assemblies of over 10,000 people, and invoking the imminent possibility of much more in the near future.[56] Interpreting freely, I think he implied something like this: Radical democracy is less an "optimism of the will" (though it is this too) than a refusal to accept depoliticized and subjugative modes of power as the basic frame of things. It is not just a refusal of the long-term finality of this frame but a refusal that seeks to lodge itself in the near term as well, searching to muster unexpected powers to alter the present course of events. It is a refusal to take the corporate megastate on its own terms—terms that would extinguish precisely the question of democracy's future. In other words, it is the determination to keep alive *the question of democracy's possibility* at each moment—and to do so strategically and *politically,* because lacking political initiatives and exemplifications, the question quickly becomes empty and impotent.

Yet the call to initiative and exemplification is a call not to a narrowly confined pragmatic politics but rather to a politics that crafts itself through a constellation of vital tensions that facilitate an intensification of widening political engagement connecting work on pressing issues to farther horizons of democratic transformation. In a world where the rules of the game are densely established in institutions, practices, and souls, a trickster politics is needed that is responsive, supple, and capable of fashioning new and powerful practices even as it masters the arts of much more cramped games. This sensibility is at the heart of what I take to be most admirable in the practice and theory of IAF-inspired organizing. Its implications are just beginning to emerge, and they may yet contribute to gathering powers necessary to change the world more radically than some critics suspect.

56. Personal conversation 2004.

CHAPTER 14

Seeing Peace:
L'Arche as a Peace Movement

Stanley Hauerwas

How L'Arche Makes Peace Visible

One of the gifts L'Arche offers Christian and non-Christian alike is its enabling us to visualize peace. Some may find this remark odd since L'Arche did not begin as a peace movement and, furthermore, the primary work of L'Arche does not seem to be about peace. Moreover, apart from questions about L'Arche there is the matter of *seeing* peace. Why do we need to *see* peace? We need to see peace because we have been taught that violence is the norm and peace the exception. In calling attention to L'Arche as a peace movement, therefore, I hope to show that peace is not an ideal waiting to be realized. Rather peace is as real—as concrete—as the work of L'Arche. By seeing the realization of peace in the communities of L'Arche, we are more able to see and enact peace in our own lives.

Christianity, like peace, is not an idea. Rather it is a bodily faith that must be seen to be believed. As we pray following Eucharist, we "eat this body" and "drink this blood" so that we might become "living members of your Son our savior Jesus Christ." We partake of the bread and wine as the body and blood of Christ, because in so doing we are taken up into Christ's vision of his creation. Given this vision, we look for Christ's presence in the world to help us live into our calling as members of his body. L'Arche, a community built on faith, turns out to be a lens that helps us see God's peace in the world.

By suggesting L'Arche is a peace movement I do not think I am forcing a category on L'Arche or Jean Vanier. Vanier, as well as the various zones of L'Arche around the world, has increasingly identified working for peace to be one of the primary purposes of L'Arche. For example, the recent newsletter of L'Arche USA Zone identified its Zone Mandate by focusing on four major themes:

- fostering vocation in L'Arche by continuing to build structures and processes that support long-term membership in our communities;

- announcing L'Arche and the gifts of people with disabilities in order to help build a more peaceful and just world;

- deepening our relationships of solidarity within the Federation of L'Arche, especially with our communities in Latin America and the Caribbean; and

- exploring new models for living the Mission that respond to current realities facing our communities.[1]

It is by no means clear, however, how "announcing" the gifts of people with disabilities can help "build a more peaceful and just world." The phrase "in order" in the second theme seems to suggest a causal connection between the work of L'Arche and the work of peace, but it remains vague as to how we should understand the relation between those two tasks. Nor is it apparent how the four themes are interrelated. How does building structures and processes that support long-term vocations serve to sustain a more peaceful world? Why is deepening relationships within the Federation of L'Arche so important, particularly as the work of peace?

I believe there are good answers to these questions to be found in the work of Jean Vanier. Accordingly, by drawing on his work I will try to spell out how Vanier understands L'Arche to be a movement for peace. I should warn the reader in doing so that Jean Vanier will often sound very much like John Howard Yoder's understanding of Christian nonviolence. I do not think that is accidental, because Jean Vanier and John

---

1. *Journey and the Dream*, 2.

Howard Yoder do strike many of the same chords, even if in quite different keys.[2]

Vanier, particularly after September 11, 200l, has increasingly and
explicitly emphasized that one of the essential tasks of L'Arche is to exemplify peace. With his usual insight into the complex character of our lives,
he often calls attention to fear as the source of our violence. The fear that
dominates our lives is not in the first instance the fear of an enemy, unless
it is acknowledged that each of us is the enemy, but rather the fear that is
the source of violence is the fear that makes us unwilling to acknowledge
the wounded character of our lives.[3] L'Arche, a place where the wounds
of each person cannot avoid being exposed and thus hopefully healed,
becomes a context in which we can learn the patient habits necessary
for being at peace. Vanier knows such an understanding of peace may
not have results for creating a more peaceful world at the international
level, but he suggests "we are all called to become men and women of
peace wherever we may be—in our family, at work, in our parish, in our
neighborhood."[4]

Though Vanier's modesty about the work of L'Arche not being a
strategy designed to end the scourge of war is admirable, I want to suggest that L'Arche is exactly the kind of peace work we so desperately need
if our imaginations are to be capable of conceiving what peace might
look like at the international level.[5] One of the problems with being an
advocate of peace, and I am a pacifist, is the widespread presumption
that violence is the rule and peace the exception. The pacifist is therefore

2. Yoder is perhaps best known for his book, *Politics of Jesus*. It would be extremely
interesting to do a close comparison of Yoder's and Vanier's reading of scripture.

3. In his book, *Following Jesus in a Culture of Fear*, Scott Bader-Saye explains how
fear possesses the lives of Americans making us incapable of following Jesus. An equally
compelling case that helps us see how liberal politics is not about the dissipation of a
pre-political fear, but about the production and manipulation of fear is developed by Dan
Bell in "Politics of Fear and the Gospel of Life."

4. Vanier quoted by Kathryn Spink in her book, *The Miracle, the Message, the Story:
Jean Vanier and L'Arche*, 225.

5. In *Befriending the Stranger*, Vanier makes the strong claim that those who become
a friend of the weak will be blessed by God by discovering that the gospel is truly "good
news," that is, "it is a solution to the deep wounds of humanity, a way to stop the cycle of
violence and war" (43). So he does think the work of L'Arche has implications for what an
alternative to war might look like. I cannot help but think that if presidents of the United
States spent one day a week in a L'Arche home they would have to think twice about their
assumption that war in inevitable.

assumed to bear the burden of proof, because violence is thought to be necessary for the maintenance of a relatively just and secure order. The question addressed to the pacifist, "What would you do if . . . ?" allegedly shows the unworkability of a commitment to peace. L'Arche is the way I believe that question must be answered.[6]

Vanier and the work of L'Arche help us see that peace is a deeper reality than violence. However, this vision—a vision that enables us to see that peace is a deeper reality than violence, because we were created to be at peace— requires training. It turns out that our teachers are the core members of L'Arche whose gift is their unprotected vulnerability.[7] In learning to live with those whom we call "the disabled"—that is, in learning to view the world through the lens L'Arche provides—we learn that questions such as "Would it not have been better if a person so disabled would not have been born?" are not ones we are tempted to ask. For the answers, even the most humane answers to such questions, too often disguise a violence cloaked in the language of compassion.[8]

6. For a more direct response to the challenge, "What would you do if . . . ?," see Yoder, *What Would You Do?* Yoder challenges the deterministic presumptions often lurking behind the question, observing that if I have told myself beforehand that there are no alternatives other than violence, then I am not free to find imaginative and creative alternatives. I believe L'Arche is the exemplification of Yoder's point. Who could have imagined L'Arche if Vanier had assumed there was no alternative to institutionalizing those with mental handicaps. Yoder asks, "Does not the Christian belief in resurrection—not simply as one bygone event but as God's pattern of action in human experience—mean that it is precisely where we do not see how a situation can possibly be worked out that God might demonstrate his saving intent?" (34).

7. For an extraordinary analysis of how an acknowledgement of vulnerability could lead to a more imaginative and "effective" foreign policy, see Muller-Fahrenholz, "What If? The Missed Opportunity of 9/11."

8. Scott Bader-Saye observes that if we attend to Scripture we must observe that ordinarily God does not choose to prevent evil and suffering, but to redeem it. Accordingly the real question is not determining "why" something happened but what kind of response is appropriate if we are to participate in God's redemptive work. Accordingly, Bader-Saye suggests that "providence is a way of giving time a story that invites a certain kind of politics. Trust in divine provision makes possible risky ventures of vulnerable love because we trust that the end of the story is in God's hands and not ours. We have been freed from the pressure of making history turn out right and thus have been set free to live the generosity, peacefulness, and hospitality that correspond to God's gracious and plentiful provision." "Figuring Time: Providence and Politics," 103–4.

THE MYSTERY OF SUFFERING

I need to explain this last remark, because it is important for understanding the kind of peace found in L'Arche. Crucial for our learning to be at peace with ourselves and one another is the ability to accept the mystery of suffering. But it turns out that is exactly what we have lost the ability to do. In an extraordinary, but unfortunately not well-known book, *Victims and Values: A History and a Theory of Suffering*, Joseph Amato argues that modernity is marked fundamentally by a transformation of how suffering is understood and responded to.[9] Amato observes that all human cultures must give meaning to suffering, but a fundamental shift in attitudes toward suffering occurred in the Enlightenment. The shift was characterized by a social sympathy for those who suffer, which led to reform movements that resulted in much social good. But that same sympathy confronted by more victims than can be cared for also led to a battle over the value of suffering.

Just at the time people developed a universal sympathy for all those who suffer—hence the significance given to the status of being a victim—they also increasingly came to believe that suffering is not an inevitable part of human experience. Thus the presumption shared by increasing numbers of people that it is wrong not to be happy. Jeremy Bentham exemplifies this attitude by his attempt to develop a social calculus that aims to do nothing less than remove all unnecessary suffering from human experience.[10] Hidden, however, in this humanism is a violence against all who suffer in ways that cannot be eliminated.[11] In the name of sympathy for the sufferer we must eliminate those who cannot be "cured."

It is against this violence that Vanier set his face by insisting on the mystery of suffering. Vanier observes, "Jesus did not come into the world to explain suffering nor to justify its existence. He came to reveal that we can all alleviate pain, through our competence and our compassion. He came to show us that every pain, every hurt we experience can become an

9. Joseph A. Amato, *Victims and Values*.

10. Amato, *Victims and Values*, 79.

11. We are all, of course, subject to suffering that cannot be eliminated, because we are all destined to die. Thus the death-denying character of so much of our lives as "modern people." Amato observes that "death ruptures our ethical world. It creates a discrepancy between what is intended and what is achieved, between what is offered and what is accepted. Death makes injustice permanent" (*Victims and Values*, 20).

offering, and thus a source of life for others in and through Jesus' offering of love to the Father."[12]

Vanier's great gift, the gift of L'Arche, is to teach us to see pain, to enter into the pain of others, without wanting to destroy those whose suffer.[13] In *Befriending the Stranger*, Vanier tells the story of Lucien, who was born with severe mental and physical disabilities. He could not talk and his twisted body meant that he had to spend his life in a wheelchair or the bed. He lived the first thirty years of his life with his mother, who could interpret his body language.[14] He was at peace with his mother,

12. Vanier, *Befriending the Stranger*, 89. I had first thought to use this occasion to explore some of the connections between Wittgenstein's and Vanier's work. I discovered, however, as I tried to write about those connections that the story was far too complicated for a short essay. However I think Wittgenstein's remarks concerning language games is very important if we are to understand the work of L'Arche and also Vanier's understanding of that work. For example, in *Culture and Value* Wittgenstein says, "The origin and the primitive form of the language game is a reaction; only from this can more complicated forms develop. Language—I want to say—is a refinement, 'in the beginning was the deed'" (31e). Accordingly Wittgenstein reminds us in the *Philosophical Investigations* that when justifications reach bedrock, "and my spade is turned. Then I am inclined to say: 'This is simply what I do'" (217). The work of L'Arche is bedrock, and Vanier tries to help us see that "this is simply what he does." It is as if Vanier, who I suspect has never read Wittgenstein, understood intuitively Wittgenstein's admonition that "we must do away with all *explanation*, and description alone must take its place" (*Philosophical Investigations*, 109). Vanier never tries to explain, at least he never tries to understand a particular action and practice as the exemplification or application of a universal idea, but rather he does the only thing he can do—that is, he holds before us the lives that have shaped his life. This means he helps us see bedrock by telling stories of L'Arche. Stories are all we have if it is true that Jesus did not come to explain suffering. Amato observes, "nothing so denies us and our stories, as the denial of our sufferings and sacrifices. If we have no sufferings or sacrifices to call our own, we have no story to tell, and with no story to tell, we are no people at all." *Victims and Values*, 210.

13. Amato provides a close analysis of the difference as well as the interrelated character of pain and suffering. He observes, "suffering is greater and more comprehensive than pain. Suffering describes a general condition, person, group, or society. While not impossible, it would be unusual to speak of the many sufferings of a person's pain, whereas we commonly speak of suffering as if it is composed of many pains. Suffering does not invite specific and immediate remedies" (*Victims and Values*, 15).

14. The significance of the body as language, and in particular the language of pain, for Vanier again suggest some fascinating connections with Wittgenstein. For example in *On Certainty*, Wittgenstein remarks: "I want to regard man here as an animal; as a primitive being to which one grants instinct but not ratiocination. As a creature in a primitive state. Any logic good enough for a primitive means of communication needs no apology from us. Language did not emerge from some kind of ratiocination" (475). By "primitive" Wittgenstein does not mean a contrast with "civilized"; rather he means to remind us, as

but he fell ill, requiring hospitalization. Losing all points of reference, screams of anguish possessed him. He came to "La Forestiere," but his constant screaming continued and nothing seemed to work to calm him. Vanier confesses that Lucien's screams pierced the very core of his being, forcing him to recognize that he would be willing to hurt Lucien to keep him quite. Vanier had to recognize that he, someone who thought he had been called to share his life with the weak, had in his heart the capacity to hate a weak person.[15]

The work of L'Arche is dangerous as it tempts us to rage against those we are committed to "help." So when Vanier tells us that "it is important to enter into the mystery of pain, the pain of our brothers and sisters in countries that are at war, the pain of our brothers and sisters who are sick, who are hungry, and who are in prison," he puts us at great risk.[16] To face the mystery of pain means we must confront the violence we harbor in our hearts, a violence created by a world we cannot force to conform to our desires. Vanier observes, "the only thing that matters is that we be truthful; that we do not let ourselves be governed by lies and by illusion."[17] But to face the truth about ourselves—the truth that we desire to eliminate those in pain—is no easy task. Yet without such truth there can be no peace.

---

he says later in *On Certainty*, "You must bear in mind that the language-game (how water behaves when boiled or frozen) is to say something unpredictable. I mean: it is not based on grounds. It is not reasonable (or unreasonable). It is there—like life" (559). L'Arche is the extended training necessary to learn the language of the body and pain. The people who speak that language—a language whose "words" are often gestures of the body—do not need to be explained. They are there—like life. Our task is to learn to listen to what they have to say.

15. Vanier, *Befriending the Stranger*, 62.

16. Ibid., 87.

17. Ibid., 61. In *Drawn into the Mystery of Jesus through the Gospel of John*, Vanier observes "but the truth is often hidden from us, which is why it takes time and the help of others to discern the truth. We often find truth only after we choose to let go of some of the illusions of life we may still have. It takes time to find inner freedom—this is the ongoing work of a lifetime. I do not have this freedom yet, but my hope is to continue to keep my heart open to receive it. Even though truth makes us free, we never *possess* it. We are called humbly to contemplate the truth that is given us, to search unceasingly in order to be drawn into truth, to let ourselves be led, in the company of others, into the unfolding mystery of truth, to be possessed by truth and to serve truth. To live in truth is to live a relationship of love with the Word of God made flesh, who is truth, compassion and forgiveness" (160).

THE POLITICS OF PEACE

In order to understand how L'Arche could be a peace movement one must recognize L'Arche as a politics. L'Arche may not seem to represent the kind of political engagement often associated with movements for a more peaceable world, but any movement for peace not determined by L'Arche-like politics will only threaten to become a form of violence. Let me try to explain this enigmatic remark. Some years ago, when many were concerned that the Cold War might result in a nuclear holocaust, I wrote an article against the presumption that "peace" could be equated with human survival and against the correlative implication being drawn by some that all life should be organized to insure that nuclear weapons were eliminated. The title of the article was "Taking Time for Peace: The Ethical Significance of the Trivial."[18] There I argued:

> Peace takes time. Put even more strongly, peace creates time by its steadfast refusal to force the other to submit in the name of order. Peace is not a static state but an activity which requires constant attention and care. An activity by its very nature takes place over time. In fact, activity creates time, as we know how to characterize duration only by noting that we did this first, and then this second, and so on, until we either get somewhere or accomplished this or that task. So peace is the process through which we make time our own rather than be determined by "events" over which, it is alleged, we have no control.[19]

I do not think that at the time I wrote "Taking Time for the Trivial" I was familiar with the work of Vanier or L'Arche. But once I discovered Vanier and L'Arche I thought I saw what peace must surely look like. If I was right that the politics of peace is a politics of time, then L'Arche is truly a fine exemplification of that. For at the heart of L'Arche is patience, which

18. The article is in my book, *Christian Existence Today: Essays on Church, World, and Living In Between*, 253–66.

19. Ibid., 258. In the letter inviting us to this symposium we were invited to address the "ontological issues related to the difference between 'being' and 'doing.'" There are metaphysical presumptions involved in this paragraph, but they challenge the presumption that ontologically being and doing are two "things." If Aquinas is right, and I certainly think he is, being is activity. See, for example, David Burrell's account of Aquinas in his Aquinas: God and Action (London: Routledge and Kegan Paul, 1979), pp. 45–48. It is crucial to avoid "intellectualistic" accounts of activity, that is, the view that for an action to be an action it must be caused by "reason." The body has its reasons making action possible.

turns out to be but another name for peace.[20] To join L'Arche at any level requires that you be ready to be slowed down. It is not just "all right" to take two hours to eat a meal with a core member or even longer to bathe a body not easily "handled," but L'Arche requires that those who do this important work learn that time is not a zero-sum game. We have all the time we need to do what needs to be done.[21]

L'Arche also teaches the significance of place. You cannot be constantly going and coming as an assistant. Core members love routines, and routines create and are created by familiarity, and familiarity makes place "a" place. Place and routine can become boring without the celebration of beauty. Thus it is crucial for L'Arche that each person's birthday be celebrated, in recognition of the beauty that is their life. Place and routine are transformed by recognizing the beauty of each person. And this celebration of each life makes trust possible, thereby making L'Arche possible. So Zone USA was right—there is a connection between building structures and processes that support long-term membership in L'Arche communities and the process through which a more peaceful and just world can come into being. Without L'Arche and communities like L'Arche we could not know what trust in its most determinative form looks like.

Alasdair MacIntyre suggests that if I am to be a trustworthy person I must be able to be relied upon even when it may be to my advantage to betray another's trust or when it may be inconvenient for me to be relied upon. Therefore trust requires that we are able to trust one another not only in the routines of everyday life, but in particular when we are a burden by reason of our disabilities. Those who have learned to trust us must know that we will be there in the times and places we have promised to be even when to be so is costly.[22] Interestingly enough, Vanier has taught

20. Patience is at the heart of John Howard Yoder's understanding of peace. See his, "'Patience' as Method in Moral Reasoning: Is an Ethic of Discipleship 'Absolute'?"

21. For my account of Vanier's understanding of time, see my essay "Timeful Friends: Living with the Handicapped." This essay also appears in *Critical Reflections on Stanley Hauerwas' Theology of Disability*, edited by John Swinton, with a response by Jean Vanier.

22. MacIntyre, *Dependent Rational Animals*, 109–10. MacIntyre has learned much from Logstrup's account of trust as a central feature arising spontaneously from our relations with one another. Yet he thinks Logstrup fails to distinguish between the initial trust of children, some element of which is preserved throughout our lives, and mature trust, for which we can sometimes give good reasons. See MacIntyre, "Human Nature

us that we learn to trust from those whom we first thought must come to trust us. Mutual vulnerability makes a trust between assistant and core member possible that is otherwise unimaginable.

Such trust, moreover, not only makes possible but necessary, as L'Arche USA suggests, the task to deepen its relationship with other L'Arche communities in other parts of the world. I often call attention to the Mennonite poster with the slogan: "A Modest Proposal for Peace—Let the Christians of the World Agree They Will Not Kill One Another." Peace is to know others in a manner that makes impossible any thought of their destruction in the interest of "wider loyalties." It is hard to imagine anyone who has lived in a L'Arche community thinking that violence must be used in the name of a "good cause." The trust that the timefulness and placedness of a L'Arche way of life provides an alternative to the violence of the world shaped by speed and placelessness. And it is just such a world in which we find ourselves. For if Paul Virilio is right, the dominant form violence takes in modernity is speed. According to Virilio contemporary war is shaped by mechanisms of mass communication that make war less and less about territory and more about the management of information. As a result, our perceptions are mediated by logics of violence in the form of speed creating a new vision of the world in which everyone "naturally" understands themselves to be part of the war machine. Local space and time disappear to be replaced by a single, global, and virtual "real time." This, according to Virilio, is "what the doctrine of security is founded on: the saturation of time and space by speed, making daily life the last theater of operations, the ultimate scene of strategic foresight."[23]

Chris Huebner argues that Virilio's account of violence as speed helps us see why peace cannot simply be understood as an alternative to war. Too often such alternatives reproduce the violence hidden in the very terms we use to underwrite a peace that is no more than the absence of overt hostilities. Rather what is needed is a community, a people, who are shaped by practices that force them to acknowledge that God has given them all the time in the world—a world that thinks it has no time to receive peace as a gift. Huebner argues, I think quite rightly, that John Howard Yoder's non-Constantinian understanding of the church helps

and Human Dependence."

23. Paul Virilio, *Popular Defense and Ecological Struggles*, 92. I am indebted to Chris Huebner for some of the wording describing Virilio's work found in his book, *A Precarious Peace*, 119–20.

us to see what such a people might look like.[24] I am suggesting that in a similar fashion L'Arche is a community necessary to train us to see the hard, difficult, but happy work peace is.

Vanier is surely right that the only thing that matters is that we be truthful. A "peace" that is anything less than truthful cannot but hide from us the violence we perpetrate in the name of peace. Commenting on Yoder's epistemology of non-violence, Huebner observes that truthfulness is an utterly contingent gift that can only be given because truth "emerges at the site of vulnerable interchange with the other."[25] Surely "vulnerable interchange with the other" is as good a description of L'Arche we can have.

The Witness of L'Arche In and To the World

Yet Vanier believes the peace we see in L'Arche cannot be limited to L'Arche, because we are creatures created to be at peace with ourselves and one another. According to Vanier, "Absolutely everything is engraved in our being. So the experience of being loved by God does not change our lives completely, yet something is changed when we realize that God loves us just as we are, not as we would like to be nor as our parents or society would have liked us to be."[26]

Vanier's confidence that L'Arche but manifests the peace that is engraved in our being is correlative of his conviction that God, through the mystery of the Incarnation, has entered into our very being.[27] That is why suffering does not need to be explained, for what has been given

24. Huebner, *A Precarious Peace*, 126–32. I find it quite interesting that Vanier has increasingly become critical of Constantinian developments in which "Church and State became intertwined" and, as a result, the building of huge and beautiful buildings became more important than "being attentive to the poor and seeing them at the heart of the church." Vanier, *Drawn Into the Mystery*, 236.

25. Huebner, *A Precarious Peace*, 126.

26. Vanier, *Befriending the Stranger*, 32. It would be fascinating to explore Vanier's understanding of these matters in relation to the debates occasioned by De Lubac's understanding of the relation of nature and grace. My hunch is that Vanier might exemplify De Lubac's insistence that grace is not extrinsically related to nature but rather is a gift that makes possible a narrative of our lives otherwise unavailable. This is an extremely important matter because I fear some may confuse Vanier's Christian humanism with a secular humanism that is the antithesis of the Gospel. John Milbank provides a good account of De Lubac's Christian humanism in his *The Suspended Middle: Henri de Lubac and the Debate Concerning the Supernatural*, 9–11.

27. Vanier, *Befriending the Stranger*, 55.

to us is not an explanation, but the practice of charity through which we are drawn into the very life of God. That practice, the practice of charity, Vanier often identifies with learning not just to wash the feet of the disabled but to have our feet washed by the disabled. By having our feet washed by the disabled we may begin to recognize that we must first learn to receive if we are to give. A receiving, moreover, that requires that our own wounds be acknowledged.[28]

The Christological center that shapes Vanier's understanding of the work of L'Arche is why he burns with a passion to be in conversation with those from other faiths or no faith. For him, such a conversation is possible because of what he has learned by having his feet washed by the disabled. In his November/December letter to L'Arche, he reports on the meeting organized by the community Sant'Egidio to celebrate the first international meeting called in 1996 by John Paul II. Muslim leaders, Jewish rabbis, and Bishops came together "to share and pray for peace and to be a sign of peace and of prayer." Vanier participated in a workshop on "the love of God and the love of people," in which he shared the life of "Ghadir, a young Muslim girl with severe disabilities whom we had welcomed in our L'Arche community near Bethany and how my encounter with her had been a sign of God and a place of transformation for me." That Ghadir exists means it might just be the case that Muslims and Christians might discover common work necessary for us to be at peace.

In chapter 7, "The Politics of Gentleness,"[29] I suggested that L'Arche cannot be L'Arche if it loses its animating center, that is, faith in Jesus as the one who has redeemed time. Of course L'Arche communities shaped by other religious or non-religious convictions are possible. But they are possible because a Jean Vanier exists to exemplify what happens to a life that has learned what it means to have one's feet washed by the least of

28. Vanier reports a lesson he learned from a letter he read written by the psychologist Carl Jung. (Vanier has a genius for learning from people I distrust and dislike.) Jung observed that he admired Christians for seeing Jesus in the hungry and thirsty, but what he did not understand was Christians' failure to see Jesus in their own poverty. Christians it seems always want to do good to the poor outside ourselves, but we often deny the poor person that resides in our own lives. This leads Vanier to acknowledge that he could not help Lucien unless he was open to and ready to accept his own wounds and seek help—help that comes from the very ones that Vanier sought to help (*Befriending the Stranger*, 64).

29. See [XREF] above.

these.[30] In this respect the work of L'Arche is analogous to John Howard Yoder's understanding of "the pacifism of the Messianic community." Such a pacifism affirms

> Its dependence upon the confession that Jesus is Christ and that Jesus Christ is Lord. To say that Jesus is the Messiah is to say that in him are fulfilled the expectations of God's people regarding the one in whom God's will would perfectly be done. Therefore, in the person and work of Jesus, in his teachings and his passion, this kind of pacifism finds its rootage, and in his resurrection it finds its enablement.[31]

Yoder notes that one of the disadvantages of such a pacifism is that it cannot promise to "work."[32] Yet I take it that that is exactly what his understanding of peace shares with the work of L'Arche. For L'Arche does not exist to "work," but to testify to what will be missed if we only attempt what we assume will work. Such a witness, however, cannot be sustained unless a people exists whose work only makes sense in light of the peace they have seen in the body and blood of Christ. So must our vision be trained to recognize Christ's peace in the work of such a people—people like Jean Vanier and communities like L'Arche. For to see the peace of L'Arche is to see the peace of Christ.

30. This way of putting the matter I owe to Dan Morehead.

31. Yoder, *Nevertheless*, 133–34.

32. Yoder, *Nevertheless*, 137.

CHAPTER 15

A Conversation

Coles: You know, Stanley, when I first read your response to me in "A Haunting Possibility," I was tempted to *affirm* your suspicion (following your Augustinian response to the questions I posed to Yoder) that your response to me could be read as a problematic "attempt to change the subject."[1] I found interesting and valuable your sense of how "Christians might help contribute to the work of radical democracy. . . . [which] requires the facing down of death, making possible a politics alternative to the politics of glory."[2] Yet I wondered if there were questions of jealousy and heterogeneity that you avoided in your response, and hence I wasn't entirely persuaded that changing the subject was wholly a good move. The more I ponder it, however, the more I think that this question of the relation to death and the possibility of an alternative to the politics of glory goes to the heart of the matter.

Thus I want to respond to your response with some questions about the politics of death and fear, which I think are related to some of the questions that Peter Dula and Alex Sider raise to you in their article in "Radical Democracy, Radical Ecclesiology" in the Winter 2006 issue of *Cross Currents*.[3] As I read it, your interpretation of Augustine is quite close to themes that Rowan Williams pursues in an essay he wrote on Augustine a couple decades ago.[4] Williams is critiquing the politics of Roman pagan glory as a terrible terror-driven consequence of not having

1. See page 28 above.
2. Ibid.
3. Dula and Sider, "Radical Democracy, Radical Ecclesiology," 482–505.
4. Williams, "Politics and the Soul."

come to terms with death. He argues that Augustine's critique is not only right concerning the Romans, and is not only pertinent to the cruder in-carnations of empire and greed in our times, but moreover that the dele-terious consequences of striving for immortality through glory are visibly at work in the writing of Hannah Arendt. I think he is partly right. Yet the question that concerns me here is to what extent Williams's critique might be generalized as a wider suspicion about non-Christian radical democ-racy? Will radical democracy inexorably tend to (de)generate patterns of immortality-seeking and impatience that undermine its best intentions? Stanley, my strong hunch is that your essay is deeply animated by this worry, even if you are too modest in this context to say it outright. My guess is that this is where you suspect Christianity can make a contribu-tion to radical democracy that not only supports radical democracy's best aims, but without which they are incoherent and probably untenable.

My questions, then, concern what *political practices and institu-tional consequences* might flow from this line of thinking (both within the church and in relation to the wider world). In your response to Peter and Alex, you have defended orthodoxy—which risks a kind of hier-archy—and I think you do so out of a sense that it is a crucial condi-tion for engendering a people who don't fear death and who, therefore, might resist the politics of empire, capitalism, and the megastate (and the cultures that come with these). Do you end up with a paradox here? Namely, that, undemocratic institutions linked to orthodoxy often would be the condition of radical democracy? As is obvious from my discussion of authority in the "Of Tensions and Tricksters" essay in this volume, it should be clear that I think some version of this paradox is immanent in radical democracy itself. But it is strung differently, and I think there are important political stakes. The direction in which I'm thinking and act-ing is that a radical-democratic ethos might be cultivated from a variety of traditions and emergent struggles, and that key to cultivating a people with capacities for this engagement is the proliferation of liturgies—body practices—that habituate people to patience, receptive generosity, dia-logue, care, the expression of eccentric gifts, courage to resist injustice and subjugation, and so forth. This requires a certain articulation of au-thority (with a certain resonance, oddly, with orthodoxy—Ella Baker is a member of the community of democratic saints, which also means she was *not* perfect). Yet this is an articulation of authority that is democratic precisely for its capacity to invigorate an insurgent dialogical ethos and insurgent dialogical practices and powers "from below," and "from beyond" those currently countenanced. As such, democratic authority must find its expression there and thus again and again. This is part of what I mean by the radical ordinary. I suspect that this liturgical sensibility is quite close to what Peter and Alex are getting at—quite close to what animates their concerns about orthodoxy. Might not institutional hierarchy vitiate the liturgies of radical *ecclesia*—and therefore *its* authority? One could say that Yoder, Williams, and Vanier are radically orthodox in some important senses, yet they articulate this orthodoxy in ways that might also be called more radically democratic than *some* of your articulations (e.g., when you name your position "high-church Mennonite"). Can you help us get clearer about your understanding of the entwinements, tensions, paradoxes, and liturgical-institutional stakes here?

Hauerwas: The first thing I need to say is that I defend "orthodoxy" because I think the hard-won wisdom of the church is true. Too often it is forgotten that, for example, that the cannon of the Scripture is "orthodoxy." If the church had not decided against Marcion—that is, if the church had followed Marcion in eliminating the Old Testament and the Gospels because they were too Jewish—then we would have appeared more coherent, but we would have lost the tension that is at the heart of the Christian faith: Christians worship the Lord of Israel. It is too often forgotten that "trinity" names a reading rule that demands Christians read the Old Testament as "our" scripture. That means we can never avoid the challenge of Jewish readings to our readings. So "orthodoxy" is not the avoidance of argument. Orthodoxy is the naming of arguments across time that must take place if we are to be faithful to Jesus.

"Bishop" is the name of the office that God has given the church to ensure that the dead—who are not dead, but who live with God in the communion of the saints—get to continue in the debates that are Christian tradition. Bishops do not need to be theologians—though some have been spectacularly so (Augustine)—because their task is to be agents of memory (Yoder[5]) for the church across time and space, to ensure that the arguments and conversations that the gospel demands are not cut short. Put differently, the bishop is the agent of unity, to ensure

5. For Yoder's account of the church's "agents of memory," see *Priestly Kingdom*, 30.

that one liturgical assembly does not isolate itself from other liturgical assemblies in such a manner that the complexity that is the gospel is lost: which means, for example, that the American church cannot tell the story of our reception of the gospel without being challenged by how the gospel is being received in Africa or Asia. I realize that this may seem "ideal," but I think it rightly suggests how God has given the church gifts over time to make us vulnerable to challenge by the Holy Spirit.

Does this mean that I am a Catholic? Do I think that the bishop of Rome has a special place in the church? Yes, I do. For no other reason than that the office of Rome can be held accountable for the disunity of the church. That John Paul II confessed Rome's sin for the division of the church in the Reformation is significant. People tend to think, and Rome too often acts to confirm, that Rome is a tyranny that puts the lid on difference. But that is not what Rome does. Because the unity of the church is to be found in Eucharistic assemblies around the world, not all have to be the same. Protestant demands that we all have to have the same reading of Scripture are unknown to Rome. Because the unity of the church is given through the Spirit, Rome exists to encourage many readings of Scripture. If you think Rome is the office of uniformity, then you have never been in the same room with Jesuits and Dominicans.

I realize that this may not seem the kind of answer you, Peter, or Alex wanted—you are responding with ecclesial examples—but I want to say that if you understand hierarchy this way, then there is a sense that the church has always exemplified the kind of conversations that you name as radically democratic. Such a response may seem too "easy" because it fails to deal with the abuses that seem more the rule than the exception. But crucial for me is the reality of God, who never lets his people alone, which means at the very least that authority in the church is exemplified in lives of holiness—lives that always call those "in power" to account.

Jim Burtchaell, CSC, was fond of using the example of a mass in India at which Mother Teresa was present. The priest had the power to celebrate, but no one doubted who had authority in that liturgical assembly. The first task of those who hold power in the church is always to point to those who are holy. That the church must recognize that it is always in need of reform (this includes the Anabaptists) is the condition of possibility for the rightful exercise of authority. When the papacy does not recognize that it is less than it should be—just to the extent that it fails to acknowledge the gifts it receives from the Anabaptists—it is not fulfilling its office.

This is my way of responding to what you identify as the "paradox" that undemocratic institutions linked to orthodoxy may be the condition of radical democracy. I do not see why that is a paradox. Hierarchy is a given. The question is, what holds hierarchy accountable to the service it is to perform for the community? To be a "high-church Mennonite" is my way to suggest that I believe the time in which we live is one in which God is leading us back to the profound unity of Christians—a unity found in our refusal to kill one another in the name of national loyalties. However, with Yoder, I have am quite open to the different ways that the church might find to organize itself institutionally. For example, I think it quite possible that those called to the ministry of word and sacrament (and I understand that some may not like the language of sacrament) be chosen by lot. I think it a very good test to ask, what kind of community do you need to be for those in leadership to be chosen by lot and, after a time, to return to what they were doing before they were chosen? I think it is, moreover, crucial for the church to produce a leadership capable of acknowledging mistakes and, even more important, wrongs done in the name of being "responsible." I assume that the ability to acknowledge wrongs is a given, because integral to the liturgy that makes the church the church is the confession of sins. The question I must ask you is, what do radical democrats do if they do not have confession of sin?

Coles: Ok, I'll try to respond to that a bit further on in our conversation. But first let me follow with a question about what you just said, namely, that the church needs to *recognize* the need for reform, and that it *includes* the Anabaptists. This seems an important insight, and yet it also skirts a difficulty that perhaps drives home the paradoxical character of the tensions here. Do Anabaptists want to be *included?* Within the current high-church institutional and liturgical power structure? Don't they by and large seek a communion that would radically reform this structure? So the issue isn't really inclusion and recognition (you're starting to sound like a "liberal," Stanley!) as much as reformation in the face of a vine that needs to be clipped back to the roots (Yoder's imagery). And reformation aims at ways that the principalities and the powers—and sin—endlessly reestablish themselves in the church and need to be taken away, given up, in the name of reforming a penitent politics of Jesus: reformation aims at

re-beginning, deepening and extending dialogical liturgies of reconciliation. Those invested in powers and unclipped vines rarely give them up.
Since we're in Durham, North Carolina, and it is summertime, kudzu is
never far from my mind. The question, then, is how to think about liturgies and institutions that can both better articulate and better sustain the
tensions that emerge when one realizes the illuminating power of two
non-identical insights. On the one hand, *authority is an integral element
of radical democracy and radical ecclesia that enhances flourishing* insofar
as nurturing conversation, patience, and intense struggle that remains
dialogical is an incredibly difficult art. Sustaining conversation, patience,
and struggle is a craft requiring those who are skilled, such that they can
keep memories before us when we'd rather forget, recognize people who
are not getting heard in the present, and call us to the heights of energetic
daily investments in such practices in a world where we'd rather shop.
On the other hand, *radical democracy and radical ecclesia are integral to
any worthwhile authority* insofar as the authority begins to lose sight of
and become a barrier to insurgent grassroots practices, or to the politics
of Jesus, as soon as it ceases to be not only accountable to but also fundamentally formed by dialogics from "below and beyond." I'm asking less
for "strong views" here and more for how you might inform our thinking
about this tension, which I think you and I both want to acknowledge.
I want to name it as tension and paradox, because when we cease to do
so, our yearning for consolation, comprehension, and so forth, tends to
slide us into relations of power that become profoundly bad. It seems to
me that Yoder is willing to venture into discussions of church practices
and institutions in ways that are at once provocative and shaped, and
at the same time that avoid a certain dogmatic stance or tone. Is your
strategy in relation to the tensions more to avoid these institutional questions? Can you, given how integral these would seem to be if one is to
take the liturgical formation of peoplehood seriously in either Christian
or radical-democratic terms? I'm looking less for answers and more for
further ways to inform the questions, such that the dangers of hierarchy
are addressed in a way that is—what?—more robust? more supple? more
intransigent? Do these questions seem fair and pertinent to you? In other
words, what kind of church practices and institutions might be more
disposed not only to recognize and include, but also to listen to and to
risk radical reformation in the face of those such as, say, Yoder, Romero,
King, and Day—past, present, and future? Perhaps this has to do with

memory? A church that could keep a memory of an insurgent St. Francis? Rather than a memory that echoes the assimilated memory that the U.S. government keeps of MLK Jr.? I'm asking—provocatively—whether a church articulated through profoundly hierarchical power structures and temporal imaginaries of endless unclipped growth is inherently invested in obfuscating practices of memory, much analogous to the way nation-states tend to be so?

Hauerwas: I wish that I had said what you just said. Putting the matter of authority in terms of memory seems just right to me. You know that you have a problem when Saint Francis is remembered primarily as someone holding a rabbit, preaching to birds. Holding rabbits and preaching to birds is a good thing, but you can forget that he was about reforming the church by challenging the presumptions about wealth. I am reminded of Dorothy Day's response when it was suggested to her that she was a saint: "you are not going to get rid of me that easily."

I once asked Rowan Williams why we should remain Protestant. He said we remain Protestant to remind the Romans of the sinfulness of the church. Interesting enough, that was also John Yoder's view. No institution, no set of offices, can ensure that the church itself is free of sin. The question is always what forms we need to help us name the powers that possess us.

So you are quite right to draw attention to Yoder's vine image. The church does need pruning. Indeed, this is what I assume is happening in our day. The church is losing its power over the "West." I think that a very good thing. So you are quite right that the Anabaptists do not want to be included, but rather from the Anabaptists we might learn (and they have lost many of the skills) as church to live by our wits, because we no longer can assume a power position.

But this still does not get at the challenge that you rightly present, namely, what institutional forms do I envision that need to exist in order that the ongoing need for reformation not be repressed? I think my answer (and I would be the first to recognize that it may not be adequate) is that a polity must exist that refuses to silence the "lesser member." Every time the pope has anything to say, I wish he might think, "what must the church be to sustain the work of Jean Vanier?" The same principle, I assume, would apply to radical democracy. That is why I think you are quite right to see the liturgical significance of footwashing. A people who have learned to have their feet washed just might be able to remember Martin Luther King Jr., and by remembering him to know that they cannot go to war.

Coles: I'm interested in pursuing further the question of the communion of saints. In "A Haunting Possibility," you argue that this communion is that of those who seek to live toward an alternative glory in having "died victorious because they broke forever the fatal victim/victimizer logic." For Christian Roman martyrs, "their dying was part of [this] story."[6] If I understand correctly, one could say that "orthodoxy" for you is the protection and passing on of this story. Ultimately, this story is the story of Jesus, and so you write that "'orthodoxy' but names the developments across time that the church has found necessary to help us keep the story of Jesus straight. Therefore, rather than being the denial of radical democracy, orthodoxy is the exemplification of the training necessary to form a people who are not only capable of working for justice, but who are just."[7] Now—returning to the tension, the paradox—authority and hierarchy are necessary on this account precisely for "keeping the story straight." No doubt this is a crucial part of what one might call the more "teleological" aspect of Christian tradition. But it seems to me that Chris Huebner, following Yoder, gives traditioning a twist in *A Precarious Peace*—a twist that you note in a footnote, and that I want to hear you discuss further.

A certain way of intonating, "keeping the story straight," might risk reifying the communion of saints. In the name of protecting the "straight story," a focus on *telos* and on associated institutional hierarchies of those closest to it, is organized in order to "keep the story going," if you will. And this requires disciplining belonging in ways that—especially when combined with the frailties of people in positions of power—is extremely dangerous. What seems vitally important about Huebner's account of martyrdom is that it is a radically *eschatological* act more than it is a teleological act. Recalling your summary of Chris Huebner's account, "martyrdom is an eschatological act through which the world as we know it is stripped of its apparent givenness, and strange new possibilities emerge. . . . martyrs do not have a 'solid identity' but rather call into question all

6. See page 25 above, including note 11.
7. See page 248 above.

our assumptions that we can secure our identity through our actions."[8] Now, for Huebner, there is a story to be passed on, a story that churches must discern seriously and patiently. But it is a story that radically decenters even itself as it does so. It is a story that continually invites eschatological inbreaking and constitutes a community through this invitation. This means that there is a constitutive tension in the story between the straight and the queer. Because church happens in that tension, Yoderian Christians are called to "keep the story going" in a different way than are those Christians with more teleological intonations. Indefinite pause, patience, midcourse correction, and unexpected newness become utterly vital to the task of becoming church. This patience opens to the manifoldness of gifts within and outside the church in a way that likely suspects and resists the potential growth of reified (and hierarchical) politics that might consolidate in new (and old) forms of insistent consolations fueled by the denial of a death to which one remains radically unreconciled. Selves in Huebner's eschatological communion have to reconcile with death more profoundly than those selves who might think that they know too well what it would mean to get the story straight. This reconciling with death is likely to make the selves in Huebner's eschatological communion more humble in relation to others.

I see such motifs all over your writing about virtually everything— one could indeed call them quintessentially "Hauerwasian." Yet sometimes I think that your straining against a certain kind of liberal takeover in the church leads you to accent a teleological voice at odds with this deeper current. And sometimes I wonder if there isn't a teleological accent that ought to be reconsidered even apart from these polemical questions? For example, in *Naming the Silences,* which I read as political theory, I think, there's a point where you draw too sharp a distinction between the kind of suffering and death that is cross-like in the more obvious, immediate sense, on the one hand, and the kind of suffering and death that is radically senseless and ungraspable, like the death of a child due to awful contingencies like a purely random genetic malfunction, on the other. You warn against the will to put the senseless kind of suffering into a narrative, while you say that the cross-like kind (like martyrdom and political sacrifice, for example) can more easily be put into a narrative. Perhaps. But I think, actually, that the virtues you discuss in relation

8. See page 25 above, note 11.

to the senseless suffering that cannot and should not be given a narrative—sitting quietly on the mourning bench, giving a gap, recognizing modes of redemption that might become possible only as we abandon any sense of redemption through narratives that we could prepare or advance or possess—I think that these virtues are crucial *political virtues too.* I think they are virtues with which we should approach even the most ostensibly cruciform suffering. I think they are one of the deepest themes in your work. Don't you think, however, that they profoundly disrupt the motif of "getting the story straight" ("disrupt" is not the same as "call us to abandon")? Don't they also profoundly disrupt tendencies toward "high church"? Don't they disrupt time-as-narrative in important ways? Don't they leaven the body of Christ with a radically democratic and plural ethos—one tending toward more radically democratic practices and institutional modes as the heart of the church? Not just what the church prepares people for?

Hauerwas: By calling attention to martyrdom I mean to suggest two gifts God has given the church: first, the defeat of victimization; and, second, patience. Martyrdom means, "you can kill us, but you cannot determine the meaning of our death." In order to have such patient defiance as a form of resistance to state power, you've got to have a community that is an alternative—that is, a community of memory. And so Christians have to negotiate memory, because martyrs are not easily remembered. So Christians hope that they are remembering martyrs the way that God remembers them; we have exemplifications of what it means to be glorified. So I think that the defeat of victimization is at the heart of what it means for the church to be an alternative to the politics of glory, to the politics that says, "America is the greatest country in the world." Martyrdom is not heroism. Rather martyrdom names the death of those who have been witnesses to the God who makes this kind of death serve a community across time—a community that will not be subjected to the temptation that we have to make a difference. Now, patience comes exactly to the extent that you are not subjected to the temptation to believe that you have to make a difference, because you can take the time—in a world that doesn't think it has any time—to live lives in quiet humility and truthfulness. I would hope this humble and truthful patience would make a contribution not only within the Christian community, but also without the Christian community. That's the way I think about the "interruption" (what you once called the "pause") that the martyr represents. The martyr obviously doesn't go to martyrdom to be martyred, because 1) they are trying to avoid having their killer be guilty of murder, and 2) they know that their business is in escaping—they want to live! God created us to live! So death is a bad thing. What I take to be the pause is that the martyr dies in confidence, but they do not die knowing what God would do with the death. Is that the pause you're asking about? Of course, I think Huebner is right, moreover, that martyrdom is an eschatological act more than it is a teleological act, but I think he learned that way of putting the matter from me via Yoder. Eschatology names the radical possibility that it did not have to happen that way. My way of putting the matter is that the past is not the past until it has been redeemed. The martyrs make possible a world otherwise unimaginable. Ella Baker could not be imagined given the world of segregation, but, by God, she exists.

Coles: Amen, Ella Baker! Yet, still, I'm also trying to get at the question about what kind of story, tradition, and memory is being kept and formed by the community? The straight story easily becomes a pauseless narrative that engenders its own impatience within the community. What kind of narrative and nonnarrative strategies might the community try to perform in order to become this politics of patience "within" itself in relation to its "exterior" edges?

Hauerwas: I guess I just assume that there's always going to be conflict. The story that is the gospel is one that produces different tellings because the story requires witness. And when you witness, oddly enough, strangers receive the witness, become witnesses, and then they tell the story back to you in ways that you had never anticipated. I think it makes all kinds of sense for people to say, "You know, I don't get the doctrine of the atonement. Why do I need a doctrine of the atonement?" Indeed, I'm one of those people—I don't think I need a doctrine of atonement. So there's always going to be a give-and-take in that sense of the ongoingness of the tradition. It's such a basic thing—and I think MacIntyre has named the necessity of conflict in any living tradition—and I assume that the Christian tradition is exemplary of being an argument across time. And that's why mission is constitutive of Christianity, because when you have to go beyond where you were, then you will discover things that you hadn't known were part of your story. Now, I don't know if that's sufficient or not to respond to your worry about keeping the story straight, but it's the best I can do. You asked the question once: how do I learn from radical democrats? And you asked whether or not a kind of syncretic radical-democratic tradition exists that Christianity could learn from. I just assume that Christianity is a syncretic tradition because, as I suggested above, we can never be free (nor should we want to be free) of being challenged by God's promised people: the Jews. So that's the way I think of Christianity in terms of its being the kind of argument that is unending. And that's why it's so interesting—and why it's such a political tradition, because the gospel requires vulnerability if it is to be true to itself.

Coles: Yes, I know you think that, but I'm still trying to push you. Let me go back to *Naming the Silences*, because one of your fears there is that the will to narrate becomes this sort of oblivion to the suffering of the other. I mean, it's one thing to narrate your *own* suffering, which might be dicey in itself. But it's really dicey to narrate the death of a child, say, as being redeemed as part of the parents' learning process. And one of the things that Iris Murdoch repeatedly probes is the way that this narrative—and many other narratives that provide consolation—becomes a deceptive machine. In this way, you get wedded to "keeping the story of Jesus straight" because you need to win that game in order to get out of the game of "winning and results." One can get addicted to and driven by consolation in the victory of the "straight story."

Hauerwas: That's exactly right.

Coles: And then, in fighting the politics of death, one inadvertently re-inscribes this politics in one's own protective relationship to the story of Jesus. So aren't decentering, pausing, and resisting certain intensities of consolation in fact paradoxically a *central* thing that must be kept, remembered, invited, and prepared for? They are not something you can assume, say, as the inexorability of conflict, because that intense and deceptive energy that Iris Murdoch talks about, and that you talk about in *Naming the Silences,* is a huge part of what we do to console suffering and thereby act foolishly with respect to death.

Hauerwas: I have thought for what seems like my whole life about Murdoch's claim that the very assumption that we can narrate our lives cannot help but be a comfort bought at the price of illusion. Truth requires the acknowledgment of the absolute pointlessness of life, she argues. Otherwise we fail to have the capacity to acknowledge the beauty of the contingent. Beauty is crucial for me, but I believe we can learn to see the contingent only because we must learn to receive it as gift. Gift, of course, entails a narrative of creation. I think Murdoch is wrong to think that narrative is but a comforting illusion. How can she think this, given the story of the Jews?

Crucial for me is the presumption that the gospel is a story meant to train us to live without explanation. Explanation presumes that if I can just account for why what happened did happen, then I will be able to live with what has happened. In modernity, this hunger for explanation often takes the form of mechanistic cause-and-effect relations that ironically attempt to give people who have such a view of the world the presumption that they are in control. I think Christianity is the training for learning how to live without being in control: You learn to live in the silences, and you learn what the politics of living in the silences might look like. I always think of nonviolence as crucial to this. Just think about this: what does it mean to try to end a war—the war in Iraq—when people feel that if you end it, they could not explain the meaninglessness of the deaths of the people who have died so far? So you've got to somehow make the deaths successful. But to learn to live patiently in a world where you have no answers, it seems to me, gives you political alternatives that otherwise would not exist—through hope. And I don't care whether the people who are able to do this are called Christians or not. I mean, I assume that God will show up in all different kinds of ways. That's how I try to conceive of what it means to live hopefully without explanation. You don't have to explain the death of a child. That will kill you. That will kill you.

Coles: Right. Is there any loneliness for Christians? I mean, when you talk about Murdoch, especially in *Wilderness Wanderings* (following your much earlier discussion of Murdoch in *Vision and Virtue*) you bring up this question of loneliness as a marked difference from Christian existence, noting that Murdoch's world is too lonely for Christians.[9] And I take it that in some ways there's at least the insinuation that the loneliness of, say, a Murdoch has a tendency toward getting reabsorbed into, and

9 Hauerwas, "Significance of Vision," 30–47.

maybe even fueling, the politics of glory. What's interesting in *Naming the Silences* is that it seems that you come close to acknowledging some kind of loneliness as an appropriate Christian sentiment, though not a loneliness of permanent solitude.

Hauerwas: Right. That's why friendship is so important. I would like to hear you say something about loneliness, and how radical democracy is a response to loneliness.

Coles: OK. Well, let's see, I don't know if you know Primo Levi's book that just came out called *A Tranquil Star*? It's a posthumous collection of short stories. Late last night I was reading the last story in the volume, "A Tranquil Star." It begins with him imagining a far off tranquil star in a manner that can only be described as apophatic. It is a star of such immensity in every way that our grandest adjectives can only dull rather than vivify our sense of it. It turns out that the "tranquil star" is actually a "capricious star," somehow occupied by "an imbalance or infection as happens to some of us." The star undergoes an unfathomable explosion that moves outward in an inferno "spreading in all directions." Imagining a planet in its solar system, Levi writes:

> After ten hours, the entire planet was reduced to vapor, along with all the delicate and subtle works that the combined labor of chance and necessity, through innumerable trials and errors, had perhaps created there, and along with all the poets and wise men who had perhaps examined that sky, and wondered what was the value of so many little lights, and had found no answer. That was the answer.[10]

If you want to talk about radical contingency and cosmic loneliness this is a pretty good image! And Levi poignantly conveys this contingency and loneliness at a micro level too, as when he is talking about a deformed molecule in a story titled "The Molecule's Defiance" as: "a symbol of other ugly things without reversal or remedy that obscure our future, of the prevalence of confusion over order, and of unseemly death over life."[11] Levi, of course, knows what he's talking about, and he also makes clear that even his breathtaking stories are themselves insufficient evocations

10. Levi, *A Tranquil Star*, 167.
11. Ibid., 155.

of the immensity of the inferno named "holocaust" that he somehow endured and lived to express.

So there is this colossal annihilation of space, time, and meaning as endurance—and yet. *And yet* Levi's story is populated with philosophers, poets, astronomers—people looking up at the stars in wonder; an Arab astronomer who, centuries ago, "equipped only with good eyes, patience, humility and the love of knowing the works of his God, had realized that this star, to which he was very attached, was not immutable"; a contemporary Peruvian astronomer who mysteriously lives for the stars (in a way that impinges on his family). These people are not extinguished by the explosion. They remain in Levi's story with their wonder, their simple love, their complex love. They populate the universe with sensuous gratitude and the stories of lives thus lived.

There may at any moment be an explosion that will extinguish all wondrous gazes and all stories of such gazes. What then? Levi's story raises a question, for me anyhow, about our normal measures—our territorial measures, thinking back to Rowan Williams's discussion. It raises the question of whether extensive magnitudes of spatial and temporal duration—however much we do and in some good ways *ought* to seek such continuities—are the final measure of meaning and value. In the sheer intensity of wonder, gratitude, and care for being (always so indebted to past experiences and practices and cultivated memories of these)—what Iris Murdoch calls 'love', which is the most complicated, difficult, and messy thing there is—there emerges a contending unfathomable measure. Even as love seeks to endure, perhaps its significance lies more in the intensity of witness and care. Love's intensity births and raises the question—in the face of catastrophes that are immense beyond measure, of whether *this* immensity is the last word. Wonder and love refuse to grant such immensity and its loneliness the last word. They proclaim: "we happened," "we are happening," and thus, crying out into the night sky, they call (and denounce) the territorial imagination that is brought to *despairing* silence in the explosion of stars, to another kind of silence: silence in the face of an utterly different and greater significance—a different measure. A different way to live. The fact of Levi, the event of his apophatic stories, his atheistic love, his story of his friend Sandro who embodied exuberant wonder until he was the first person in the resistance shot dead by the

Italian fascists—Levi's storied love for Sandro refuses Auschwitz the last word.[12]

Hauerwas: So the beauty overcomes the loneliness?

Coles: Does it overcome it? It at least puts loneliness radically into question and orients us toward witnessing and seeking to embody another kind of nonterritorial light. There is a certain warmth in this, though to say so directly like this definitely takes us to the edge of blasphemy in the midst of catastrophe piling up relentlessly over time. ("Certain truths, when said, become untrue," as we heard from Rowan Williams.) And the warmth of wonder and love are never untroubled by territorial catastrophes, because even as they are born in an intensity that has no extension, they immanently yearn to radiate outward and extend in time and space. So the beauty and love exceed the loneliness of catastrophe but nevertheless engender and maintain a distinct and radical vulnerability to it.

Yet I do think this: to recall Ella Baker, Bob Moses, Septima Clarke, and Myles Horton—their event, their memory, the passing on of their memory, and the effort to form selves in communities of their memory—is, I think, to be witness to an event of human relationship, care, and intense struggle so miraculous (with all its imperfections) that it is not clear to me that any extinction of space and time could possibly diminish it (even one that annihilates their memory and all future possibility). Even as they call us more profoundly than most to extend and deepen the legacy they leave us—and this is the work we *must* do, I remain tempted to say: these events of the "radical ordinary" are so incredible as to call into question the possibility that they could be diminished. Of course, Benjamin is right, even the dead are not safe from dying again at the hands of the "victors," so the work of memory and extension is imperative and urgent. And yet this work, for me, is sustained by a contingent intensity that exceeds duration and extension even as it is requires such duration and extension—yearns for them, and is radically vulnerable in so doing. This opens radical democracy to myriad complexities torn between an ethos of radical receptive generosity and wanting a legacy to survive and flourish. Yet such democracy negotiates these complexities with its weight (and lightness) in the radical ordinary.

12. See Levi, "Iron," in *The Periodic Table*.

Hauerwas: This is an antagonistic question: Why choose Ella Baker and Myles Horton and not America as a kind of project to also engage in a new politics that the world has never seen etc. etc.? Why isn't that also a sign of intervention?

Coles: It is not impossible that "America" can sometimes embody the intensity and traditions of relationship, care, and struggle that I am talking about. Howard Zinn's histories are replete with examples of struggles that have sometimes linked up with a subversive image and memory of America. MLK Jr. at his best employs this in profoundly radical ways. Yet the more dominant "America" is by its own definition a jealous and proprietary secular god that wants to exclude and/or subordinate all other attachments. It has so often been a project that subverts democracy and proliferates imaginary communities that are more the stuff of capital, mega-state, and empire.

The miraculous aspect of radical-democratic wonder, tending, and struggle is—like Iris Murdoch's love—*profoundly difficult*. To experience the intensities of these is to become deeply aware of insufficiencies at the heart of the very moments that are miraculous. This awareness, in turn, immanently calls for a deepening sense of the very specific histories of those who are engaged in the ethical and political work of co-existence. This is about memory and the effort to cultivate ongoing relationships. It is especially hard to do this at the level of the nation-state—partly because of scale, and largely because of the dense operations of power that are constitutive of its dominant institutions and practices. It is not that there is no point in trying—it is that in terms of cultivating a democratic care for the radical ordinary you and I find much more hope in specific relationships: It is infinitely more probable in Bob Moses telling people to go and sit at the feet of the sharecroppers. It's going to play basketball with the kids of parents who won't talk to you yet. It is specific bodies marching together and enduring blows as they advance nonviolently through public space for basic justice and more. It is the incredible work of people weaving their lives and struggles together—with all the difficult differences in Durham—to engage in creating and caring for goods of the city. The elements of specificity and relationships of tending are more possible here, these have far greater potential to resist the dominant obfuscations and, behold!, find us "doing a new thing." So this is where I would cultivate a radical hope. "America" has too often been used to deny precisely these qualities domestically and abroad. "Baghdad" might be the short answer to "why not America?"

Hauerwas: It seems to me that you and I presuppose a lot about, for example, the liberal subversion of democracy. And when I ask you, why America? you're presupposing something like Wolin's understanding of the liberal subversion of democracy. Now, what may not be all that clear is how the liberal subversion of democracy relates, then, as a narrative—how it relates to issues of death. I think liberalism is a grand narrative that promises worldly salvation in a way that has terrible results for people who are subjected to the ethos of freedom. And I think we share this in common.

Coles: We do, but I wouldn't limit my critique here to liberalism. I mean that the ugly faces of America have all sorts of liberal, illiberal, conservative, fundamentalist, and radical forms, and I want to keep that complexity in our memory—as well as an eye for certain gifts that, remarkably, we inherit from some of the most questionable places, ideologies, and developments.

And I want to say this: I am sympathetic with your general idea that there are central strands of the formation and legacy of the United States of America that are fundamentally oriented toward worldly salvation. You can see in the writing of Hamilton, for example, ways in which this salvation is understood as extension in space (via empire) and duration in time (via a stable republic, in contrast to the tempestuous ancients). A dominant imaginary of the U.S. nation-state tends toward global dominance and immortality—it was born in that dream. There are other American dreams (which were generally also *dreams that also had other* sources) that have far more of a call to me: those of Abolitionists, many of the women in Seneca Falls in 1847, those of many of the radical-democratic populists in the nineteenth century, Debs, labor organizing, MLK Jr., and so forth; but all these greatly risk succumbing to the salvific dream of America, and many have, in ways that have gotten very ugly. At the most profound level, perhaps, what the liturgies of the radical-democratic ordinary and of the radical ecclesia cultivate, is a nonterritorial, nonimmortal relation to death. That is, sitting on front porches, leaning into the stillness of the present, and listening in order to cultivate different voices and visions: what I was calling wonder, love, struggle, care; what is going on here is the genesis of imaginaries that provide striking alternatives to the political imaginary of the U.S. nation-state. In terms of the question of death, if you read Ella Baker and early SNCC through Iris Murdoch, you could think of SNCC liturgies as daily training in a politics of "right dying." What I mean is a politics that moves into relationships with others without an instrumental agenda based on a preestablished imperative frame in light of which you seek to manipulate whomever you need to, in order to get what you want. Right dying is sitting at the feet of the sharecropper and listening. I mean, learning redemption little by little in letting die your will to impose monologically, and instead seeking life in radically receptive relationships. This isn't something that you ever possess. It is difficult, and we're always falling away from it. It has to be reborn in each relationship at every minute. You could say, then, that what we're up to in this book is the work of recollecting, reflecting upon, and summons-ing liturgical practices that might engender a postsecular politics. I'm thinking of this also in terms of Talal Asad's claims about the way the secular nation-state strives to monopolize the spatial and temporal framework for significant political contestation. We're probing possibilities of a politics through which, in manifold ways, peoples might reconstitute a more labyrinthine politics (in Wolin's sense) as an alternative to such secularization.

Hauerwas: I think about your first response to my "Haunting Possibility" as you were sitting in California thinking about the dead that are not remembered. My view is that liberalism is exactly the project that compels us to forget the dead—particularly the ones that have been killed in the name of "civilization." How do you remember what was done that is so wrong that there is nothing to be done to make it right? Maybe one of the ways is, as you suggest, to take the time to listen to the wisdom of those who have been about the everyday work of living. I think we have that in common, and that's why we both look for smaller politics. And I hope that's not an attempt to escape confronting what is at the heart of the challenge before us today. I would like to think that what one might learn from radical democrats is an exemplification for how one reclaims the time it takes to listen.

Coles: Yes, I agree. Wolin's critique of Rawls and social-contract theory seems much to the point in this regard. In terms of framing the politics in our book as "smaller politics"—this makes me somewhat uneasy. Because, say, in terms of remembering the dead, I'd say we are suggesting a much more *expansive* politics of time. And in terms of space, I think Mennonite missionary work, the kinds of transnational initiatives discussed by Gibson-Graham in *Postcapitalist Politics*, transnational networks of indigenous peoples who live locally *and* organize and cultivate relations with other traditions and localities—I think all these are examples of ways in which our politics is spatially more *expansive* than that of the nation-state. What we are saying, it seems to me, is that specificity and enduring relationships of tending, and a sense for the complexities and nuances of distinct places and histories, are elemental aspects of the kind of politics we endorse. These are most often less difficult in localities. But they can be cultivated in painstaking ways on other scales too. And they should not be conceived as a barrier against larger scales but rather as the sites and practices without which people will likely lack the experiences, relationships, and knowledge necessary to inhabit larger scales without succumbing to "seeing like a state," or like a Walmart, or like an NGO that has lost receptive contact with people beyond its staff. I am putting a lot of eggs in the basket of specific practices of tending democratically to the radical ordinary. We need to formulate and to form many of our struggles in this way. I think we need to collect a growing manifold of such stories and to draw them toward one another in tensional relationships from which we might learn. Yet I don't want them to congeal in a way that Murdoch warns against: consoling metanarratives that become an escape from seeing the specificity before us; metanarratives that impose their orders to secure their threatened consolation. That scares me a great deal. And it scares me when I see it in most Christian formations—not all; and when radical democrats do it, it scares me too.

Hauerwas: I'm uncomfortable—and I hate that phrase—but I don't like calling the gospel a metanarrative. To say the gospel is metanarrative can suggest that the gospel occupies an epistemological space that assumes superiority over all other narratives. Such a presumption betrays the content of the gospel, that is, that the gospel just is this particular story of Jesus, the Son of God, known through cross and resurrection. Learning that story is every bit as difficult to learn as sitting at the feet of the sharecropper. So it's not like the gospel is some grand story that helps me get the world straight. It is a story that helps me discover who I should worship. And worshipping God turns out to be a very demanding business indeed—which is like the death that comes through listening to the sharecropper's story, because it teaches me: God is God, and I ain't.

Which brings us back to Levi's astronomer. You know, Christians believe that God is going to kill us all in the end. The human species is not the apple of God's eye. All of creation is the apple of God's eye. So the survival of the human species is not what is at stake for us. It is rather that, in the time that God has given us, we are to enjoy God and God's salvation. What do we need more than that? Any idea that Christianity is about ensuring the significance of the human as crucial to God's life makes no sense to me at all.

Coles: Could you say something about that in relation to Yoder, in relation to the places where he claims that the "fifth act" and God's victory are already assured, and that's what makes possible peacemaking?

Hauerwas: I think it is very simple. Because we believe that the end has come, through the death and resurrection of Jesus we see what God would have us be; it means that as Christians, we can live eschatologically. To so live means that we don't have to live in a way to make sure that God's purpose comes out all right. We can rest easy in God's creation—to take time to listen to the sharecropper—and that this is the kind of training that comes from learning the story of Jesus and of the people of Israel. John (rightly, I think) saw how nonviolence is the prismatic form taken by God's care of all of that is; and that nonviolence requires such a patient and conflictual politics exactly because we have the time to have the conflicts we need, in order to learn to live in peace with each other.

Coles: Yes. But isn't that a little at odds with what you were saying before? I mean, I read Yoder as saying that the church is somehow written into a major story; humans have a major part in this story.

Hauerwas: True, but if Sam Wells is right in what he is saying in *Improvisation* about how we live in between the times, then we live in the fourth act. So we don't get to speculate about how the fifth act is going to work out. That is God's problem. To be sure, we live in the tension between the third and fifth acts, but that is a wonderful place to be. We do not have to triumph over others, because God has triumphed. Only in the light of that triumph do we believe it possible to live with the patience that makes nonviolence not only possible but necessary.

Coles: That's wonderful.

Hauerwas: But then I take it that I won't be surprised to see this elsewhere in people who do not know the name of Christ, because we have all been created by God to live that way. I love how, in *For the Nations*, John says,

> Yet when "the nature of things" is properly defined, the organic relationship to grace is restored. The cross is not a scandal to those who know the world as God sees it, but only to the pagans who look for what they call wisdom, or the Judeans, who look for what they call power. This is what I meant before, when I stated that the choice of Jesus was ontological: it risks an option in favor of a restored vision of how things really are. It has always been true that suffering creates shalom. Motherhood has always meant that. Servanthood has always meant that. Healing has always meant that. Tilling the soil has always meant that. Priesthood has always meant that. Prophecy has always meant that. What Jesus did—and we might say it with reminiscence of Scholastic Christological categories—was that he renewed the definition of kingship to fit with the priesthood and prophecy. He saw that the suffering servant is king as much as priest and prophet. The cross is neither foolish nor weak, but natural.[13]

That's natural theology. I believe that, so I expect to see it in people tilling the soil. Now the question then becomes: how does being articulate help you? The gospel helps you become articulate about what it is you're doing in a way that otherwise you are constantly tempted toward misdescription.

Coles: Which gets to the question I was raising about the narrative becoming its own end.

Hauerwas: Right. You're collecting the stories. . . . I suppose I just want to say, "Well, I'm ready to see the results—and see if I can be of any help."

13. Yoder, *For the Nations*, 212.

What I refuse to do is to think that I must show you that somehow you need me—a Christian. I want you to enjoy what I enjoy, but I don't want you to do it out of need.

Coles: It's interesting. We actually enjoy a lot of the same things, but I actually think the joy is intensified by immanence, which is not so different from how you think of it. But it's not clear to me what's gained by God-talk in the passage you just mentioned from Yoder. I'm closer to Wendell Berry when he says (somewhere in *The Art of the Commonplace*) that he is not that enamored with talk of "virtue." Rather, he says, talk about how you put a bridle on a horse, talk about how the plough should run along the contours of this place on earth—those are the virtues: right there in the specific contingency of people, places, relationships, and practices.[14]

Hauerwas: What I want to know is, where does Wendell Berry get the skills to articulate that, and how do you pass that on to another generation?

Coles: I think there are many answers to that—like Highlander. It's poets like Adrianne Rich; it's stories like those of Primo Levi; it is the memory of SNCC; it's the work of Durham CAN. We need a thick, rich, dense pedagogy of stories and practices that help bring forth the next generations. The thing that I'm stepping back from (but it sounds like you are, too, in resisting metanarrative) is the idea that radical democrats are going to accumulate something that puts them at the cutting edge and thus engenders the temptation to stay there by any means necessary.

Hauerwas: When you say that Berry doesn't want the virtues—he wants to know how to put on the bridle—surely it's the case that the teacher who will teach you how to put on the bridle has somewhere become articulate about the virtues (in particular patience) that are constitutive of the skills it takes to learn how to put on the bridle. And good communities require those kinds of theory—or philosophical articulation—that help us notice what we otherwise might miss as constitutive of our ability to put on bridles.

14. Berry, *Art of the Common Place*, 233–35.

Coles: Right. But isn't a central part of that articulation a recognition of our inarticulateness? Not just for scholars; but somehow we need to find languages in which people every day are called to a modesty about how inarticulate we humans ought to recognize that we are.

Hauerwas: Absolutely. But that comes not just from the languages but from a community calling you into account. That means you've really got to have a concrete community across time that has developed those skills. What bothers me a bit about the Wolinian fugitive character of democracy is that I don't know who is going to carry that story across time.

Coles: Right. As you know my Wolin is not quite as fugitive.

Hauerwas: I think radical democracy has a problem with the concrete community, and it may be a problem it wants to have.

Coles: It may be; and it may be that some kinds of Christianity have this same problem. Yoder talks about Anabaptism as this incredibly discontinuous community in time and space.

Hauerwas: I don't think that's a right reading of John. I think that John sees God as never abandoning the world of faithful witness—even in the midst of the most Constantinian church. The very fact that priests were not allowed to kill at least suggests that Christians have a problem with killing. The tension is still there (the discontinuity is there), but he didn't want to say that in the sixteenth century the church started again.

Coles: That's true, but that move makes me nervous. It sounds a little like democrats who say, "Well we've always valued an idea of equality, so we've always had a nervousness about the slaves . . ." At that point, we stop talking about the movement of daily care that we're summons-ing.

Hauerwas: I used to say that I represent a minority position within Christianity, but then Cathy Rudy once said to me, "No, that's not true because most women throughout the history of Christianity were not permitted to kill. So why aren't they the majority?" But how you narrate the history therefore shows how you narrate continuity and discontinuity. Why let the mainstream tell you that Christianity is primarily carried by bishops and popes and not women?

Coles: And that strikes me as a move similar to what Wolin is doing with naming a different America. It's not a linear time so much as it is strange connections that disrupt "reality," which is what I'm talking about. And, perhaps, by remembering histories of struggle to enact co-existence as tending, and by extending ourselves thus to the smallest places and times we might cultivate the greatest potential for provoking larger disruptions and grander alternatives.

Hauerwas: Right. Jesus was a very small thing; Israel a small nation.

Bibliography

Adorno, Theodor W. *Minima Moralia: Reflections from Damaged Life.* Translated by E. F. N. Jephcott. London: New Left, 1974.

———. *Negative Dialectics.* Translated by E. B. Ashton. New York: Continuum, 1973.

Albert, Michael. *Parecon: Life after Capitalism.* London: Verso, 2003.

Alinsky, Saul D. *Reveille for Radicals.* Chicago: University of Chicago Press, 1946.

———. *Rules for Radicals: A Practical Primer for Realistic Radicals.* New York: Random House, 1971.

Alperovitz, Gar. *America beyond Capitalism: Reclaiming Our Wealth, Our Liberty, and Our Democracy.* Hoboken, NJ: Wiley, 2005.

Anscombe, G. E. M. *Intention.* 2d ed. Cambridge, MA: Harvard University Press, 2000.

Amato, Joseph Anthony. *Victims and Values: A History and a Theory of Suffering.* With the assistance of David Monge. Foreword by Eugen Weber. New York: Praeger, 1990.

Arendt, Hannah. *The Human Condition.* 2d ed., with an introduction by Margaret Canovan. Chicago: University of Chicago Press, 1998.

———. *On Revolution.* New York: Penguin, 1990.

Asad, Talal. *Formations of the Secular: Christianity, Islam, Modernity.* Cultural Memory in the Present. Stanford: Stanford University Press, 2003.

———. *On Suicide Bombing.* Wellek Library Lectures. New York: Columbia University Press, 2007.

Augustine, Saint. *Concerning the City of God against the Pagans.* Translated by Henry Bettenson. Harmondsworth: Penguin, 1972.

Bader-Saye, Scott. "Figuring Time: Providence and Politics." In *Liturgy, Time, and the Politics of Redemption,* edited by Randi Rashkover and C. C. Pecknold, 91–111. Grand Rapids: Eerdmans, 2006.

———. *Following Jesus in a Culture of Fear.* The Christian Practice of Everyday Life. Grand Rapids: Brazos, 2007.

———. "Listening: Authority and Obedience." In *The Blackwell Companion to Christian Ethics,* edited by Stanley Hauerwas and Samuel Wells, 156–68. Blackwell Companions to Religion. Maldnen, MA: Blackwell, 2004.

Bakhtin, Mikhail. *Problems of Dostoevsky's Poetics.* Translated by Caryl Emerson. Theory and History of Literature 8. Minneapolis: University of Minnesota Press, 1984.

347

Baldwin, James. "Many Thousands Gone." In *The Price of the Ticket: Collected Nonfiction, 1948–1985*, 65–78. New York: St. Martin's, 1985.

Barrois, Georges A., translator. *The Fathers Speak: St. Basil the Great, Saint Gregory of Nazianzus, St. Gregory of Nyssa*. Crestwood, NY: St. Vladmir's Seminary Press, 1986.

Bell, Daniel. "The Politics of Fear and the Gospel of Life." *Journal for Cultural and Religious Theory* 8 (2007) 55–80.

Benjamin, Walter. "Critique of Violence." In *Reflections: Essays, Aphorisms, Autobiographical Writings*, edited and with an introduction by Peter Demettz. Translated by Edmund Jephcott. New York: Schocken, 1986.

———. "Theses on the Philosophy of History." In *Iluminations: Essays and Reflections*. Edited and with an Introduction by Hanna Arendt. Translated by Harry Zohn. New York: Schocken, 1968.

Berry, Wendell. *The Art of the Commonplace: The Agrarian Essays of Wendell Berry*, edited and introduced by Norman Wirzba. Washington DC: Shoemaker and Hoard, 2002.

Bérubé, Michael. "Making Yourself Useful." In *Critical Reflections on Stanley Hauerwas' Theology of Disability: Disabling Society, Enabling Theology*, edited by John Swinton, 31–43. Binghamton: Haworth, 2004.

Bloch, Ernst. *The Principle of Hope*. Translated by Neville Plaice, et al. 3 vols. Studies in Contemporary German Social Thought. Cambridge: MIT Press, 1986.

Block, Fred, et al., "Symposium: Poor People's Movements." *Perspectives on Politics* 1(2002) 707–35.

Bourdieu, Pierre. *Outline of a Theory of Practice*. Translated by Richard Nice. Cambridge Studies in Social Anthropology 13. Cambridge: Cambridge University Press, 1990.

Bonilla-Silva, Eduardo. *Racism without Racists: Color-Blind Racism and the Persistence of Racial Inequality in the United States*. Lanham: Rowman and Littlefield, 2006.

Boyte, Harry C. *Everyday Politics: Reconnecting Citizens and Public Life*. Philadelphia: University of Pennsylvania Press, 2004.

Budgen, Sebastian, et al., editors. *Lenin Reloaded: Towards a Politics of Truth*. Durham: Duke University Press, 2007.

Burner, Eric. *And Gently He shall Lead Them: Robert Parris Moses and Civil Rights in Mississippi*. New York: New York University Press, 1994.

Campbell, Will D. *And Also With You: Duncan Gray and the American Dilemma*. Franklin: Providence House, 1997.

———. *Brother to a Dragonfly*. 25th anniversary edition. New York: Continuum, 2000.

———. *Forty Acres and a Goat: A Memoir*. Atlanta: Peachtree, 1986. Reprint, Eugene, OR: Wipf & Stock, 1998.

———. *The Glad River*. Nashville: Rutledge Hill, 1982.

———. *Providence*. Atlanta: Longstreet, 1992.

Campbell, Will D., and James Y. Holloway. "Forword." In *The Failure and the Hope: Essays of Southern Churchmen*, 7–10. Reprint, Eugene: Wipf & Stock, 2005.

———, editors. *The Failure and the Hope: Essays of Southern Churchmen*. Reprint, Eugene: Wipf and Stock, 2005.

———. *Up to Our Steeples in Politics*. Reprint, Eugene: Wipf and Stock, 2005.

Carnoy, Martin, and Derek Shearer. *Economic Democracy: The Challenge of the 1980s.* White Plains, NY: M. E. Sharpe, 1980.

Carson, Clayborne. *In Struggle: SNCC and the Black Awakening of the 1960s.* Revised edition with new preface and epilogue. Cambridge, MA: Harvard University Press, 1995.

Chambers, Edward T. *Organizing for Family and Congregation.* New York: Industrial Areas Foundation, 1978.

Chambers, Edward T., with Michael A. Cowan. *Roots for Radicals: Organizing for Power, Action, and Justice.* New York: Continuum, 2003

Chappell, David L. *A Stone of Hope: Prophetic Religion and the Death of Jim Crow.* Chapel Hill: University of North Carolina Press, 2004.

Clifford, James. *Routes: Travel and Translation in the Late Twentieth Century.* Cambridge: Harvard University Press, 1997.

Cohen, Joshua, and Joel Rogers, editors. *Associations and Democracy.* The Real Utopias Project 1. London: Verso, 1995.

Coles, Romand. *Beyond Gated Politics: Reflections for the Possibility of Democracy.* Minneapolis: University of Minnesota Press, 2005.

———. "Democracy, Theology, and the Question of Excess: A Review of Jeffrey Stout's *Democracy and Tradition.*" *Modern Theology* 21 (2005) 301–21.

———. "Feminists of Color and the Torn Virtues of Democratic Engagement." In *Beyond Gated Politics: Reflections on the Possibility of Democracy,* 185–212. Minneapolis: University of Minnesota Press, 2005.

———, "Hunger (of Mind/of Belly), Ethics, and the University." In *Ethics and Higher Education,* edited by J. Peter Euben and Elizabeth Kiss. Durham: Duke University Press, forthcoming.

———. "Merleau-Ponty." In *Self/Power/Other: Political Theory and Dialogical Ethics,* 99–169. Ithaca: Cornell University Press, 1992.

———. "Moving Democracy: Industrial Areas Foundation Social Movements and the Political Arts of Listening, Traveling, and Tabling." *Political Theory* 32 (2004) 678–705.

———. "Moving Democracy: The Political Arts of Listening, Traveling, and Tabling." In *Beyond Gated Politics: Reflections for the Possibility of Democracy,* 213–38. Minneapolis: University of Minnesota Press, 2005.

———. *Rethinking Generosity: Critical Theory and the Politics of Caritas.* Ithaca: Cornell University Press, 1997.

———. *Self/Power/Other: Political Theory and Dialogical Ethics.* Ithaca: Cornell University Press, 1992.

———. "Storied Others Possiblities of *Caritas*: Milbank and Neo-Nietzschean Ethics." *Modern Theology* 8 (1992) 331–51.

———. "Of Tensions and Tricksters: Grassroots Democracy between Theory and Practice." *Perspectives on Politics* 4 (2006) 547–61.

———. "The Wild Patience of Radical Democracy: Beyond Zizek's Lack." In *Radical Democracy: Politics between Abundance and Lack,* edited by Lars Tønder and Lasse Thomassen, 68–85. Manchester: Manchester University Press, 2005.

Collier, Charles. "A Nonviolent Augustiniansm? History and Politics in the Theologies of St. Augustine and John Howard Yoder." PhD diss., Duke University, forthcoming.

Collins, Patricia Hill. *Black Feminist Thought: Knowledge, Consciousness, and the Politics of Empowerment*. Rev. 10th anniversary edition. New York: Routledge, 2000.

Connolly, William E. "A Letter to Augustine." In *Identity and Difference: Democratic Negotiations of Political Paradox*. Minneapolis, MN: University of Minnesota Press, 1991.

Crews, Harry. *A Childhood: The Biography of a Place*. New York: Harper and Row, 1978.

Daley, Brian E. "Building the New City: The Cappadocian Fathers and the Rhetoric of Philanthropy." *Journal of Early Christian Studies* 7 (1999) 431–61.

Davis, Christina. "An Interview with Toni Morrison." In *Conversations With Toni Morrison*, edited by Danille Taylor-Guthrie, 223–33. Jackson, MS: Univerity Press of Mississippi, 1994.

Derrida, Jacques. "The Principle of Reason: The University in the Eyes of its Pupil." *Diacritics* 13 (1983) 3–20.

———. *Specters of Marx: The State of the Debt, the Work of Mourning, and the New International*. Translated by Peggy Kamuf, with an introduction by Bernd Magnus and Stephen Cullenberg. New York: Routledge, 1994.

DiFranco, Ani. "Grand Canyon." *Educated Guess*. Righteous Babe Music. B0000VV4HM. 2004.

———. "Not So Soft." *Like I Said*. Righteous Babe Music. B0000058MM. 1994.

Dodaro, Robert. "Eloquent Lies, Just Wars and the Politics of Persuasion: Reading Augustine's City of God in a 'Postmodern' World." *Aug Stud* 25 (1994), 77–138.

Dula, Peter, and Alex Sider. "Radical Democracy, Radical Ecclesiology." *Cross Currents* 55 (2006) 482–505.

Duke, Paul D. "John 13:1–17, 31b–35: Between Text and Sermon." *Interpretation* 49 (1995) 399–402.

Dunn, John. *Democracy: A History*. New York: Atlantic Monthly Press, 2005.

Euben, J. Peter. "Creatures of a Day: Thought and Action in Thucydides." In *Political Theory and Praxis: New Perspectives*, edited by Terence Ball, 28–56. Minneapolis: University of Minnesota Press, 1977.

Euben, Roxanne L. "Traveling Theorists and Translating Practices." In *What Is Political Theory?* edited by Stephen K. White and J. Donald Moon, 145–73. Thousand Oaks: Sage, 2004.

Forbath, William E. "Short-Circuit: A Critique of Habermas's Understanding of Law, Politics, and Economic Life." In *Habermas on Law and Democracy: Critical Exchanges*, edited by Michael Rosenfeld and Andrew Arato, 272–86. Berkeley: University of California Press, 1998.

Foucault, Michel. "What is Enlightenment?" In *Ethics: Subjectivity and Truth*, edited by Paul Rabinow, 303–20. The Essential Works of Foucault 1. New York: New Press, 1997.

Fung, Archon, and Erik Olin Wright, editors. *Deepening Democracy: Institutional Innovations in Empowered Participatory Governance*. The Real Utopias Project 4. London: Verso, 2003.

Gaines, Kevin K. *Uplifting the Race: Black Leadership, Politics, and Culture in the Twentieth Century*. Chapel Hill: University of North Carolina Press, 1996.

Gates, Henry Louis, Jr., and Cornel West. *The Future of the Race*. New York: Knopf, 1997.

Gecan, Michael. *Going Public* Boston: Beacon, 2002.

Gibson-Graham, J. K. *A Postcapitalist Politics.* Minneapolis: University of Minnesota Press, 2006.

Gilmore, Glenda Elizabeth. *Gender and Jim Crow: Women and the Politics of White Supremacy in North Carolina, 1896–1920.* Gender and American Culture. Chapel Hill: University of North Carolina Press, 1996.

Goldberg, David Theo. *The Racial State.* Oxford: Blackwell, 2002.

Graber-Miller, Kieth. "Mennonite Footwashing: Identity Reflections and Altered Meanings." *Worship* 66 (1992) 148–70.

Grant, Joanne. *Ella Baker: Freedom Bound.* New York: Wiley, 1998.

Gregory of Nazianzus. "On Love for the Poor." In *Select Orations,* translated by Martha Vinson, 39–71. Washington DC: Catholic University of America Press, 2003.

Greenberg, Cheryl Lynn, editor. *A Circle of Trust: Remembering SNCC.* New Brunswick: Rutgers University Press, 1998.

Gustafson, James. "The Sectarian Temptation: Reflections on Theology, the Church, and the University." *Proceedings of the Catholic Theology Society* 40 (1985) 83–94.

Hauerwas, Stanley. *After Christendom? How the Church Is to Behave If Freedom, Justice, and a Christian Nation Are Bad Ideas.* Nashville: Abingdon, 1999.

———. *Christian Existence Today: Essays on Church, World, and Living In Between.* Durham: Labyrinth, 1988. Reprint, Grand Rapids: Brazos, 2001.

———. *Naming the Silences: God, Medicine, and the Problem of Suffering.* Grand Rapids: Eerdmans, 1990.

———. "The Non-Violent Terrorist: In Defense of Christian Fanaticism." In *Sanctify Them in the Truth: Holiness Exemplified,* 177–90. Nashville: Abingdon, 1998.

———. *The State of the University: Academic Knowledges and the Knowledge of God.* Malden, MA: Blackwell, 2007.

———. "Timeful Friends: Living with the Handicapped." In *Sanctify them in the Truth: Holiness Exemplified,* 143–56. Nashville: Abingdon, 1998. Also in *Critical Reflections on Stanely Hauerwas' Theology of Disability: Disabling Society, Enabling Theology,* edited by John Swinton, 11–25. Binghamton: Haworth, 2004.

———. *Vision and Virtue.* Notre Dame: University of Notre Dame Press, 1981.

Hauerwas, Stanley, and Charles Pinches. *Christians among the Virtues: Theological Conversations with Ancient and Modern Ethics.* Notre Dame: University of Notre Dame Press, 1997.

Hauerwas, Stanley, and Samuel Wells, editors. *The Blackwell Companion to Christian Ethics.* Blackwell Companions to Religion. Malden, MA: Blackwell, 2004.

———. "The Gift of the Church and the Gifts God Gives It." In *The Blackwell Companion to Christian Ethics,* edited by Stanley Hauerwas and Samuel Wells, 13–27. Blackwell Companions to Religion. Malden, MA: Blackwell, 2004.

Hawkins, Merrill M. Jr. *Will Campbell: Radical Prophet of the South.* Macon: Mercer University Press, 1997.

Heschel, Abraham J. *The Prophets.* New York: Harper, 1962

Higginbotham, Evelyn Brooks. *Righteous Discontent: The Women's Movement in the Black Baptist Church.* Cambridge, MA: Harvard University Press, 1993.

Holman, Susan R. *The Hungry are Dying: Beggars and Bishops in Roman Cappadocia.* Oxford Studies in Historical Theology. Oxford: Oxford University Press, 2001.

hooks, bell. "Black Women Intellectuals." In *Breaking Bread: Insurgent Black Intellectual Life* by Bell Hooks and Cornel West, 147–64. Boston: South End, 1991.

———, and Cornel West. *Breaking Bread: Insurgent Black Intellectual Life.* Boston: South End, 1991

Huebner, Chris. "Unhandling History: Anti-Theory, Ethics, and the Practice of Witness." PhD diss., Duke University, 2002.

———. *A Precarious Peace: Yoderian Explorations on Theology, Knowledge, and Identity.* Scottdale: Herald, 2006.

Huebner, Harry. "Learning Made Strange: Can a University be Christian?" In *God, Truth, and Witness: Engaging Stanley Hauerwas*, edited by L. Gregory Jones et al., 280–308. Grand Rapids: Brazos, 2005.

Johnson, Kristen Deede. *Theology, Political Theory, and Pluralism: Beyond Tolerance and Difference.* Cambridge Studies in Christian Doctrine 15. Cambridge: Cambridge University Press, 2007.

Jones, L. Gregory, et al., editors. *God, Truth and Witness: Engaging Stanley Hauerwas.* Grand Rapids: Brazos, 2005.

Kant, Immanuel. "An Answer to the Question: 'What is Enlightenment?'" In *Kant: Political Writings*, edited with an introduction by Hans Reiss, 54–60. Translated by H. B. Nisbet. 2d enlarged edition. Cambridge Texts in the History of Political Thought. Cambridge: Cambridge University Press, 1991.

Katongole, Emmanuel. "Greeting: Beyond Racial Reconciliation." In *The Blackwell Companion to Christian Ethics*, edited by Stanley Hauerwas and Samuel Wells, 68–81. Blackwell Companions to Religion. Malden, MA: Blackwell, 2004.

Katznelson, Ira. *City Trenches: Urban Politics and the Patterning of Class in the United States.* Chicago: Chicago University Press, 1981.

Kierkegaard, Søren. *Philosophical Fragments.* Originally translated and introduced by David Swenson. New introduction and commentary by Niels Thulstrup. Translation revised and commentary translated by Howard V. Hong. Princeton: Princeton University Press, 1967.

Killilea, Alfred. *The Politics of Being Mortal.* Lexington: University Press of Kentucky, 1988.

King, Martin Luther, Jr. *A Testament of Hope: The Essential Writings of Martin Luther King Jr.* Edited by James M. Washington. San Francisco: Harper and Row, 1986.

———. *Where Do We Go From Here: Chaos or Community?* New York: Harper and Row, 1967.

Kling, Joseph M., and Prudence S. Posner, editors. *Dilemmas of Activism: Class, Community, and the Politics of Local Mobilization.* Philadelphia: Temple University Press, 1990.

Kluger, Richard. *Simple Justice: The History of Brown vs. Board of Education and Black America's Struggle for Equality.* New York: Knopf, 2004.

Levi, Primo. *The Periodic Table.* Translated by R. Rosenthal. New York: Schocken, 1984.

———. *A Tranquil Star.* Translated by Ann Goldstein and Alessandra Bastagli. New York: Norton, 2007.

Lutz, Christopher Stephen. *Tradition in the Ethics of Alasdair MacIntyre: Relativism, Thomism, and Philosophy.* Lanham, MD: Lexington, 2004.

Macpherson, C. B. *The Real World of Democracy*. New York: Oxford University Press, 1972.

Kluger, Richard. *Simple Justice: The History of Brown vs. Board of Education and Black America's Struggle for Equality*. New York: Knopf, 2004.

MacIntyre, Alisdair C. *Dependent Rational Animals: Why Human Beings Need the Virtues*. Paul Carus Lecture Series 20. Chicago: Open Court, 1999.

———. "Human Nature and Human Dependence: What Might a Thomist Learn from Reading Lostrup?" In *Concern for the Other: Perspectives on the Ethics of K. E. Lostrupp*, edited by Sven Andersen and Kees van Kooten Niekerk, 147–66. South Bend, IN: University of Notre Dame Press, 2007.

———. *Three Rival Versions of Moral Enquiry: Encyclopedia, Genealogy and Tradition*. Gifford Lectures. Notre Dame: University of Notre Dame Press, 1990.

Maclean, Norman. *A River Runs Through It, and Other Stories*. Chicago: University of Chicago Press, 1976.

Mahmood, Saba. *Politics of Piety: The Islamic Revival and the Feminist Subject*. Princeton: Princeton University Press, 2005.

Markus, R. A. *Christianity and the Secular*. Blessed Pope John XXIII Lecture Series in Theology and Culture. Notre Dame: University of Notre Dame Press, 2006.

Marsh, Charles. *The Beloved Community: How Faith Shapes Social Justice, From the Civil Rights Movement to Today*. New York: Basic, 2005.

Marx, Karl, and Friedrich Engels. "The Communist Manifesto." In *The Marx-Engels Reader*, edited by Robert C. Tucker. 2d ed. New York: Norton, 1978.

McCarthy, Thomas A. *Ideals and Illusions: On Reconstruction and Deconstruction in Contemporary Critical Theory*. Cambridge, MA: MIT Press, 1991.

McGuckin, John A. *Saint Gregory of Nazianzus: An Intellectual Biography*. Crestwood NY: St Vladimir's Seminary Press, 2001.

Mignolo, Walter D. *The Idea of Latin America*. Blackwell Manifestos. Malden, MA: Blackwell, 2005.

Milbank, John. *The Suspended Middle: Henri de Lubac and the Debate Concerning the Supernatural*. Grand Rapids: Eerdmans, 2005.

Mouffe, Chantal. *The Democratic Paradox*. Phronesis. London: Verso, 2000.

Mueller, Carol. "Ella Baker and the Origins of 'Participatory Democracy.'" In *Women in the Civil Rights Movement: Trailblazers and Torch Bearers: 1941–1965*, edited by Vicki L. Crawford, et al., 51–70. Bloomington: Indiana University Press, 1993,

Müller-Fahrenholz, Geiko. *America's Battle for God: A European Christian Looks at Civil Religion*. Grand Rapids: Eerdmans, 2007.

Naples, Nancy A., editor. *Community Activism and Feminist Politics: Organizing across Race, Class, and Gender*. Perspectives on Gender. New York: Routledge, 1998.

———. *Grassroots Warriors: Activist Mothering, Community Work, and the War on Poverty*. Perspectives on Gender. New York: Routledge, 1998.

Nation, Mark Thiessen. "Washing Feet: Preparation for Service." In *The Blackwell Companion to Christian Ethics*, edited by Stanley Hauerwas and Samuel Wells, 441–51. Blackwell Companions to Religion. Malden, MA: Blackwell, 2004.

Nietzsche, Friedrich. *Thus Spoke Zarathustra*. Translated by Walter Kauffman. New York: Penguin, 1954.

Norris, Frederick W. *The Apostolic Faith: Protestants and Roman Catholics*. Collegeville: Liturgical, 1992.

————. *Faith Gives Fullness to Reasoning: The Five Theological Orations of Gregory Nazianzen*. Translated by Lionel Wickham and Frederick Williams. Supplements to Vigiliae Christianae. Leiden: Brill, 1991.

————. "Gregory Contemplating the Beautiful: Knowing Human Misery and Divine Mystery through and Being Persuaded by Images." In *Gregory of Nazianzus: Images and Reflections*, edited by Jostein Bortnes and Tomas Hagg, 19–35. Copenhagen: Museum Tusculanum Press, 2006.

————. Introduction to *Faith Gives Fullness to Reasoning: The Five Theological Orations of Gregory Nazianzen*, 1–80. [AQ] Translated by Lionel Wickham and Frederick Williams. Supplements to Vigiliae Christianae. Leiden: Brill, 1991.

Nussbaum, Martha C. *Frontiers of Justice: Disability, Nationality, Species Membership*. The Tanner Lectures on Human Values. Cambridge, MA: Belknap/Harvard University Press, 2006.

Pateman, Carole. *Participation and Democratic Theory*. Cambridge, MA: Cambridge University Press, 1970.

Payne, Charles. *I've Got the Light of Freedom: The Organizing Tradition and the Mississippi Freedom Struggle*. Berkeley: University of California Press, 1997.

Percy, Walker. "The Failure and the Hope." In *The Failure and the Hope: Essays of Southern Churchmen*, edited with an introduction by Will D. Campbell and James Y. Holloway, 13–28. Reprint, Eugene: Wipf and Stock, 2005.

Piven, Frances Fox, and Richard A. Cloward. *Poor People's Movements: Why They Succeed and How They Fail*. New York: Vintage, 1979.

Polanyi, Karl. *The Great Transformation: The Political and Economic Origins of our Time*. Boston: Beacon, 1957.

Ransby, Barbara. *Ella Baker and the Black Freedom Movement: A Radical Democratic Vision*. Gender and American Culture. Chapel Hill: University of North Carolina Press, 2003.

Reinders, Hans S. *The Future of the Disabled in Liberal Society: An Ethical Analysis*. Revisions. Notre Dame: University of Notre Dame Press, 2000.

————. "The Virtue of Writing Appropriately, Or: Is Stanley Hauerwas Right in Thinking He Should Not Write Anymore on the Mentally Handicapped?" *In God, Truth and Witness: Engaging Stanley Hauerwas*, edited by L. Gregory Jones, et al., 53–70. Grand Rapids: Brazos, 2005.

Rich, Adrienne. *A Wild Patience Has Taken Me This Far: Poems, 1978–1981*. New York: Norton, 1981.

Rogers, Mary Beth. *Cold Anger: A Story of Faith and Power Politics*. Denton, Texas: University of North Texas Press, 1990.

Ryan, Alan. "Cosmopolitans." *New York Review of Books* 53 (2006) 48–49.

Ryan, Mark. "Agency and Practical Reason: The Critique of Modern Moral Theory from Anscombe to Hauerwas." PhD diss., University of Virginia, 2006.

Sacks, Karen Brodkin. *Caring by the Hour: Women, Work, and Organizing at Duke Medical Center*. Urbana: University of Illinois Press, 1988.

Santer, Eric L. *On the Psychotheology of Everyday Life: Reflections on Freud and Rosenzweig*. Chicago: University of Chicago Press, 2001.

Santos, Boaventura de Sousa. *The Rise of the Global Left: The World Social Forum and Beyond*. London: Zed, 2006.

————. "The World Social Forum: Toward a Counter-Hegemonic Globalization. Presented at the Twenty-Fourth International Congress of the Latin American Studies Association, Dallas, Texas, March 28, 2003. Originally published at http://www.ces.fe.us.pt/bss/fsm.php.

Schlabach, Gerald W. "Breaking Bread: Peace and War." In *The Blackwell Companion to Christian Ethics*, edited by Stanley Hauerwas and Samuel Wells, 360–74. Blackwell Companions to Religion. Malden, MA: Blackwell, 2004.

Scott, James C. *Seeing Like a State: How Certain Schemes to Improve the Human Condition Have Failed*. Yale Agrarian Studies. The Yale ISPS Series. New Haven: Yale University Press, 1998,

Smith, Ted A. *The New Measures: A Theological History of Democratic Practice.* Cambridge: Cambridge University Press, 2007.

Snyder, Sharon L., and David T. Mitchell. *Cultural Locations of Disability*. Chicago: University of Chicago Press, 2006.

Spink, Kathryn. *The Miracle, the Message, the Story: Jean Vanier and L'Arche*. Mahwah, NJ: Hidden Spring, 2006.

Stout, Jeffrey. *Democracy and Tradition*. New Forum Books. Princeton: Princeton University Press, 2004.

————. "The Spirit of Democracy and the Rhetoric of Excess." *Journal of Religious Ethics* 35 (2007) 9–21.

Swinton, John, editor. *Critical Reflections on Stanely Hauerwas' Theology of Disability: Disabling Society, Enabling Theology*. Binghamton: Haworth, 2004.

Szasz, Andrew. *EcoPopulism: Toxic Waste and the Movement for Environmental Justice*. Social Movements, Protest, and Contention 1. Minneapolis: University of Minnesota Press, 1994.

Thomas, John Christopher. "Footwashing within the Context of the Lord's Supper." In *The Lord's Supper: Believers Church Perspectives*, edited by Dale R. Stoffer, 169–75. Scottdale, PA: Herald, 1997.

Todorov, Tzvetan. *Mikhail Bakhtin: The Dialogical Principle*. Translated by Wlad Godzich. Theory and History of Literature 13. Minneapolis: University Minnesota Press, 1984.

Unger, Roberto Mangabeira. *False Necessity: Anti-Necessitarian Social Theory in the Service of Radical Democracy; From Politics: A Work in Constructive Social Theory*. Politics 1. New York: Verso, 2004.

————. *What Should the Left Propose?* London: Verso, 2005.

Unger, Roberto Mangabeira, and Cornel West. *The Future of American Progressivism: An Initiative for Political and Economic Reform*. Boston: Beacon, 1998.

Vanier, Jean. *Befriending the Stranger*. Grand Rapids: Eerdmans, 2005.

————. *Community and Growth*. Translated by Ann Shearer. London: Darton, Longman and Todd, 1979.

————. *Community and Growth: Our Pilgrimage Together*. Revised edition. New York: Paulist, 1989.

————. *Drawn into the Mystery of Jesus through the Gospel of John*. New York: Paulist, 2004.

————. "L'Arche: Its History and Vision." In *The Church and Disabled Persons*, edited by Griff Hogan, 50–60. Springfield, IL: Templegate, 1983.

———. *Made for Happiness: Discovering the Meaning of Life with Aristotle*. Translated by Kathryn Spink. London: Darton, Longman and Todd, 2001.

———. *Made for Happiness: Discovering the Meaning of Life with Aristotle*. Translated by Kathryn Spink. Toronto: House of Anansi, 2001.

———. *The Scandal of Service: Jesus Washes our Feet*. Ottawa: Novalis, 1996.

Virilio, Paul. *Popular Defense and Ecological Struggles*. New York: Semiotext(e), 1990.

Warren, Mark E. *Democracy and Association*. Princeton: Princeton University Press, 2001.

Warren, Mark R. *Dry Bones Rattling: Community Building to Revitalize American Democracy*. Princeton Studies in American Politics. Princeton: Princeton University Press, 2001.

Wells, Samuel. *God's Companions: Reimagining Christian Ethics*. Challenges in Christian Theology. Oxford: Blackwell, 2006.

———. *Improvisation: The Drama of Christian Ethics*. Grand Rapids: Brazos, 2004.

West, Cornel. "Afterword." *Theory and Event* 10 (2007). No pages. Online: http://muse.jhu.edu /journals/theory_and_event/ v010/10.1west.html.

———. *The American Evasion of Philosophy: A Genealogy of Pragmatism*. The Wisconsin Project on American Writers. Madison: University of Wisconsin Press, 1989.

———. "Beyond Eurocentrism and Multiculturalism." *Prophetic Thought in Postmodern Times*, 3–30. Monroe: Common Courage, 1993.

———. "Black Strivings in a Twilight Civilization." In Henry Louis Gates Jr., and Cornel West. *The Future of the Race*, 53–113. New York: Knopf, 1996.

———. "The Black Underclass and Black Philosophers." In *Prophetic Thought in Postmodern Times*, 143–57. Beyond Eurocentrism and Multiculturalism 1. Monroe: Common Courage, 1993.

———. *The Cornel West Reader*. New York: Basic Civitas, 1999.

———. "The Crisis of Black Leadership." In *Race Matters*, 33–46. Boston: Beacon, 1993.

———. "Decentering Europe: A Memorial Lecture for James Snead." *Critical Quarterly* 33 (1991) 1–19. Reprinted in Cornel West. *Prophetic Thoughts in Postmodern Times*, 119–42. Beyond Eurocentrism and Multiculturalism 1. Monroe: Common Courage, 1993.

———. *Democracy Matters: Winning the Fight against Imperialism*. New York: Penguin, 2004.

———. "The Dilemma of the Black Intellectual." In *Keeping Faith: Philosophy and Race in America*, 67–88. New York: Routledge, 1993.

———. "The New Cultural Politics of Difference." In *Keeping Faith: Philosophy and Race in America*, 3–32. New York: Routledge, 1993.

———. *Keeping Faith: Philosophy and Race in America*. New York: Routledge, 1993.

———. "The Paradox of African-American Rebellion." In *Keeping Faith: Philosophy and Race in America*, 271–92. New York: Routledge, 1993.

———. *Prophesy Deliverance!: An Afro-American Revolutionary Christianity*. Philadelphia: Westminster, 1982.

———. *Race Matters*. Boston: Beacon, 1993.

———. *Prophetic Thought in Postmodern Times*. Monroe: Common Courage, 1993.

Wiebe, Joseph. "Inheriting John Howard Yoder: A New Generation Examines His Thought." Paper presented at Toronto Mennonite Theological Centre, May 25–26, 2007.

Wilken, Robert Louis. *The Spirit of Early Christian Thought: Seeking the Face of God*. New Haven: Yale University Press, 2003.

Williams, Rowan. "Afterword." In *The Blackwell Companion to Christian Ethics*, edited by Stanley Hauerwas and Samuel Wells, 495–98. Blackwell Companions to Religion. Malden, MA: Blackwell, 2004.

———. *Christ on Trial: How the Gospel Unsettles Our Judgment*. Grand Rapids: Eerdmans, 2000.

———. "Politics and the Soul: A Reading of the city of God." *Milltown Studies* 19/20 (1987) 55–72.

———. "Trinity and Pluralism." In *On Christian Theology*, 167–80. Challenges in Contemporary Theology. Oxford: Blackwell, 2000.

———. *The Truce of God*, with a foreword by Robert Cantuar, former Archbishop of Canterbury. Grand Rapids: Eerdmans, 2005.

———. *Resurrection: Interpreting the Easter Gospel*. Harrisburg, PA: Morehouse, 1982.

———. *The Wound of Knowledge: Christian Spirituality from the New Testament to Saint John of the Cross*. Cambridge: Cowley, 2003

———. *Where God Happens: Discovering Christ in One Another*. Boston: New Seeds, 2005.

———. *Writing in the Dust: After September 11*. Grand Rapids: Eerdmans, 2002.

Wittgenstein, Ludwig. *Culture and Value*. Chicago: University of Chicago Press, 1980.

———. *On Certainty*. New York: Harper Torchbooks, 1969.

———. *Philosophical Investigations*. New York: MacMillan, 1953.

Wolin, Sheldon S. "Agitated Times." *Parallax* 11 (2005) 2–11.

———. "The Destructive Sixties and Postmodern Conservatism." In *Reassessing the Sixties*, edited by Stephen Macedo, 129–57. New York: W.W. Norton, 1997.

———. "Fugitive Democracy." In *Democracy and Difference: Contesting the Boundaries of the Political*, edited by Seyla Benhabib, 31–45. Princeton Paperbacks. Princeton: Princeton University Press, 1996.

———. *Hobbes and the Epic Tradition of Political Theory*. Los Angeles: William Andrews Clark Memorial Library, University of California, Los Angeles, 1970.

———. "Invocations of Political Theory." In *Vocations of Political Theory*, edited by Jason A. Frank and John Tambornino, 3–24. Minneapolis, MN: University of Minnesota Press, 2000.

———. "A Look Back at the Ideas That Led to the Events." *New York Times*, July 26, 1998, Arts Section, 37.

———. "Norm and Form: The Constitutionalizing of Democracy." In *Athenian Political Thought and the Reconstruction of American Democracy*, edited by J. Peter Euben, et al., 29–58. Ithaca: Cornell University Press, 1994.

———. "Political Theory: From Vocation to Innovation." In *Vocations of Political Theory*, edited by Jason A. Frank and John Tambornino, 3–22. Minneapolis: University of Minnesota Press, 2000.

———. "Political Theory as a Vocation." In *Machiavelli and the Nature of Political Thought*, edited by Martin Fleischer, 23–75. Studies in Political Theory. Atheneum 189. New York: Macmillan, 1972.

————. *Politics and Vision: Continuity and Innovation in Western Political Thought.* Boston: Little, Brown, 1960.

————. *Politics and Vision: Continuity and Innovation in Western Political Thought.* Expanded edition. Princeton: Princeton University Press, 2004.

————. Preface to the Expanded Edition of *Politics and Vision*, xv–xxii. Princeton: Princeton University Press, 2004.

————. *The Presence of the Past: Essays on the State and the Constitution.* The Johns Hopkins Series in Constitutional Thought. Baltimore: Johns Hopkins University Press, 1989.

————. *Tocqueville: Between Two Worlds; The Making of a Political and Theoretical Life.* Princeton: Princeton University Press, 2001.

————. "Transgression, Equality, Voice." In Dēmokratia: *A Conversation on Democracies, Ancient and Modern*, edited by Joseph Ober and Charles Hedrick, 63–90. Princeton Paperbacks. Princeton: Princeton University Press, 1996.

Wolin, Sheldon S., and John H. Schaar. *The Berkeley Rebellion and Beyond: Essays on Politics and Education in the Technological Society.* New York Review Book. New York: New York Review, 1970.

Xenos, Nicholas. "Momentary Democracy." In *Democracy and Vision: Sheldon Wolin and the Vicissitudes of the Political*, edited by Aryeh Botwinick and William E. Connolly, 25–38. Princeton: Princeton University Press, 2001.

Yoder, John Howard. *Body Politics: Five Practices of the Christian Community before the Watching World.* Nashville: Discipleship Resources, 1992.

————. "Christ the Hope of the World." In *The Original Revolution: Essays on Christian Pacifism*, 148–82. Scottsdale, PA: Herald, 1971. Reprint, Eugene, OR: Wipf & Stock, 1999.

————. "The Disavowal of Constantine: An Alternative Perspective on Interfaith Dialogue." In *The Royal Priesthood: Essays Ecclesiological and Ecumenical*, edited by Michael Cartwright. Grand Rapids: Eerdmans, 1994.

————. *For the Nations: Essays Public and Evangelical.* Grand Rapids: Eerdmans, 1997. Reprint, Eugene, OR: Wipf & Stock, 2002.

————. *Nevertheless: Varieties of Religious Pacifism.* Scottsdale, PA: Herald, 1992.

————. "'Patience' as Method in Moral Reasoning: Is an Ethic of Discipleship Absolute?" In *The Wisdom of the Cross: Essays in Honor of John Howard Yoder.* Edited by Stanley Hauerwas et al., 24–42. Grand Rapids: Eerdmans, 1999.

————. "The Power Equation, the Place of Jesus, and the Politics of King." In *For the Nations: Essays Public and Evangelical*, 125–47. Grand Rapids: Eerdmans, 1997.

————. *The Priestly Kingdom.* Notre Dame, IN: University of Notre Dame Press, 1984.

Zinn, Howard. *SNCC: The New Abolitionists.* The Radical Sixties 1. Cambridge, MA: South End Press, 2002.

Zwick, Mark, and Louise Zwick. *The Catholic Worker Movement: Intellectual and Spiritual Origins.* New York: Paulist, 2005.

Index